THE ELEMENTS OF PUBLIC SPEAKING

SECOND EDITION

THE ELEMENTS OF PUBLIC SPEAKING

JOSEPH A. DEVITO

Queens College, City University of New York

1817

HARPER & ROW, PUBLISHERS, New York

Cambridge, Philadelphia, San Francisco, London, Mexico City, São Paulo, Sydney

Sponsoring Editor: Louise Waller
Project Editor: Karla Billups Philip
Designer: Gayle Jaeger
Production Manager: Debi Forest-Bochner
Photo Researcher: Maggie Berkvist
Compositor: Ruttle, Shaw & Wetherill, Inc.
Printer and Binder: The Murray Printing Company
Cover: Abner Graboff

THE ELEMENTS OF PUBLIC SPEAKING, Second Edition

Library of Congress Cataloging in Publication Data
DeVito, Joseph A., 1938-
   The elements of public speaking.

   Includes bibliographies and indexes.
   1. Public speaking. I. Title.
PN4121.D389   1984   808.5'1   83-16630
ISBN 0-06-041649-1

CONTENTS IN BRIEF

APPENDIXES

CONTENTS IN DETAIL

CONTENTS OF BOXED ESSAYS

PREFACE

It is important to explain (1) the point of view that underlies this book, (2) the general structure or plan of the book, (3) the major changes between the first edition and this second edition, and (4) the "payoffs"—the benefits that the student should derive from both this text and from a course in public speaking.

A POINT OF VIEW

I believe that every course you take and every textbook you read should benefit you in some way: you should become a somewhat different and more effective person; otherwise, you have wasted your time and energy. This book is designed to enable you to derive specific benefits and provide you with the materials to realize these benefits (principles, theories, guidelines, exercises, model speeches).

My point of view is pragmatic and practical: the function of the book is to develop and improve your public speaking skills—as a speaker, as a listener, as a critic. My point of view is transactional: each aspect of the public speaking situation is in a constant state of interaction with all other aspects; the speaker does not merely influence the audience, rather, audience and speaker interact; each influences the other. My point of view is that public speaking has an ethical dimension: Because public speaking influences the thoughts and behaviors of human beings, it involves ethical issues—issues of right and wrong. I assume here that each person involved in the public speaking transaction has ethical obligations—the speaker to present information fairly and with consideration for the welfare of the audience; the audience to listen fairly and openly to the speaker; the critic to evaluate honestly the public speaking effort. My point of view recognizes the necessity of free and open communication on significant social, political, economic, and psychological issues if a democratic society is to survive and prosper. These points of view permeate the entire book; they influence what is included and what is omitted; they influence the treatment of each of the various topics and particularly the value statements included throughout the text.

THE PLAN OF THE BOOK

The Elements of Public Speaking is designed to enable you to achieve the goals and benefits of public speaking with relative ease and with considerable personal enjoyment and satisfaction. The book is divided into 22 short units rather than traditional long chapters. Each unit is short enough to be read in its entirety in one average study period but long enough to cover a coherent, complete body of material. Brevity also facilitates flexibility; the order of the units may be rearranged to suit any number of specific purposes.

The 22 units are organized into six major parts that focus on the major dimensions of the public speaking transaction: "Preliminaries to Public Speaking," "Audiences of Public Speaking," "Organizing the Public Speech," "Types of Public Speaking," "Style and the Public Speech," and "Delivery in Public Speaking." In addition to these six parts, two of the appendixes deal with "Asking and Answering Questions" and "The Small Group Encounter"—two topics that are often included in courses in public speaking. Further, "Stimuli for Speech Topics" is included as Appendix C, which should help a great deal in suggesting suitable topics for a wide variety of speeches. Appendix D contains speeches (two with annotations) that should prove helpful in visualizing the principles of effective public speaking.

Integrated throughout the text is a series of Experiential Vehicles (or exercises) designed to enable you to work effectively and actively with the concepts covered in the preceding units. By working with these Experiential Vehicles you will find that the principles discussed throughout the text become more easily understandable and more clearly relevant and applicable to your own public speaking tasks. These vehicles also make learning public speaking more enjoyable and personally satisfying.

Twenty-five "How to" essays are also included throughout the text. These are brief practical essays dealing with a wide variety of issues relevant to public speaking, for example, how to develop confidence as a public speaker, how to deal with a mixed audience, how to secure and maintain audience attention, how to improve your memory, how to dress for a public speech, and so on. These "How to" essays are set off from the text proper and may be read in any order although their placement in the text is particularly appropriate to the unit topic.

I have included early in the text (Unit 2) a summary of the essential steps in the public speaking process so that you may begin almost immediately to prepare and present public speeches. In this way you will be able to put theory into practice from the start and may be in a position to profit both from the increased understanding of the theory as developed in this book and in your course, and from your own performance—your successes and your errors. With the aid of criticism from both your instructor and your fellow classmates (as well as from your own responses and intuitions), you should be able to refine and polish your skills as they are being developed. This early summary will also provide you with a convenient picture of the public speaking transaction as a whole; it will then be easier to see where and how the various more specific considerations developed in the remainder of the book fit into this total picture.

In developing *Elements* I have relied heavily on the insights of numerous theorists and researchers—on the classical rhetoricians, the "new" rhetoricians, the general semanticists, the generative grammarians, the transactional psychologists, the psycholinguists and the sociolinguists, and, in fact, on any individual or "group" that provided insight into public discourse. Likewise, I have utilized both theoretical insights and experimental research findings and have attempted to blend these into a meaningful and comprehensive whole. For the sake of clarity I have omitted the names of researchers and theorists, books and journals, from the text proper and have put these into the Sources that appear at the end of each unit. Thus, the Sources represent both my indebtedness to those whose ideas I have utilized as well as my suggestions for further reading. In public speaking, more so than with other subjects, it will prove useful for you to see these principles explained in a different way and from a different perspective, so I urge you to make use of the wealth of information available on public speaking, only a small part of which is recorded in these end-of-unit Sources.

I have tried to write *Elements* as I would talk with my own students, for example, using an informal style and keeping jargon and other technical vocabulary to a minimum. Where such terminology cannot be avoided, I have defined the terms and provided sufficient examples so that the concepts are clear and meaningful.

The ability to prepare and present effective public speeches is one of the most important competencies you can develop. This book will assist you in that development.

MAJOR CHANGES

This second edition enables me to improve on a number of topics presented in the first edition and to include a number of additional topics. The most general revisions are the inclusion of a more focused progressive sequence for the development and presentation of the public speech, and the inclusion of a wider variety of options that the student may add to her or his arsenal of public speaking strategies.

More specifically, the major change is in the discussion of the types of speeches. Informative and persuasive speeches are more clearly defined in terms of their types and their supporting materials than they were in the first edition. Two units are devoted to informative speaking (Units 13 and 14) and three units to persuasive speaking (Units 15, 16, and 17). Unit 18, on special types of speeches, has been expanded to include speeches of presentation and acceptance.

The Toulmin model for analyzing arguments and the motivated sequence have been presented to provide additional perspectives on persuasion and attitude change. An extended discussion of the thesis statement has been added to this edition to make the process of selection and organization of main ideas easier and more effective for the student. This discussion appears in Unit 9, "General Principles of Organization." The material on style and delivery has been more carefully integrated and is developed in two units each. These materials have also been given a more practical focus.

Each of the six parts of the text begins with an introductory unit dealing with "general principles" and covers the essentials of each of the six major topics. The remaining units within each part then develop the relevant issues in greater detail. I have retained those features that proved helpful and popular in the first edition: the unit format, the informality of style, the experiential learning materials, and the practical focus.

THE PAYOFFS

Fair questions to ask before beginning any book are "What will I get out of it?," "What will I be able to do after reading this book that I am not able to do well now?," or "What is the payoff?" Here are some general "payoffs"—some general objectives you should be able to meet after reading this text:

1 Analyze a wide variety of audiences and effectively adapt your informative, persuasive, and special occasion speeches to their unique characteristics and attitudes.

2 Effectively research a wide variety of topics and issues of both contemporary and historical significance.

3 Organize materials into a meaningful public message so that introduction, body, and conclusion (and their subdivisions) are integrated into a coherent and purposeful whole.

4 Support ideas and points of view (with amplification, psychological appeals, evidence, and argument) so that they are both understandable and persuasive in their effects on the audience.

5 Listen to public messages of all kinds more efficiently and more effectively.

6 Critically analyze and appraise the arguments and appeals of others (as well as your own) and therefore more effectively evaluate a wide variety of messages.

7 Give criticism to others that is constructive and meaningful and receive and respond to the criticisms of others nondefensively.

8 Effectively present yourself to an audience so that you will be perceived as believable.

9 Reduce or more effectively control any fear or apprehension of the public speaking experience.

10 Effectively word public messages so that they are clear, persuasive, and easily remembered by an audience.

11 Deliver public messages to a wide variety of audiences with effective use of both voice and bodily action.

In sum, you should be able to construct and deliver a wide variety of informative, persuasive, and special occasion speeches to a wide variety of audiences with considerable effectiveness and be able to listen critically and responsibly to the public speeches of others.

ACKNOWLEDGMENTS

It is a pleasure for me to express my appreciation to the many people who influenced the development and production of this text. The first and most obvious debt is to those who have contributed to the research and theory in public speaking that I have reported in this volume. Without them this book could not have been written. Second, I want to thank those who read the manuscript at various stages of development (or who commented on the first edition) and who offered criticisms, suggestions for improvement, and the feedback so important in turning a manuscript into a useful and relevant textbook. The following persons were most helpful: John E. Baird, Jr., Modern Management Methods; Parke G. Burgess, Queens College; James Chesebro, Queens College; Joseph Giordano, University of Massachusetts; Bradford L. Kinney, Wilkes College; Cal M. Logue, University of Georgia; Janice Peterson, University of California, Santa Barbara; Ellen Ritter, University of Missouri; Malcolm O. Sillars, University of Utah; Mary Ann Smith, University of Vermont; Ralph R. Smith; Debra Stenger, Mississippi State University; William E. Wiethoff, Indiana University; and Russel R. Windes, Queens College. I especially wish to thank Donald Egan, Emerson College, and Stephen Coletti, Ithaca College, who shared their students' comments on the first edition with me; these were most rewarding and most helpful.

On the more personal side, my major debt is to Boo who taught me so much about communication and about teaching, writing, and living in general. As always and from the beginning, Maggie gave me the support and encouragement essential to this type of task.

The people at Harper & Row, were also of great help. I especially want to thank Louise Waller, Executive Editor, for her guidance, her wise editorial judgment, and her concern at all stages of development. I am particularly thankful for the opportunity to have again worked with Karla Billups Philip who, for the seventh time, supervised the editorial and production processes with her customary good humor and good sense. It is a pleasure to thank Gayle Jaeger for developing a design for this book that is both attractive and functional. To all of these and many others I am most thankful.

Joseph A. DeVito

THE ELEMENTS OF PUBLIC SPEAKING

PART ONE

PRELIMINARIES TO PUBLIC SPEAKING

PART ONE

UNIT 1

General principles of public speaking

OBJECTIVES

After completing this unit, you should be able to:

1 *define* public speaking
2 *diagram and explain the public speaking transaction*
3 *define and explain the role of each of the following components of public speaking: speaker, listeners (audience), noise, effect, context, and messages and channels*
4 *describe at least three benefits to be derived from the study of public speaking*

Of all the courses you will take in your college career, public speaking will surely be one of the most demanding, satisfying, frustrating, stimulating, ego-involving, and useful now and throughout your professional life. This book explains the nature and principles of effective public speaking and will provide you with the theoretical foundations and the specific practical techniques for increasing your own effectiveness as a public speaker, as a consumer of public communications, and as an analyst or critic of public speeches.

WHAT IS PUBLIC SPEAKING?

Although the entire book will, in effect, define what public speaking is, for now let us look briefly at the historical development of public speaking and explore a brief definition.

A brief history

Public speaking is both an ancient and a modern art. Theories of public speaking were probably formulated shortly after people began to speak, for if there was a need to speak, there was a need to speak effectively. The earliest known attempt to theorize about public speaking dates as far back as 3000 B.C. An Egyptian essay, written on parchment and addressed to the son of the pharaoh, contains some elementary advice on effective speaking. It was in Greece in the fifth century B.C., however, that significant theories of effective public speaking developed. And when we think of the contributions of the Greeks, we think of Plato and especially of Aristotle, whose *Rhetoric*—written some 2300 years ago—has probably influenced the development of public speaking more than any other single work. The Latin rhetoricians (public speaking theorists)—for example, Cicero, Quintilian, and St. Augustine—followed Aristotle in according great educational emphasis to effective speaking and wrote extensively on the art.

Since this "classical period" there have been many different schools of thought and many different emphases given to the study of public speaking. Ramistic, stylistic, and elocutionary movements concentrated on public speaking in terms of style and delivery. Whereas the works of Aristotle and Cicero focused primarily on the substance of the speech (what was referred to as "invention"), these theorists focused on the language and delivery of the speech. The classical rhetoricians of sixteenth-, seventeenth-, and eighteenth-century England and the classical rhetoricians in America during the twentieth century went back to the classics, particularly to Cicero, and again emphasized substance—the development of arguments, reasoning, strategies of persuasion, and a host of other issues to be discussed throughout this book.

Today this classical rhetorical tradition has been supplemented by insights from information theory, psycholinguistics, social psychology, transactional analysis, communication theory, and numerous other developments. It is not surprising, therefore, that we do not have any one theory that is universally accepted and powerful enough to justify excluding the others. The theory of public speaking presented here actually contains ideas drawn from many different theoretical positions. All theories, however, are selected and developed with the intention of presenting you with those insights related to the practical and important task of improving your own public speaking abilities—as speaker, as listener, as critic.

A brief definition

In order to best explain public speaking—what it is and how it works—let us first review briefly the act of one person talking with another. This interpersonal communication act may be represented as in Figure 1.1.

Each of the two individuals is designated as *speaker/listener* to emphasize that both persons serve the roles of speaker and listener. Connecting them is the *message*, which consists of both verbal and nonverbal elements: words, facial expressions, body movements, increases and decreases in vocal intensity, and numerous other signals. In its path from one person to another, the message is subjected to invasion by *noise*—anything that interferes with or detracts from the message being sent from one person to the other. Throughout the process of interpersonal communication, each person sends the other person *feedback*—messages that tell the other person how his or her message, or reactions to the message, are being received. A shake of the head indicating disagreement, a smile, an intense glance saying "continue, I'm listening," an additional example to clarify a statement, or a simple "Am I making sense?" are examples of feedback messages. The entire interpersonal communication act takes place in a *context*, or environment, that is part physical (the actual room or place) and part social-psychological

FIGURE 1.1   The interpersonal communication act

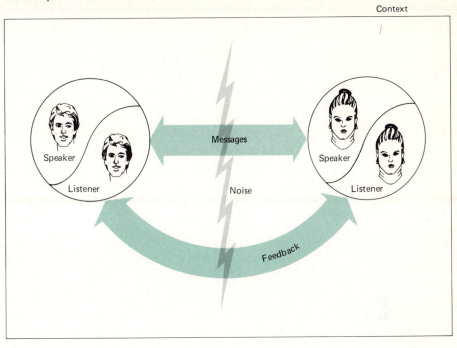

(the culture, the friendliness of the participants, the relationship between the two people).

Public speaking may be seen as a variation and extension of this interpersonal communication act. *Public speaking* may be defined as that form of communication in which a speaker addresses a relatively large audience with a relatively continuous discourse, and usually in a face-to-face situation. A student delivers a report to an economics class, a teacher lectures on the Roman Empire, a minister preaches a sermon, a politician delivers a campaign speech, and thousands of similar examples are all public speaking situations.

Unlike the interpersonal situation where the only "audience" is one listener, the public speaking audience is "relatively large," but the range of "relatively large" is wide—from a group of 10 or 12 to an audience of hundreds of thousands. During interpersonal communication, the role of speaker shifts repeatedly from one person to another, whereas the public speech is a relatively continuous address by one speaker. This does not mean that only the speaker communicates; both speaker and audience communicate throughout the public speaking situation—the speaker in delivering the speech and the audience in responding to the speech with feed-back.

Although this book and this course will concentrate on face-to-face public speaking, we must also consider the significant role of the various media, particularly television. When the president delivers a speech to the nation over television or when a station manager editorializes, each is clearly engaged in public speaking, but it is channelled through a television—it is not a face-to-face encounter. Although this media factor does not make the two speeches completely different, it does introduce a number of additional complexities. The face-to-face situation is logically the primary one: Expertise in public speaking through the media rests on expertise in face-to-face situations. As we proceed, then, we will concentrate on face-to-face public speaking situations but will recognize and take into consideration the role of the mass media. The nature of public speaking and its various components will be further clarified in our discussion of how public speaking works.

REMEMBER: Public speaking is a form of communication in which the speaker addresses a relatively large audience with a relatively continuous discourse, usually in a face-to-face situation.

HOW PUBLIC SPEAKING WORKS

Figure 1.2 presents a diagrammatic model that clearly illustrates what public speaking is and how it works. The following discussion focuses on six major *elements* (or *components*) in this model: speaker, listener, noise, effect, context, and messages and channels.

Speaker

As a public speaker you bring to the public speaking situation all that you are and all that you know, as well as all that the audience *thinks* you are and *thinks* you know. When you prepare and deliver a public speech, everything about you becomes significant and contributes to the total effect of your speech: your knowledge of the subject, your purpose in speaking to this audience, your speaking ability, your attitudes toward your subject and toward your audience, and a host of other factors. Furthermore, the audience will have its own perceptions of who you are and will make judgments concerning your competence, your trustworthiness, your speaking ability, your logic, and so on. All of these factors will interact both during and after the public speaking event.

The speaker, as noted in the model (Figure 1.2), is the center of the transaction. Although a speaker usually physically faces the audience, the speaker appears in the center of the model here to illustrate psychological centrality; that is, the audience members "look to" the speaker, who embodies the reason for the gathering.

FIGURE 1.2   A public speaking model

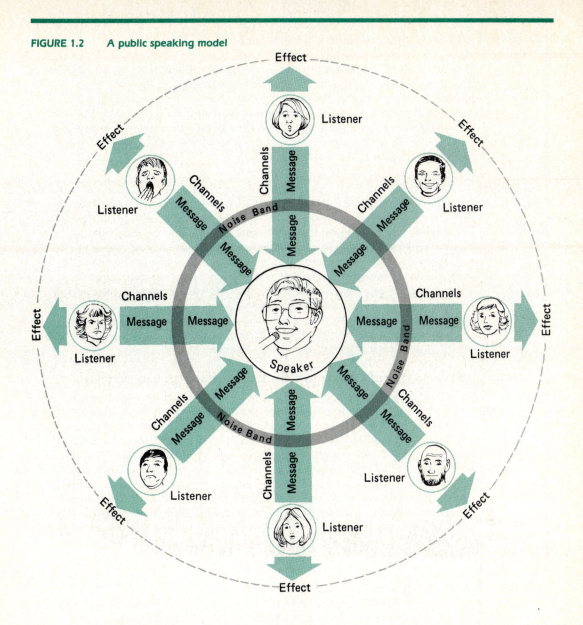

Listeners

The listeners are indicated as separate individuals to emphasize that each is unique. Although we often speak of "the audience" as a collective body—often implying an absence of diversity—we should not forget that it is composed of separate and distinct individuals. Each of these individual

One of the most important qualities separating the effective from the ineffective public speaker is confidence. Confidence also seems to separate the speaker who derives enjoyment from the speaker who derives nothing but pain and anxiety. Fortunately, confidence is not something magical that some people have and others do not; rather, it is a quality that we can all develop and improve. Here are a few suggestions for developing your self-confidence as a public speaker.

1. PREPARE THOROUGHLY

This is probably the major factor in instilling confidence in a speaker. Preparation would include everything you do from the time you begin thinking about your speech to the time you deliver it. Most important is the thorough research of the topic. This will help to eliminate any fears you may have of not being able to answer questions (should there be a question period following your speech) or of saying something that may be perceived as incorrect or naive. The more you know about your topic, the more confident you will feel and the more confidence you will project to your audience. Thorough preparation also includes learning your speech well so that you will not have to rely on your notes. Eliminating the fear of forgetting what you want to say will go a long way toward building your self-confidence.

2. FAMILIARIZE YOURSELF WITH THE PUBLIC SPEAKING SITUATION

The more familiar you are with the public speaking situation—the room in which you will speak, the arrangement of the chairs, the type of audience you will address, and so on—the more confident you will become. Familiarity with any situation increases one's ability to control it; the public speaking situation is no exception. If you are speaking in your regular classroom, then you are already familiar with the situation, but it would also help if you could view the room from the point of view of the speaker. Perhaps a day or two before you are to speak, stand in front of the room, look it over, and try to imagine the entire speaking situation as it will be when you deliver your speech. Then, when you do go to the front of the room to give your first speech, you will face the familiar instead of the unexpected and your confidence will probably increase.

3. DEVELOP THE DESIRE TO COMMUNICATE

This is a most difficult suggestion to follow and yet it seems most helpful to the development of self-confidence as a public speaker. Too often we rehearse negative "scripts"; we tell ourselves over and over again how much we will dislike the public speaking experience and how terrible we are as speakers. If you approach the public speaking situation negatively—with a firm desire to get the experience over with as soon as possible—you will project this image to the audience and will inevitably lower your own self-confidence. Substitute positive "scripts." Tell yourself that the experience can be an enjoyable one (it really can be!). With time, you will find that you are operating with a more positive and a more confident view of the entire public speaking encounter.

4. REHEARSE

Rehearsing your speech and its presentation is most essential for increasing self-confidence. Often a lack of confidence is brought on by thoughts of failure; with increased rehearsal we lessen our chances and our thoughts of failure and of course increase our general effectiveness and our general self-confidence.

One general rule to follow in rehearsal is to rehearse as a confident, fully-in-control public speaker; rehearse with a positive attitude and perspective. Do not give yourself negative criticism during rehearsal. When you then present the actual speech, you will find that you can present the speech as you rehearsed it, with confidence. This self-confidence will be communicated to the audience in a variety of ways—by the way you walk, the way you stand, the way you maintain direct eye contact with the audience, the way you deliver your ideas, the way you handle audience questions, and so on.

Each public speaking experience—like each rehearsal—should add to your self-confidence. Repeated public speaking experiences will help to further develop your self-confidence. After five or six speeches, you should be looking forward to subsequent speaking engagements in a more positive frame of mind and with much greater self-confidence.

5. DEVELOP A COMMUNICATOR SELF-IMAGE

By a "communicator self-image," I mean a view of yourself as a capable, proficient, and most importantly, confident communicator, a person who is effective in getting her or his message across to others. This image may be enhanced by thinking of ourselves as confident speakers and perhaps equally important, by acting as if we are confident speakers. Acting confidently will go a long way toward making us view ourselves as confident and eventually in actually making us confident. The process, it seems, occurs in three steps: (1) we act as if we are confident; (2) we come to think of ourselves as confident; and (3) we become confident. All this is not to suggest that we should fool ourselves or that we should engage in self-deception. Rather, it is to suggest that we can build positive qualities by acting as if we already possess them. This "acting as if" will help make these positive qualities a more integral part of our thinking and our behavior.

listeners comes to the public speaking situation with different purposes, different motives, different expectations, different knowledges, and different attitudes, beliefs, and values. Consequently, each listener is going to view you and your speech somewhat differently than the next listener; each listener is going to respond differently to the entire public speaking encounter.

Noise

Noise is anything—audible or not—that interferes with the transmission or reception of the message. The circle around the speaker (Figure 1.2), labeled "noise band," indicates how noise interferes with the messages as the speaker intends them to be received and how the audience actually receives them. Noise may originate from outside the immediate context (passing cars, screaming children, wind and rain) as well as from within the immediate context (listeners talking, microphone static, papers rustling, stereotypes and prejudices in the minds of speaker or listener). Sunglasses that prevent the listeners from reading the messages communicated by your eyes and a lectern that prevents the listeners from seeing your body movements would also be regarded as noise. The message you think of, the message you communicate, and the message received are all different—in part due to noise interference, in part due to other variables to be discussed throughout the text. It is important to note here that the "message" at one point in the public speaking process is not the same at any other point. Some noise sources may be eliminated or their effects lessened, but it is impossible to eliminate all noise. Instead of attempting to eliminate all noise, you should learn to combat its effects by, for example, increasing your volume, repeating important assertions, and gesturing to reinforce the verbal messages.

Effect

Public speeches are designed and delivered to have some effect on the listeners; were it not to have some effect, speeches would not be given. Politicians would not give campaign speeches were it not for their desire to secure your vote; advertisers and salespersons would not give sales pitches were it not to get you to buy their products; teachers would not give lectures were it not to have some effect on their students.

In the model of public speaking, each effect is shown separately to emphasize that, just as each listener is unique, each effect is also unique. From the very same speech, one listener may respond with total agreement, another with total disagreement, and still another with gross misunderstandings. In public speaking situations we should always speak of the multiple effects of a speech—never of a single effect because each listener experiences and reacts differently.

In considering the effects of your speech, keep in mind that effects are not isolated and stored separately in our minds. Communication is cumulative because messages that a person receives are added to each other. They are not compartmentalized but are combined with everything else in our memories. Thus, for example, the information derived from hearing a speech on the recognition of Cuba will be combined with everything that we already know about Cuba, and about the recognition of other nations—with our facts, our attitudes, our beliefs, our preconceptions. Similarly, the messages derived about a speaker will interact with all the other facts, attitudes, and beliefs that were derived about the speaker from previous transactions, from rumor and gossip, from stereotypes concerning the racial, religious, or national group to which the speaker belongs, and so on.

This principle is important for you as a public speaker because your speech will interact with all other information the audience has about the topic and you. The relative success or failure of the speech will depend upon this interaction and not merely on the speech proper. Consequently, if you are to be an effective speaker, you must know what information, attitudes, and beliefs the audience has about the topic and you. Your credibility—your reputation in the eyes of the audience (discussed in depth in Unit 4)—will influence the way the audience perceives your speech. Thus, a speech on making advertising more ethical could hardly be delivered effectively by someone who has a reputation for dishonesty or unethical behavior. Likewise, a speech on abortion could not ignore the preconceptions of the audience—as either a right-to-life or a right-to-abortion group because the speech would be received differently by each. It would, for all practical purposes, be a different speech.

Context

The speaker and listeners in Figure 1.2 operate in a context that consists of the physical and the social-psychological dimensions of the environment. As in interpersonal communication, these context variables influence the audience, the speaker, the speech, and the effects of the speech and, therefore, must be measured in planning and in preparing the speech. A speech in a small intimate room and a speech in a sports arena must be approached differently. Similarly, a supportive and a hostile atmosphere cannot be treated in the same way. The effects of the speech are illustrated partially within and partially outside the immediate context to indicate that some of them may be confined to and others may extend beyond the immediate context. The effects of the speech may not appear until long after it is over: a senator may receive votes for a speech made two years earlier. Sometimes the effects are not even identified by the listeners as having been due to the speech. Fortunately, the context for your first speeches will remain relatively stable; your speeches will most likely be presented in the same physical environment to the same audience. But this should not lead you to ignore the importance that context plays in public speaking; the context always exerts significant influence and therefore needs to be analyzed and adjusted to for all public speaking situations.

Messages and channels

All messages pass through one or more channels on their way from speaker to listener and from listener to speaker. A channel is a medium that carries message signals from sender to receiver. This book concentrates on the vocal-auditory channel, the channel concerned with speech and hearing. But the visual channel is also important; significant messages are sent by means of eye contact (and the lack of it), body movement, hand and facial gestures, and by clothing. To a lesser extent messages are sent and received even through the sense of touch. The handshake and the pat on the back are perhaps the clearest examples of tactile communication relevant to public speaking even though they usually occur just prior to or just following the speech proper. Visual messages are sent and received simultaneously with vocal messages. Such message combinations are effective as they reinforce and supplement each other and ineffective as they contradict each other. For example, if a speaker avoids direct eye contact (a nonverbal message) but claims to feel strongly about his or her topic, this speaker is sending conflicting messages and the audience will generally perceive the negative message (eye avoidance) as the one most indicative of the speaker's true feelings.

SEE EXPERIENTIAL VEHICLE 1.1.

REMEMBER that public speaking involves at least the following elements:

1 **speaker**
2 **listeners**
3 **noise**
4 **effect(s)**
5 **context**
6 **messages and channels**

BENEFITS OF PUBLIC SPEAKING

There are numerous benefits to be derived from the study of public speaking and from the improvement of your own public speaking skills. A few general benefits may be mentioned here as a way of rounding out what public speaking is and as a kind of preface to the remaining units.

Public speaking abilities

At the most obvious level, this book and this course should enable you to improve your skills in public speaking. You should emerge from this course-and-text experience a more competent, a more confident, and a more effective public speaker. You should emerge as a more effective listener—more open and yet more critical, more discriminating yet more empathic—and a more competent and discerning critic of public communication. And, since valid and insightful criticism is essential to the improvement of any art (public speaking is no exception), your increased critical competence will in turn help to set higher standards and explain how such higher standards may be achieved.

Speakers are not born but made. Through instruction, through exposure to different models, through feedback, and, in general, through our individual learning experiences, we become the speakers we are. Some have developed considerable competence while others have not. Regardless of your present level of competence, you can improve through proper training

Enhanced academic and professional skills

Learning public speaking consists of learning a wide variety of skills central, but not limited, to public speaking. These skills should serve you in numerous and diverse areas of your academic and professional life. For example, the ability to do the research stressed throughout this book will be useful throughout college. Four units are devoted to the principles and techniques of organization, perhaps the most important single skill for success in college and one that so many students seem to lack. The ability to support an argument logically, to understand human motivation and be able to use your insights in persuasive encounters, the qualities of effective style and how to utilize these in all your communications, the elements of credibility and how they make you a more effective and persuasive individual in all your interactions are additional skills that will prove to be of considerable value in your educational growth.

Personal and social competencies

We all know individuals who function effectively in the academic environment but who are totally inept socially and interpersonally. They may have learned the principles of economics or computer science or mathematics, but the skills of social adjustment and social interaction are sorely lacking. In public speaking, the social and the academic aspects are inseparable. In this book and in your course these will always be treated together. Not only will you be expected to master the body of material contained in this text—as you would in a sociology, geology, or linguistics course—but you will also be expected to apply that material, to use that material, and to make that material an integral part of your communication experiences. Numerous such personal skills are covered in depth in the pages that follow, for example, self-awareness, self-confidence, and dealing with communication apprehension. This book is not concerned with public speaking in the abstract. Rather, it is concerned with you as a public speaker, as a consumer, and as an analyst of public communications. In all discussions of all principles, you as a speaker-listener-critic are the central component.

The preservation of a free and open society

Our society is sustained and improved largely through open and free communication. As Justice Felix Frankfurter said: "In the last analysis we are governed either through talk or through force." One of the lessons to be learned from history is that when communication is restricted, it is the people who lose. Communication is rarely, if ever, restricted for the benefit of the people as a whole. It is restricted for the benefit of those who would attempt to gain and wield power at the expense of others.

As educated leaders—roles that you will assume in the near future—you will need to possess the skills of effective communication so that the values of a free and open society can be preserved. These skills are applicable to the speaker concerned with getting his or her message understood and accepted, to the listener needing to evaluate and critically analyze ideas and arguments before making decisions, and to the critic concerned with evaluating and judging with insight and taste various public communications. The more comfortable you are as a public speaker, the more willing you will be to speak out—supporting what you feel should be supported and resisting what you feel should be resisted. The study of public speaking is, therefore, an essential part of any student's attempt to develop into a more effective individual and social leader.

REMEMBER: The study of public speaking may lead to a number of significant benefits:

1 the improvement of public speaking abilities, as speaker, as listener, and as critic

2 the enhancement of related academic and professional skills in organization, research, style, and the like

3 the improvement of the skills of personal and social adjustment and interaction

4 the improvement of our society in general through the maintenance of free and open communication

SOURCES

On interpersonal communication see my *The Interpersonal Communication Book*, 3d ed. (New York: Harper & Row, 1983), especially Units 1 to 3. The nature of public speaking is considered in numerous and excellent sources. Three of the best are James C. McCroskey, *An Introduction to Rhetorical Communication*, 4th ed. (Englewood Cliffs, N.J.: Prentice-Hall, 1982); Douglas Ehninger, Alan H. Monroe, and Bruce E. Gronbeck, *Principles and Types of Speech Communication*, 8th ed. (Glenview, Ill.: Scott, Foresman, 1978); and Karlyn Kohrs Campbell, *The Rhetorical Act* (Belmont, Calif.: Wadsworth, 1982). On the importance of public speaking see Mortimer J. Adler, *How to Speak, How to Listen* (New York: Macmillan, 1983). On self-confidence as it relates to public speaking, see Dale Carnegie, *How to Develop Self-Confidence and Influence People by Public Speaking* (New York: Pocket Books, 1956). For interesting perspectives on the importance of speech communication in general and public speaking in particular, see Bert E. Bradley, "Speech Communication and Liberal Education," *Southern Speech Communication Journal* 45 (Fall 1979):1–11, and Donald K. Smith, "Rhetoric of and in the Learning Society," *Communication Education* 28 (May 1979):97–103. An interesting exercise of value in many public speaking courses may be found in Kaylene A. Long and Karen Bruner Stroup, "Making Orators Interesting to Students: The Speaker Resume," *Communication Education* 32 (April 1983):243–246.

UNIT 2

Preparing a public speech: An overview

OBJECTIVES

After completing this unit, you should be able to:

1 *identify the three major types of speeches*
2 *explain the distinction between speeches of information and speeches of persuasion*
3 *identify and explain the various steps that a speaker would go through in constructing a public speech*

In Unit 1, "General Principles of Public Speaking," the public speaking process was defined. Here I continue that discussion by focusing on the public speech as a coherent body of messages—designed for a specific audience in order to achieve a specific purpose—and by identifying the steps you should take in preparing and presenting the public speech. Here, then, a capsule summary of the entire public speaking preparation-presentation process will be presented to provide you with enough specific guidance to start preparing and presenting your initial speeches. By following the eight steps outlined, you should be able to prepare and present effective public speeches.

This initial presentation will enable you to put the theory into practice as soon as possible. Another reason for presenting these steps is that they will provide a framework for structuring all of the remaining information in the text. The rest of the text may be seen, then, as an elaboration of these eight steps. As the course progresses and as you continue reading, we will return to each of the principles and further clarify them so that you may perfect and improve your public speaking competencies. For each of the eight steps, I have noted where in the text you may find additional information.

Before examining these eight steps, it is important to realize that the steps are presented in a linear fashion (one after the other) but that the process of constructing a public speech often does not follow such a logical and linear sequence. That is, you will probably not progress simply from Step 1, to 2, to 3, and so on. Instead, your progression might go more like this: Step 1, to Step 2, back again to Step 1, to Step 3, back again to Step 2, and so on throughout the preparation of your speech. For example, after selecting your subject and purpose (Step 1), you may progress to Step 2 and analyze your audience. On the basis of this analysis, however, you may wish to go back and modify your subject, your purpose, or both. Similarly, after you research the topic (Step 3), you may find that you need additional information on your audience and may have to go back to Step 2. All this back and forth should not throw you off track. This is the way most people prepare their speeches as well as their written communications. So, although the steps are presented as a linear sequence and in the general order one would follow, remember that you are in charge of the process. Use the order of these steps as guidelines but break the sequence, going back or jumping forward, as the specific circumstances seem to warrant. As long as you cover all eight steps thoroughly, you should accomplish your goal.

1. SELECT THE TOPIC AND PURPOSE

The first step in preparing a public speech is to select the subject on which you will speak and the general and specific purposes you hope to achieve. Each of these is considered in turn.

The topic

Many beginning student speakers spend an inordinate amount of time selecting a topic. Millions of topics—political, social, economic, philosophical, psychological, and anthropological, to say nothing of those on communication—are available.

Select a topic that is worthwhile and will prove relevant and interesting to both the audience and to you. After all, you will invest a great deal of time and energy in studying and organizing the topic, and you should derive something of value from the topic itself as well as from the application of the public speaking principles.

If your initial speech is to be persuasive, one in which you attempt to influence the attitudes or behaviors of your audience, it would be best to select a topic about which both you and the audience agree and attempt to strengthen rather than to change their existing attitudes. Or you might select a topic about which the audience is relatively neutral and attempt to persuade them to feel either positively or negatively, as you think best. Be certain to limit and narrow your topic to manageable proportions; do not try to cover too much. It would be much better to cover a limited aspect of a topic in depth than to attempt to cover a broad topic but only superficially.

See Appendix C, "Guidelines and Stimuli for Speech Topics," for guidelines on what constitutes a suitable and appropriate speech topic and for numerous topic suggestions. Experiential Vehicles 1.2 and 1.3 also offer subject suggestions.

The purpose

Generally, three types of speeches are distinguished. The type of speech selected will depend on your purpose in making the speech, although in many instances the dividing lines between the different types are not always easy to draw. Recognize that some of the distinctions are made for practical and pedagogical purposes rather than because these distinctions always exist in clear form. The three purposes of speeches are to inform, to persuade, and to serve some ceremonial or special occasion function.

HOW TO . . . Narrow and Limit a Topic

Perhaps the best way to narrow and limit a topic is to begin with a general topic and divide it into its component parts. Then, take one of these parts and divide it into its component parts. Continue with this general process until the topic seems manageable, as one that can reasonably be covered in some depth in the allotted time. For example, take the topic of *television programs* as the first general topic area. This might then be divided into such subtopics as *comedy, children's programs, educational programs, news, movies, soap operas, quiz programs,* and *sports.* You might then take one of these topics, say comedy, and divide it into subtopics. Perhaps you might consider it on a time basis and divide comedy into its significant time periods as presented on television: pre-1950, 1950–1960, 1960–1970, and 1970 to the present. Let us say you are most interested in the current period, 1970 to the present. Divide this into further subtopics such as *major programs*—"Three's Company," "Happy Days," "Mork and Mindy," and so on. You might then take some portion of this subtopic and begin to construct a speech around a specific topic. Some such topics might be "Women in Television Comedy," "Race Relations in Situation Comedy," "Comedy Spinoffs," and so on. The important point, regardless of whether you would have subdivided the topics in this way or not, is that the resultant topic is at least beginning to look manageable, whereas *television programs* without some specificity would take a lifetime to cover adequately.

Construction of tree diagrams—similar to those used in linguistics to illustrate the parts of a sentence and their relationship to each other and to the sentence as a whole—might clarify the general procedure involved in narrowing a topic. Let us say, for example, that you are interested in literature. You might develop a tree diagram developing branches for the division that interests you most. Thus *literature* can be divided into *fiction* and *nonfiction.* If you are more interested in *fiction*, then develop branches from *fiction: novel, drama, poetry,* and *short story.* Now, let us say that it is the *novel* that most interests you. In this case you would create branches from *novel,* and so on. You would keep dividing the topic until you got to something that was significant, appropriate to you, your audience, and the occasion, and manageable in the allotted time. "The Contributions of Truman Capote to Contemporary Fiction," "A Thematic Analysis of Norman Mailer's Novels," "Vonnegut's Appeal Among College Students," and "The Rewriting of Vidal's Novels for Film" might be possible topics. Even though these topics are still broad, they should illustrate what I mean by manageability and the procedures involved in narrowing a topic.

SEE
EXPERIENTIAL
VEHICLE 1.2.
The *informative speech* is designed to create understanding—to clarify, to enlighten, to correct misunderstandings, to demonstrate how something works, to explain how something is structured. In this type of speech we rely most heavily on materials that amplify—on examples, illustrations, definitions, testimony, visual aids, and the like.

SEE
EXPERIENTIAL
VEHICLE 1.3.
The *persuasive speech*, on the other hand, is designed to influence attitudes or behaviors—to strengthen existing attitudes or to change the beliefs of the audience; to motivate behavior or redirect the way in which audience members act. In this type of speech we rely most heavily on materials that offer proof—on evidence, argument, and psychological appeals, for example. Any persuasive speech is in part an informative speech and as such contains materials that amplify, illustrate, define and so on. It would probably be impossible to persuade an audience of something without informing them as well. But in its concern with strengthening or changing attitudes and behaviors, the persuasive speech must go beyond amplification to the use of evidence, argument, motivational appeals, and the like.

The *special occasion speech* contains elements of information and persuasion; yet it is distinctive enough to merit a special division. By "special occasion" I mean speeches designed, for example, to introduce another speaker or a group of speakers; to present a tribute to some individual, institution, or event; and, perhaps most importantly, to secure good will—for an individual, for an institution, for a way of life, for a point of view. This special occasion speech, as you can easily appreciate, is most closely related to the persuasive speech.

The informative speech is covered in Units 13 and 14, "General Principles of Informative Speeches" and "Amplifying the Informative Speech." The persuasive speech is discussed in Units 15–17, "General Principles of Persuasive Speeches," "Developing Arguments for Persuasive Speeches," and "Motivating Behavior in Persuasive Speeches." Special occasion speeches are discussed in Unit 18, "Special Types of Speeches."

SEE
EXPERIENTIAL
VEHICLE 1.4.
Whether you intend to inform, to persuade, to praise, or to introduce, you must narrow your specific purpose. Too many beginning speakers attempt to cover too much in too little time. If your specific purpose is narrow enough, you can go into some depth on those aspects of the topic you do choose to cover. The audience benefits most from a speech that covers a small area in some depth. Otherwise, you will find that you will be telling them essentially what they already know or will be giving them so many new facts and data that they could not possibly retain even a small part of them. Select a few main issues within the topic and illustrate, explain, describe, and support them in a variety of ways.

2. ANALYZE THE AUDIENCE

If you are to inform or persuade your audience, you must know them. Who are they? What do they already know? What would they want to know more about? What special competencies do they have? What opinions, attitudes, and beliefs do they have? Where do they stand on the issues you wish to address? What needs do they have? Specifically, you might wish to focus on some of the following variables, asking yourself what are their implications for your subject, purpose, and method of construction and presentation, and, in fact, for any and all aspects of public speaking.

Age   What is the general age of the audience? How wide is the range? Are there different age groups that will have to be addressed differently? Does the age of the audience impose any limitations on the topic? On the language that will be used? On the examples and illustrations to be selected?

Sex   What is the predominant sex of the audience? Do men and women view the topic differently? If so, how? Do men and women have different backgrounds and experiences and knowledge about the topic? How will this influence the way in which the topic is developed?

Cultural and subcultural factors   How does the audience break down in terms of ethnic and racial background? What implications are there for the topic? For the purpose? For the method of development? Do the experiences, backgrounds, and knowledge of these groups differ so that adjustments must be made in the way in which the speech is constructed? Will the audience identify with you or see you as an outsider—as one outside their own cultural or subcultural group—and what are the implications of this?

Occupation, income, and status of the audience   What are the main occupations of the audience? How might this influence your speech? Does the income of the audience have any implications for the subject chosen, or the way in which it will be developed? What about the general status of the audience members? Might this influence the speech in any way?

Religion and religiousness   What is the dominant religious affiliation of the audience? What are the implications of this for the speech? What is the strength of their belief? How might this relate to the speech topic?

Other factors   What other factors will influence the way in which your speech is prepared and presented? Is marital status relevant? Does the audience have special interests that might be noted in the speech?

Occasion   Is it a special occasion? Does it impose any restrictions on what may or may not be considered appropriate? Are there any implications for the way in which the speech is prepared or presented?

Context   Will the context influence what you discuss or the way in which your speech is presented? Will the context impose any restrictions? Are there appropriate facilities for showing slides? Is there a blackboard? Is there adequate light? Are there enough seats? Is there a podium? Is a microphone necessary?

Units 7, "General Principles of Audience Analysis and Adaptation" and 8, "Adapting to Your Audience," provide more detail on these factors.

3. RESEARCH THE TOPIC

If the speech is to be worthwhile and if you and the audience are to profit from it, you must research the topic. For your first speeches, this will probably entail research in the library. First read some general source—an encyclopedia article or a general article in a journal or magazine. You might pursue some of the references in the article or seek a book or two on the topic from the card catalog. You might also consult one or more of the guides to periodical literature for recent articles in journals, magazines, and newspapers. For some topics, you might want to consult individuals—professors, politicians, physicians, or any person or group of persons with specialized information of value to the development of your speech.

Principles of research and useful sources are considered in depth in Unit 5, "Research for the Public Speech."

4. FORMULATE YOUR THESIS AND IDENTIFY THE MAJOR PROPOSITIONS

The thesis of your speech is simply the main assertion; it is the essence, the core, of what you want your audience to derive from your speech. If your speech is an informative one, then your thesis is the main idea that you want your audience to understand. For example: "Human blood consists of four major elements," or "Speeches may be delivered in four general ways."

If your speech is to be a persuasive one, then your thesis is the main proposition that you wish your audience to accept, to believe in, or to follow. For example: "We should buy Brand X," or "We should contribute to the college athletic fund."

Once the thesis statement is formulated, ask yourself—as would an audience—questions about the thesis in an attempt to identify its major components. In an informative speech, the questions that seem most relevant are What? or How? So, to the thesis "Human blood consists of four major elements," the logical question seems to be: *What are they?* To the thesis "Speeches may be delivered in four general ways," the logical question seems to be: *How?* or *What are they?* In answering these questions, you, in effect, identify the major propositions that should be covered in your speech. The answer to the question *What are the major elements of the blood?,* in the form of a brief public speech outline, would look something like this:

Thesis: "There are four major elements in the human blood." (*What are they?*)
  I. Plasma
 II. Red blood cells (erythrocytes)
III. White blood cells (leukocytes)
IV. Platelets (thrombocytes)

In the persuasive speech, the questions an audience would ask would be more often of the *Why?* type. If your thesis is "We should buy Brand X," then the inevitable question is *Why should we buy Brand X?* Your answers to this question will then enable you to identify the major parts of the speech, which might look something like this:

Thesis: "We should buy Brand X." *(Why should we buy Brand X?)*
 I. Brand X lasts longer.
 II. Brand X is cheaper.
 III. Brand X does a better job.

If your thesis is "We should contribute to the college athletic fund," the inevitable question is *Why should we contribute?* and the answers again enable you to identify the major issues to be covered in the speech. Such a speech outline might look like this:

Thesis: "We should contribute to the college athletic fund." *(Why should we contribute?)*
 I. Your money will increase the positive reputation of the school.
 II. Your money will increase the number of sports that are made available.
 III. Your money will make athletic scholarships available to needy students.

The thesis statement is discussed in greater detail in Unit 9, "General Principles of Organization."

5. SUPPORT THE MAJOR PROPOSITIONS

Now that you have identified your thesis and your major propositions, you must support each of them. You now need to devote attention to telling the audience what it needs to know about plasma and white blood cells. You need to convince the audience that Brand X does in fact last longer and does a better job, and that by contributing to the college athletic fund the positive reputation of the school will be increased.

In the informative speech, your support primarily amplifies—describes, illustrates, defines, exemplifies—the various concepts being discussed. You want the "causes of inflation" to come alive to the audience, to stand out as real, significant, and relevant. Amplification accomplishes this. Specifically, you might use examples and illustrations and the testimony of various authorities or of eyewitnesses to reconstruct an event, for example, a crime of some sort. Presenting definitions especially make the audience conversant with what you are talking about and breathe life into concepts that may otherwise be too abstract or vague. Statistics (summary figures that explain various trends) are essential for certain topics. Audiovisual aids—charts, maps, actual objects, slides, films, audiotapes, records, and so on—will enliven normally vague concepts.

In a persuasive speech your support is proof—material that offers evidence, argument, and motivational appeal and that establishes the credibility and reputation of the speaker—designed to convince the audience to agree with you. If you want to persuade the audience that Brand X should be their choice and if you are going to accomplish this, in part, by demonstrating that Brand X is cheaper, then you must give them good reasons for believing that this is true. You might, for example, compare the price of Brand X with five or six other brands and/or you might demonstrate that the same amount of Brand X will accomplish twice the work as other brands selling at the same price.

Generally, we support our propositions with reasoning from specific instances, from general principles, from analogy, and from causes and effects. These may be thought of as logical support. Also, we support our position through the use of motivational appeals—to the audience's desire for status, for financial gain, for increased self-esteem. We also add persuasive force to our propositions through our own personal reputation or credibility. If the audience members see us as competent, of high moral character, and as charismatic, they are more likely to believe what we say.

Supporting materials are discussed in Unit 14, "Amplifying materials in Informative Speeches," 16, "Developing Arguments for Persuasive Speeches," and 17, "Motivating Behavior in Persuasive Speeches." Credibility is discussed in Unit 4, "Public Speaking Ethics and Credibility."

6. ORGANIZE THE SPEECH MATERIALS

The material must be organized if the audience is to understand and retain it. You might, for example, select a simple *topical pattern*. This involves taking the main points of your speech, treating them as coordinate and equal items, and organizing the various supporting materials under the appropriate items. The body of the speech, then, might look like this:

I. Main point—I
   A. Supporting material for I
   B. Supporting material for I
II. Main point—II
   A. Supporting material for II
   B. Supporting material for II
   C. Supporting material for II
III. Main point—III
   A. Supporting material for III
   B. Supporting material for III

Or you might, in describing the events leading up to a specific happening, choose a temporal pattern, arranging the main issues in chronological order. Say, for example, your topic is war movies and you want to explain some of the changes that have taken place in them. A temporal organizational pattern might be appropriate and might look like this:

I. Movies about World War II
   A. *The Best Years of Our Lives*
   B. *From Here to Eternity*
   C. *Sands of Iwo Jima*

II. Movies about the Korean War
   A. M*A*S*H
   B. *The Manchurian Candidate*
   C. *Pork Chop Hill*
III. Movies about the Vietnam War
   A. *Coming Home*
   B. *The Deer Hunter*
   C. *Apocalypse Now*

For a persuasive speech you may wish to consider other organizational patterns. For example, a *problem-solution pattern* might be effective for a number of topics. Let us say you want to persuade your listeners that communication courses should be required in high schools. You might use a problem-solution pattern; your speech in outline form might look like this:

I. Students cannot communicate. (problem)
   A. They are inarticulate in expressing ideas. (problem 1)
   B. They are ineffective listeners. (problem 2)
   C. They are not critical. (problem 3)
II. Communication courses should be established in high school. (solution)
   A. Communication courses will train students to express themselves. (solution 1)
   B. Communication courses will train students in listening skills. (solution 2)
   C. Communication courses will train students to be critical. (solution 3)

In general, the pattern for a persuasive speech looks like this:

I. Assertion 1
   A. Reason for accepting I
   B. Reason for accepting I
      1. Reason for accepting B
      2. Reason for accepting B
II. Assertion 2
   A. Reason for accepting II
      1. Reason for accepting A
      2. Reason for accepting A
   B. Reason for accepting II

The two assertions (I and II) would, in turn, support the general purpose of the speech. Thus, for example, your specific purpose might be to persuade the audience that they should invest in real estate. Assertions I and II would be reasons why people should invest in real estate. Support A and B would be reasons why we should accept assertions I and II. In short, each item should persuade the audience to accept the item it supports.

These obviously are not the only patterns that might be used; they are merely some of the most popular and ones that beginning speakers seem to be able to develop facility with over a short period of time.

Organizational principles are considered in Units 9, "General Principles of Organization," 10, "The Body of the Speech," and 12, "Outlining the Speech."

7. WORD THE SPEECH

It is obvious that you cannot simply read the outline to the audience. You have to put flesh on the bones and that is the function of language and wording the speech. This step should not be taken as a suggestion to write out your speech word for word; this would result in a stilted and artificial speech, something you clearly want to avoid and something the audience likewise wants to avoid. Rather, in wording the speech you should be concerned with putting your main ideas as well as your supporting materials into language that will be readily understood by your audience. The audience will hear your speech only once. Consequently, make what you are saying instantly intelligible. Do not speak down to your audience but make your ideas, even complex ones, easy to understand at one hearing.

Use words that are simple rather than complex, concrete rather than abstract. Use personal and informal rather than impersonal and formal language. Use simple and active rather than complex and passive sentences. In wording the speech be careful that you do not offend members of your audience. Remember that not all doctors are men and not all secretaries are women; not all persons are or want to be married. Not all persons love parents, dogs, and children. The hypothetical person does not have to be male.

In wording the persuasive speech try to phrase your main assertions in a convincing manner. Be forceful. If the audience you are addressing is hostile or holds a position very different from yours, your wording might be more conciliatory. If you wish to strengthen the position of an already favorable audience, you might be more direct at the start.

For additional insight into style in public speaking and for specific suggestions on wording the speech, see Units 19 and 20, "General Principles of Style" and "Effective Style and the Public Speech."

8. CONSTRUCT THE CONCLUSION AND THE INTRODUCTION

For your early speeches, you may wish to outline the conclusion or write it out word for word. As you develop facility in speech preparation, you will construct the conclusion in the way that works best for you. For now use whatever system seems easiest. Although conclusions may serve a number of different functions, you should try in the initial speeches to have your conclusion serve two major purposes. First, summarize the speech. Identify the main points again and recapitulate essentially what you have told the audience. Second, try to wrap up your speech in some way; seek

HOW TO . . . Rehearse Your Speech

There are many benefits to rehearsing your speech, it will enable you to (1) see how the speech will flow as a whole, (2) make changes and improvements as necessary, (3) learn the speech effectively, and (4) determine how best to present it to your audience. The rehearsal, then, should enable you to improve both the speech and the delivery of it. Here are some suggestions for rehearsal that should enable you to get the most from the experience.

1   Rehearse the speech as a whole, from beginning to end. Do not rehearse the speech in parts; rehearse it from getting out of your seat through the introduction, the body, and the conclusion, to returning to your seat. This will enable you to connect the parts of the speech into a whole and to see how they interact with each other.

2   Rehearse the speech under conditions as close to the actual ones under which you will deliver the speech. If possible, rehearse the speech in the same room in which you will present the speech. If this is impossible, try to simulate the actual conditions as best you can—in your living room or even bathroom if necessary. If possible, rehearse the speech in front of a few supportive listeners. It is always helpful (but especially for your beginning speeches) that your listeners be supportive rather than overly critical. Merely having listeners present during your rehearsal will further simulate the conditions under which you will eventually speak. A most useful procedure is for three or four students in the class to get together in an empty classroom where you can each serve as speaker and listener.

3   Rehearse the speech (if not for the first time, at least during the second or third rehearsal) in front of a full-length mirror. This will enable you to see yourself and to see how you will appear to the audience. This will be extremely difficult at first and you may have to force yourself to watch yourself. After a few attempts you will begin to see the value of this experience.

4   Make any changes in the speech that seem appropriate between rehearsals; do not interrupt your rehearsal to make notes on changes. If you do, you may never experience the entire speech from beginning to end.

5   Rehearse the speech as often as seems necessary. Two useful guides are these: (1) rehearse the speech at least three or four times; less than this is sure to be too little, and (2) rehearse the speech as long as your rehearsals are resulting in improvements in the speech or in your delivery of it.

some kind of closure, some crisp ending. Do not let the speech hang. End the speech clearly and distinctly. For a persuasive speech you may also wish to provide one final push in the direction you want, one final motivational appeal.

The introduction should be the last major part to be constructed because you must know in detail all that you are going to say before you prepare it. It will also be easier to prepare once you have constructed the major part of the speech. Your introduction should first gain the attention of the audience. Most often, your coming to the front of the room will attract their attention; however, as you start to speak you may lose them if you do not make a special effort to hold their attention. A provocative statistic, a little-known fact, an interesting story, or a statement explaining the significance of your topic will secure this attention. Second, try to establish some kind of relationship with the topic and the audience. That is, tell the audience why you are speaking on this topic—why you are concerned with the topic, why you are addressing the audience on this topic, why you are competent to address them, and so on. These are questions that most audiences will automatically ask, and as a speaker you should tell them before they ask. Lastly, the introduction should orient the audience: prepare them for what you are going to say in the order you are going to say it.

For additional consideration of the functions and types of conclusions and introductions, see Unit 11, "Introductions and Conclusions."

REMEMBER the basic steps in preparing a public speech:

1 Select the topic and purpose
2 Analyze the audience, occasion, and context
3 Research the topic
4 Formulate the thesis and identify the major propositions
5 Support the major propositions
6 Organize the major ideas, subdivisions, and supporting materials
7 Word the speech
8 Construct the conclusion and the introduction

SOURCES

All public speaking books treat the nature and general structure of the informative speech. Those by Ehninger, Monroe, and Gronbeck and by McCroskey, cited in Unit 1, provide additional insight into this type of speech. Another useful source is Clark S. Carlile's *Project Text for Public Speaking,* 4th ed. (New York: Harper & Row, 1981), which provides numerous suggestions for informative speeches along with practical suggestions for their preparation and presentation.

For the theory, research, and practical applications of persuasion, the following should prove especially useful: Wayne N. Thompson, *The Process of Persuasion: Principles and Readings* (New York: Harper & Row, 1975); Kenneth E. Andersen, *Persuasion: Theory and Practice,* 2d ed. (Boston: Allyn & Bacon, 1978); Winston L. Brembeck and William S. Howell, *Persuasion: A Means of Social Influence,* 2d ed. (Englewood Cliffs, N.J.: Prentice-Hall, 1976); Joseph A. Ilardo, *Speaking Persuasively* (New York: Macmillan, 1981); Raymond S. Ross and Mark G. Ross, *Understanding Persuasion* (Englewood Cliffs, N.J.: Prentice-Hall, 1981); and Mary John Smith, *Persuasion and Human Action: A Review and Critique of Social Influence Theories* (Belmont, Calif.: Wadsworth, 1982). Two useful brief paperbacks covering the substance of this unit are John Quick, *A Short Book on the Subject of Speaking* (New York: Washington Square Press, 1978) and Leon Fletcher, *How to Speak Like a Pro* (New York: Ballantine Books, 1983).

UNIT 3

Critical listening and evaluation

OBJECTIVES

After completing this unit, you should be able to:

1 *define* listening
2 *explain at least four principles of effective listening*
3 *explain at least three tendencies to avoid in listening*
4 *define and explain the nature of criticism*
5 *identify and explain at least five principles to follow in giving criticism*

The preparation and presentation of the public speech is only one-half of the process; the other half is critical listening and evaluation. This unit is devoted to the principles of listening to and evaluating a speech.

LISTENING AND CRITICISM: TWO DEFINITIONS

Before identifying the principles of effective listening and criticism, we need to define what is meant by each of these activities.

Listening

Listening is an *active*, not a passive process. Listening is not merely hearing. Listening is the active process of receiving aural stimuli. Listening does not just happen. We make it happen through a considerable expenditure of energy. Listening involves *receiving* stimuli, not merely allowing them to pass through our ears. By "receiving stimuli" I mean that these stimuli are processed or used by the individual, that they are retained at least for some period of time, and that they are integrated with whatever other information is in our memories. Lastly, listening involves *aural stimuli*—stimuli received by the auditory mechanism. Listening, therefore, is not limited to the reception of words and sentences but includes all signals that are auditory—noise as well as words; unintentional as well as intentional sounds; grunts, groans, and sighs as well as poetry. It is important to note, however, that even though we receive the speech auditorily, our total response to the speech is influenced by various nonauditory factors as well—by the speaker's physical mannerisms, dress, and general appearance, by the physical and psychological context, by our own expectations, and, in general, by all those factors that influence the public speaking transaction.

SEE
EXPERIENTIAL
VEHICLE 1.5.

Listening is a most imperfect process. When we listen to a speech, we derive a meaning that is actually a composite of what the speaker has said and all that we already have in our minds and bring to bear on this particular message (prejudices, knowledge, values, opinions, and so on). Meaning is thus in the minds of listeners, not in the message itself. As listeners our job in understanding a speaker is to approximate as closely as we can the meaning that is in the mind of the speaker. As speakers our job is to communicate messages that will enable listeners to most effectively reproduce in their minds what is in ours. In this unit a number of suggestions are offered to improve our listening behavior in order to make us more effective and more efficient consumers of oral messages. Throughout the text, suggestions are offered to enable us to construct and deliver messages that listeners will find (at a minimum) relevant to their needs and interests, understandable, convincing, and persuasive.

Criticism

More difficult than listening critically is the process of evaluating or criticizing a public speech. By criticism or evaluation I do not mean miscellaneous fault-finding. Actually, the term *criticism* comes from the Latin *criticus* meaning "able to discern," "to judge." There is nothing inherently negative about criticism. Rather, by criticism I mean the process by which we apply standards to a particular speech and render a judgment of the speech. The judgment or evaluation may be positive as well as negative, praise as well as blame, applause as well as censure.

PRINCIPLES OF EFFECTIVE LISTENING

In his most recent book, *How to Speak, How to Listen,* philosopher Mortimer J. Adler criticizes our educational system for ignoring the teaching of listening: "How utterly amazing is the general assumption that the ability to listen well is a natural gift for which no training is required. How extraordinary is the fact that no effort is made anywhere in the whole educational process to help individuals learn how to listen well—at least well enough to close the circuit and make speech effective as a means of communication." The following principles should help significantly to "close the circuit." Listening improvement will be facilitated if you listen actively, listen for total meaning, listen with empathy, listen with an open mind, and listen critically.

Listen actively

Perhaps the first step in listening improvement is the recognition that it is not a passive activity; it is not a process that will happen if you simply do nothing to stop it. You may hear without effort but you cannot listen without effort.

Listening is a difficult process; in many ways it is more demanding than speaking. In speaking you are in control of the situation; you can talk about what you like in the way you like. In listening, however, you are forced to follow the pace, the content, and the language set by the speaker.

Perhaps the best preparation for active listening is to act like an active listener. This may seem trivial and redundant. In practice, however, this may be the most often abused rule of effective listening. Students often, for example, come into class, put their feet up on a nearby desk, nod their head to the side, and expect to listen effectively. It just does not happen that way. Recall, for example, how your body almost automatically reacts to important news. Almost immediately you assume an upright posture, cock your head to the speaker, and remain relatively still and quiet. You do this almost reflexively because this is how you listen most effectively. This is not to say that you should be tense and uncomfortable but only that your body should reflect your active mind.

Listen for total meaning

In listening to another individual you need to learn to listen for total meaning. The total meaning of any communication act is extremely complex, and you can be sure that you will never get it all. However, the total meaning is not only in the words used. The meaning is also in the nonverbal behavior of the speaker. Sweating hands and shaking knees communicate just as surely as do words and phrases.

Along with the verbal and nonverbal behaviors you should also recognize that the meaning of a public speech lies also in what is omitted. The speaker who talks about racism solely in the abstract, for example, and who never once mentions a specific group is communicating something quite different from the speaker who talks in specifics.

Listen with empathy

It is relatively easy to learn to listen for understanding or for comprehension. But this is only a part of public speaking. You also need to *feel* what the speaker feels—to empathize with the speaker. To empathize with others is to feel what they feel, to see the world as they see it, to walk in their shoes. Only when you achieve this will you be able to fully understand another's meaning.

There is no fast method for achieving empathy with another individual. But it is something you should work toward. It is important that you see the teacher's point of view, not from that of your own, but from that of the teacher. And, equally, it is important for the teacher to see the student's point of view from that of the student. If students turn in late papers, teachers should attempt to put themselves in the role of the students to begin to understand the possible reasons for the lateness. Similarly, if teachers get disturbed because they are late, students should attempt to put themselves in the role of teachers and attempt to understand the reason for the disturbance.

William V. Pietsch, in his imaginative *Human BE-ing*, makes the point that most of our education has been concerned with objective facts to the almost total neglect of subjective feelings. We need to recognize that understanding and problem solving cannot be achieved solely with reference to the intellect; the emotions as well need to be examined. "Real listening," says Pietsch, "means 'tuning in' to what the other person is *feeling* so that we *listen to emotions*, not simply to 'ideas.' "

Listen with an open mind

Listening with an open mind is difficult. It is not easy to listen to arguments against some cherished belief. It is not easy to listen to statements condemning what you so fervently believe. It is not easy to listen to criticisms of what you think is just great.

In counseling students one of the most difficult tasks is to make them realize that even though they may dislike a particular teacher, they can still learn something from him or her. For some reason many people attempt to punish the people they dislike by not listening to them. Of course, if the situation is that of teacher and student, then the student suffers by losing out on significant material.

It is difficult for most people to continue listening fairly after some signal has gone up in the form of an out-of-place expression or a hostile remark. Listening often stops when such a remark is made. Admittedly, to continue listening with an open mind is difficult; yet, it is when hostile feelings first develop that it is particularly important that listening continues.

Listen critically

Although I emphasize that you should listen with an open mind and with empathy, I do not mean that you should listen uncritically. Quite the contrary, you need to listen fairly but critically if meaningful public speaking is to take place. As an intelligent and educated citizen, it is your responsibility to critically evaluate what you hear. This is especially true in the college environment. While it is easy simply to listen to a teacher and take down what is said, it is extremely important that what is said be evaluated and critically analyzed. Teachers have biases too; at times consciously and at time unconsciously these biases creep into scholarly discussions. They need to be identified and brought to the surface by the critical listener. Contrary to what most students will argue, the vast majority of teachers will appreciate the responses of critical listeners. It demonstrates that someone is listening.

REMEMBER these principles of effective listening:

1   Listen actively
2   Listen for total meaning
3   Listen with empathy
4   Listen with an open mind
5   Listen critically

LISTENING TENDENCIES TO AVOID

Your listening effectiveness should improve if you do not prejudge the speech or speaker, do not rehearse your responses, do not filter out unpleasant messages, and do not focus attention on style and delivery. Each of these needs to be explained a bit more fully.

Don't prejudge the speech or speaker

Whether in a lecture auditorium or in a small group of people there is a strong tendency to prejudge the speeches of others as uninteresting or irrelevant to our own needs or to the task at hand. Often we compare these speeches with something we might say or with something that we might be doing instead of "just listening." Generally, listening to others comes in a poor second.

By prejudging a speech as uninteresting, you are in effect lifting the burden of listening from your own shoulders. If you have already determined that the speech is uninteresting, for example, there is no reason to listen. So you may just tune out the speaker and let your mind recapture last Saturday night.

All speeches are, at least potentially, interesting and relevant. If you prejudge them and tune them out, you will never be proven wrong. At the same time, however, you close yourself off from potentially useful information. Most important, perhaps, is that you do not give the other person a fair hearing.

Don't rehearse your responses

For the most part we are, as Wendell Johnson put it, our own most enchanted listeners. No one speaks as well or on such interesting topics as we do. If we could listen just to ourselves, listening would be no problem.

It often happens that a speaker may say something with which you disagree; for the remainder of that speaker's time you may rehearse your response or rebuttal or question. You then imagine his or her reply to your response and then your response to his or her response and so on and on. Meanwhile, you have missed whatever else the speaker had to say—perhaps even the part that would make your question unnecessary or irrelevant or which might raise other and more significant questions.

If the speech is relatively long, it is perhaps best to jot down the point at issue and go back to listening. If the situation makes this impossible, simply make mental note of what you want to say and perhaps keep this in mind by relating it to the remainder of what the individual is saying. In either event the important point is to get back to listening.

Don't filter out unpleasant messages

I once had a teacher who claimed that whatever he could not immediately understand was not worth reading or listening to; if it had to be worked at, it was not worth the effort. I often wonder how he managed to learn, how he was intellectually stimulated if indeed he was. Depending on our own intellectual equipment, many of the messages that we confront will need careful consideration and in-depth scrutiny. Listening will be difficult, but the alternative—to miss out on what is said—seems even less pleasant than stretching and straining our minds a bit.

Perhaps more serious than filtering out difficult messages is filtering out unpleasant ones. None of us want to be told that something we believe in is untrue, that people we care for are unpleasant, or that ideals we hold are self-destructive. And yet, these are the very messages we need to listen to with great care. These are the very messages that will lead us to examine and reexamine our implicit and unconscious assumptions. If we filter out this kind of information we will be left with a host of unstated and unexamined assumptions and premises that will influence us without our influencing them. That prospect is not very pleasant.

Don't focus attention on style or delivery

For many people in communication, having studied language and style for so long, it is difficult not to concentrate on the stylistic peculiarities of an individual. In hearing a clever phrase or sentence, for example, it is difficult to resist the temptation to dwell on it and analyze it. Similarly, it is difficult for many to ignore various gestures or particular aspects of voice. Focusing on these dimensions of communication only diverts time and energy away from the message itself. This is not to say that such behaviors are not important, but only that you can fall into the trap of devoting too much attention to the way the message is packaged and not enough to the message itself.

REMEMBER to avoid these obstacles to listening:
1   Prejudging the speech or speaker
2   Rehearsing your responses
3   Filtering out unpleasant messages
4   Focusing attention on style or delivery

EVALUATING THE SPEECH

Now that the basic steps of speech preparation and the principles of effective listening have been identified, the issue of critical evaluation should be explored. Two major issues are relevant here. First, we need to identify some guidelines for criticism: What do we look for—what do we focus on—when criticizing or evaluating a public speech? Second, how we can best express our criticism so that it has the effect we want it to have? Each of these two issues is considered in turn.

Guidelines for speech criticism

As a beginning guide to the criticism of public speeches, focus on the following questions as the basis for your criticism and evaluation. All of these questions are drawn from topics considered in Unit 2 and elaborated on in greater detail in the units to follow. You should also find these questions a useful checklist for your own speeches, to make sure that you have appropriately followed the various principles of public speaking. These questions are in no way exhaustive; there are many additional issues on which criticism may focus. These questions provide you only with some initial guidance in criticism. Additional issues for critical evaluation, as well as refinements of these questions, are presented throughout the rest of the text.

The subject and purpose
1   Is the subject a worthwhile one?
2   Is the subject relevant and interesting to the audience and to the speaker?
3   Is the information presented of benefit to the audience in some way?
4   What is the general purpose of the speech (to inform, to persuade, to secure good will, etc.)?
5   Is the specific topic sufficiently narrow to be covered in some depth in the time allotted?
6   Are the general and specific purposes clear to the audience? Is this clarity (or lack of it) appropriate to this specific speech for this specific audience?

The audience, occasion, and context
7   Has the speaker taken into consideration the age; sex; cultural and subcultural factors; occupation, income, and status; and religion and religiousness of the audience? How are these factors dealt with in the speech?
8   Is the speech topic appropriate to the specific occasion?
9   Is the speech topic appropriate to the general context?

Research
10   Has the speech been thoroughly researched?
11   Do the sources appear reliable and up-to-date?
12   Does the speaker seem to have a thorough understanding of the subject?
13   Is this competence communicated in some way to the audience?

The thesis and major propositions
14   Is the thesis of the speech clear and limited to one main idea?
15   Are the main propositions of the speech clearly related to the thesis?
16   Are the thesis and the major propositions clear to the audience?
17   Are there an appropriate number of major propositions in the speech (not too many, not too few)?

Supporting materials
18   Is each major proposition adequately supported?
19   Are the supporting materials appropriate to the speech and to the propositions?

20 Do the supporting materials amplify what they purport to amplify? Do they prove what they purport to prove?
21 Are there a variety of supporting materials used?
22 Are enough supporting materials used so that each of the major propositions are clearly and forcefully presented?
23 Does the speaker's own personal reputation or credibility add persuasive force to the propositions? How?

Organization
24 How is the body of the speech organized? What pattern of organization is used?
25 Is the pattern of organization used appropriate to the speech topic? To the audience?
26 Is the pattern of organization clear to the audience?

Style and language
27 Does the language used enable the audience to understand clearly and immediately what the speaker is saying? For example, are simple rather than complex, concrete rather than abstract, words used? Are personal and informal terms and sentence patterns used? Are simple and active sentences used?
28 Is the language offensive to any person or group of persons?
29 Are the assertions intended to be persuasive phrased in as convincing a manner as possible?

The conclusion and the introduction
30 Does the conclusion effectively summarize the main points identified in the speech?
31 Does the conclusion effectively wrap up the speech and provide a recognizable closure?
32 In a persuasive speech, does the conclusion help to further motivate the audence in the direction the speaker wishes?
33 Does the introduction gain the attention of the audience?
34 Does the introduction establish a relationship between the speaker on the one hand and the audience and the topic on the other?
35 Does the introduction provide an adequate and clear orientation to the subject matter of the speech?

Delivery
36 Does the speaker maintain eye contact with the audience?
37 Are there any distractions (of mannerism, dress, or vocal characteristics) that will divert attention from the speech?
38 Can the speaker be easily heard?
39 Is the volume and rate appropriate to the audience, occasion, and topic?
40 Are the voice and bodily actions appropriate to the speaker, subject, and audience?

Expressing criticism

The major purpose of criticism in the classroom is to improve public speaking. Through constructive criticism you, as a speaker and as a listener-critic, will learn the principles of public speaking more effectively. Feedback is essential to improvement. By seeing these guidelines in operation, by dissecting them, and by evaluating their applications in various speeches, you will come to understand and appreciate them better and ultimately internalize them. Through criticism, you will be better able to see what worked and what did not work and what should be retained, enlarged upon, modified, or eliminated. Yet, for all its benefits critical evaluations are often fiercely resisted—especially by the beginning student. The main source of resistance seems to be that the evaluations are often expressed in a manner that encourages defensiveness and often appear to be personal attacks. To counteract that resistance and to make the evaluations effective and even enjoyable learning experiences, the following suggestions on expressing our critical evaluations are offered.

SEE EXPERIENTIAL VEHICLE 1.6.

Say something positive   Remember that egos are fragile and that public speaking is extremely personal, especially for the beginning speaker. We all want compliments. We are all like Noel Coward when he said, "I love criticism just as long as it's unqualified praise." Recall that part of your function as a critic is to strengthen the already positive aspects of someone's public speaking performance. Positive criticism is particularly important in itself but is almost essential as a preface to negative comments. In fact, my own practice is to make only positive comments on all first speeches, not to give grades, and in general to use the critical period to build a positive and a supportive atmosphere to strengthen the positive aspects. I reserve the more complex negative criticism for future speeches. There are enough positive characteristics to easily occupy considerable time and it is more productive to concentrate on them first.

Be specific   In any criticism, you should help the speaker improve his or her public speaking efforts. You achieve this by being as specific as you can. To say, "I thought your delivery was bad" or "I thought your examples were good" does not specify what the speaker might do to improve delivery or to capitalize on the examples used. In commenting on delivery, refer to such specifics as eye contact, vocal volume, or whatever else is of consequence.

In giving negative criticism, specify and justify—to the extent that you can—positive alternatives. For example, "I thought the way in which you introduced your statistics was somewhat vague. I wasn't sure where the statistics came from or how recent or reliable they were. It might have been better to say something like 'The 1980 U.S. Census figures show that. . . .' In this way we would know that the statistics were recent and the most reliable available."

Be objective   Objectivity is perhaps the most difficult of all principles of speech criticism; we seem inherently subjective creatures. We see things and respond to them through our unique perceptual apparatus, an apparatus that is made up almost solely of subjective feelings, desires, preferences, prejudices, and the like. In criticizing a speech you should, first of all, acknowledge your own subjectivity, your own biases. Second, try to transcend these as best you can and see the speech as objectively as possible. If, for example, you are strongly in favor of women's right to abortion and you encounter a speech diametrically opposed to your position, you need to take special care not to dismiss the speech because of your own bias. Rather, you need to examine the speech from the point of view of the (detached) critic and evaluate, for example, the validity of the arguments and their suitability to the audience, the language of the speech, the supporting materials, and in fact all the ingredients that went into the preparation and presentation of the speech. Conversely, you need to take special care that you do not evaluate positively a speech simply because it puts forth a position with which you agree. This speech needs to be evaluated based on the same factors—the validity of the arguments, the supporting materials, and so on. When evaluating a speech by a speaker you feel strongly about—whether positively or negatively—you must be equally vigilant. A disliked speaker may give an effective, well-constructed, well-delivered speech, whereas a well-liked speaker may give an ineffective, poorly constructed, poorly delivered speech.

The more strongly you feel about the speech purpose or about the speaker, whether positively or negatively, the less likely you are to be objective. In fact, you can never be totally objective. You can only strive to become more aware of your own biases and to limit their influence on your evaluations and criticisms. Keep Matthew Arnold's definition of criticism in mind. Criticism, he noted, is a "disinterested endeavour to learn and propagate the best that is known and thought in the world."

Limit criticism   If criticism is to help the speaker improve, cataloging 10 or 12 weak points will overwhelm and not help the speaker. If you are the sole critic, your criticism naturally will need to be more extensive. If you are one of many critics, your criticism should be more limited. In all cases, your guide should be the value your comments have for the speaker.

Be constructive   Criticism should be constructive. It is not to demonstrate your own expertise on the subject. Nor should it be a forum to air your own contrary views. Some of this can hardly be avoided. Certainly there is no need to hide your knowledge of the subject or that you hold different views. Yet, the demonstration of such knowledge or viewpoints should not be your primary goal. Your primary goal should be to provide the speaker with the insight that you feel will prove useful in future public speaking transactions.

Support the speaker during the speech   Criticism is given not only after a speech but during it as well. As listeners in any public speaking effort, you should demonstrate support for the speaker throughout the speech. Listen attentively and otherwise respond actively. When you agree,

Criticism is an inevitable part of public speaking and of life in general. Receiving criticism is one of the most significant ways in which we learn to improve our skills, and yet it is one of the most difficult experiences we have to deal with. Here are a few suggestions for receiving criticism and making positive use of it.

You will benefit from criticism if you, as a speaker, learn to control your defensiveness, to separate criticism of the speech from criticism of the self, to seek clarification when needed, and to understand the reasons for the criticisms and the suggested changes.

CONTROL DEFENSIVENESS

Whenever we are evaluated, especially when negatively, we tend to become defensive, perhaps in an effort to protect ourselves from psychological harm or to preserve our egos or to otherwise save our positive self-concept. But defensiveness seals off effective communication and prevents us from taking in the very information that may prove helpful to our future efforts. After all, we are in a public speaking class to improve our public speaking and not merely to be patted on the back.

SEPARATE SPEECH CRITICISM FROM CRITICISM OF THE SELF

Speech—and, in fact, all aspects of your communication behavior—is so ego-involving that it is difficult (often impossible) to separate it from yourself as a person. And yet, if you are to improve your public speaking performance and yet not be psychologically crushed by negative evaluations, you should recognize that when some aspect of your speech is criticized, your personality or your worth as an individual is not being criticized. Try to externalize critical evaluations so that you view them and analyze them dispassionately.

SEEK CLARIFICATION

Critics, assuming that what is very clear to them must also be clear to everyone else, often tend to state their comments in vague and general terms, so in many instances the criticism will not be clear. You should not hesitate, when this is the case, to ask for clarification. Also ask for clarification if you do not see how to apply the criticism to improve your future efforts. Thus, for example, if it is unclear when you are told that your specific purpose was too broad, ask how you might narrow down the specific purpose. Your critics—instructor and fellow students—should welcome such attempts to seek clarification.

UNDERSTAND REASONS

Try to understand the reasons for the criticism; that is, why certain aspects of the speech or its presentation were criticized and why the suggested alterations would make a more effective speech. Once you understand the *basis* for the criticism, you will be in a better position to incorporate these suggestions into your future public speaking efforts.

let the speaker see that you agree by a head nod, a smile, or some other signal. To the public speaker new to the experience nothing seems worse than to look out at an audience and see total indifference written on everyone's face. So, not only is it important to say something positive after the speech, it is also important to demonstrate positiveness during the speech.

Remember the irreversibility of communication Communication is irreversible. Once something is said, it cannot be unsaid. Remember this when offering criticism, especially criticism that may be too negative. If in doubt, it is better to err on the side of gentleness.

REMEMBER, when giving criticism:

1 **Say something positive**
2 **Be specific**
3 **Be objective**
4 **Limit criticism**
5 **Be constructive**
6 **Support the speaker during the speech**
7 **Remember the irreversibility of communication**

SOURCES

For listening see, for example, Lyman K. Steil, Larry L. Barker, and Kittie W. Watson, *Effective Listening: Key to Your Success* (Reading, Mass.: Addison-Wesley, 1983); Ella Erway, *Listening: A Programmed Approach* (New York: McGraw-Hill, 1969); Baxter and Corinne Geeting, *How to Listen Assertively* (New York: Monarch, 1976); and Andrew D. Wolvin and Carolyn Gwynn Coakley, *Listening* (Dubuque, Iowa: Brown, 1982). Ralph Nichols and Leonard Stevens, *Are You Listening?* (New York: McGraw-Hill, 1957) is perhaps the classic in the field of listening and still is valid. Brief but useful accounts of listening are provided by C. William Colburn and Sanford B. Weinberg, *An Orientation to Listening and Audience Analysis* (Chicago: Science Research Associates, 1976) and Robert O. Hirsch, *Listening: A Way to Process Information Aurally* (Dubuque, Iowa: Gorsuch Scarisbrick, 1979). A different approach to listening may be found in Robert R. Bostrom and Carol L. Bryant, "Factors in the Retention of Information Presented Orally: The Role of Short-Term Listening," *Western Journal of Speech Communication* 44 (Spring 1980):137–145. For a philosopher's viewpoint, see Mortimer J. Adler, *How to Speak, How to Listen* (New York: Macmillan, 1983).

On criticism and evaluation see, for example, Craig R. Smith, *Speech Criticism* (Chicago: Science Research Associates, 1976). Also see Sidney B. Simon's *Negative Criticism* (Niles, Ill.: Argus Communications, 1978) for an approach to criticism that focuses on what it does to an individual and how to deal with it. On feedback see, for example, Barrie Hopson and Charlotte Hopson's *Intimate Feedback: A Lover's Guide to Getting in Touch with Each Other* (New York: New American Library, 1976) and B. Aubrey Fisher's *Perspectives on Human Communication* (New York: Macmillan, 1978).

Most of the works on criticism and evaluation are addressed to the professional critic rather than the beginning student concerned with criticizing the speeches of fellow students and most effectively utilizing criticism received. For those who do wish more advanced reading, the following few sources should prove useful: Robert Scott and Bernard Brock, eds., *Methods of Rhetorical Criticism: A Twentieth Century Perspective*, 2nd ed. (Detroit, Mich.: Wayne State University Press, 1980); Karlyn Kohrs Campbell, *Critiques of Contemporary Rhetoric* (Belmont, Calif.: Wadsworth, 1972); Lester Thonssen, A. Craig Baird, and Waldo Braden, *Speech Criticism* (New York: Ronald Press, 1970); and James R. Andrews, *The Practice of Rhetorical Criticism* (New York: Macmillan, 1983). A most useful work for speaker and critic alike is Hendrie Weisinger and Norman M. Lobsenz, *Nobody's Perfect: How to Give Criticism and Get Results* (New York: Warner Books, 1981).

UNIT 4

Public speaking ethics and credibility

OBJECTIVES

After completing this unit, you should be able to:

1 *identify and explain the guidelines for evaluating the ethics of a speaker*
2 *define speaker credibility*
3 *explain the ways in which credibility impressions may be formed*
4 *distinguish among initial, derived, and terminal credibility*
5 *explain the three components of credibility*
6 *identify at least 10 suggestions for increasing your credibility*

In this unit two related issues will be explored: ethics and credibility. Both concern the character of the speaker. *Ethics* refers to the rightness or wrongness of behavior; it refers to the morality-immorality of actions. *Credibility*, on the other hand, refers to the audience's perception of the character of the speaker.

SPEAKER ETHICS

After Watergate, notes Fred Hechinger writing for *The New York Times* (August 28, 1979), "the public saw bribery in high places, disregard of civil liberties and of people's privacy, scandals in Congress, misuse of Medicaid by many doctors and reports of flagrant cheating on college campuses by those who would be tomorrow's doctors, lawyers, executives, politicians." In 1977 the Carnegie Corporation and the Rockefeller Brothers Fund underwrote an examination of the place of ethics, of moral principles, and of standards of right and wrong in higher education. A number of basic goals have emerged from this study.

One goal is to understand the existence and importance of an ethical point of view. Human beings exist in relationships, and decisions made by one person may deeply affect others, bringing pain or happiness. Because of this interrelationship among all of us, decisions have a moral dimension. Another goal is to recognize and appreciate that numerous social, psychological, and political issues are intimately connected to moral and ethical questions and that decisions in these areas also involve questions of right and wrong, morality and immorality. And perhaps most importantly, we have to appreciate the very real personal responsibility each of us bears for the maintenance of a democratic society and the protection of the rights and freedoms of others. These goals are not new; they have been recognized by theorists of public speaking since classical times. And yet, in light of recent political and social events, it is perhaps appropriate that ethical issues be reexamined and reemphasized.

In this discussion of ethics, I am specifically concerned with the rightness or wrongness of the public speaker's behaviors *and* the listener's behaviors. I am concerned with looking at the speaker and the listener and asking what standards they should adhere to—what principles they should follow—if their public speaking behaviors are to be considered ethical.

All criteria or principles that are advanced must be based on some ethical system. Standards do not exist in a vacuum; rather, they grow out of some coherent systematic analysis of human interaction. The standards applied here to the public speaker and to the listener grow out of the fundamental belief that each person has a right to make his or her own choices and that each person has a right to the information and the knowledge necessary to make informed choices. I assume that the individual is intellectually and emotionally capable of making reasoned and reasonable choices and that these choices will not restrict or prevent other persons from making their choices. Thus, young persons, mentally ill persons, and those who would prevent others from exercising their right of choice cannot always and everywhere be given the freedom to exercise their own choices. Mothers and fathers, doctors and psychiatrists, and judges and law enforcement officers may have to prevent the exercise of some individual choices. But with these few exceptions, I think it is helpful to visualize our standards and guidelines for the speaker-listener as growing out of this fundamental assumption that people have the right to make their own choices and the right to secure valid and reliable information relevant to the making of these choices.

The aim of this unit is not to prime you to accept the ethical position set forth here, but rather to provide you with one point of view that will serve as a starting point for a personal examination of your own system of ethics. You will eventually formulate a system of ethics of public speaking that you find useful, workable, justifiable, and consistent with your own beliefs and values.

ETHICAL GUIDELINES

Five guidelines might be used in evaluating the ethics of your behavior as a public speaker. My primary purpose in presenting these guidelines is to stimulate you to think about your own ethical standards and behaviors. These are not the only guidelines that may be used and certainly they do not answer all the questions that might be raised about the ethics of public speaking. Yet, they should provide an initial framework for structuring your own.

Be truthful   First, be truthful. Present the truth as best you understand it. Your audience does not expect universal Truths (with a capital T). But it does have a right to expect that you speak the truth as you see it. Obviously you should avoid lying but should also avoid misrepresenting the truth because it better fits your purpose, or distorting some bit of information because in undistorted form it would support an alternative point of view. Edgar A. Shoaff noted that "advertising is the art of making whole lies out of half truths." And, unfortunately, public speaking is viewed by many persons in the same way. If you stick to the literal truth but imply an untruth or lead the audience to assume an untruth, you are lying just as surely as if the lie was presented stripped of this half-truth veneer.

Be informed   Second, you should be informed. If you elect to speak on a specific subject—as a teacher lecturing to a class, as a lawyer summarizing a case, or as a union official explaining a new contract—prepare yourself as thoroughly as you can so that the audience may learn information necessary to make reasoned and reasonable choices.

Be audience oriented   Third, you should have the audience's interests foremost in mind. This is not to say that you should not speak out of personal interest but that the audience should not be exploited. If the audience is asked to listen to a speech and to behave in specified ways, it should be for their ultimate benefit or for that of some larger audience—the general community, the next generation, and so on. It would be unethical, for example, to persuade an audience to take up arms in a self-destructive war or to donate money to a mismanaged or embezzling organization. It is unethical to promote a product detrimental to the audience members. To be specific, I think it is unethical for speakers, advertisers, designers, actors, writers, and the like to promote the sale of cigarettes since they have been determined to be harmful to the consumer. Some will object to this position and argue that the advertiser is merely making attractive something that the consumer already wants. Advertisers are themselves not so naive. Their function, it is true, is to make their product more attractive but their ultimate aim, in the case of cigarettes, is to encourage nonsmokers to smoke and smokers to smoke more. If they didn't, the tobacco manufacturers would lose money and they themselves would be out of jobs. Any speaker, then, who encourages destructive behavior in the audience engages in unethical behavior.

Be well prepared   Fourth, I think the audience has a right to expect that you have done your best in terms of preparation, organization, style, delivery, and all the elements that go into making a public speech. As a student you know how horrible it is to sit through class after class and listen to boring lecturers ramble on not attempting to make the lecture relevant or to deliver it in a dynamic and interesting manner or to organize it into a coherent whole with an introduction, a body, and a conclusion. Such public speaking is unethical because inept delivery, organization, and the like keep the audience uninformed and unable to make reasoned choices.

Be easily understood   Fifth, and closely related to preparedness, is the issue of understandability, a concept I take from J. Vernon Jensen's *Perspectives on Oral Communication.* The speaker has an obligation to make his or her speech understandable to the audience. To talk above the level of the audience and thus prevent the audience from clearly understanding what is being argued or explained, or to talk in oversimplified terms and allow the audience to think they understand what they really do not are both unethical practices. You can see clear examples of this practice every day—the doctor or lawyer who speaks in "medicalese" or "legalese" to prevent you from understanding what she or he means or the insurance company salesperson who makes the insurance benefits seem so simple that you think you understand fully until you file a claim and discover that the small print ruled out this particular kind of coverage.

This does not mean that it is unethical for a speaker to use irony, to phrase ideas in complex language, or to simplify abstract concepts. As with the other principles noted here, you must analyze the speaker's intention. If it is to present the audience with the information necessary for them to make their own choices, it would be basically ethical. If, on the other hand, it intends to prevent the audience from securing such information, it would be basically unethical.

SEE EXPERIENTIAL VEHICLE 1.7.

If you put yourself in the position of the listener, you can appreciate that nothing extraordinary is being demanded of you. You are merely asked to be truthful, informed, concerned with the interests of the audience, to do the best you can in terms of preparation and presentation, and to be easily understood.

REMEMBER the ethical public speaker is

1   **Truthful**
2   **Informed**
3   **Concerned with the audience**
4   **Prepared**
5   **Understandable**

CREDIBILITY

We have probably all had the experience of listening to a public speaker and, as a sole result of who the speaker was—apart from any arguments, evidence, or motivational appeals offered—believed or disbelieved the speaker. Often we are persuaded to believe certain information or to take certain action solely by virtue of the speaker's reputation, personality, or character. As Alexander Pope put it more poetically in his "Essay on Criticism":

> Some judge of author's names, not works, and then
> Nor praise nor blame the writings, but the men.

This quality of believability is referred to as *speaker credibility*. In this section I will explain what constitutes speaker credibility, how we form credibility impressions, and, most importantly, how we can increase our own credibility.

SEE EXPERIENTIAL VEHICLE 1.8.

Speaker credibility is that quality of persuasiveness that depends on the audience's perception of the moral character of the speaker. Note that I said "the audience's *perception* of the character of the speaker" rather than simply the character of the speaker. The reason for this distinction is a most important one: Credibility is something that a listener or receiver perceives a speaker to have; it is not something that the speaker has or does not have in any objective sense. In reality the speaker may be a stupid immoral person, but if perceived by the audience as intelligent and moral then that speaker is said to have high credibility and will, research tells us, be believable.

Writing some 2300 years ago Aristotle said in his *Rhetoric:* "There are three things which inspire confidence in the orator's own character—the three, namely, that induce us to believe a thing apart from any proof of it: good sense, good moral character, and good will."

Much contemporary research has been directed at the question of what makes a person believable. As can be appreciated, it is a question of vital concern to many. Advertisers are interested because it relates directly to the effectiveness or ineffectiveness of their ad campaigns. Is James Garner an effective spokesperson for Polaroid? Is Bill Cosby an effective spokesperson for Jello? For Texas Instruments? Credibility is important to the politician because it determines in great part how people vote. It influences education since the students' perception of teacher credibility will determine the degree of influence the teacher has on a class. There are probably few communication encounters that will not be influenced by considerations of credibility.

Forming credibility impressions

We form a *credibility impression* of a speaker on the basis of (1) the reputation of the speaker (as perceived in our minds), and (2) how that reputation is confirmed or refuted by what the speaker says and does during the public speaking situation. Most of us would find it difficult to operate with the philosophy of Henry Ford who observed, "It is all one to me if a man comes from Sing Sing or Harvard. We hire a man, not his history." Most of us—and the results of numerous experimental investigations clearly support this observation—do consider a person's history, weighing it very heavily in the total evaluation, and do combine that information from history with the more immediate information derived from present interactions. Information from these two sources—from history and from present encounters—interact and the audience forms some collective final assessment of your credibility.

There are, then, three types of credibility that should be considered: *initial credibility, derived credibility,* and *terminal credibility.* Each of these will be discussed briefly.

Initial credibility   *Initial credibility* is based on the speaker's reputation and on what we know of the speaker's history. It is the credibility that we perceive a speaker to have *before* she or he begins to speak. In your classroom you have probably made an initial credibility assessment of every other student, especially if the course has been in progress for some time. You may not have verbalized this assessment or even thought about it consciously. Yet, if you do think about it, you will probably realize that you feel high credibility for certain of your fellow students and lower credibility for others. This may be because of various experiences. Perhaps you have heard each student give a few speeches and on that basis you

3. *Stress the particular competencies of your sources if your audience is not aware of them.* Thus, for example, instead of saying simply, "Senator Smith thinks . . . ," also establish the Senator's credibility by saying "Senator Smith, who headed the finance committee for three years and who was formerly a professor of economics at MIT, thinks . . . ." In this way it becomes clear to the audience that you have chosen your sources carefully and with a view toward providing the most authoritative sources possible.

4. *Demonstrate confidence with your materials and with the speech situation generally.* Having rehearsed the speech and having familiarized yourself with the unique context in which you will deliver your speech, you should be able to communicate the resulting confidence—the feeling of being comfortable and at ease—to the audience. If, for example, you are using visual aids, then become so familiar with them that you know exactly what order they are in and exactly at what point you will use each.

5. *Demonstrate your command of the language.* Your use of language and your voice will greatly influence the audience's perception of your credibility. Be especially careful to learn the correct pronunciations of terms or names about which you may be in doubt, and make certain that any potential grammatical errors have been eliminated.

6. *Do not needlessly call attention to your inadequacies as a spokesperson or to any gaps in your knowledge.* No one can know everything and your audience does not expect you to be the exception. But it is not necessary to remind them—stress your competencies, not your inadequacies.

Character   We will perceive a speaker as credible if we perceive that speaker as having what Aristotle referred to as a high moral *character*. Here we would be concerned with the individual's honesty and basic nature. We would want to know if we could trust that person. A speaker who can be trusted is apt to be believed. An individual's motives or intentions are particularly relevant in judging one's character. The salesperson who says all the right things about a product is often doubted because his or her intentions are perceived as selfish; credibility is therefore low. The salesperson is less believable than a consumer advocate who evaluates a product with no motives of personal gain. Of course, it is extremely difficult to judge when individuals are concerned with our good or with theirs, but when we can make the distinction, it greatly influences our perception of a person's character.

As a speaker you need to demonstrate those qualities of character that will increase your credibility. A few suggestions may be added to those noted for demonstrating competence.

7. *Stress your fairness.* If delivering a persuasive speech, stress that you have examined both sides of the issue (if, indeed, you have). If you are presenting both sides, then make it clear that your presentation is an accurate and fair one. Be particularly careful not to omit any argument the audience may have already thought of—this is a sure sign that your presentation is not a fair and balanced one. Make it clear to the audience that you

would not advocate a position if it were not the conclusion derived from an honest and fair evaluation of the various alternatives.

8. *Stress your concern for enduring values.* Speakers who appear to be concerned with small and insignificant issues are generally seen as less credible than are speakers who demonstrate a concern and a commitment to lasting truths and general principles. Thus, in your speech make it clear to the audience that your position—your thesis—is related to higher order values and, of course, show them exactly how this is true.

9. *Stress your similarity with the audience, particularly your beliefs, attitudes, values, and goals.* Generally, we perceive as believable people who are like ourselves, especially in basic values. The more similar people are to our own attitudes and beliefs, goals and ambitions, the more likely it is that they will be perceived as credible. Closely related to this is the issue of "common ground." When people align themselves with what we align ourselves, they establish common ground with us and are generally perceived as more believable than people who do not establish this common ground.

10. *Demonstrate your long-term consistency.* Generally, we feel more comfortable putting our trust in someone who has been consistent over time. We become leery of persons who flit from one issue to another or from one team to another. If you have been in favor of XYZ for the last three years, then tell the audience this somewhere in your speech.

11. *Demonstrate a respect and a courtesy for the audience members.* To talk down to them or to insult their intelligence or ability to comprehend will only result in your own credibility suffering. Audiences generally look up to people who treat them with respect.

12. *Make it clear to the audience that you are interested in their welfare rather than simply seeking self-gain.* If the audience feels that you are "out for yourself," they will justifiably downgrade your credibility. Make it clear that the audience's interests are foremost in your mind.

Charisma   Charisma is best viewed as a composite of the speaker's personality and dynamism as seen by the audience. Generally, we perceive as credible or believable speakers we like rather than speakers we do not like; speakers who have what we commonly call a "pleasing personality"; speakers who are friendly and pleasant rather than aloof and reserved. Similarly, we seem to favor the dynamic over the hesitant, nonassertive speaker; the shy, introverted, soft-spoken individual is perceived as less credible than the extroverted and forceful individual. The great leaders in history have generally been dynamic people. Perhaps it is because we feel that the dynamic speaker is open and honest in presenting herself or himself whereas the shy, introverted individual may be seen as hiding something. Even though we may not come close to Billy Graham or John Kennedy or Martin Luther King, we all possess varying degrees of charisma. As speakers there is much that we can do to increase our charisma and hence our perceived credibility.

13. *Demonstrate a positive orientation to the public speaking situation and to the entire speaker-audience encounter.* We seem to like listening to positive rather than negative people and so it will help if you accentuate the positive and eliminate the negative, as the old song goes. Positive and forward-looking people are seen as more credible than negative and backward-looking people. Perhaps we reason that they have "gotten themselves together" and so are in a better position to know what is right and what is wrong. We would be leery of accepting marital advice from an unhappily married couple, perhaps for a similar reason. If they cannot solve their own problems, we reasonably doubt their ability to help us.

14. *Demonstrate assertiveness.* Show the audience that you are a person who will stand up for your rights and will not back off simply because the odds may be against you or because you are outnumbered.

15. *Be enthusiastic.* The lethargic speaker, the speaker who somehow plods through the speech is the very opposite of the charismatic speaker. Try viewing a film of Martin Luther King or Billy Graham speaking; they are totally absorbed with the speech and with the audience. They are excellent examples of the enthusiasm that makes speakers charismatic.

SEE
EXPERIENTIAL
VEHICLE 1.10.

16. *Be emphatic.* Use language that is emphatic rather than colorless and indecisive. Use gestures that are clear and decisive rather than random and hesitant. An emphatic speaker demonstrates commitment to the position advocated and the audience will be much more likely to agree with a speaker who is convinced of the proposition being presented.

General guidelines   In addition to these specific suggestions for projecting competance, character and charisma, here are four general guidelines that will assist you in putting these suggestions into operation most effectively.

17. *Develop or strengthen these characteristics as a person as well as as a speaker.* Enhance your competence, character, and charisma. I know that this is easy to say but may be extremely difficult to put into practice. Nevertheless, it is important to have these as goals because their actual development is the best insurance that they will function to make you credible in public speaking situations as well as in your everyday interactions.

18. *Demonstrate your possession of these three components of credibility, especially in your introduction.* Whether you introduce your own speech or whether someone else does it, it is important to legitimize yourself to the audience. If you have a broad knowledge of the topic or, say, first-hand experience, tell the audience of this knowledge and experience as early as possible. If there is some sort of formal introduction to your speech, you may have some important references integrated into this introduction to help establish your credibility. Thus, for example, if you are to speak on living under wartime conditions, the audience should know that you have in fact lived under these conditions and you should supply the person introducing you with the pertinent data. When teachers introduce them-

selves to their classes they often establish their credibility with references to their degrees, where they studied, the textbooks that they themselves have written, or to some research project on which they are working. At first glance this may seem immodest. But note that as long as the references are true, such credibility-establishing references allow the audience to appreciate better the information they will receive and to evaluate it in different ways.

SEE
EXPERIENTIAL
VEHICLE 1.11.

19. *Exercise moderation.* Be careful that you do not emphasize your competence so much that the audience concludes that you therefore must be incompetent. It is rather like people who keep telling us that they are telling the truth. They say it so often and forcefully that we conclude that they must be lying. "Doubt the man," advises Louise Colet, "who swears to his devotion." So, while you should stress your credibility, do so modestly and always truthfully.

20. *Use a variety of methods to establish your credibility.* Do not rely on the same few methods to build your credibility. Use a number of different methods and be sure to give consideration to all three components of credibility: competence, character, and charisma.

REMEMBER the components of credibility:
1 **Competence**
2 **Character**
3 **Charisma**

SOURCES

On ethics and communications see Thomas R. Nilsen, *Ethics of Speech Communication*, 2d ed. (Indianapolis: Bobbs-Merrill, 1974) and Richard L. Johannesen, *Ethics in Human Communication* (Columbus, Ohio: Charles E. Merrill, 1975). Jane Blankenship, *A Sense of Style: An Introduction to Style for the Public Speaker* (Belmont, Calif.: Dickenson, 1968), provides an insightful discussion of ethics and language. Two recent and thorough treatments of ethics are Sissela Bok, *Lying: Moral Choice in Public and Private Life* (New York: Pantheon Books, 1978) and Charles Fried, *Right and Wrong* (Cambridge, Mass.: Harvard University Press, 1978). On understandability see J. Vernon Jensen, *Perspectives on Oral Communication* (Boston: Holbrook Press, 1970). For different approaches to ethics, see Michael McGuire, "The Ethics of Rhetoric: The Morality of Knowledge," *Southern Speech Communication Journal* 45 (Winter 1980):133–148, and Ralph T. Eubanks, "Reflections on the Moral Dimension of Communication," *Southern Speech Communication Journal* 45 (Spring 1980):240–248. On ethics and the media, of great relevance to any consideration of the ethics of public speaking, see the thorough review by Clifford G. Christians, "Fifty Years of Scholarship in Media Ethics," *Journal of Communication* 27 (Autumn 1977):19–29.

Credibility is a variable that has always been a major part of the study of public speaking and has been the subject of numerous experimental studies and is considered in most of the available texts. A summary of early research is contained in Kenneth Andersen and Theodore Clevenger, "A Summary of Experimental Research in Ethos," *Communication Monographs* 30 (1963):59–78. A number of researchers have addressed the issue of the components of credibility, for example, David Berlo, J. B. Lemert, and R. Mertz, "Dimensions for Evaluating the Acceptability of Message Sources," *Public Opinion Quarterly* 33 (1969):563–576; James C. McCroskey, "Scales for the Measurement of Ethos," *Communication Monographs* 33 (1966):65–73; and Jack L. Whitehead, "Factors of Source Credibility," *Quarterly Journal of Speech* 54 (February 1968):59–63. Wayne N. Thompson, *The Process of Persuasion: Principles and Readings* (New York: Harper & Row, 1975) provides an excellent analysis together with selected readings. Perhaps the best single source is James C. McCroskey, *An Introduction to Rhetorical*

Communication, 4th ed. (Englewood Cliffs, N.J.: Prentice-Hall, 1982). For some of the differences in the credibility of men and women see Virginia P. Richmond and James C. McCroskey, "Whose Opinions Do You Trust?," *Journal of Communication* 25 (Summer 1975): 42–50. A constructivist approach to credibility is presented by Jesse G. Delia, "A Constructivist Analysis of the Concept of Credibility," *Quarterly Journal of Speech* 62 (December 1976):361–375. For a rhetorical study of the credibility of a contemporary speaker, see, for example, David Ross, "The Projection of Credibility as a Rhetorical Strategy in Anwar el-Sadat's Address to the Israeli Parliament," *Western Journal of Speech Communication* 44 (Winter 1980): 74–80. For an up-to-date review of credibility in persuasion, see Ruth Ann Clark, *Persuasive Messages* (New York: Harper & Row, 1984).

UNIT 5

Research for the public speech

OBJECTIVES

After completing this unit, you should be able to:

1 *identify at least four general principles for conducting research*
2 *explain at least eight items of information that are contained on a library card in a card catalog*
3 *explain the information usually retained in the library's vertical file*
4 *identify at least three sources for biographical material*
5 *identify at least three newspaper, magazine, and journal indexes*
6 *explain some of the types of information that are available in government publications*

In this unit speech research will be presented in two parts. First, I will focus on some general principles for conducting research, principles that should prove useful regardless of what your topic is or whether you are planning to prepare a speech, write a paper, or simply inform yourself about a topic. Second, I will focus on some research sources that should prove useful in researching any topic for any purpose.

GENERAL PRINCIPLES OF RESEARCH

The following are principles of research applicable to your immediate task of researching your speech topics, and are also relevant to your entire college and professional experience. You will always need to find information, so here are some ways to handle this task more efficiently and effectively. You should modify these general principles as appropriate to your specific needs, to your specific subjects, to your specific strengths and weaknesses.

1. Begin by examining what you know

Perhaps the best way to begin searching for information on a particular topic is to analyze what you already know. This is essentially the procedure followed by Edward Gibbon, the famed English historian and author of *The History of the Decline and Fall of the Roman Empire*. Before he would begin to write a new book or on a new topic, he would take a long walk or sit alone and attempt to recall everything he knew about the topic. Only after doing this did he move on to other sources of information. Winston Churchill followed the same procedure when preparing his speeches.

Write down what you do know—the names of the persons connected with the idea, the books or articles you have seen on the topic, the persons you know or know of who you think know something about the topic. In this way you can attack the problem systematically and not waste effort and time.

2. Work from the general to the more specific

Before dealing with the specifics of any aspect of any topic, first obtain a general overview. An encyclopedia or journal article will often serve this purpose quite well. This will enable you to see the topic as a whole and to see how its various parts fit together. It may also suggest approaches to a topic. Many of these general articles will contain bibliographies to direct the next stages of your research.

After securing this general overview, consult increasingly specific and specialized source materials. Progress from the general to the specific: You will educate yourself gradually to understand and to make use of the most specific and generalized sources available. For example, when consulting indexes to locate articles in magazines and journals, begin with a general index such as *Readers' Guide to Periodical Literature*, and then go on to more specific indexes such as *Index to Legal Periodicals*, *Education Index*, *Humanities Index*, or whatever specialized index is most appropriate. These and numerous other indexes are explained later in this unit.

3. Keep an accurate research record

The more accurate your record is, the less time you will waste going back to sources to check on a date or spelling or even to consult sources read but forgotten.

I find a looseleaf book best to keep everything—a list of sources consulted, quotations, ideas, arguments, suggested references, and so on—relating to an article or speech. In this way I don't waste time looking through several different places to pull all the material together. Another advantage of the looseleaf book is that I can xerox book pages, articles, and the like and insert them in appropriate places. Do not waste time copying long quotations and statistics; xerox them and insert them in the appropriate places.

4. Use research time effectively

There never seems to be enough time to do all the things we want to do. Consequently, the time we do have must be managed effectively and efficiently. For example, before going to the library to check out a book, examine what other purposes this trip can serve—to get books you need for other courses and to return due books, and so on. Single-purpose visits are genrally inefficient.

If you are going to give two speeches on the same topic, say an informative and a persuasive speech, do the research for the two at the same time. Don't wait until the first speech has been completed to begin researching the second. For example, divide the looseleaf book into two sections and insert the material with appropriate cross references.

5. Get to know the available sources of information

I suspect that research is such a chore for many people—not only for students but for many who devote a sizeable portion of their time to speaking, writing, or research—because they are unfamiliar with the available sources of information. Those who have difficulty researching are invariably those who have not learned to do it effectively and efficiently. To the extent that you know how to research, it will be easy, pleasant, and generally rewarding. To the extent that you lack this information, research throughout your college and professional career will be understandably hateful and wasteful. Learn what is available, where and how. For example, spend a few hours in the library learning where some of the most useful source materials are located. Where are the encyclopedias? The almanacs? The indexes to the various journals? Where is the vertical file and how is it used in your library? How are newspapers and journals maintained in your library? What material is on microfilm (reels of film)? What is on microfiche (pieces of film containing perhaps 100 frames on approximately 4 × 6-inch cards)? What is on microcards (printed rather than filmed material)? What is on ultramicrofiche (pieces of film containing up to 1200 pages on a 2 × 2-inch card)? How do you use the machines to read this material?

How does your library operate interlibrary loans? How long do such loans take to secure? May journals or only books be borrowed? Are there any restrictions? What other libraries are available in your area? Are there municipal libraries that might complement your college library? In what ways? Do other colleges allow students from your college to use their facilities? Are they better equipped in certain areas?

REMEMBER to follow these general principles in researching your speech topics:

1   Begin by examining what you know
2   Work from the general to the more specific
3   Keep an accurate research record
4   Use your research time effectively
5   Become familiar with the available sources of information

SOURCES FOR RESEARCH

It is estimated that over 30 million different books have been published since the beginning of printing. Currently, approximately 400,000 titles are published each year. Millions of articles are published each year in thousands of different journals and magazines. It is estimated that there are over 100,000 journals and magazines in the area of science alone. From these

SEE
EXPERIENTIAL
VEHICLE 1.12.

figures or from roaming through any fair-sized library, you should appreciate that the amount of information currently available on just about any topic is so vast that it is understandably daunting for many people. Here I would like to try to make the initial search procedure easier and less forbidding by identifying some of the more significant sources of information.

The experts

The faculty at your college is one of the best, if rarely used, sources of information for almost any speech topic. Regardless of what your topic is, someone on the faculty of some department knows a great deal about the topic or at least can direct you to the appropriate sources. Your speech communication instructor should be able to direct you to the appropriate department and perhaps even to the appropriate staff member. Experts in the community would serve similar functions. Local politicians, religious leaders, doctors, lawyers, museum directors, and the like are often suitable sources of information.

Another obvious expert is the librarian at your college or local library. A librarian is a professional who knows the contents and mechanics of libraries. She or he had graduate training in the very issues that may be giving you trouble, for example, finding suitable biographical material, appropriate indexes of current articles, materials in specialized collections at other libraries or nearby institutes or museums, and so on. The librarian is there to serve as a competent resource person to assist you in locating the right materials in the shortest possible time. It would serve you well to seek out the librarian for guidance during the initial stages or for more specialized and advanced direction.

The card catalog

Each library catalogs its books in a slightly different way, depending on its size and the needs of its users. Most, however, make use of some form of card catalog. Generally, you will find three types of cards: title cards, subject cards, and author cards. Thus, if you know the title or the author of the book you want, go to these cards to find out exactly where the book is located in your library. If, as is more usually the case, you just have a general subject heading, then go to the subject cards. These identify all the books on this subject that your library has.

In cataloging books, libraries use one of two systems, the Dewey Decimal System or the Library of Congress System. The Dewey Decimal System, designed by the nineteenth-century librarian Melvil Dewey, catalogs books into 10 general categories; the Library of Congress System uses 20 categories. The general categories and their designations in the two systems are presented in Table 5.1.

Each of these categories is further divided. For example, in the Dewey Decimal System, the Social Sciences are divided as follows:

300   Social Sciences
310   Statistics
320   Political Science
330   Economics
340   Law
350   Public Administration
360   Social Welfare
370   Education
380   Public Services and Utilities
390   Customs and Folklore

As you might suspect, each of these divisions is further subdivided. You should learn the numbers used for those areas you will be investigating in your speeches and for those subjects you will be concentrating on in college.

TABLE 5.1 Library cataloging systems

Dewey Decimal System		Library of Congress System	
000	General Works	A	General Works
100	Philosophy	B	Philosophy, Religion
200	Religion	C	History, Auxiliary Sciences
300	Social Sciences	D	History and Topography (except American)
400	Languages	E–F	North and South America
500	Science	G	Geography, Anthropology
600	Technology	H	Social Sciences
700	Fine Arts and Recreation	J	Political Science
800	Literature	K	Law
900	History	L	Education
		M	Music
		N	Fine Arts
		P	Language and Literature
		Q	Science
		R	Medicine
		S	Agriculture, Plant and Animal Industry
		T	Technology
		U	Military Science
		V	Naval Science
		Z	Bibliography and Library Science

FIGURE 5.1 A sample catalog card. There is such a great deal of information on each card in the library's card catalog that most people never even notice. This information can save you a great deal of time because it may enable you to pinpoint the specific book you want without having you search through 10 or 20. Here is a sample card with notes on the various types of information contained on it.

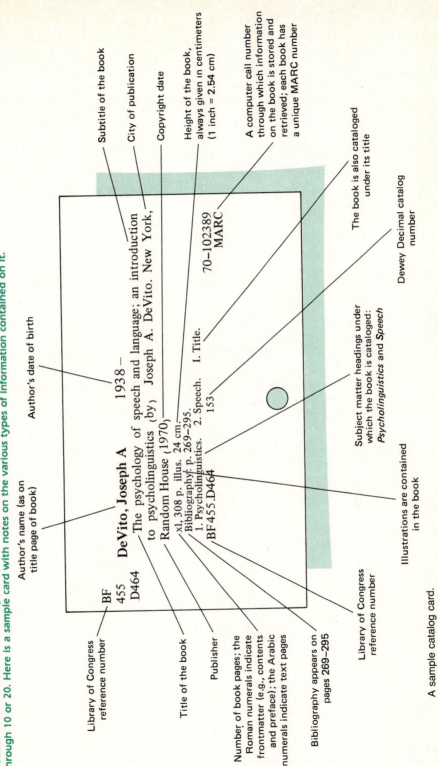

Author's name (as on title page of book)

Author's date of birth

Subtitle of the book

City of publication

Copyright date

Height of the book, always given in centimeters (1 inch = 2.54 cm)

A computer call number through which information on the book is stored and retrieved; each book has a unique MARC number

The book is also cataloged under its title

Dewey Decimal catalog number

Library of Congress reference number

Title of the book

Publisher

Number of book pages; the Roman numerals indicate frontmatter (e.g., contents and preface); the Arabic numerals indicate text pages

Bibliography appears on pages 269–295

Library of Congress reference number

Illustrations are contained in the book

Subject matter headings under which the book is cataloged: *Psycholinguistics* and *Speech*

BF 455 D464

DeVito, Joseph A 1938 –
The psychology of speech and language; an introduction to psycholinguistics (by) Joseph A. DeVito. New York, Random House (1970)
xl, 308 p. illus. 24 cm.
Bibliography: p. 269–295.
1. Psycholinguistics.   2. Speech.   I. Title.
BF 455.D464   153
                                                        70-102389
                                                        MARC

A sample catalog card.

The vertical file

The vertical file (sometimes called the "information file") is a frequently overlooked source because many students are unaware of its existence or of what type of information it contains. Basically, the vertical file is a collection of clippings from newspapers and magazines, pamphlets, and other materials, such as photographs or letters, organized by topic and arranged in files. Your librarian will be able to direct you to and explain the use of the vertical file in your library.

Encyclopedias

One of the best places to start to investigate your topic is a standard encyclopedia. You will get a general overview of the subject and suggestions for additional reading. Perhaps the most comprehensive and the most prestigious is the *Encyclopaedia Britannica*, which consists of 30 volumes in its current edition. The *Macropaedia* (19 volumes) contains the detailed articles that have made the *Britannica* popular since its inception in Scotland in 1771. The *Micropaedia* (10 volumes) contains short entries that provide general information on the subject and identify the articles in which the topic is covered in the 19-volume *Macropaedia*. The thirtieth volume, the *Propaedia*, contains an outline of knowledge and general essays on each of the major topics in the *Encyclopaedia*, for example, matter and energy, the earth, human life, human society, technology, religion, and others. The annual *Britannica Book of the Year* updates the encyclopedia as a whole. *Collier's Encyclopedia* and the *Encyclopedia Americana* are also excellent and comprehensive works that should provide much insight into just about any subject you might look up. The *Americana* consists of 30 volumes and, as its title implies, is especially devoted to American issues. The articles are generally shorter and easier to read than those in the *Britannica*. *Collier's* consists of 24 volumes and is less detailed and scholarly than either the *Britannica* or the *Americana*. It is distinguished by its illustrations and attractive format. A number of one-volume encyclopedias, useful for locating dates, essential facts, brief biographies, and the like, are now within a price range that most college students can afford—about the price of four or five 8-tracks or just one pair of designer jeans. Perhaps the two best are *The Columbia Encyclopedia* and the *Random House Encyclopedia*.

There are also numerous specialized encyclopedias. *The New Catholic Encyclopedia* (15 volumes) is the best and most scholarly source for general information on the Catholic Church and such topics as philosophy, science, and art as these have been influenced by and have influenced the Church. *Encyclopedia Judaica* (16 volumes) emphasizes Jewish life and includes numerous biographies and detailed coverage of the Jewish contribution to world culture. *Encyclopedia of Islam* and *Encyclopedia of Buddhism* cover the development, beliefs, institutions, and personalities of Islam and Buddhism, respectively.

For the physical, applied, and natural sciences there is the 15-volume *McGraw-Hill Encyclopedia of Science and Technology* complemented by the annual supplement, the *McGraw-Hill Yearbook of Science and Technology. Our Living World of Nature* is a 14-volume popular encyclopedia dealing with natural history from an ecological point of view. The *International Encyclopedia of the Social Sciences* concentrates on the theory and methodology of the social sciences in 17 scholarly, well-researched volumes.

Biographical material

It is often necessary for the speaker to secure information on particular individuals. This is a difficult task if you are unfamiliar with the available sources; if you know where to go, the task is simplified by numerous and excellent sources for biographical material.

The *Biography Index* is perhaps the first work to consult. It contains an index to biographies appearing in various sources—magazines, books, letters, and diaries. This work is particularly useful for locating information on living persons who have not yet had thorough biographies written on them.

The *Dictionary of National Biography* (DNB) actually consists of two sets of volumes: *From the Earliest Times to 1900* and *The Twentieth-Century Dictionary of National Biography* contain articles on famous deceased British men and women and is the most authoritative source for such biographical data. *The Dictionary of American Biography* (DAB), modeled after the DNB, contains articles on famous deceased Americans from all areas of accomplishment—politics, sports, education, art, industry, and so on. *The Dictionary of Canadian Biography* (DCB), only some volumes of which have been published so far, is arranged chronologically rather than alphabetically and concentrates on those who have contributed significantly to Canada. In all three works (DNB, DAB, DCB) the articles are signed and contain useful bibliographies to consult for additional information. Another useful source is *The New York Times Obituaries Index* which indexes those obituaries (approximately 400,000) that have appeared in *The New York Times* since 1858. Since *The New York Times* is on microfilm in most libraries, this index should prove helpful to most speakers.

For living individuals the best single source is *Current Biography,* issued monthly and in cumulative annual volumes. Beginning in 1940 *Current Biography* contains articles of one to two pages in length, most with photographs and brief bibliographies. The essays in *Current Biography* are written by an editorial staff and, consequently, include both favorable and unfavorable comments. The essays in *Who's Who in America,* which also covers living individuals, are compiled from questionnaires returned by the biographees and, hence, are more favorable and often omit crucial details that may reflect negatively on the individual. In addition to these there are a host of other more specialized works whose titles in most instances indicate their scope: *Directory of American Scholars* (where biographies of many of your teachers will be found), *International Who's Who, Who Was Who in America, Who's Who* (primarily British), *Who's Who in Germany, Who's Who in Italy, Who's Who in Australia, Prominent Personalities in the U.S.S.R., Dictionary of Scientific Biography, American Men and Women of Science,* and so on. For every group of people there seems to be a suitable and comprehensive biographical sourcebook.

Newspaper, magazine, and journal indexes

The indexes to the various newspapers, magazines, and professional journals are extremely useful. *The New York Times Index,* published since 1913, is important because it indexes one of the leading newspapers in the world and certainly the most widely available and carefully indexed. The index is published twice a month with cumulative annual issues. It enables you to locate important news stories, book, play and movie reviews, sports accounts, obituaries, complete texts of important speeches, and political, economic, and social commentaries; it also contains brief summaries of major news items and lists the major events in chronological order so that you can get, at a glance, an overview of the major developments of many events. This index is also useful since it enables you to locate the specific dates on which events occurred, which will in turn facilitate your use of other materials such as local newspapers. Also useful is *The Wall Street Journal Index,* published since 1958, which indexes perhaps the most important newspaper for financial and business news. The *Newspaper Index,* published since 1972, indexes such newspapers as the *Chicago Tribune,* the *Los Angeles Times,* and the *Washington Post.*

For magazine articles, the *Reader's Guide to Periodical Literature* covers the period from 1900 to the present. This guide indexes by subject and by author (in one convenient alphabetical index) articles published in some 180 different magazines. There is also an *Abridged Readers' Guide,* which indexes about 60 publications and is often more convenient to use, at least in initial searches, than the longer version. *Readers' Guide* is extremely valuable for its broad coverage but is limited in that it covers mostly general publications and only a few of the more specialized ones.

For more advanced materials you should consult some of the more specific and specialized indexes noted below. Also, you will have to consult other indexes for other popular but perhaps less conservative periodicals. For example, *Readers' Guide* does not index such publications as *Mother Jones, Rolling Stone,* and *Crawdaddy.* These and similar publications are indexed in the *Popular Periodical Index,* published since 1973 and now carried by many libraries. The *Alternative Press Index,* published since 1970, indexes almost 200 magazines, newspapers, and journals which might be considered "radical." This index is particularly valuable for many speakers dealing with such issues as the Third World, minority groups and minority rights, socialism, and the like.

For the period from 1802 to 1907 see *Poole's Index to Periodical*

Literature which covers both British and American periodicals. *Poole's Index* was started by William Frederick Poole while he was a student at Yale because he felt such a guide would be indispensable to college students. The *Education Index*, published since 1929, serves much the same function but indexes articles from about 330 journals and magazines relevant to education at all levels. It also indexes most of the speech communication journals and government periodicals. *The Catholic Periodical and Literature Index* indexes approximately 120 Catholic perodicals and includes an annotated bibliography of books relevant to Catholicism. *The Social Sciences and Humanities Index* covers periodicals in such areas as history, language, sociology, political science, and philosophy. Although these subjects are covered in greater depth in more specialized indexes, this one is useful for its cross-disciplinary coverage. Among the more specialized indexes that will prove useful to many speakers are the *Business Periodicals Index*, *Art Index*, *Applied Science and Technology Index*, *Biological and Agricultural Index*, *General Science Index*, *Index to Legal Periodicals*, *Humanities Index*.

In addition to indexes to articles appearing in periodicals, there is also a useful index to periodicals. The *Standard Periodical Dictionary*, published since 1970, lists about 70,000 periodicals under both title and subject headings. This directory is particularly useful for locating specialized periodicals that you might not have known existed.

In addition to these indexes, which are guides to locating material within a general subject area, there are numerous abstracts with which you should be familiar. One of the most comprehensive is *Psychological Abstracts* which provides short summaries of articles that appeared in psychology journals and books; it is indexed by subject and by author. *Sociological Abstracts*, *Language and Language Behavior Abstracts*, and *Communication Abstracts* are other important abstracts. All of these abstracts devote considerable attention to articles dealing with speech communication in all its forms. As each discipline expands, it becomes increasingly difficult for researchers and teachers to keep up with the new developments. Abstracts allow teachers and researchers to keep abreast of what is happening in the field as a whole and also direct them to those articles that would prove particularly meaningful.

A somewhat different abstract is *Resources in Education*, a monthly journal published by ERIC (Education Resources Information Center), operated by the National Institute of Education of the U.S. Department of Health, Education and Welfare. ERIC stores a wide variety of documents on such subjects as speech, listening, communication, reading, language and linguistics, counseling, tests and measurements, handicapped and gifted children, and so on, and publishes abstracts of these in *Resources in Education*. Documents appearing in *Resources* may be obtained from ERIC on microfiche or photocopy. This service is particularly useful for obtaining copies of papers delivered at professional conferences and conventions and which are not available in journals and magazines. Thus, ERIC not only serves to inform you of the available resources but also disseminates them for a modest fee. For a more extended survey of the literature on a particular topic, you can secure a computer search (again, for a fee) of the ERIC documents on a specific subject. From this search you will receive a computer printout containing the titles, authors, abstracts, and price of all the documents on this topic that are stored in the ERIC system.

Almanacs

One of the best single sources for information of all kinds is the almanac. Numerous inexpensive ones published annually are perhaps the most up-to-date source on many topics. The most popular is *The World Almanac & Book of Facts*. Others include *Information Please Almanac, Reader's Digest Almanac and Yearbook*, and *The New York Times Encyclopedic Almanac*. *Whitaker's Almanac* is the best of the British almanacs and *Canadian Almanac and Directory* is the best source for things Canadian.

SEE EXPERIENTIAL VEHICLE 1.13.

More detailed information of a statistical nature may be found in *Statistical Abstracts of the United States* which summarizes just about any facts and figures you might be interested in which the United States government and various private agencies have collected.

Government publications

The United States government is the country's largest publisher, printing more pages per year on a vast number of topics than any other publisher: government, history, population, law, farming, and numerous others. Here is just a small sampling of the publications that are available in most libraries or directly from the Government Printing Office in Washington, D.C. The United States Bureau of the Census publishes *Statistical Abstract of the United States* (from 1878 to the present) and *Historical Statistics of the United States, Colonial Times to 1957* (with various supplements). Together these volumes contain the most complete information on immigration, economics, geography, education, population, and various other topics that has been collected during the various census counts. The *Official Congressional Directory* (1809 to date) and the *Biographical Directory of the American Congress (1774–1961)* contain biographical information on government personnel, maps of congressional districts, and various other helpful information to those concerned with the workings of Congress. Perhaps most important is the *Congressional Record* (1873 to date). Issued daily when Congress is in session, the *Record* details all that was said in both houses of Congress as well as materials added that members of Congress wish inserted into the *Record*.

REMEMBER the main functions of the major research sources:

1 The faculty and other experts
2 The card catalog
3 The vertical file
4 Encyclopedias

SOURCES

There are a number of excellent guides to research, libraries, and reference materials. I would recommend the following: Mona McCormick, The New York Times *Guide to Reference Materials* (New York: Popular Library, 1971); Robert O'Brien and Joanne Soderman, *The Basic Guide to Research Sources* (New York: New American Library, 1975); Robert B. Downs and Clara D. Keller, *How to Do Library Research*, 2d ed. (Urbana: University of Illinois Press, 1975); Alden Todd, *Finding Facts Fast* (Berkeley, Calif.: Ten Speed Press, 1979); and Charlotte Gorden, *How to Find What You Want in the Library* (Woodbury, N.Y.: Barron's Educational Series, 1978). On taking notes see Judi Kesselman-Turkel and Franklynn Peterson, *Note-Taking Made Easy* (Chicago: Contemporary Books, 1982).

UNIT 6

Speaker apprehension

OBJECTIVES

After completing this unit, you should be able to:

1 *define speaker apprehension*
2 *identify four suggestions for dealing with speaker apprehension*
3 *identify three suggestions listeners might follow to help the speaker deal with apprehension*

Of all the speaker-related variables, speaker apprehension is perhaps the most salient from the point of view of the speaker. Speaker apprehension is of most concern to the beginning public speaker but to many experienced speakers as well. There are numerous terms for the same basic phenomenon. Stage fright is perhaps the most popular and certainly the oldest, but there are others—speech fright, reticence, shyness, audience sensitivity, unwillingness to communicate, and communication apprehension. Although each theorist defines the concept a bit differently, all terms refer to a state of fear or anxiety about communication interaction. I use the term *speaker apprehension* to emphasize that the phenomenon is speaker centered.

SEE
EXPERIENTIAL
VEHICLE 1.14.
James McCroskey and Lawrence Wheeless, in their excellent *Introduction to Human Communication*, note that "communication apprehension is probably the most common handicap that is suffered by people in contemporary American society." According to a nationwide survey conducted by Bruskin Associates in 1973, speaking in public was ranked as the number one fear of adult men and women. (Fear of heights, of insects and bugs, of financial problems, and of deep water were ranked second, third, fourth, and fifth, respectively.) According to surveys of college students noted by McCroskey and Wheeless, between 10 and 20 percent suffer "severe, debilitating communication apprehension" while another 20 percent "suffers from communication apprehension to a degree substantial enough to interfere to some extent with their normal functioning."

WHAT IS SPEAKER APPREHENSION?

Pooling the insights of the various researchers and theorists who have investigated this phenomenon, speaker apprehension may be defined from at least two perspectives: cognitive and behavioral. That is, speaker apprehension may be defined in terms of how a person thinks and feels (cognitive) or how a person behaves (behavioral).

Cognitively, speaker apprehension would be a fear of engaging in communication transactions. That is, people develop negative feelings and predict negative results as a function of engaging in communication interactions. They feel that whatever gain would accrue from engaging in communication is clearly outweighed by the fear.

Behaviorally, speaker apprehension would be a decrease in the frequency, the strength, and the likelihood of engaging in communication transactions. That is, speakers avoid communication situations and, when forced to participate, participate as little as possible.

Trait and state apprehension   The distinction between trait and state apprehension will clarify speaker apprehension as a public speaking issue. *Trait apprehension* refers to fear of communication generally, regardless of the specific situation: it would appear in dyadic, small group, public speaking, and mass communication situations. *State apprehension*, on the other hand, is a fear that is specific to a given communication situation. For example, a speaker may fear public speaking but have no difficulty with dyadic communication, or a speaker may fear job interviews but have no fear of public speaking, and so on. State apprehension is extremely common; it is experienced by most persons for some situations. For example, most persons would experience apprehension in public speaking situations or in important job interviews.

Differences in degree   Speaker apprehension exists on a continuum. Persons are not either apprehensive or not apprehensive; we all experience some degree of apprehension. Some people are extremely apprehensive and become incapacitated in a communication situation. They suffer a great deal in a society oriented, as ours is, around communication and in which success depends on one's ability to communicate effectively. Others are so mildly apprehensive that they appear to experience no fear at all when confronted by communication situations; they actively seek out communication experiences and rarely experience even the slightest apprehension. Most of us lie between these two extremes. We fear some situations more than others. For some of us this apprehension is debilitating and hinders personal effectiveness in dealing with people. On the other hand, apprehension energizes and makes others of us all the more alert, active, and responsive, and aids us in achieving our goals.

REMEMBER the distinction between trait and state apprehension:
1   *Trait apprehension* is a fear of communication generally, regardless of the specific situation
2   *State apprehension* is a fear of one or more specific communication situations

Apprehension: Is it normal? Is it harmful?

Stage fright, speaker apprehension, or whatever else it is called, is normal. Everyone experiences some degree of fear in the relatively formal public speaking situation in which you are the sole focus and are to be evaluated. Public speaking is perhaps the most anxiety-provoking communication situation, therefore, experiencing fear or anxiety is not strange or unique. Very likely your instructor experienced speaker apprehension as a student and, perhaps, experiences it even now as a teacher. I have experienced speaker apprehension and, in fact, still do in a variety of situations. In most cases, I think, it actually helps me. It leads me to prepare my lectures very thoroughly and to rehearse a great deal, and it keeps me alert and energized throughout the speaking transaction. Once you recognize that you are not unique in experiencing speaker apprehension, you will have taken a most important first step in managing your own apprehension.

Apprehension is not necessarily detrimental. As noted, fear can energize us and may even get us to work a little more to produce a speech that will be better than it would have been if we had not experienced some apprehension. Gerald Phillips, for example, has noted that "learning proceeds best when the organism is in a state of tension." Phillips cites the results of studies which followed groups of students with speaker apprehension for one and three years after instruction in dealing with communication apprehension. Almost all of the students were able to deal effectively with the originally difficult communication situations but they still experienced the same level of tension. "Apparently," notes Phillips, "they had learned to manage the tension; they no longer saw it as an impairment, and they went ahead with what they had to do."

The apprehension symptoms that most speakers experience cannot be seen by the audience. Even though you may think that the audience can feel your heart beat faster and faster, they cannot. They cannot see your knees tremble; they cannot sense your dry throat—at least not most of the time.

Why apprehension develops

There are numerous specific reasons for speaker apprehension, but the general underlying reason seems to be that we have been *conditioned* to respond to communication situations as we do. Thus, the person who avoids communication situations learned to avoid them as a child: by being required to remain silent at various times, by being scolded for talking, and otherwise rewarded for communication avoidance and punished for communication. As the child grows up, significant demands are placed upon him or her to communicate. An obvious conflict is established between the conditioning to remain silent and the current pressures to communicate. This conflict is experienced as fear: fear of avoiding the communication situation (because of the need to communicate) and, at the same time, fear of communication (because of the previous conditioning). The inability to resolve this conflict causes the fear to grow and spiral to the point where, at times, the person becomes so gripped with fear that he or she cannot communicate.

DEALING WITH SPEAKER APPREHENSION

In the public speaking context we are concerned with dealing with speaker apprehension. Specifically, what does a person with apprehension do? What does one do as a listener-critic in dealing with persons with high apprehension?

It is most important to realize that one cannot *eliminate* speaker apprehension: It may be lessened and it may be controlled, but it probably cannot be totally eliminated. The suggestions offered here will help you to lessen and manage apprehension, but not necessarily eliminate it. It is also important to realize that these suggestions are addressed to persons with low and moderate levels of apprehension. Persons who experience extremely high levels of speaker apprehension, who are so fearful of the speaking situation that they simply cannot function, should seek professional assistance. Being forced into public speaking situations and being made to go through the motions will not help their speaker apprehension; it might aggravate it.

Speaker guidelines

1. Prepare and practice thoroughly Inadequate preparation—not having rehearsed the speech adequately, for example, or not having researched it thoroughly and fearing questions you cannot answer—is reasonable cause for anxiety. Much of the fear we experience is a fear of failure. Adequate and even extra preparation will lessen the possibility of failure and the accompanying apprehension.

2. Experience helps Experience has been touted as being the cure-all for just about everything. It is not; but it does help—in most cases. As noted, if you are an extremely apprehensive speaker, experience will probably not help you—although there are techniques that will—and you should pursue other techniques for reducing apprehension before you take on the actual experiences themselves. Experience will help normal or moderate degrees of apprehension a great deal. Experience will show that a public speech can be effective despite these fears and anxieties, that the resultant feelings of accomplishment are most rewarding, and that public speaking can be an intellectually rewarding, as well as enjoyable, experience. The situation is similar to learning to drive a car or ski down a mountain. With experience the initial fears and anxieties give way to feelings of control, comfort, and pleasure.

3. Put apprehension in perspective First, maintain realistic expectations for yourself and your audience. You do not have to be perfect. You do not have to be a Winston Churchill, an Adlai Stevenson, or a Steve Martin to be an effective speaker. You do not have to be the best in the class or even as good as the person sitting next to you. You should be the best you can—whatever that is. Compete with yourself. Your second speech does not have to be better than the speech of your friend or of the previous speaker, but it should be better than your own first one.

Your audience does not expect perfection, either. Your classmates are not there to cut you down but to help you become a more effective public speaker, as you are there to help them become more effective public speakers. Persons who habitually find fault with everything and everyone—and there are a few of these in every class—create difficulties, but not insurmountable ones. Deal with their comments as if well-intentioned (it is conceivable that they are) and try to derive as much benefit as you can from them.

Second, place the public speaking situation, the entire class, and the specific apprehension in perspective. Although you should obviously try to give the best speeches you can, recognize that an actual speech in a public speaking classroom lasts about 5 to 10 minutes. Even if you give six 10-minute speeches—a fair estimate—you are only speaking for 60 minutes . . . one hour . . . 1/24th of a day . . . 1/35,064th of your four-year college life. By all calculations it is an extremely short time. Your public speaking class is one of perhaps 40 courses—again a very small part of your college career. So put it in perspective. Let your apprehension motivate you to produce a more thoroughly prepared and rehearsed speech, but do not let it debilitate you or upset you to the point where it harms your other activities.

4. Physical activity and deep breathing help   Apprehension is generally eased or lessened by physical activity, by gross bodily movements as well as by the small movements of the hands, face, and head. If you are apprehensive, you might work into your speech some writing on the blackboard or some demonstration that requires considerable movement. You could use a visual aid: Manipulating the aid or showing slides temporarily diverts attention from you and allows you to expend your excess energy. Obviously, the movement should be integral to the speech. Do not walk around for the sake of walking around; do not use a visual aid just so that you might move about. Integrate such activities into your speech.

Deep breathing relaxes the body. By breathing deeply a few times before getting up to speak, you will sense your body relax and you will overcome your initial fear of getting out of your seat and walking to the front of the room. If you find yourself getting a bit more nervous than you want during your actual speech, again try breathing deeply during a pause.

REMEMBER these guidelines in dealing with speaker apprehension:
1   **Prepare and practice thoroughly**
2   **Experience helps**
3   **Put apprehension in perspective**
4   **Physical activity and deep breathing help**

Listener guidelines

Listeners can do a great deal to assist the speakers with their apprehension. I offer here just a few suggestions.

Positively reinforce the speaker A nod of the head, a pleasant smile, and, perhaps most important, an attentive appearance throughout the speech are most helpful in putting the speaker at ease. Resist the temptation to pick up the newspaper or to talk with a friend. Try to make it as easy as possible for the speaker. Obviously, attend those classes when other students are speaking. Speakers often have a particular fear that the audience will not show up ("They know I'm a terrible speaker and so they're not going to come today").

Ask questions in a supportive manner If there is a question period after the speeches, ask questions as information-seeking attempts rather than as critical challenges. Instead of saying, for example, "Your criticism of disco music is absurd," you might say "Why do you find the lyrics of disco songs meaningless?" or "What is there about the beat of disco music that you find offensive?" Ask questions in a tone and a manner that do not make the speaker defensive and that do not signal conflict between you and the speaker.

Do not focus on errors If the speaker fumbles in some way, do not focus on it by putting your head down, covering your eyes, or otherwise nonverbally communicating your intense awareness of the fumble. Instead, continue listening to the content of the speech. Nonverbally, try to communicate to the speaker that you are concerned with what is being said and that the bungling of a sentence is not all that important. In the total scheme of things, of course, it isn't.

SOURCES

The area of speaker apprehension owes much to the theoretical and experimental research of James C. McCroskey, and that of reticence to the work of Gerald M. Phillips. Both researchers have contributed significantly to our understanding of apprehension and the entire communication process. For general overviews, I would suggest James C. McCroskey, "Oral Communication Apprehension: A Summary of Recent Theory and Research," *Human Communication Research* 4 (Fall 1977):78–96; "Classroom Consequences of Communication Apprehension," *Communication Education* 26 (January 1977):27–33; Gerald M. Phillips, "Reticence: Pathology of the Normal Speaker," *Communication Monographs* 35 (March 1968):39–49; and "Rhetoritherapy Versus the Medical Model: Dealing with Reticence," *Communication Education* 26 (January 1977):34–43. Another useful survey is contained in James C. McCroskey and Lawrence R. Wheeless, *Introduction to Human Communication* (Boston: Allyn & Bacon, 1976). Specific studies dealing with issues relevant to this unit include: James C. McCroskey, John A. Daly, and Gail Sorensen, "Personality Correlates of Communication Apprehension: A Research Note," *Human Communication Research* 2 (Summer 1979):376–380; James C. McCroskey, John A. Daly, Virginia P. Richmond, and Raymond Falcione, "Communication Apprehension and Self-Esteem," *Human Communication Research* 3 (Spring 1977):269–277; John A. Daly, "Communication Apprehension and Behavior: Applying a Multiple Act Criteria," *Human Communication Research* 4 (Spring 1978):208–216; H. Thomas Hurt and Raymond Preiss, "Silence Isn't Necessarily Golden: Communication Apprehension, Desired Social Choice, and Academic Success Among Middle-School Students," *Human Communication Research* 4 (Summer 1978):315–328.

On the measurement of apprehension, see Michael D. Scott, James C. McCroskey, and Michael E. Sheahan, "Measuring Communication Apprehension," *Journal of Communication* 28 (Winter 1978):104–111. There is also a listener apprehension test: see Michael J. Beatty, Ralph R. Behnke, and Linda S. Henderson, "An Empirical Validation of the Receiver Apprehension Test as a Measure of Trait Listening Anxiety," *Western Journal of Speech Communication* 44 (Spring 1980):132–136. An excellent attempt to compare the various approaches to dysfunctional communication is presented by William T. Page, "Rhetoritherapy vs. Behavior Therapy: Issues and Evidence," *Communication Education* 29 (May 1980):95–104. Also see the replies to this article by Gerald M. Phillips and James C. McCroskey in this same issue of *Communication Education*. For an up-to-date report on the treatment of apprehension, see Susan R. Glaser, "Oral Communication Apprehension and Avoidance: The Current Status of Treatment Research," *Communication Education* 30 (October 1981):321–341. For a thorough discussion of apprehension and how it relates to other similar behaviors, see Lynne Kelly, "A Rose by any Other Name Is Still a Rose: A Comparative Analysis of Reticence, Communication Apprehension, Unwillingness to Communicate, and Shyness," *Human Communication Research* 8 (Winter 1982):99–113.

HOW TO . . . Evaluate Your Preliminary Speech Preparations: Part One Checklist

Yes	No	
■	■	1. Is the speech topic a worthwhile one?
■	■	2. Is the purpose appropriate to the audience?
■	■	3. Is the topic sufficiently narrow in scope?
■	■	4. Has the audience, occasion, and context been analyzed and adapted to?
■	■	5. Has the topic been researched appropriately?
■	■	6. Have the thesis and major propositions of the topic been clearly identified and adequately supported?
■	■	7. Have these propositions and their supporting materials been organized for easy comprehension by the audience?
■	■	8. Has the speech been worded with simple rather than complex words and sentences?
■	■	With personal and informal rather than impersonal and formal language?
■	■	With nonoffensive language?
■	■	9. Does the introduction gain attention?
■	■	Establish a speaker-audience relationship?
■	■	Orient the audience as to what is to follow?
■	■	10. Does the conclusion summarize the speech?
■	■	Provide crisp closure?
■	■	11. Do you as a public speaker demonstrate competence?
■	■	Character?
■	■	Charisma?

EXPERIENTIAL VEHICLES FOR PART ONE

1.1 DIAGRAMMING THE PUBLIC SPEAKING TRANSACTION

This exercise is designed to introduce some significant issues that will be considered in greater depth in the following units. The questions should stimulate you to think of the public speaking situation and of yourself as a public speaker-listener-critic.

Construct a diagrammatic model of the public speaking transaction as you see it taking place in this class. Incorporate the following elements and processes: speaker, speech, communication channel, listeners, feedback, critics, context, effect, and noise. After you have constructed this model, respond to the following questions.

1. How would you characterize yourself as a public speaker? How would you characterize yourself as a listener? As a critic? How would you characterize the others in your class as speakers? As listeners? As critics? On what do you base these conclusions?

2. How would you define a public speech? What communication channels would be involved in the speeches to be given in this class?

3. What are some topics that you would like to speak on? What are some topics that you would like to hear others speak on? What topics would turn you off?

4. What form can feedback take? What functions may feedback serve?

5. What do you see to be the function of the critics?

6. How will the context influence the public speaking transaction? How might the context be changed to make it more conducive to effective public speaking?

7. What type of effects do you think can be achieved in the speeches that you will deliver and hear in this class? Why?

8. How might noise enter the public speaking transaction? What might be done about it?

The following suggestions will assist you in your initial search for appropriate informative speech subjects. Additional suggestions may be found in Appendix C.

Speech of self-introduction

Prepare a speech in which you introduce yourself to your class. Base your speech on a collage of how you see yourself. The collage should be constructed from pictures taken from magazines or other sources and objects and arranged on some kind of cardboard. Your speech would consist of a brief introduction in which you give such information as your name, your college major, your professional goal, and some idea of what you do in college—aside from attend classes. Also, your introduction should provide the audience with some idea as to how you will discuss your collage—that is, it should orient. The body of the speech should explain the collage. The conclusion should summarize the speech (for example, "As you can see my life currently revolves around sports, my two children, and three dogs") and wrap it up in some crisp fashion.

Biography speech

Prepare and present a speech in which you explain the contributions of one of the following historical figures.

Clement Attlee	Giuseppe Garibaldi	Charles Steward
Bernard M. Baruch	Joseph Goebbels	Parnell
Otto von Bismarck	Patrick Henry	Cardinal de Richelieu
Simon Bolivar	Adolf Hitler	Maximilien Robespierre
Golda Meir	Benito Juarez	Eleanor Roosevelt
William Jennings Bryan	John Kennedy	Carl Schurz
Ralph Bunche	Nikita Khruschev	William H. Seward
John C. Calhoun	Kublai Khan	Joseph Stalin
Chiang Kai-shek	Joseph McCarthy	Sukarno
Winston Churchill	Malcolm X	Sun Yat-sen
Henry Clay	Mao Tse-tung	Leon Trotsky
DeWitt Clinton	Lorenzo de Medici	Daniel Webster
Jefferson Davis	Benito Mussolini	Emiliano Zapata
Benjamin Franklin	Jawaharilal Nehru	
Mohandas K. Gandhi	Eva Peron	

These clearly are not the only names that might be used: they suggest suitable subjects for a biographical speech.

Ethnic contribution speech

Prepare a speech in which you explain some of the contributions of one of the following ethnic groups (or one not noted here) to our current society:

Arab	Greek	Philippino
Argentinian	Indian	Polish
Australian	American Indian	Portuguese
Austrian	Iranian	South African
Brazilian	Irish	Spanish
British	Israeli	Swedish
Canadian	Italian	Swiss
Chinese	Japanese	Syrian
Cuban	Kenyan	Thai
Czechoslovakian	Korean	Turkish
Danish	Mexican	Ugandan
Dutch	Mongolian	Russian
Egyptian	Morocco	Vietnamese
French	Norwegian	Yugoslavian
German	Pakistani	Zambian

Obviously, these randomly selected groups are not the only contributing ones.

Sports speech

Prepare a speech in which you explain the nature of one of the following sports:

archery	dog racing	rowing
automobile racing	fencing	skiing
baseball	football	sky diving
basketball	golf	swimming
bowling	gymnastics	tennis
boxing	hockey (field, ice)	volleyball
bridge	horse racing	weight lifting
canoeing	ice skating	wrestling
chess	polo	yachting
cycling	pool	

Holiday speech

Prepare a speech to explain one of the following holidays. In your speech, consider, for example, how the holiday originated, how it is celebrated, the particular customs that are associated with it, its purpose, and why it is relevant today to your listeners.

Christmas	Candlemas	Purim
New Year's Day	Good Friday	Chanuka
Thanksgiving	Independence Day	Yom Kippur
Easter	Election Day	Mother's Day
Passover (Pesach)	Robert E. Lee's	Father's Day
George Washington's	Birthday	Armed Forces Day
Birthday	Shrove Tuesday (Mardi	Magna Carta Day
Lincoln's Birthday	Gras)	Labor Day
Columbus Day	Flag Day	American Indians
St. Patrick's Day	Halloween	Day
Epiphany	General Pulaski	Veterans Day
Martin Luther King	Memorial Day	Sadie Hawkins Day
Day	All Saint's Day	Loyalty Day
Memorial Day	St. Valentine's Day	Rosh Hashana
Russian Orthodox New	United Nations Day	Palm Sunday
Year	Ash Wednesday	
Groundhog Day		

Abstract terms speech

Explain one of the following abstract concepts:

freedom	caring	patience
trust	creativity	misery
truth	ugliness	honor
justice	success	jealousy
love	failure	greatness
happiness	strength	friendship
beauty	masculinity	forgiveness
hatred	femininity	cruelty
equality	sorrow	cowardice
reverence	pride	bravery
fear	power	confidence
anxiety	peace	loyalty
depression		

1.3 PERSUASIVE SPEECH PROJECTS

Prepare a persuasive speech of approximately four to seven minutes in length in which you attempt to (1) strengthen an existing attitude, (2) change an attitude from positive to negative or from negative to positive, or (3) get the audience to behave in a certain way.

The following topics suggest the types of issues that may prove suitable for such speeches. Naturally, you will have to phrase your own (very) specific purpose. The 25 topics listed here are merely general suggestions. Additional suggestions may be found in Appendix C.

1. Vote in the next election (college, city, state, national)
2. Support college athletics
3. Support the college theater program
4. Take a specific course as an elective
5. Contribute time (or money) to a specific cause
6. Teachers, police, and firefighters should (not) be permitted to strike
7. Read a specific book, see a specific film, or watch a specific television show
8. Buy (don't buy) a particular product or service
9. Military recruitment should (not) be allowed on college campuses
10. Alcohol should be prohibited (permitted) on college campuses
11. Marriage licenses should be denied to any couple not knowing each other for at least one year
12. Nuclear plants should be abolished (expanded)
13. The government should (not) support the expansion of solar energy utilization
14. Required college subjects should (not) be abolished
15. College athletics should (not) be abolished
16. Gay men and lesbians should (not) be permitted to teach in elementary school, high school, or college
17. Cheating on an examination should result in automatic dismissal from college
18. This country should (not) establish comprehensive health insurance for all citizens
19. This country should (not) establish a system of free legal services for all its citizens
20. Church property should (not) be taxed
21. Personal firearms should be prohibited (permitted)
22. Travel to a specific place
23. Do (not) marry
24. Gay men and lesbians should (not) be permitted to marry
25. Capital punishment should be abolished (extended)

1.4 NARROWING THE TOPIC

For one of the following, narrow the topic sufficiently for a five-minute informative or persuasive speech. Once you have selected a suitably limited subject, formulate a specific purpose phrased in terms of behavioral objectives.

1 history	14 philosophy
2 emotions	15 language
3 family	16 film
4 communication problems	17 energy
5 psychology	18 television
6 education	19 health
7 mass media	20 work
8 nonverbal communications	21 play
9 politics	22 economics
10 religion	23 conflict
11 the United States	24 love
12 war	25 society
13 sex	

1.5 THE LISTENING PROCESS

This exercise provides convincing support for the proposition that listening is difficult and requires a considerable expenditure of energy. It also enables students to focus on some of the changes that result when messages travel from source to source. The procedure is as follows.

Six students participate as subjects; the remaining students serve as observers. Five of the subjects leave the room while a brief verbal message* is read to the one remaining subject. This subject tries to retain as much of the message as possible and repeats it as accurately as possible to the next person who enters the room after the message has been read to the first subject. The third subject then enters the room and hears the second subject's version of the message, tries to

* A message that works particularly well is the following, taken from William Haney's "Serial Communication of Information in Organizations," in Joseph A. DeVito, *Communication: Concepts and Processes,* 3d ed. (Englewood Cliffs, N.J.: Prentice-Hall, 1981):

Every year at State University, the eagles in front of the Psi Gamma fraternity house were mysteriously sprayed during the night. Whenever this happened, it cost the Psi Gams from $75 to $100 to have the eagles cleaned. The Psi Gams complained to officials and were promised by the president that if ever any students were caught painting the eagles, they would be expelled from school.

retain as much as possible, and repeats it to the fourth subject. The process continues until all six subjects have had an opportunity to hear and repeat the message. The sixth subject should repeat the message to the class as a whole. After this sixth reproduction, focus on some of the following processes that are normally considered in the passage of messages from source to source:

1   What was omitted? Can you describe the specific omissions that were made? Why do you suppose such omissions were made?
2   What was distorted? Can you describe the specific distortions that were made? Why do you suppose they were made?
3   What was added? Describe the specific additions that were made. Why do you suppose they were made?

What are the implications of this experience for the public speaker? For the listener? That is, what specific recommendations would you be willing to advance for the public speaker and for the listener as a result of this exercise?

1.6 STIMULATING POSITIVE EVALUATION

This exercise aims to increase your awareness of positive criticism and evaluation—specifically, to make you more aware of the wide variety of positive comments that could be addressed to a speaker, and to provide some "rehearsal" for voicing positive comments. Incidentally, this exercise will also provide a useful review of the qualities that make for speaker and speech effectiveness.

Each person should conduct a private "brainstorming" session and write down a list of positive comments that might be said to a speaker. Generate at least 10 or 12 comments on each of the following general topics: (1) the speech itself, (2) the delivery of the speech, and (3) the speaker. Before beginning this "brainstorming" session, review the first five units. These units identify those characteristics and principles that would logically stimulate positive criticism and evaluation. Pay particular attention to the suggestions offered for giving criticism in Unit 3.

After generating these topics, share them with others either in small groups of five or six or with the class as a whole. There is no "punch line" here. The objective of this exercise will have been achieved if you become more sensitive to the nature and function of positive criticism and to the multitude of possible comments that could be made.

This exercise raises some of the significant issues concerning the ethics of public speaking and should stimulate you to consider the way in which you think you should act in each of the following situations.

Read over the following situations and respond to each of the questions posed.

A   You are pressed to deliver a speech in your public speaking class. You find a *Reader's Digest* article which, it seems, could be used without anyone being aware that it was not your work. Should you use this article for your speech? Should you use it if there were no chance of anyone finding out?

B   You are speaking on behalf of Paul Robinson's candidacy for state senator. You are constructing your speech—to be delivered by you on the campuses of the state university—around his experience and accomplishments as a member of the city council, as deputy mayor, and as a member of the President's Commission on Education. In all of these positions Robinson has consistently advocated liberal views on almost all issues, which is consistent with your own attitudes and with those of the students you will be addressing. You want to concentrate on these. However, on a number of other issues Robinson has taken positions that your audiences would probably view negatively. For example, he has consistently voted against the Equal Rights Amendment, against the various bills proposing equal rights for homosexuals and lesbians in employment and housing, and against state funding for abortion. Probably few people in your audience will know how he voted on these issues and yet you wonder if you can ethically omit mention of this in your campaign speeches for Robinson. What should you do?

C   You have been put in charge of an advertising campaign to sell Flytrap Soap—a new deodorant hand soap. You are considering printing ads with sexual terms and symbols embedded in the soap bubbles below the level of conscious awareness. This technique, you understand, is used quite often by some of the leading advertisers. It sells liquor, cars, and perfume and should be effective in selling soap as well. Would this be ethical?

D   You are running for student body president and need to deliver speeches to the various clubs on campus. But you do not have the time or the abilities needed to construct these speeches. A few friends offer to write your speeches for a slight fee which you could easily afford. Would this be ethical?

1.8 SOME IDEAL SPEAKERS

Identify the ideal speaker—in terms of specific characteristics and competencies—for each of the following propositions. That is, describe the qualifications, background, experience, knowledge, and so on, needed for you and your classmates to believe the speaker.

1. Tuition should be raised 25 percent.
2. Required courses should be abolished.
3. Qualification tests should be administered after completion of sophomore year to determine if the student should be permitted to continue in college.
4. You should tell your best friend all your secrets.
5. You should undergo therapy.
6. The ERA (Equal Rights Amendment) should be reintroduced.
7. Puerto Rico should be made the fifty-first state.
8. The country is on the verge of a recession.
9. A program of comprehensive health insurance should be adopted by the federal government.
10. College admission standards should be abolished—anyone with a high school diploma or equivalent should be guaranteed admission.

Discuss the characteristics noted for the "ideal" speakers, the reasons offered for the inclusion of the various characteristics, the diversity of opinions certain to manifest itself and the reasons for such diversity, and the difficulty of describing the "ideal" speaker for propositions one strongly opposes. Lastly, consider the implications of the responses in terms of understanding the competencies of the public speaker and speaker credibility.

1.9 CREDIBILITY AND THE FAMOUS PERSON

Listed here are 20 famous persons. For each person identify the subject matter area(s) in which each person would be perceived as credible and give at least one reason why you think so. Use your public speaking class as the target audience.

Edward Kennedy	S. I. Hayakawa	Truman Capote
Francis Ford Coppola	Coretta King	Abigail Van
Elizabeth Taylor	Henry Kissinger	Buren
Calvin Klein	George Lucas	Edward Albee
Leo Buscaglia	Yoko Ono	Margaret
James Baldwin	Linus Pauling	Thatcher
David Brinkley	Ronald Reagan	George P. Shultz
John Ehrlichman		

After completing this exercise, discuss your responses with others, either in small groups or in the class as a whole. From an analysis of these responses, the following should be clear and may also serve as springboards for further discussion:

1   Each individual will be perceived in a somewhat different way by each other individual.

2   Each person—regardless of "expertise" or "sophistication"—will be perceived as credible on some topics by some audiences.

3   Credibility exists in the perception of the audience rather than in the person-speaker.

1.10 SPEAKER CREDIBILITY

Each of the following excerpts are examples of attempts by speakers to establish their credibility. Examine each with special reference to the components of credibility and record the specific means used by each of the speakers to establish their credibility. The time span of over 200 years illustrates, I think, that the techniques for establishing credibility have not changed very much.

1   I am certain that my fellow Americans expect that on my induction into the Presidency I will address them with a candor and a decision which the present situation of our Nation impels. This is preeminently the time to speak the truth, the whole truth, frankly and boldly. Nor need we shrink from honestly facing conditions in our country today. This great Nation will endure as it has endured, will revive and will prosper. So, first of all, let me assert my firm belief that the only thing we have to fear is fear itself—nameless, unreasoning, unjustified terror which paralyzes needed efforts to convert retreat into advance. In every dark hour of our national life a leadership of frankness and vigor has met with that understanding and support of the people themselves which is essential to victory. I am convinced that you will again give that support to leadership in these critical days.

—Franklin Delanor Roosevelt, First Inaugural Address

2   Mr. Chairman and Gentlemen of the Convention: I would be presumptuous, indeed, to present myself against the distinguished gentlemen to whom you have listened if this were a mere measuring of abilities; but this is not a contest between persons. The humblest citizen in all the land, when clad in the armor of a righteous cause, is stronger than all the hosts of error. I come to speak to you in defense of a cause as holy as the cause of liberty—the cause of humanity.

—William Jennings Bryan, The Cross of Gold Speech

3   The people of this state, the state which sent John Quincy Adams and Daniel Webster and Charles Sumner and Henry Cabot Lodge and John Kennedy to the United States Senate, are entitled to representation in that body by men who inspire their utmost confidence.

For this reason, I would understand full well why some might think it right for me to resign. For me this will be a difficult decision to make.

It has been seven years since my first election to the Senate. You and I share many memories—some of them have been glorious, some have been very sad. The opportunity to work with you and serve Massachusetts has made my life worthwhile.

And so I ask you tonight, People of Massachusetts, to think this through with me. In facing this decision, I seek your advice and opinion. In making it, I seek your prayers. For this is a decision that I will have finally to make on my own.

—Edward M. Kennedy, Speech on Chappiquiddick

4   Then, in 1942, I went into the service. Let me say that my service record was not a particularly unusual one. I went to the South Pacific. I guess I'm entitled to a couple of battle stars. I got a couple of letters of commendation.

But I was just there when the bombs were falling. And then I returned to the United States, and in 1946 I ran for the Congress.

When we came out of the war, Pat and I—Pat during the war had worked as a stenographer, and in a bank, and as an economist for a government agency and when we came out, the total of our savings, from both my law practice, her teaching, and all the time that I was in the war, the total for that entire period was just a little less than $10,000—every cent of that, incidentally, was in government bonds—well, that's where we start, when I go into politics.

—Richard Nixon, Checkers Speech

5   For my own part, I consider it as nothing less than a question of freedom or slavery; and in proportion to the magnitude of the subject ought to be the freedom of the debate. It is only in this way that we can hope to arrive at truth, and fulfill the great responsibility which we hold to God and our country. Should I keep back my opinions at such a time, through fear of giving offense, I should consider myself as guilty of treason towards my country, and of an act of disloyalty toward the Majesty of Heaven, which I revere above all earthly kings.

—Patrick Henry, Liberty or Death Speech

1.11 CREDIBILITY ANALYSIS

Analyze one of the speeches in Appendix D, "Speeches for Study and Enjoyment," in terms of speaker credibility. Specifically, analyze how the speaker established or failed to establish his or her credibility. Focus on the following:

1   Did the speaker establish his or her competence? How or why not?
2   Did the speaker establish his or her character? How or why not?
3   Did the speaker establish his or her charisma? How or why not?

1.12 REFERENCE WORKS

In order to become more familiar with some of the more useful sources of information available in most libraries, each student might select one reference work identified briefly in Unit 5 and examine it carefully. In a brief speech of say three or four minutes, each student would report to the class as a whole the structure and major functions of the reference work and its location in the college library.

An alternative is to have each student prepare a brief written report on one of the reference works noted. These reports would then be reproduced and distributed to all class members. After each member has had a day or two to carefully examine these annotations, a class meeting might be devoted to a question-and-answer session on the various reference works.

1.13 INFORMATION SEARCH

In order to gain some familiarity with some of the ways of locating information, each student should select or be assigned one of the following items of information and should report back to the class the answer and the reference work(s) he or she used to find the answer. In reporting how the answer was found, report on unproductive as well as productive sources.

1   the Japanese flag during WWII
2   the ethnic population of Nebraska
3   the age of the author of this text
4   the ingredients of a Harvey Wallbanger
5   the first capital of the United States
6   the current president of the Speech Communication Association, The American Psychological Association, or the International Communication Association

7   the world's largest library and the number of volumes it contains
8   the actress who won the Academy Award in 1952 for best actress
9   the literacy rate for China
10 the main languages of Cambodia
11 the prime interest rate for today
12 the faculty-student ratio for Harvard
13 the film grossing the largest amount of money and the amount of money it has grossed to date
14 the profits for the Exxon corporation for last year
15 the author of the following quotation: "Though it be honest, it is never good to bring bad news"
16 the birthplace and real name of John Wayne
17 the full name of the journals usually abbreviated QJS, JC, CM, CE
18 the use and origin of the word *meathead*
19 the early years of John Travolta
20 the number of votes received by Stephen Douglas from Illinois in the Lincoln-Douglas presidential election of 1860
21 the text of Winston Churchill's speech "After Dunkirk"
22 the political configuration of Europe in 1942
23 the graduate program in communication at Indiana University
24 births and deaths in Chile over the past 30 years
25 the number of books published last year by Harper & Row and by Prentice-Hall publishers
26 the amount of money *Playboy* pays for an article
27 the amount of money charged for a full page, four-color advertisement in *Reader's Digest*
28 the characteristics of the Hudson River school of painting
29 the rules for playing "Bughouse Chess"
30 contemporary speeches on United States energy problems

1.14 APPREHENSION QUESTIONNAIRE*

The following questionnaire, the PRCA (Personal Report of Communication Apprehension), was developed by James McCroskey to measure speaker apprehension. Now complete the accompanying questionnaire, following the directions provided by McCroskey.

* James C. McCroskey, *An Introduction to Rhetorical Communication*, 4th ed. (Englewood Cliffs, N.J.: Prentice-Hall, 1982). Reprinted by permission of James C. McCroskey.

Directions: This statement is composed of 24 statements concerning your feelings about communication with other people. Please indicate in the space provided the degree to which each statement applies to you by marking whether you (1) Strongly Agree, (2) Agree, (3) Are Undecided, (4) Disagree, or (5) Strongly Disagree with each statement. There are no right or wrong answers. Many of the statements are similar to other statements. Do not be concerned about this. Work quickly, just record your first impression.

QUESTIONNAIRE

_____ 1 I dislike participating in group discussions.

_____ 2 Generally, I am comfortable while participating in group discussions.

_____ 3 I am tense and nervous while participating in group discussions.

_____ 4 I like to get involved in group discussions.

_____ 5 Engaging in a group discussion with new people makes me tense and nervous.

_____ 6 I am calm and relaxed while participating in group discussions.

_____ 7 Generally, I am nervous when I have to participate in a meeting.

_____ 8 Usually, I am calm and relaxed while participating in meetings.

_____ 9 I am very calm and relaxed when I am called upon to express an opinion at a meeting.

_____ 10 I am afraid to express myself at meetings.

_____ 11 Communicating at meetings usually makes me uncomfortable.

_____ 12 I am very relaxed when answering questions at a meeting.

_____ 13 While participating in a conversation with a new acquaintance, I feel very nervous.

_____ 14 I have no fear of speaking up in conversations.

_____ 15 Ordinarily I am very tense and nervous in conversations.

_____ 16 Ordinarily I am very calm and relaxed in conversations.

_____ 17 While conversing with a new acquaintance, I feel very relaxed.

_____ 18 I'm afraid to speak up in conversations.

_____ 19 I have no fear of giving a speech.

_____ 20 Certain parts of my body feel very tense and rigid while giving a speech.

_____ 21 I feel relaxed while giving a speech.

_____ 22 My thoughts become confused and jumbled when I am giving a speech.

_____ 23 I face the prospect of giving a speech with confidence.

_____ 24 While giving a speech I get so nervous I forget facts I really know.

Scoring

To obtain your PRCA score, follow these instructions provided by Mc-Croskey.

The PRCA permits computation of one total score and four subscores. The subscores relate to communication apprehension in each of four common communication contexts: group discussions, meetings, interpersonal conversations, and public speaking. To compute your scores merely add or subtract your scores for each item as indicated below.

Subscore Desired	Scoring Formula
Group discussions	**18 + scores for items 2, 4, and 6;** **− scores for items 1, 3, and 5.**
Meetings	**18 + scores for items 8, 9, and 12;** **− scores for items 7, 10, and 11.**
Interpersonal conversations	**18 + scores for items 14, 16, and 17;** **− scores for items 13, 15, and 18.**
Public speaking	**18 + scores for items 19, 21, and 23;** **− scores for items 20, 22, and 24.**

To obtain your total score for the PRCA, simply add your four subscores together.

Each subscore should range from 6 to 30; the higher the score the greater the apprehension. "Any score above 18," according to McCroskey, "indicates some degree of apprehension." Most people score above 18 for the public speaking context, so if you scored relatively high in this subdivision, you are among the vast majority of people. Most people also score higher on public speaking than on any of the other subdivisions.

PART TWO

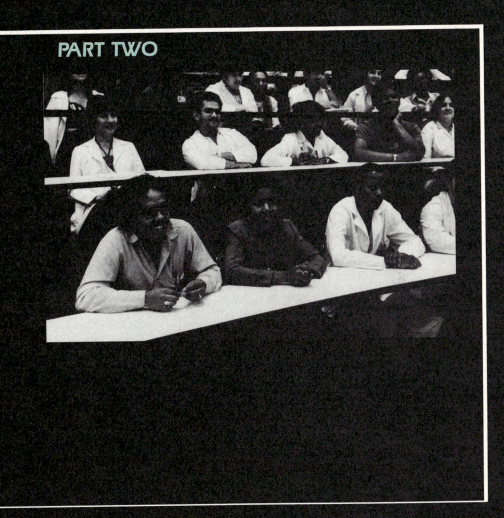

AUDIENCES OF PUBLIC SPEAKING

PART TWO

General principles of audience analysis and adaptation

OBJECTIVES

After completing this unit, you should be able to:

1 *define audience*
2 *identify at least five characteristics that need to be included in an audience analysis and explain why they must be considered in audience adaptation*
3 *identify and explain at least three context characteristics and their role in audience analysis and adaptation*

"People have one thing in common," noted Robert Zend. "They are all different." Because of these differences the public speaker has to analyze and adapt the speech to a specific audience—an audience that is different from every other audience.

Public speaking audiences vary so much that a very specific and restricted definition of an audience would be useless. The thousands at Yankee Stadium listening to Pope John Paul II or Billy Graham, the several hundred in an auditorium listening to a commencement address, the 35 in a classroom listening to a lecture, the 5 to 10 listening to a street orator standing on the proverbial soap box all constitute public speaking audiences. The characteristic that seems best define such an audience would be common purpose: An *audience* is a group of individuals gathered together to hear a speech.

The public speaking transaction exists for a speaker to effect some kind of change in the minds or behavior (or both) of the listeners. That is, the speaker speaks to inform or to persuade the audience in some way. The teacher lectures on colloidal chemistry to increase understanding, the minister talks against adultery to influence behaviors and attitudes, the football coach chews out the team after a particularly bad showing to motivate them to improve, and so on. All of these persons are concerned with producing some kind of change. If that is to be done effectively, we must know something about the nature of the audience. We need to construct a detailed profile of our specific audience. We cannot, obviously, give the same speech on, say, the advantages of retirement to a group of college students and to a group of senior citizens. The same speech on the value of physical fitness would not be effective with physical education majors and expectant mothers. Both need to be physically fit, but the means and specific goals differ considerably. Consequently, the speeches will have to be different. The differences may be quite obvious; not so obvious are the factors involved in analyzing an audience. The remainder of this unit describes these factors.

ANALYZING AUDIENCE CHARACTERISTICS

The following characteristics will affect the attitudes, beliefs, and values of the audience; what they know and what they want; what they will or will not understand. In short, you must consider these characteristics if you are to select the appropriate supporting materials, effectively structure and clearly and appropriately word the speech, and so on. They are: (1) age, (2) sex, (3) cultural and subcultural factors, (4) educational and intellectual levels, (5) occupation, income, and status, and (6) religion and religiousness. In any discussion of this nature, generalizations (sometimes broad ones) have to be made and will often prove incorrect when applied to specific cases. You should, therefore, test what I say here against what your own experience indicates.

SEE
EXPERIENTIAL
VEHICLE 2.1.

Age

The age of the listeners is one of the most obvious, most important, and most overlooked of all audience variables. Although we are aware of age—sometimes painfully, as when we are too young or too old to go somewhere or to do something—throughout our entire lives, it is not a factor that speakers often weigh as they develop their speech. Listeners of different ages will generally respond differently in a number of important ways.

Since experience molds our values, attitudes, and beliefs, different age groups are going to have different values, attitudes and beliefs simply because they have had different experiences. These differences must be taken into consideration by the speaker.

Age groups also differ in their goals. The goal of many college students is to get out of college and do "nothing" for a year or two—tour Europe, see the rest of the country, live on their own, and so on. The goal of a somewhat older group might be to achieve status in their occupation or profession, buy a home, and settle down with a family. To a much older group, the goal might be to retire, sell the home, and move to a warmer climate. Thus, for example, a speech on achieving corporate success would be significant to our second group, ultimately but not immediately relevant to our first group, and totally irrelevant to our third group.

Age groups differ in their day-to-day concerns. To the recently married couple in their twenties, salt in baby foods, methods of birth control and abortion rights, community property laws and divorce laws might all be very important. But people in their sixties would find such issues personally irrelevant. Interests will differ depending upon age. Certain ages are more sports-minded than others, especially when we think of participant sports. The 25-year-old may still enjoy basketball but it would be a rare 55-year-old who enjoyed it in the same way. A person's credibility is often age related. Thus, an audience will consider not only your topic and the way you handle it but also your age in judging you. In the very first course I taught on the college level, I was the youngest person in the room—younger than every one of the students. Although I was not aware of it then, I am sure I had credibility problems because of my youth.

The young are traditionally more liberal than the old. And yet, this varies greatly with the times. Some 15 years ago, college students were "extremely liberal" to the point of being revolutionaries. Today, they seem much more conservative, much more concerned with traditional values that were normally thought the preserve of their parents—money, security, a steady job, and status, for example. The young seem more optimistic than the old and perhaps with good reason—they have greater opportunity and freedom to construct their own reality. Older persons, with additional responsibilities, may not have the luxury of optimism.

The young generally take in information at a more rapid pace than do the old. Consequently, the speaker should keep up a relatively steady and swift pace with a young audience, lest they get bored, and a more moderate pace with older persons.

The young, perhaps because of television, seem more visually oriented than do the old. Persons over 40, for example, can easily remember being without television; persons under 30 probably cannot; they always had television and are used to visual information. Speakers should exploit this and perhaps employ visuals. As many older persons have trouble with their vision and generally rely less on the visual, speakers should depend less on visuals when addressing them. Charts that 20- and 25-year-olds can see readily may prove difficult for an older audience.

Age, then, influences a great deal. It influences the subjects that are thought appropriate and inappropriate, relevant and irrelevant, interesting and uninteresting. It influences how the speech is developed—the arguments that will prove effective and those that will fall flat, the appeals that will work and those that will not, the amplifying materials that will make for clarity and those that will confuse. And finally, it influences the language used—the level of complexity, the degree to which slang or subcultural language would be appropriate, and so on.

Sex

Today sex is one of the most important and most difficult of all audience variables. It is particularly difficult because of the rapid changes in roles (particularly in women's, but also in men's), and because so many women and men are currently experiencing conflicts and displaying numerous inconsistencies in their behaviors as a result of these conflicts. Despite the difficulties, all speakers must deal with the sex variable.

One of the most widely replicated findings on sex differences in regard to communication is that women are more persuasible than men and tend to generalize the effects of persuasion more than do men. This finding is not difficult to understand when we realize that women have been raised to take the word of men whereas men have been trained to be critical, ask questions, and make up their own minds. This, it is true, is changing rapidly and in the next few years we may see this sex difference disappear.

Both sexes, but women more so, experience conflicts between their training and their experience, on the one hand, and their views as to what a liberated individual should feel and act like. These conflicts often create inconsistencies in behaviors and attitudes. For example, many college women feel that they should be able to ask men out for dates (first dates as well as follow-up dates) and take the sexually aggressive role in first encounters generally. Many of these same women will note that they themselves have been unable to ask men out or assume this aggressive role. This discrepancy between attitudes and behaviors creates dissonance (a state of psychological discomfort).

The sex of the audience will influence a number of significant factors. For example, the topics that the audience finds interesting and relevant will, in part, be sex related; abortion, rape, equal pay for equal work, and hundreds of other issues may be of interest to all persons but especially to women. The attitudes that you can anticipate toward these various issues and numerous others will also, in part, be a function of the sex of the listeners. The most effective supporting materials and language to use will be heavily influenced by sex, even though all is in a rapid state of change.

A 1978 survey conducted by *Time* may be instructive in this regard. The statement "A wife should put her husband and children ahead of her career" was "completely believed" by 39 percent and "partially believed" by 39 percent of the respondents. Twenty-two percent "completely believed" and 30 percent "partially believed" the statement "It is still the wife's responsibility to make sure the house is clean and neat even if she works as hard as her husband." Twenty-seven percent "completely believed" and 26 percent "partially believed" that "Marriages are stronger when the wife stays at home and doesn't go out to work." "Children suffer when the mother goes to work" was "completely believed" by 32 percent and "partially believed" by 37 percent. Consider these findings reported in the *American Journal of Sociology* (January 1978): 25 percent of college men claim to be openly chauvinistic and 50 percent claim to be trying to be supportive but are not doing a good job of it; 16 percent talk "a good game but have not changed their chauvinistic ways"; only 9 percent are considered "genuinely liberated college men." And a Harris poll indicated that in 1976, 65 percent of Americans were in favor of the Equal Rights Amendment; in 1978 the percentage in favor of ERA dropped to 55 percent. And, more recently, the ERA went down in defeat. I cite these statistics to illustrate that sex is a crucial and ever-changing characteristic in any attempt at audience analysis.

Cultural and subcultural factors

Such factors as nationality, race, subcultural identity and identification are important in audience analysis. Largely because of training and different experiences, the interests, values, and goals of the listeners will differ. Generally, for example, groups that have been oppressed—for example, blacks, women, homosexuals, to name just a few—are today concerned with immediate goals and have little patience with the more conservative posture of the majority that argues that they should be content with evolutionary (rather than revolutionary) changes and that all will come to those who wait. Such oppressed groups will generally have a more practical orientation to education, to employment, and to life in general. For example, blacks and Hispanics will often major in practical job-related fields of study rather than pursue the generally "impractical" liberal arts. They will study communications, education, sociology, and other areas where jobs are generally more plentiful. Many women too will choose practical occupationally related majors, perhaps with the idea that they will be able to pursue this, have a family, and return to it later when the children have grown. For years, teacher education programs were crammed with women who thought this way. Urged on largely by their "practical" parents, they pursued such occupations as nurse (rather than doctor) and secretary (rather than manager).

Stereotypes of homosexuals, of women, of blacks, of Orientals, of Chicanos, and of any minority group are significant because they influence what most speakers will expect of members of these groups. This seems true even if the speaker or listener denies believing such stereotypes.

The level of trust-distrust will vary greatly depending on the subcultural identification of the speaker or listener. For example, a white speaking of jobs for inner city residents may well be distrusted by blacks or Chicanos who have tried in vain to get such jobs. A male speaking of management jobs for women might be distrusted by women who have failed to secure such positions.

Educational and intellectual levels

An individual may be well educated but not very intelligent and, conversely, an intelligent individual may not be well educated. Even with education, distinctions should be made between formal education (college and graduate school, for example) and informal education (experience, individual reading, and the like). With these qualifications in mind, however, education and intellectual level may be considered together since they are related and influence the reception of the speech in similar ways.

Generally, the more education an individual has the more liberal his or her views will be. College seems to liberalize people—though, again, not all people and not all people to the same extent. Nevertheless, the liberalizing influence of a college education is, perhaps, its most significant feature. The educated are more concerned than the uneducated with issues outside their immediate field of operation; they are concerned with international affairs, economic issues, and the broader philosophical and sociological issues confronting the nation and the world. The educated tend to recognize that these issues do affect them in many ways; many of the uneducated do not see the connection. The more uneducated the audience, then, the more you will need to focus on their own immediate needs, interests, and surroundings.

The educated are more active socially and politically. Perhaps they recognize that social and political issues bear direct relationship to their own well-being or they feel that they must assume the role of guardians in our society. Regardless of why the educated are more active—and there are different explanations for each individual's activity—the speaker must recognize not only this activity but the relative inactivity of the uneducated. With an audience of mixed educational level, the speaker will find the uneducated extremely difficult to move. Whereas appeals to humanitarian and broad social motives may work with the educated, the speaker will have to concentrate on the value of this social activism to the specific individuals, to their immediate needs, and to the satisfaction of their immediate goals.

Education trains one to recognize the value of long-range goals, of planning for the future, and of suffering a bit now so that tomorrow will be better. The uneducated—and again this is a broad generalization—more often focus on the present. Long-range goals are viewed with some irrelevance since their immediate needs may be difficult to satisfy.

The more educated an audience, the more critical they will be of your arguments and your evidence. They will be more skeptical of generalizations, as you may and should be of my generalizations here. They will question the validity of the statistics and frequently demand better substantiation of your propositions. The educated will be less persuaded by appeals to emotions and authorities. The uneducated, on the other hand, will not be as skeptical and will often be more moved by emotional appeals than by appeals to logic and reasoning.

Perhaps the most obvious difference between the educated and the uneducated is the amount of general and specific knowledge they have and that you, as a speaker, may assume. For example, if you are speaking on Lebanon or Nicaragua, you would be able to assume a great deal more specific information on the part of the educated audience than you would on the part of the uneducated audience. Consequently, you would have to fill in the uneducated audience with, for example, something about the geographical location of these areas, their population, and their importance to our country and to the world community. This same principle will hold with names of noted personalities, with complex terms, with theoretical assumptions, and, in fact, with anything that takes time to learn.

Occupation, income, and status

Like education and intelligence, the variables of occupation, income, and status are not identical. An individual may have no occupation but may have great income and status from family millions. Or a person may have a high status occuptation—the poet, the minister, the college professor, for example—but moderate income. Generally, however, the occupation an individual has will determine income and together these determine status. Consequently, it seems reasonable to consider these together.

The higher an individual's occupation, income, and status the more concerned he or she will be with long-range goals and with the needs and goals of others. In this they are similar to the educated group previously noted. And, of course, they are among the better educated; the bonuses of education are a better job, greater income, and higher status.

All or at least a vast majority of persons see topics and issues through their occupations. Samuel Johnson expressed this well: "No man forgets his original trade: the rights of nations, and of kings, sink into questions of grammar, if grammarians discuss them." As an obvious extreme, consider, for example, the topic of tenure for an audience of college teachers, of federal health insurance for an audience of doctors, of tax shelters for persons making $10,000 a year, and of a four-day work week for an audience of management. Topics are analyzed in terms of what they mean to "my job." This both helps and hinders speakers. It helps by providing speakers with an almost sure way of relating a topic to the immediate concerns of the audience members—show them that your topic or your proposal will benefit their job or working conditions and you will gain their attention and support. It is a hindrance that few issues in the real world affect the jobs of a wide variety of listeners in the same way. Thus, for example, when teachers' salaries go up, it is great for teachers but not very good for taxpayers and for students paying tuition. When food prices go up, it may be fine for the farmers, but it is bad for the restaurants who have to raise their prices, and it is bad for the average citizen who wants to eat out once in a while.

We live in a society that regards one's occupation as almost sacred. Attempts to tamper with job security, to eliminate certain jobs, to cut benefits or salaries, to close down factories and offices will meet with what seems to many to be extreme resistance. Any speaker attacking the audience's job security will face monumental obstacles and had better proceed most cautiously.

In general, as one's occupation, income, and status improve, one enjoys much more leisure time; in general, the poor have little. Consequently, the speaker needs to recognize when speaking on a wide variety of issues that time is extremely valuable to the poor and that to ask anything that would take their time is to demand a great deal—perhaps more than many can afford. No one would deny that the poor should get involved in voter registration drives, in working for political candidates and worthy charities, and in volunteer work in hospitals, but many have to spend their available time making "a living wage."

Religion and religiousness

Compared with 20 or even 10 years ago, there is today great diversity within each religion and the diversity seems to be getting greater each year. Whereas each religion was once almost totally of one mind concerning matters of morals and morality, for example, today there are wide differences within each religion. Almost invariably there are conservative, liberal, and middle-of-the-road factions within each religion. As the differences within each religion widen, the differences between religions seem to narrow. Different religions are coming closer together on various social and political, as well as moral, issues.

The speaker has to deal with religious affiliation and the strength of belief and adherence to religion generally and to one religion specifically in analyzing the audience. These—like some of the other characteristics—are difficult to assess since attitudes and behaviors do not always coincide and because expressed and internally held beliefs do not always match. Although some may claim total alienation from the religion in which they were raised, they may still have strong emotional ties to that religion, its beliefs, and its values.

One correlation that seems valid (and holds more for some religions than for others) is between religiousness and conservatism. Despite the amount of change going on in many religions today, they and their adherents are still relatively conservative in their political and social attitudes. Again, there are many people who are deeply religious but who are extremely liberal, even revolutionary.

SEE
EXPERIENTIAL
VEHICLE 2.2.
You will generally have to take into consideration the religion of your listeners whether or not the topic of the speech deals specifically with religion. In the minds of the religious, the speaker must recognize, all topics will be in some way related to religion. Consider a few such instances. On a most obvious level you have such issues as birth control, abortion, and homosexuality; but other issues not so clearly linked to religion are less obvious, for example, obedience to authority, beliefs concerning what is right and what is wrong for a nation and an individual, and guilt from engaging in some "wrongful" or "criminal" act. Likewise, premarital sex, marriage, children, money, unmarrieds living together, responsibilities toward parents, and thousands of other issues are clearly related to religion and religiousness.

Other factors

No list of audience variables can possibly be complete; the list presented here is no exception. You will need another category—"other factors"—to identify any additional characteristics that might be significant to a particular audience. Such factors might include the following.

Expectations   The expectations that the audience has about a speaker will influence their reception of the speech and should influence what you as a speaker will do. This does not mean that you should always give the audience what it expects, simply that you must take into consideration these expectations whether you intend to fulfill them or explode them. If your audience expects you to be humorous, you must either be humorous or explain why you won't be.

In the classroom, teachers face this problem all the time. Students will frequently come to a course with expectations based on the reputation of the department or the individual instructor or on the course material. These expectations must be faced squarely and dispelled if they are incorrect or met if they are correct.

Marital status   Are the audience members married? Single? Divorced? Widowed? Do the members wish to get married? Are they content in their present state or do they wish to change in some way? Are they without primary relationships or are they in such relationships?

Special interests   What kind of special interests do the audience members have? Do they have hobbies that you might refer to? What occupies their leisure time? Do they have an interest in films? Television? Community projects?

Organizational memberships   Are the members of the audience joiners? Nonjoiners? What organizations do they belong to and how might these organizations influence what you as a speaker might say or expect? Are they members of NRA? KKK? AMA? KC? DAR? CORE? NGTF? SCA? FALN?

Political affiliation   Are members of the audience identified with any particular political party? Democrat? Republican? Socialist? Communist? Are they liberal in their politics? Conservative? Are they uninvolved and uninterested? What does this mean to the development of your speech?

REMEMBER to consider the following factors in analyzing an audience:

1   Age
2   Sex
3   Cultural and subcultural factors
4   Educational and intellectual levels
5   Occupation, income, and status
6   Religion and religiousness
7   Other factors—expectations, marital status, special interests, organizational memberships, political affiliation

HOW TO . . . Deal with a "Mixed" Audience

All audiences are mixed; all audiences consist of members who are different from one another. Yet, some audiences represent more differences than others. And, generally, the more differences existing among members of your audience, the more difficult will be your task of informing or persuading. Here are a few general propositions that may help in addressing mixed audiences.

1 The greater the homogeneity of the audience, the easier will be the analysis and subsequent adaptation and the less the chance of making serious mistakes as a speaker.

   Consider an audience whose members are all middle-aged men working in nonunion sweat shops, earning the minimum wage, sharing the same religion and cultural background, and with less than an eighth-grade education. This audience—albeit to an unrealistic extreme—is homogeneous; the members share a number of important characteristics. Consequently, it will be relatively easy to analyze and adapt to them; easier than analyzing and adapting to an audience of men and women, rich and poor, management and labor, with different religions, educational backgrounds, and cultural heritages.

2 When the audience is too heterogeneous, it is sometimes helpful to subdivide it and appeal to each section separately. Thus, for example, if the audience consists of college students and their parents, your supporting materials (examples, illustrations, arguments) must differ to appeal to both groups or be so general as to appeal to all persons regardless of age, marital status, and so on. It might be better for the speaker first to use materials that appeal to the students without attempting to involve the older group directly and then to include materials to appeal to the older group without attempting to involve the younger group directly. Another frequently encountered case is the audience consisting of men and women. Say the topic is abortion on demand. To limit yourself to arguments that would appeal equally to men and women might seriously damage your case. You should consider concentrating first on arguments that men can relate to and then on those that women can relate to, or vice versa. You thus avoid using supporting materials that fall in between the groups.

3 Homogeneity does not equal attitudinal sameness. Generally, the audience that is similar in age, sex, educational background, and so on, will also share attitudes and beliefs. However, this does not always hold true. Variety directly relates to the size of the group. This is a simple anthropological axiom. As any group expands in size, their characteristics diversify. You may recall the same principle from statistics: As a sample size increases, all characteristics of the group will approach closer to a bell-shaped curve. This is crucial for you, as a speaker, to recognize. Generally, college professors would be liberal on most social and political issues. However, as the group of college professors examined is expanded, their liberalness will approach a bell-shaped curve with a small percentage extremely liberal, another small percentage conservative, and the

vast majority somewhere in between these extremes. This does not mean that this bell-shaped curve will be the same as, say, that for Midwestern farmers (generally more conservative than professors), but only that within each group there will be a diversity that will increase with the size of the group. The speaker who ignores this simple truism—the college teacher who assumes that all English majors enjoy literature; the priest who assumes that all Catholics are against abortion; the parent who assumes that all parents want to be parents, and so on—encounters difficulties.

ANALYZING CONTEXT CHARACTERISTICS

In addition to analyzing specific listeners, you will have to devote some attention to the specific context in which you will speak. Here I identify just a few of the characteristics on which you might focus: (1) the size of the audience, (2) the physical environment, and (3) the occasion. These factors are not totally separate and distinct from those considered in the previous section under "Analyzing Audience Characteristics." The topics considered under "Analyzing Audience Characteristics" are relatively stable or static characteristics; they are what is technically called "demographic characteristics." The factors considered here under "Analyzing Context Characteristics" are more closely related to the ever-changing nature of the specific context; they are characteristics that are temporary and dynamic (always changing).

Size of the audience

A few years ago I gave a speech at East Stroudsburg State College in Pennsylvania. I was told that, because of the number of competing events and the fact that the students had no classes for that week, there would be approximately 15 or 20 people in the audience. I therefore reworked my speech, incorporating questions to the audience, to a dialogue format. When I walked into the audience there were several hundred students, which precluded any dialogue format. Fortunately, I had previously prepared a continuous, public speaking format speech and was able to make the adjustment. But the situation still vividly reminds me of the importance of audience size. In your class you will not have this problem; you will know the size of each audience (at least approximately) for each speech. But this does not negate the fact that in all public speaking situations you should know beforehand the size of the audience. Generally, the larger the audience, the more formal the presentation. With a small audience, you may be more casual and informal. Also, the larger the audience is, the more heterogeneous the members and the broader your supporting materials must be. You will have in a large audience more different religions, a greater range of occupations, more different income levels, and so on. All the variables noted earlier will be even more varied in the large audience.

A large audience also presents difficulties with visuals. When I taught psycholinguistics to 30 students, I was able to construct relatively small charts of important concepts. Now, in a class of over 200, these would be totally inadequate and I must use transparencies, slides, and other materials more suited to a large audience.

The physical environment

The physical environment—indoors or outdoors, room or auditorium, sitting or standing audience—is important.

A few minutes of time could erase or lessen the problem of entering the public speaking environment totally cold. Even if you will be giving your speech in a familiar classroom, you should spend some time in front of the room, seeing the room from the perspective of the speaker before you are ready to speak. When you walk into the room, take a second and stand in the front and survey the entire room—look at the windows, the back wall, the desks, the students, and so on. See the room as you will as a speaker. The same is even more true for rooms that are totally unfamiliar to you.

Another factor in speech effectiveness is audience density. Whether the listeners are close or far apart will influence their interaction and your persuasiveness. Generally, audiences are easier to persuade if they are sitting close together than if they are spread widely apart. As a teacher, I always exceed the limit on the number of students allowed in my class because I find that physical closeness encourages students to get to know one another and to interact freely, which makes for a more effective class.

The occasion

The occasion will greatly influence the nature and the reception of the speech. Whether the speech is a class exercise (as most of your early speeches will be) or some invited address (as most of your professional-life speeches will be) will influence much of the speech. When the speech is given as a class assignment, for example, you will probably be operating under a number of restrictions—time limitations, the type of purpose you can employ, the types of supporting materials to be emphasized, and various other matters as well. When your speech is invited because of who you are, you have a great deal more freedom to talk about what interests you, which by virtue of the invitation will also interest the audience.

The type of occasion will dictate in part the kind of speech required. A wedding speech will differ drastically from a funeral speech, which will differ drastically from one at a political rally. What is appropriate in terms of topic, treatment, language, and of all the variables of public speaking will be influenced by the occasion. In constructing the speech, focus on each element in relation to the occasion. Ask yourself in what way the particular public speaking variable (language, organization, supporting materials, for example) might be made more responsive to this particular occasion.

These are not the only characteristics that affect the context, but they are a few that should keep you productively busy as you master the art of public speaking. As you progress you will find that these analyses become easier and easier to do; with greater experience you will come to know almost intuitively what to expect, how to adjust to a large versus a small audience, how to deal with hostility or indifference, and so on.

REMEMBER to consider the following factors in analyzing the public speaking context:
1   **Size of the audience**
2   **Physical environment**
3   **Occasion**

SOURCES

Audience analysis is covered in the sources noted in the following unit as well as in the numerous and excellent works on persuasion. See, for example, Herbert W. Simons, *Persuasion: Understanding, Practice, and Analysis* (Reading, Mass.: Addison-Wesley, 1976); Winston Brembeck and William S. Howell, *Persuasion: A Means of Social Influence* (Englewood Cliffs, N.J.: Prentice-Hall, 1976); and Raymond S. Ross and Mark G. Ross, *Understanding Persuasion* (Englewood Cliffs, N.J.: Prentice-Hall, 1981). An excellent source for any speaker, and one from which I drew for the research data discussed under sex, is Barry Tarshis, *The "Average American" Book* (New York: Atheneum SMI, 1979). On differences in the expectations between males and females see, for example, Cynthia L. Berryman and James R. Wilcox, "Attitudes toward Male and Female Speech: Experiments on the Effects of Sex-Typical Language," *Western Journal of Speech Communication* 44 (Winter 1980):50–59. An interesting and relevant analysis of students in beginning communication courses is Glen E. Hiemstra and Ann Q. Staton-Spicer, "Communication Concerns of College Undergraduates in Basic Speech Communication Courses," *Communication Education* 32 (January 1983): 29–37. A recent work on persuasion with much on audience analysis is Ruth Ann Clark, *Persuasive Messages* (New York: Harper & Row, 1984).

UNIT 8

Adapting to your audience

OBJECTIVES

After completing this unit, you should be able to:

1 *explain at least five of the dimensions of an audience*
2 *explain how the public speaker might adapt to audiences differing on the five dimensions*
3 *explain at least three guidelines for dealing with a mixed audience*

Now that some of the general characteristics of audiences have been identified, we need to look into some additional ways in which audiences differ. In focusing on these differences, keep in mind the observation of Blaise Pascal: "The more intelligent a man is, the more originality he discovers in men. Ordinary people see no difference between men."

In pursuing these differences I find it helpful to view an audience as existing on a number of different continua, each of which suggests a different dimension. Most (if not all) audiences can be indexed on scales such as those depicted in Figure 8.1.

SEE
EXPERIENTIAL
VEHICLE 2.3.

Any audience may be described by its willingness to listen to the speech, the degree to which it is favorable to the specific purpose of the speaker, and so on. This is not to say that you can analyze all audiences on all continua, but only that each audience does in reality exist on these various continua. By indicating on each scale where a particular audience is (or is thought to be), you may construct a profile that, theoretically at least, will be unique for each audience. First, however, you should understand the various dimensions.

WILLINGNESS

Audiences gather to hear a speaker with varying degrees of willingness. Some are anxious to hear the speaker and might even pay substantial admission prices. The "lecture circuit," for example, is one of the most lucrative aspects of public life; public figures often earn substantially more from speaking than they do from their regular salaries. *The New York Times* (December 15, 1982 and June 10, 1983) reported, for example, that lecture fees of prominent speakers range from $500 to $25,000 per lecture. Alexander M. Haig, Jr. seems to be the highest priced lecturer, earning from

FIGURE 8.1   The dimensions of an audience

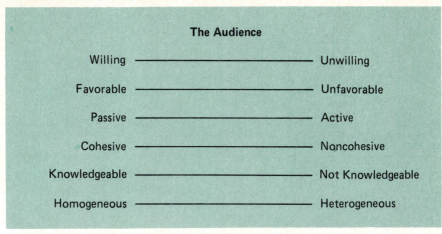

The Audience

Willing	Unwilling
Favorable	Unfavorable
Passive	Active
Cohesive	Noncohesive
Knowledgeable	Not Knowledgeable
Homogeneous	Heterogeneous

$20,000 to $25,000 per speech. Henry Kissinger gets upward of $15,000 and Gerald R. Ford, from $10,000 to $15,000. Columnists who are popular on the lecture circuit include Art Buchwald ($12,500), William Safire ($12,000), Ann Landers ($10,000), and Jack Anderson ($6,000 to $7,500). Television newscasters command a similar fee: David Brinkley earns from $7,500 to $12,000, Diane Sawyer earns $8,500, Sam Donaldson earns around $7,500, and Jessica Savitch earns around $7,000. Polly Bergen and Jane Bryant Quinn (a financial expert) earn around $7,000 to $8,000; Pearl Bailey around $7,000 (for speaking only); Bess Myerson and Cicely Tyson around $5,000 to $6,000; and Celeste Holm around $5,000. Ralph Nader, Joyce Brothers, Arlene Dahl, and Letitia Baldrige (an etiquette expert) earn around $4,000 to $5,000 while John Dean earns $2,000 to $2,500. All in all, not a bad evening's work. And this surely is a far cry from the first paid public speaker in American history, Ralph Waldo Emerson, who received $5 and oats for his horse. Daniel Webster was reportedly the first to receive a fee of $100 and Henry Ward Beecher the first to receive $1,000.

While some audiences are willing to pay considerable sums to hear a speaker, others do not seem to care one way or the other, and some are literally dragged and forced to listen (or at least to sit in the audience). A group of people who gather in the street to hear Jane Fonda are there willingly. They want to be there and they want to hear what Fonda has to say. On the other hand, some groups gather of necessity—because the union contract demands that members show up, or because administrators require teachers to attend college and department meetings. These people may not wish to be there but they do not want to risk losing their jobs or their vote. In a college classroom, the willingness of the students varies greatly. In some classes the students seem to come willingly, not from fear of attendance checks or of missing work for an examination. Some come simply to enjoy listening to a relevant lecture on a topic in which they are interested; others cut all classes, dread the thought of attending class, and only sit through a class when there is no alternative. The willingness with which students attend a public speaking class will vary greatly from one school to another, from one class to another, and from one session to another. Student speakers should realize that a number of students may be there under duress—much as you will attend at times under pressure from the instructor or from your friends who are speaking.

Adapting to the unwilling audience

The unwilling audience demands special and delicate handling. First, as early in the speech as possible, secure their interest and attention and seek to reinforce this throughout the speech. Using little-known facts, quotations, startling statistics, examples and illustrations, visual aids, and the like, will help you to secure and maintain the attention of an initially unwilling audience (see "How to Secure and Maintain Audience Attention" in Unit 11).

Second, reward the audience for being there to hear your speech and for attending it throughout—and do this in advance of your main arguments. Let the audience know that you are aware that they are making a sacrifice in coming to hear your speech and that you appreciate it. One student, giving a speech close to mid-term time, said simply, "I know how easy it is to cut classes during mid-term time to finish the unread chapters and do everything else that has to be done, and so I especially appreciate your being here this morning. But I think what I have to say will interest you and will be of direct benefit to all of you." Once said, it is difficult for an audience to continue to feel unwilling.

Third, in selecting your topic and your supporting materials that will amplify or bolster your position, pay special attention to materials that relate directly to the audience's needs and wants (see especially Unit 17). Show the audience how they can save time, make more money, solve their problems, enjoy leisure time more, become more popular, and so on. If you fail to do this, then your audience has a good reason for not listening.

FAVORABLENESS

Audiences may or may not agree with the speaker's proposition. One group may be totally in favor of a speech that seeks to persuade the audience that comprehensive health insurance should be provided all citizens; another group may be totally against the very same proposition. If you intend to change an audience's attitudes, beliefs, or behaviors, you must fully understand their present position.

The audience may vary as much in their attitude toward you as toward your topic. At times the audience may have no real feeling, positive or negative, toward you as the speaker; at other times they will have very clear feelings that must be confronted. Thus, when Richard Nixon addressed the nation after Watergate, it was impossible to avoid his negative image and the audience's unfavorable attitude toward him as a person. Sometimes the degree of favorableness will depend not only on the specific speaker but on certain of the speaker's characteristics. Thus, a group of male physicists may resent listening to a woman lecture on thermodynamics (although these men may not be conscious of their unfavorable attitude at the time). Similarly, audiences may have favorable or unfavorable responses to speakers because of their racial or ethnic origin, because of their religion, their status, their relative wealth or poverty, and so on. The speaker needs to ascertain, therefore, how the audience perceives not only the speech purpose but also the speaker.

Adapting to the unfavorably disposed audience

Perhaps the first and most important strategy to follow in addressing an audience that is unfavorable toward you or your position is to build on commonalities. Emphasize not the differences but the similarities; stress what you and the audience share as people, as advocates, as interested citizens, as fellow students. Persuasion, as viewed by theorist and critic Kenneth Burke and by numerous other contemporary rhetoricians, is achieved through identification, by the speaker identifying with the audience members—with their needs, their attitudes, their beliefs. Only when an audience finds some common ground between itself and the speaker will it be favorably disposed to the speaker and to the speaker's position.

Second, build your speech from areas of agreement, through areas of slight disagreement, up to the major point of difference. Always proceed in small steps. Thus, if management was attempting to persuade labor to accept a particular wage offer, a speaker might begin with such areas of general agreement as the mutual desire for improved working conditions, for the economic growth of the entire plant, for the continued operation of the factory, and so on. In any disagreement—in any polarized argument—there are still areas of agreement, areas of commonality, and these should be emphasized.

Third, if you are facing an unfavorable audience, be satisfied with small gains. Do not try to convert a pro-life group to contribute money for the new abortion-on-demand clinic in a five-minute speech. Be content to get them to see some validity in your position; be content to get them to listen fairly. About-face changes take a long time to achieve. To try to attempt too much persuasion, too much change, can only result in failure or resentment.

PASSIVITY–ACTIVITY

During the Korean War, we developed an idea of the audience as a passive mass that could be manipulated easily by cleverly constructed propaganda. One of the horrors of the war, we were told, was brainwashing, where an individual's mind was changed and values, attitudes, and beliefs once cherished and defended at all costs were abandoned for their antithesis.

This most passive view of the audience attributed all of the change to the speaker-propagandist. Clearly, some people are passive and easily molded to another's way of thinking. We all know such people. But most persons are active listeners; they do not merely take in the information and use it as instructed, but they work actively with it. They analyze it, critically evaluate it, question it, add it to what they already know, challenge it with previously learned data, and otherwise work it over. The audience is the final arbiter of what is believed, of what is held to be true, of what is thought to be right. It is probably easier to force the horse to drink than to get the horse to want to drink. The same is true with men and women. We may force them to do certain things but it is much more difficult to get them to want to do them. Thus, it is relatively easy for a college teacher to secure daily, faithful (though passive) class attendance; however, it is much more difficult for the instructor to secure an audience that is active and willingly in attendance.

There is a second kind of passive audience—the audience that public speakers dread. This is the audience that simply doesn't care about you, about your speech, or about your position. Its members may be physically present at your speech but emotionally and intellectually they are somewhere else, "tuned out." These listeners must be "awakened" and made to care, made to feel concern.

Adapting to the passive audience

The passive audience, like the unwilling audience, must be shown why they should listen to your speech and why they should be concerned with what you are saying. During your speech, first answer the listeners' inevitable questions: "Why should I listen?" "Why should I care about what you are saying?" "Why should I bother to clutter up my mind with this information, with these arguments?" Second, involve the audience as directly as you can in your speech. Ask questions and pose problems directly to the audience members, pausing a reasonable amount of time to get them to consider a response to what you are saying. Third, use material that has attention-gaining and interest-securing power. Once you get the audience to pay attention, they will begin to really listen to what you are saying and to internalize some of your arguments and information. Fourth, focus on a few (even one) very strong issues rather than diffuse your energies and time on many issues, none of which may awaken the truly passive audience. You want your audience to stop thinking there is no reason to care, no reason to be concerned. If you give them four or five poorly developed reasons, they may still feel there is no reason to care. But if you spend all your energies on your one best argument, it will be difficult for them to continue in a passive frame of mind.

COHESIVENESS

Groups vary greatly in cohesiveness, that is, the degree to which there is closeness among the members. This factor, not often considered in the public speaking situation, is actually most significant, especially when dealing with audience interaction after the speech. A cohesive audience is more likely to discuss the speech. A group with little cohesiveness is more likely to quickly disband. Discussion or lack of it will significantly influence the eventual effect of the speech.

With a cohesive group, the members of the audience will probably also interact during the speech itself. Verbally or nonverbally, the members will share opinions, voice disagreements, offer counterexamples, and so on, as you are speaking. Although this interaction is often disconcerting, it is probably inevitable and you should learn to live with it rather than attempt to change "human nature."

With a cohesive audience, you are also likely to find that audience members are more willing to disagree with you during the question-and-answer period, should there be one. Listeners who feel supported by their peers are generally more apt to voice their real feelings even when these feelings are in disagreement with those of the speaker.

Adapting to the cohesive audience

If you are in basic agreement with a cohesive audience and your main function is to reinforce their beliefs or attitudes or to provide them with additional information on a topic they are already concerned about, addressing the cohesive audience poses no real problem. A cohesive audience, however, does pose difficulties when you, the speaker, are in disagreement with them. When you find yourself in this situation, the following guidelines may prove helpful.

First, emphasize commonalities. Your task here is to become less of an outsider, less of a nonmember. You want your audience to look upon you and see similarities with themselves. Obviously, you should stress those commonalities that are relevant to the subject of your speech.

Second, be especially careful not to state opinions with which the audience disagrees too boldly or too early in your speech. Proceed from the agreement to the disagreement and, again, proceed slowly and in small steps. Audiences high in cohesiveness are continually communicating with each other nonverbally. When a speaker states a position with which there is obvious and strong disagreement, the audience tends to become even more cohesive and invariably more polarized with you on one side and them on the other.

Third, concentrate on the opinion leaders in the group. Cohesive audiences tend to discuss the speech and the speaker after the speech is concluded. When this discussion takes place, the opinion leaders, generally the better educated and the higher status members, exert significant influence and will often influence the other members in these after-the-speech discussions.

KNOWLEDGE

Audiences differ greatly in terms of the knowledge that the members have. Some audiences will prove most knowledgeable about the topic; others will prove almost totally ignorant. The really difficult audiences are those with a mixture. In graduate courses in communication, for example, in psycholinguistics, my major problem in structuring a lecture is accommodating the varied knowledge levels of the audience. When some students have had three or four related courses and others do not even know what psycholinguistics is, the task is not easy for the speaker.

If you are unaware of the audience's knowledge, you will not know what to assume and what to explain. You will not know what amount of information will overload the channels and what amount will bore the audience to sleep.

Perhaps you will show that previous knowledge is now inadequate. Perhaps you will show a new slant to old issues. Or perhaps what you have to say will not repeat but instead will build on the already extensive knowledge of the audience. However you accomplish this, you need to secure from the audience the understanding that what you have to say is new, that you will not simply repeat what they already know. Further, it is especially important with this type of audience to emphasize your credibility, especially your competence in this general subject area. You need to make the audience aware that you have in fact earned the right to speak and that what you have to say is based on a competent and firm grasp of the material.

Adapting to the knowledgeable and unknowledgeable audiences

Audiences that lack knowledge of the topic need to be treated very carefully. Be especially careful that you do not talk down to these members of your audience. This is perhaps the greatest communication error that teachers make. After having taught a subject for 10 to 30 years, they face, semester after semester, students who have no knowledge of the topic. Many teachers, as a result, will often talk down to the audience and in the process lose them. No one wants to listen to a speaker putting them down.

Do not confuse a lack of knowledge with a lack of intelligence. An audience may have no knowledge of your topic but may be quite capable of following a clearly presented idea or a logically developed argument. Try especially hard to use concrete examples, visual aids, and simple language. Avoid jargon and specialized terms that may be clear to you but would not be to someone new to the subject.

Audiences with a great deal of knowledge also require special handling because their response may well be, "Why should I listen to this? I already know about this topic." With this audience it is important that you emphasize as early as possible that what you have to say will not be redundant to them—that you are going to deal with newly discovered facts and information.

HOMOGENEITY–HETEROGENEITY

Audiences vary in homogeneity—the degree to which they possess similar characteristics, values, attitudes, knowledge, and so on. Some audiences are composed of individuals who are very much alike; some are composed of widely different individuals.

In your public speaking class, you will probably address the most homogeneous group of persons you will ever find. They are all college students, they are taking a course in public speaking, and they are all approximately the same age (in many evening classes, this will not be true). Many will come from similar socioeconomic, ethnic, racial, and religious backgrounds. They will share many goals. In some classes all students will be majoring in business, in others all will be majoring in the arts, and so on.

SEE
EXPERIENTIAL
VEHICLE 2.4.
Outside the classroom, the same degree of homogeneity would be difficult to find. Even in union meetings, for example, although the individuals may be of the same general socioeconomic level, they differ widely in age, in religion, in education, in ethnic and racial background, and so on.

Obviously, it is easier to address a homogeneous group than a heterogeneous group. You may use similar supporting materials. If the listeners are so alike, the arguments will be as effective for one as another. The language appropriate to one will be appropriate to another, and so on, through all the variables of the public speaking transaction. With a heterogeneous group, however, this does not hold. The argument that works with one subgroup will not work with another; the language that is appropriate to the educated members will not be appropriate to the uneducated. Consequently, the speaker addressing a heterogeneous audience must compromise.

Homogeneity-heterogeneity also relates to the previous five dimensions just considered. Thus, audience homogeneity-heterogeneity applies to their willingness to listen, their favorableness, their passivity, their cohesiveness, and their knowledge. Some audiences will be extremely similar (homogeneous) in their willingness to listen; others may contain members who differ widely in their willingness to listen; and so on, for all of the dimensions noted.

Adapting to the heterogeneous audience

The most difficult audience to address is not the unwilling or the unfavorable or the unknowledgeable but the mixed audience; the audience consisting of some who do and some who don't, of some who care and some who don't, of some who know and some who don't. At times, addressing this type of audience will seem an impossibility—it isn't. Teachers face this type of audience every day as do politicians and advertisers. Because this issue is applicable to all dimensions of an audience, it is covered in the box, "How to Deal with a Mixed Audience," Unit 7.

SEE
EXPERIENTIAL
VEHICLE 2.5.

Employ these six dimensions to analyze all audiences. The relative importance of each dimension will naturally vary greatly from one situation to another. This is inevitable. As a speaker, concentrate your efforts on those dimensions that are most relevant to your specific speech situation.

SOURCES

For audience adaptation see, for example, Paul D. Holtzman, *The Psychology of Speakers' Audiences* (Glenview, Ill.: Scott, Foresman, 1970); James W. Gibson and Michael S. Hanna, *Audience Analysis: A Programmed Approach to Receiver Behavior* (Englewood Cliffs, N.J.: Prentice-Hall, 1976); and the early but still excellent Theodore Clevenger, *Audience Analysis* (Indianapolis: Bobbs-Merrill, 1966). Excellent and more recent treatments may be found in Loren Reid, *Speaking Well*, 4th ed. (New York: McGraw-Hill, 1982), and Rudolph F. Verderber, *The Challenge of Effective Speaking*, 5th ed. (Belmont, Calif.: Wadsworth, 1982).

HOW TO . . . Evaluate Your Audience Analysis and Speech Adaptation: Part Two Checklist

Yes No

☐ ☐ 1. Have you analyzed your audience members and adapted to them on the basis of their willingness to listen to you?

☐ ☐ Their favorableness-unfavorableness toward you and your position?

☐ ☐ Their passivity-activity?

☐ ☐ Their cohesiveness or noncohesiveness?

☐ ☐ Their knowledge or lack of it?

☐ ☐ Their homogeneity-heterogeneity?

2. Have you taken into consideration the following audience characteristics?

☐ ☐ Age?

☐ ☐ Sex?

☐ ☐ Cultural and subcultural factors?

☐ ☐ Educatonal and intellectual levels?

☐ ☐ Occupation, income, and status?

☐ ☐ Religion and religiousness?

☐ ☐ Expectations, marital status, special interests, organizational memberships, and political affiliations?

☐ ☐ 3. Have you taken into consideration the size of the audience?

☐ ☐ The physical environment in which the speech is to be given?

☐ ☐ The occasion?

Presented in Table 8.1 is an Audience Analysis and Adaptation Form in which the audience characteristics and dimensions are laid out in chart format. Ideally, for each speech, this form or a form similar to it should be completed in detail. On the left are spaces for you to write down a detailed description of the audience. Here you would record your impressions of the audience's willingness to hear your specific speech, their favorableness toward you, your speech, and your purpose, and so on. Also included here are the variables— the audience characteristics such as age, sex, and the like. Here you would record what you know about the make-up of your audience or your best guesses if you have not faced or seen the audience before. On the right are spaces for you to record your proposed adaptation for this specific speech and specific purpose. That is, what will you do in light of their willingness-unwillingness to listen to you? What will you do on the basis of your analysis of their age? Their sex? Their expectations? What will you do to adapt to the physical environment? Admittedly this is a most time-consuming and difficult process to go through for every speech and this is at least one of the reasons why prominent politicians and business leaders maintain extensive speech writing staffs. For a beginning speaker, however, there is no better experience than to analyze at least one audience in depth and to propose adaptations on the basis of these analyses. Each and every fact you learn about your audience should mean something to you in constructing your speech; each audience characteristic should somehow be written into your speech. Put differently, your speech should be modified for each and every discovery you make about your audience. *(continued)*

TABLE 8.1 Audience analysis and adaptation form

SPEECH TOPIC:
THESIS:
GENERAL PURPOSE:
SPECIFIC PURPOSE:

AUDIENCE DESCRIPTION	*AUDIENCE ADAPTATION*
Age:	
Sex:	
Cultural, subcultural factors:	
Occupation, income, status:	
Expectations:	
Marital status:	
Special interest:	
Organizational memberships:	
Political affiliations:	
Audience size:	
Physical environment:	
Occasion:	
Willingness:	
Favorableness:	
Passivity-activity:	
Cohesiveness:	
Knowledge:	
Homogeneity-heterogenity:	

EXPERIENTIAL VEHICLES FOR PART TWO

2.1 ANALYZING AN AUDIENCE

This experience should familiarize you with some of the essential steps in analyzing an audience on the basis of relatively little evidence and in predicting their attitudes.

The class should be broken up into small groups of five or six members. Each group will be given a different magazine and their task is to analyze the audience (i.e., the readers or subscribers) of that particular magazine in terms of the characteristics discussed in Unit 7. The only information the groups will have about their audience is that they are avid and typical readers of the given magazine. Pay particular attention to the type of articles published in the magazine, the advertisements, the photographs or illustrations, the editorial statement, the price of the magazine, and so on.

Appropriate magazines for analysis are: *Gentlemen's Quarterly, Movie Life, Ms., Playboy, Playgirl, Scientific American, Field and Stream, Family Circle, Good Housekeeping, Reader's Digest, National Geographic, Modern Bride, Gourmet, Architectural Digest, Christopher Street, Essence, Personal Computing.* Magazines differing widely from each other are most appropriate for this experience.

After the audience has been analyzed, try to identify at least three favorable and three unfavorable attitudes that they probably hold. On what basis do you make these predictions? If you had to address this audience advocating a position with which they disagreed, what adaptations would you make? That is, what strategies would you use in preparing and presenting this persuasive speech?

Each group should share with the rest of the class the results of their efforts, taking special care to point out not only their conclusions but the evidence and reasoning they used in arriving at the conclusions.

2.2 AUDIENCE ANALYSIS AND ADAPTATION

Analyze one of the speeches in Appendix D, "Speeches for Study and Enjoyment" in terms of audience analysis and adaptation. Specifically, attempt to discover in what ways the speaker demonstrated (or failed to demonstrate) a consciousness of and an adaptation to the audience. You may wish to consider those factors discussed in Unit 7, for example: age; sex; cultural and subcultural factors; educational and intellectual level; occupation, income, and status; religion and religiousness.

Since you will have relatively little information about the specific audience addressed, you will not be able to state with great certainty the extent to which the speaker analyzed and adapted to the audience. Here you will have to make some educated guesses.

2.3 DIVERSITY WITHIN GROUPS

This exercise should sensitize you to the diversity that exists within any group.

Select a group of which you are a member—for example, a racial, ethnic, religious, occupational group—and prepare a brief talk in which you explain the diversity within this group. Base your talk on information secured not only from personal observation and experience of your group but also on pertinent sociological, anthropological, and psychological data.

2.4 AUDIENCE ATTITUDES

This exercise will enable you to deal with some of the issues involved in audience analysis and adaptation.

Try to predict the attitudes of your class members toward each of the following propositions by indicating how you think the majority of the class members feel about each. Write the number of the attitude you predict the majority of the members hold in the space provided on the left. Use the following scale:

1 = strongly in favor of the proposition as stated
2 = mildly in favor of the proposition as stated
3 = neutral
4 = mildly against the proposition as stated
5 = strongly against the proposition as stated

After you have completed the predictions for all propositions, select one that you predicted the audience to be "strongly against" and indicate what kinds of adaptations you would make to get your audience to accept the proposition or at least to feel more positive towards it than they do now.

After all persons have completed both parts of this experience, the class as a whole or in small groups should discuss the following issues:

1   the accuracy-inaccuracy with which the various attitudes were predicted
2   the possible sources for the inaccurate and the accurate guesses
3   the appropriateness-inappropriateness of the adaptations proposed

_____ 1 Marijuana should be legalized for all persons over 18.
_____ 2 All required courses (general education requirements) should be abolished.
_____ 3 Parochial elementary and high schools should be tax supported.
_____ 4 X-rated movies (even XXX movies) should be shown on television without time restrictions.
_____ 5 Prostitution (male and female) should be legalized.
_____ 6 Puerto Rico should be made the fifty-first state.
_____ 7 Members of minority groups that have been discriminated against should be given preferential treatment in entrance into graduate and professional schools.
_____ 8 Homosexuals should be allowed to be teachers, fire fighters, and police officers without any restrictions based on affectional preference.
_____ 9 Mandatory retirement should be abolished.
_____ 10 Tenure for college teachers should be eliminated.

2.5 ANALYZING AUDIENCE DIMENSIONS

Described below are six public speaking situations. Each student should analyze the audience based on the six dimensions identified in Unit 8, then complete a set of scales (such as that presented in Figure 8.1) for each of the six situations. On the basis of this analysis, what one suggestion would you give the speaker to help her or him better adapt the speech to this audience?

In small groups or with the class as a whole, be prepared to give reasons for your decisions and to discuss your one major bit of advice for each of the six speakers.

PUBLIC SPEAKING SITUATIONS
1   A group of film students listening to George Lucas discuss the filming of the *Star Wars* movies.

2   A group of high school athletes listening to a college athletic director speaking against sports scholarships.

3   A group of pregnant women listening to an advertising agency executive speak on how advertisers try to protect the consumer.

4   A group of office managers listening to an organizational communication consultant speaking on ways to increase employee morale and productivity.

5   Your class listening to a famous actress speaking in favor of supporting the Will Rogers Institute.

6   A group of Chicago high school seniors listening to a college recruiter speak on the advantages of a small rural college.

PART THREE

ORGANIZING THE PUBLIC SPEECH

PART THREE

UNIT 9

General principles of organization

OBJECTIVES

After completing this unit, you should be able to:

1 *define the* **simple thesis** *and the* **expanded thesis**
2 *identify three uses of thesis statements*
3 *explain the principles of coordination and subordination*
4 *explain the suggested uses of internal summaries and transitions*
5 *define and explain the roles of unity, coherence, balance, and emphasis in public speaking*
6 *explain the differences between climax and anticlimax orders in speech organization*
7 *define and explain the differences between primacy and recency in speech organization*

THE IMPORTANCE OF ORGANIZATION

In this unit and the following three units, the topics of organization are considered. Organization is one of the central concerns of public speaking and is therefore considered at length. It is a skill that once learned will assist you not only in constructing a public speech but in constructing any type of message, whether written or oral.

Public speaking organization is of value to the speaker both in constructing the speech and in securing the desired response from the audience. In organizing the speech you will be able to see at a glance where the speech is weak and where it needs additional supporting materials. You will be able to see if one step follows logically from the previous one or if the two seem unrelated. From these examinations you will be able to remedy any major problems with relative ease.

Organization is also important in enabling you to construct a message that an audience will find easy to understand, to process, and to remember. We can more easily follow an oral message if it has a clear and logical organizational pattern. Think of the lectures you find easy to understand and those you have difficulty with. I suspect that at least in some instances the difference is in the presence of a clear and sensible organizational pattern versus an erratic one. Further, it is easier to process new information if we can see its relationship to other information that is being presented. Isolated and unrelated pieces of information are difficult to process and internalize. We are helped by seeing an overall structure and a relationship among the parts. Lastly, the audience will find it easier to remember your speech if it follows a clear and recognizable organizational pattern. Again, isolated and unrelated pieces of information are difficult to recall; connected and logically related items are a great deal easier to remember.

This unit will offer some general principles of organization: developing the thesis statement; coordination and subordination; the use of internal summaries and transitions; and the concepts of unity, coherence, balance, and emphasis.

THE THESIS

The first step in the development and organization of any public speech is to write out the thesis statement of your speech. I find it useful to distinguish the simple thesis from the expanded thesis.

The simple thesis

The simple thesis is your main assertion, what you want the audience to absorb from your speech. The simple thesis of Lincoln's Second Inaugural Address was that Northerners and Southerners should now work together for the good of the entire country. The simple thesis of Richard Nixon's "Checker's Speech" was "I am innocent of any wrongdoing." The simple thesis of the "Rocky" movies was that the underdog can win.

Let us say, for example, that you are planning to deliver a speech in favor of Senator Farrington. Your thesis statement might be something like this: "Farrington's candidacy should be supported." This is what you want your audience to believe as a result of your speech. In an informative speech the thesis statement would focus on what you want your audience to learn as a result of your speech. For example, if you were to speak on the topic of jealousy, one suitable thesis might be: "There are two main theories to account for jealousy." Note that the thesis statement is phrased as a declarative sentence. Theses as brief as "Farrington's candidacy" or "Theories of jealousy" are not suitable largely because they lack the clarity and specificity so helpful in the construction of a speech that a complete declarative sentence provides. On the basis of "Farrington's candidacy," we have no idea as to whether you will support it or attack it, and on the basis of "Theories of jealousy," we are similarly left with only a vague idea as to what you will say about it.

In addition to being phrased as a declarative sentence, and being clear and specific, the thesis statement should be limited to one central idea, focus, or purpose. Statements such as "We should support Farrington and the entire Democratic party" contain not one but two basic ideas. Limit your thesis statement to one main idea.

The expanded thesis

The expanded thesis statement builds on the simple thesis but includes the main ideas you will use to develop the thesis. For example, if "Farrington's candidacy should be supported" is the simple thesis, then we might expand this and phrase the expanded thesis to read: "Farrington's candidacy should be supported because Farrington is qualified and because the alternative candidates are not qualified." In the jealousy example, the expanded thesis might read: "The two main theories of jealousy are that it is a sign of intense love and that it is a sign of personal insecurity."

Notice that in persuasive speeches, the thesis statement puts forth a point of view, an opinion. The thesis is an arguable, debatable proposition. It is a nonneutral statement. In the informative speeches, the thesis appears relatively neutral and objective. But notice that in many ways it too states a point of view; for example, that there are two theories of jealousy and that the two main theories focus on intense love and personal insecurity. The division between information and persuasion, as has been previously noted, is an extremely thin line.

Using thesis statements

The thesis statement serves a number of useful purposes: It helps you to generate your main ideas or assertions, to suggest suitable organizational patterns and strategies, and to help focus the audience's attention on your central idea. Each of these functions should be examined briefly.

Generating main ideas Once you have phrased the thesis statement and especially the expanded thesis statement, the main divisions of your speech are readily suggested. Let us take an example: "The Hart bill will provide the needed services for senior citizens." Once stated in this form, the obvious question to address in preparing a speech with this thesis is: *What are they?* The answer to this question suggests the main parts of your speech, for example, health, food, shelter, and recreational services. Your expanded thesis should clearly identify these as well: "The Hart bill will provide the needed services for senior citizens in the areas of health, food, shelter, and recreation." These four areas then become the four main points of your speech. A brief outline illustrating how this speech would be developed would look something like this:

I. The Hart bill will provide needed health services.
II. The Hart bill will provide needed food services.
III. The Hart bill will provide needed shelter services.
IV. The Hart bill will provide needed recreational services.

The remainder of the speech would then be filled in with various supporting materials covered in Units 14, 16, and 17. Under I, for example, you would identify the needed health services and explain how the Hart bill makes provision for these services and so on with II, III, and IV.

Suggesting suitable organizational patterns The expanded thesis and the way in which you answer the questions you anticipate should provide you with a useful guideline in selecting your organizational pattern, a number of which are identified and explained in Unit 10. For example, let us suppose your thesis is: "We can improve our own college education." Your answer to the inevitable, *What can we do?*, will suggest a possible organizational pattern. If you attempt to identify the remedies in the order in which they should be taken, then perhaps a time-order pattern would be appropriate. If, on the other hand, you itemize a number of possible solutions, all of which are of approximately equal importance, then perhaps a topical pattern would be appropriate. These and other patterns are explained in detail in the following unit. All I wish to emphasize here is that the thesis statement will suggest not only the items of information or the main arguments that you will advance, but will also suggest how you might go about structuring these into a meaningful, coherent, and organized whole.

Focusing (or not focusing) audience attention   In addition to enabling you to more effectively collect and structure your material, the thesis sentence also focuses the audience's attention on your central idea. In many speeches you may wish to state your thesis early in your speech—perhaps in your introduction or perhaps early in the body of the speech. This early statement of the thesis clearly focuses the audience's attention on your central idea, on what you want them to get out of your speech.

There are instances, however, when you may not wish to state your thesis or may wish to state it late in your speech. For example, if your audience is hostile to your thesis, it may be wise to give your evidence and arguments first, in order to move them gradually into a more positive frame of mind, before stating the thesis. In other cases, you may wish to have the audience infer your thesis without you actually spelling it out. Beginning speakers especially should be careful in choosing not to state their thesis explicitly. Research has shown, for example, that audiences—especially relatively uneducated audiences—will not be persuaded by speeches in which the thesis is not explicitly stated. It seems they often fail to grasp what the thesis is and hence do not change their attitudes or behaviors.

Your decision as to when (or if) to state your thesis should be made on the basis of what will be more effective given your specific purpose and your specific audience. Generally, although there are many exceptions, I would suggest the following guidelines:

1   In an informative speech, state your thesis as early as possible and as directly and clearly as possible.
2   In a persuasive speech where your audience is neutral, state your thesis explicitly and relatively early in your speech.
3   In a persuasive speech where your audience is in favor of your position, you may leave the thesis unstated or may state it late in the speech.
4   In a persuasive speech where your audience is hostile to your position, it may be best to reserve your thesis until you have moved them somewhat closer to your position.

Wording the thesis

Although you should state the thesis as a simple declarative sentence for yourself to help you focus your thinking, your collection of materials, and your organizational pattern (as already noted), you may elect to phrase your thesis in a number of different ways when you present it to your audience. At one extreme, you may state it to your audience as you phrased it for yourself: "You should support Farrington," "My thesis is that you should support Farrington," or "I want to tell you in this brief speech why you should support Farrington."

You may decide to state your thesis as a question: "Why should you support Farrington?," "Are there valid reasons for supporting Farrington? I think so," or "What are the two main theories of jealousy?"

In persuasive speeches in which you face a hostile or mildly-opposed audience, you may wish to state your thesis in vague and ambiguous terms, for example, "I want to talk about Farrington's qualifications" or "Does Farrington deserve our support? Let's look at the evidence." In these cases you may wish to focus the audience's attention on the central area you will be talking about but not reveal your point of view until a more favorable time.

A note on thesis and purpose

It has probably occurred to you that thesis is much like purpose. They are in fact quite similar. In fact, many textbooks in public speaking do not include extended discussions of both, choosing instead to explain either the thesis or the purpose. Actually, both will prove helpful in constructing an effective public speech. Both the thesis and the purpose help guide you in selecting and in organizing your materials. Consequently, I have considered the thesis at some length here and consider purpose in depth in Units 13, "General Principles of Informative Speeches" and 15, "General Principles of Persuasive Speeches." Here I want to identify a few of the differences between thesis and purpose.

The most obvious difference between thesis and purpose is in the form of expression: The thesis is phrased as a complete declarative sentence while the purpose is phrased as an infinitive phrase (to inform . . ., to persuade . . .). A more important difference is that the thesis is more message oriented whereas the purpose is more audience oriented. The thesis identifies the central idea of your speech: it summarizes—it epitomizes—the speech content. The purpose identifies the change the speaker hopes to achieve in the audience—for example, to gain certain information, to change attitudes, to engage in a certain behavior. A related difference is that the thesis is applicable to any and all forms of communication; it is applicable to the public speech but it is also applicable to the poem, the essay, the short story, the play, the novel, the film. Purpose (in a public speaking context), on the other hand, is distinctly rhetorical; it is applicable to communications that are directed at securing specific audience responses. Some theorists and critics, of course, would argue that all communications are rhetorical, that all communications seek to change their audience in some way. Without attempting to resolve this age-old issue, it is sufficient to note that in this discussion *purpose* applies to communications that are designed to produce some change in an audience.

Further, the purpose limits what the speaker hopes to achieve given the very practical limitations of time and the audience's preconceptions, expectations, and attitudes. The thesis, on the other hand, epitomizes the speech without regard to these practical limitations. In one sense, the purpose specifies what the speaker hopes to achieve once the thesis has been established. For example, the thesis might be, "Colleges are not educating students for today's world." The purpose of this speech, however, might be (1) to persuade my audience that colleges must change to keep pace with today's world or (2) to persuade my audience to quit college.

Another distinguishing factor is that the thesis is usually stated somewhere in the speech. Often, for example, the speaker will state the thesis in the introduction or perhaps as a preface to the main ideas whereas the purpose is rarely stated. The speaker would rarely say, for example, "I want to persuade you to vote for me" or "I'm going to convince you to buy Brand X." However, the speaker might say (in thesis form), "I'm the most qualified candidate" or "Brand X is an excellent product."

Here are a few more examples to further clarify the difference between thesis and purpose (the discussions in Units 13 and 15 will develop the notion of purpose in greater depth).

Thesis: "We can reduce our phone bills by following three rules."
Purpose: To inform my audience of three ways to save on their phone bills.

Thesis: "Computer science knowledge is essential for all students."
Purpose: To persuade my audience to elect a computer science course.

Thesis: "Dunham Gresham was a great leader."
Purpose: To eulogize Dunham Gresham

SEE EXPERIENTIAL VEHICLE 3.1.

I would strongly suggest, especially in these early stages of mastering the art of public speaking, that you formulate both the thesis statement as considered here and the purpose as outlined in Units 13 and 15. With both the thesis and the purpose clearly formulated, you should be able to eliminate a great many problems faced by even experienced public speakers—speeches that lack cohesiveness, that ramble all over the field, that audiences find difficult to understand and remember.

REMEMBER the thesis statement should be:
1   phrased as a complete declarative sentence
2   clear and specific
3   limited to one central idea or focus

And is especially useful to:
4   generate main ideas
5   suggest suitable organizational patterns
6   focus (or not focus) audience attention

But may in the actual speech:
7   be phrased in various ways (as a statement, as a question, as a relatively ambiguous statement)
8   be stated early or late in the speech (or even only implied)

PRINCIPLES OF COORDINATION AND SUBORDINATION

The concepts of *coordination* and *subordination* cause some of the major problems in speech construction and yet they are extremely simple concepts. Focus on the following partial outline dealing with two areas of study, some specific courses, and some areas covered within these courses (Table 9.1). This outline, I should stress, is not intended to illustrate how a speech outline would look but only to illustrate coordination and subordination.

Focus first on the two major headings: *psychology* and *sociology*. In this outline they are equal and parallel; they are coordinate items. Within the *psychology* heading there are other coordinate items; *learning* and *motivation* are coordinate, representing two specific courses taught in psychology departments. Within the course in learning are covered *classical conditioning* and *operant conditioning*; these two approaches to learning are again coordinate items. *Development* and *current status* are likewise coordinate; they are two topics covered for each of the different theories. The same is true of the *sociology* outline. As in this outline, coordinate items are given symbols of the same order; here, for example, the coordinate items of *psychology* and *sociology* are both given Roman mumerals (I and II); the major courses are given capital letters (A and B); the specific theories taught within the course are given Arabic numerals (1 and 2); and so on.

By *subordination* I mean that two items of information are related in such a way that one item is a part of, supports, or amplifies the other. For example, *learning* and *motivation* are two courses which are a part of *psychology* and, hence, are subordinate to psychology. *Classical conditioning* and *operant conditioning* are types of *learning* and as such are subordinate to learning. Similarly, *cognitive* and *instinct* theories are subordinate to *motivation* in the same way that *prejudice* and *crime* are subordinate to *sociology*. Note that items that are immediately subordinate to another item are

TABLE 9.1 An outline illustrating coordination and subordination

I. Psychology
   A. Learning
      1. Classical conditioning
         a. Development
         b. Current status
      2. Operant conditioning
         a. Development
         b. Current status
   B. Motivation
      1. Cognitive theories
         a. Development
         b. Current status
      2. Instinct theories
         a. Development
         b. Current status
II. Sociology
   A. Prejudice
      1. Instinct theories
         a. Development
         b. Current status
      2. Learning theories
         a. Development
         b. Current status
   B. Crime
      1. Instinct theories
         a. Development
         b. Current status
      2. Learning theories
         a. Development
         b. Current status

given symbols of one order lower: items subordinate to Roman numeral items are given capital letters; items subordinate to Arabic numeral items are given small letters; and so on. This is the customary, agreed upon set of symbols for consistency and ease of comparison. The symbols and some of the coordination and subordination relationships are presented in Table 9.2.

TRANSITIONS AND INTERNAL SUMMARIES

In organizing the speech, connect the parts clearly and carefully to each other so that their relationships are clear to you *and* to the audience who, remember, hears the speech but *once*. Transitions and internal summaries will enable the audience to more effectively and efficiently understand your speech.

Transitions

Transitions are words, phrases, or sentences used to connect the various parts of your speech, and to provide the audience with guideposts that help

TABLE 9.2 An outline illustrating symbols for coordination and subordination

I. Main item
  A. Support for I
    1. Support for A
      a. Support for 1
        (1) Support for a
          (a) Support for (1)
  B. Support for I
    1. Support for B
    2. Support for B
      a. Support for 2
      b. Support for 2
        (1) Support for b
        (2) Support for b
II. Main item
  A. Support for II
  B. Support for II

them follow the development of your thoughts and arguments. In constructing and organizing the speech you should incorporate transitions between *every* two items of information. This sounds like a great deal of transitional material, but it isn't. Specifically, I suggest that you incorporate transitions between the introduction and the body of the speech and between the body and the conclusion. Also, transitions should be used from one main point to every other main point. *And,* transitions should be used between each item of information within each of the main points. Put differently, each item of information that is given a separate symbol in your outline should be connected with the next item with some kind of bridge or transition. Each item, then, should be connected to each other item by some sentence, phrase, or word. After you have reviewed the speech outline with these transitions incorporated, you may wish to omit some for stylistic or other reasons. I would suggest, however, that you keep clearly in mind the fact that your audience is going to hear this speech only once and they are undoubtedly going to miss a great deal due to inattention, preoccupation with other things, noise interference, and so on. The more transitions you can supply the better your listeners will be able to maintain attention for your speech. If you rewrote the speech for publication as an article or essay, you would remove some of the transitional statements because the reader—unlike the listener—can see the entire message and review it if some thread is momentarily lost.

Internal summaries

An *internal summary* is a statement summarizing what you have already discussed; it is a statement that usually summarizes some major subdivision of your speech. It helps if you incorporate a number of internal summaries into your speech—perhaps working them into the transitions connecting, say, the major arguments or issues.

Transitions may be single words, phrases, sentences, questions, and even short paragraphs. Here are some useful examples:

My next point . . .
A second example (argument, fact) . . .
In conclusion . . .
By way of introduction . . .
If you want further evidence, consider . . .
First . . . , Second . . .
Furthermore, . . .
But, as we will see . . .
Next consider . . .
An even better argument . . .
So, as you can see . . .
Given this situation, what should we do?
How, then, can we deal with these three problems?
It follows, then, that . . .
Not only should we . . . , but we should also . . .
Now that we understand the basic structure of the central processing unit, the memory, and the input-output system, let us look into their basic functions.
Thus, . . .
Similarly . . .
In contrast, consider . . .
On the other hand . . .
The other side of the issue is this: . . .

An internal summary that is also a transition might look something like this: "The three arguments advanced here were (1) . . . , (2) . . . , (3) . . . . Now, what can we do about them? I think we can do two things. First, . . ." Another example: "Inadequate recreational facilities, parental ignorance, and lack of adequate role models seem to be the major problems faced by Tryskillion youngsters. Each of these, however, can be remedied and even eliminated. Here is what we can do."

Note that these brief passages remind the listeners of what they have just heard and preview for them what they will now hear. The clear connection in their minds will fill in any gaps that may have been created through inattention, noise, and the like.

BALANCE, UNITY, COHERENCE, AND EMPHASIS

In your English composition class you probably heard that a paragraph or essay should be governed by unity, coherence, and emphasis. These qualities, to which I add *balance*, also govern a public speech.

Balance

First, *balance* should govern the three major parts of the speech: introduction, body, and conclusion. As a useful guideline, the introduction and the conclusion should be about the same length. Each might account for about 10 to 20 percent of the entire speech. The body should constitute approximately 60 to 80 percent. These are rough approximations based on the analysis of effective speeches.

Second, the individual parts of the body should also be in balance. If you are going to explain the five senses, each should be given approximately equal time. When you have particular difficulty applying this principle of balance, something else may be wrong in the organization of the speech. For example, assume you are going to give a speech on mass media and its influence on teenage sexual behavior. The media you feel should be covered are television, radio, film, newspapers, and magazines. But it should be clear that each of these media should not be given equal weight. Although we may differ on which exerts the most influence (I would say television), we would probably all agree that newspapers would not be in the top two or three. Let us say, then, that you also feel that television exerts the most influence and that the other media are about equal. Then, perhaps, your speech should be rephrased as dealing with "television and other media." Your first major point would deal with television and the second with radio, film, newspapers, and magazines. Your inability to devote equal attention to all the media informs you that your general purpose should be rephrased.

Third, balance should manifest itself in the type of supporting material used. A speech supported solely by reference to authority will be dull and generally ineffective, as would a speech supported solely by statistics or solely by examples. What you should strive to achieve is a judicious blending among the various types of supporting material—a balance. It should be clear, however, that the supporting materials chosen will vary greatly depending on the purpose and the topic of the speech. So I would not argue that all forms of support should be used equally. Rather, I am suggesting that there be a balance among those forms of supporting material that are effective and appropriate to the topic, purpose, audience, and so on.

Unity

Unity refers to the singularity of purpose which any well-constructed message should have. The public speech, like the written composition, should have one major purpose to which everything else in the speech relates. Each item of information must relate to that single purpose. Any item that does not relate should be cut. The same is true with longer messages, even with messages as long as books. This book, for example, has as its purpose the training of the public speaker; any unit, any experience, any topic, in fact, any sentence that is not related to that general purpose should not have been included. This does not mean that a speech (or book or article) may not have secondary purposes or hidden agenda or other goals. It is to say that the speech should have one major purpose to which everything else is subordinated.

As you are constructing your speech and considering whether or not to include any given item of information, ask how it relates to the general purpose of the speech. If you cannot answer that question, or if the answer involves a most roundabout route, cut the item out.

Coherence

Coherence (or continuity) refers to the connections among the various parts and items of the speech. In the *Phaedrus*, Plato noted: "Every speech ought to be put together like a living creature, with a body of its own, so as to be neither without head, nor without feet, but to have both a middle and extremities, described proportionately to each other and to the whole." Every part of the speech must be related to every other part, and—perhaps most importantly—the relationship must be clear to the listeners. There is little sense in including an interesting story, a provocative quotation, or some startling statistic if these bits of information are not related in some integral way to other parts of the speech. Many teachers, for example, will frequently, intersperse their lectures with some fascinating stories, but often the students remember the stories and forget the ways in which they related to the substance of the rest of the speech. In class I, for example, tell the story of how I stopped smoking with electric shock. My purpose is to illustrate the application of conditioning procedures in changing one's own behavior. Because the story is interesting—few teachers, I assume, have submitted themselves to electric shock treatment to stop smoking—I make sure that the students remember not only the story but the reason for it— the application of conditioning principles to change one's own behavior.

Make certain that the relationships among the various parts of the speech are clear to the listeners. That they are clear to you does not mean they are clear to others. You should be able to appreciate the importance of this distinction when you realize that teachers almost always know the relationships that exist among the parts of their lectures but—at least some- times—students do not. Put yourself in the position of the student listening to a lecture, and you will find it easier to remember that relationships, especially among subtle and complicated issues, need to be clearly mapped out for the audience.

Emphasis

Emphasis refers to the rather obvious principle that you should emphasize what is important. What is not obvious are the ways in which this is done. First, you cannot emphasize everything. The teacher who prefaces just about everything by saying this is "really important" soon discovers that this catch phrase is not believed and in fact is promptly disregarded by any listener. On the other hand, if one or two items per lecture are highlighted in this way, the listeners will perk up and devote special attention to material so introduced. Second, recognize that listeners will often not be able to tell what is important and what is not as important unless you, the speaker, tell them. Remember that you are very familiar with the topic, the background material, and, therefore, with the important points. Your listeners will not be so familiar with the topic and, consequently, must be told how to distinguish the very important from the not-so-important. Perhaps the best way to do this is simply to say "this is the most important argument" or "the most essential aspect to remember" or "if you forget everything else I said, I would want you to remember . . ." and so on. Teachers frequently highlight parts of their lecture by noting that such-and-such will appear on the examination or that "you'll find it useful to remember the 12 cranial nerves for the final examination."

You can also use organizational structure to add emphasis. Two organizational patterns are especially relevant: climax versus anticlimax and primacy versus recency.

Climax and anticlimax   Climax and anticlimax orders refer to the use of inductive or deductive approaches. In *climax order* you first present your evidence and then climax it with your conclusion or major thesis. For example, a speaker might say to a college class, "The athletic program will have to be cut because of inadequate funds; the student union which operates at a loss each year will have to be closed; and class size will have to be increased 40 percent because a number of faculty will have to be fired since there is no money to pay them." Given these bits of information, the speaker would climax with the main issue, that tuition must be raised. In *anticlimax order* the speaker starts out with the thesis that tuition must be raised and then gives the various reasons.

As you can easily appreciate from this example, whether you choose the climax or the anticlimax order depends a great deal on the attitudes and points of view of your audience. Generally, it is best to lead with the information the audience will object to least. If you anticipate great objection to your thesis, present your arguments and somehow soften the blow that is soon to come. In the example, your audience would willingly pay the increased tuition to save the atheltic program, the student union, and the small class size. If you anticipate little or no objection to your thesis or if your audience already supports it, lead with it and present the reasons or support for it later.

Primacy and recency   In primacy versus recency, *primacy* argues that what is heard first is remembered best and has the greatest effect. *Recency*, on the other hand, argues that what is heard last or most recently is remembered best and with the greatest effect. Research findings on this controversy are not always consistent, but there are a few useful conclusions. First, most research agrees that what is in the middle is remembered least and has the least general effect. Thus, if you have a speech with three points, put the weakest one in the middle. Second, if your listeners are relatively neutral, that is, if they have no real conviction either way, lead off with your best argument and in this way get the listeners on your side early. Research has shown that we often form a general impression of someone or something from initial contacts and then filter everything else through these initial impressions. I would follow this same reasoning with an audience that was positive or favorable to the point of view espoused. On the other hand, if you are faced with a hostile audience or at least with an audience that holds very different views than you do, put your most powerful argument last and work up to it, assuming of course that you can at least count on the listeners staying with you until the end.

Research on memory clearly demonstrates that the audience is going to remember very little of what you have said in this speech. Interesting as the speech may be, listeners will forget the vast majority of what you say. You should, therefore, repeat your main arguments—whether you put them first or last in your speech—in your conclusion.

REMEMBER to use the following general guides in organizing your speech:

1   Balance
2   Unity
3   Coherence
4   Emphasis

Arrange your arguments and supporting materials in light of the research findings on:

1   climax and anticlimax orders
2   primacy and recency

SOURCES

On thesis statements see Frank J. D'Angelo, *Process and Thought in Composition,* 2d ed. (Cambridge, Mass.: Winthrop, 1980). I relied in part on D'Angelo and on the insights of and research evidence presented by Bert E. Bradley, *Fundamentals of Speech Communication: The Credibility of Ideas* (Dubuque, Iowa: Brown, 1974). The remaining general principles of organization are covered in just about every text in public speaking. Perhaps the most thorough treatments may be found in Judy L. Haynes, *Organizing a Speech: A Programmed Guide* (Englewood Cliffs, N.J.: Prentice-Hall, 1973); Philip Amato and Donald Ecroyd, *Organizational Patterns and Strategies in Speech Communication* (Skokie, Ill.: National Textbook Company, 1975); Douglas Ehninger, Alan H. Monroe, and Bruce E. Gronbeck, *Principles and Types of Speech Communication* (Glenview, Ill.: Scott, Foresman, 1978); and James C. McCroskey, *An Introduction to Rhetorical Communication,* 4th ed. (Englewood Cliffs, N.J.: Prentice-Hall, 1982). On the importance and some effects of organization see, for example, Arlee Johnson, "A Preliminary Investigation of the Relationship between Message Organization and Listener Comprehension," *Central States Speech Journal* 21 (1970):104–107; and Douglas G. Bock and Margaret E. Munro, "The Effects of Organization, Need for Order, Sex of the Source, and Sex of the Rater on the Organization Trait Error," *Southern Speech Communication Journal* 44 (Summer 1979):364–372.

UNIT 10

The body of the speech

OBJECTIVES

After completing this unit, you should be able to:

1 *define the* **problem-solution pattern** *and identify two or three topics for which this pattern might be appropriate*
2 *define the* **temporal pattern** *and identify two or three topics for which this pattern might be appropriate*
3 *define the* **spatial pattern** *and identify two or three topics for which this pattern might be appropriate*
4 *define the* **cause-effect** *or* **effect-cause pattern** *and identify two or three topics for which this pattern might be appropriate*
5 *define the* **structure-function pattern** *and identify two or three topics for which this pattern might be appropriate*
6 *define the* **topical pattern** *and identify two or three topics for which this pattern might be appropriate*
7 *define the* **motivated sequence** *and identify two or three topics for which this pattern might be appropriate*

All speeches are difficult to understand. The audience hears a speech once and must instantly make sense of this complex mass of verbiage. Often an audience will simply tune out the speaker if the difficulty of understanding becomes too great. Because of this you must aid the listeners in any way possible. Perhaps the best way to aid comprehension is to organize what is to be said in a clear and unambiguous manner.

Each speech demands a unique treatment and no set of rules or principles may be applied without consideration of the uniqueness of the specific speech. Consequently, some general organizational schemes are presented here with the warning that they must be adopted to the needs of the specific speech, speaker, and audience.

Let us concentrate on the body of the speech. (The next unit will focus on the introduction and the conclusion.) Specifically, the following organizational patterns are considered: problem-solution pattern, temporal pattern, spatial pattern, cause-effect pattern, structure-function pattern, topical pattern, and the motivated sequence pattern. Each pattern is considered in terms of the topics to which it is most applicable and the way in which the main points and supporting materials are arranged. Examples of each are provided to further clarify the general and specific principles of organizational structure.

PROBLEM–SOLUTION PATTERN

One popular pattern of organization is to present the main ideas in terms of problem and solution. Under this system the speech is divided into two basic parts: one part deals with the problem and one part with the solution. Generally the problem is presented first and the solution second, but under certain conditions the solution may be more appropriately presented first and the problem second.

Let us say you are attempting to persuade an audience that teachers should be given higher salaries and increased benefits. Here a problem-solution pattern might be appropriate. We might for example discuss in the first part of the speech some of the problems confronting contemporary education such as the fact that industry lures away the most highly qualified graduates of the leading universities, that many excellent teachers leave the field after two or three years, and that teaching is currently a low-status occupation in the minds of many undergraduates. In the second part of the speech we might consider the possible solutions, namely, that salaries for teachers must be made competitive with salaries offered by private industry, and that the benefits teachers receive must be made at least as attractive as those offered by industry.

The speech might look something like this in outline form:

I. There are three major problems confronting contemporary education.
   A. Industry lures away the most qualified graduates.
   B. Numerous excellent teachers leave the field after two or three years.
   C. Teaching is currently a low-status occupation.
II. There are two major solutions to these problems.
   A. Salaries for teachers must be increased.
   B. Benefits for teachers must be made more attractive.

A problem-solution pattern for a persuasive speech, "No More Nukes," might look something like this:

I. Nuclear plants create too many problems.
   A. Leaks could endanger the lives of workers and the community.
   B. Nuclear plants endanger the environment.
   C. A Hiroshima-like explosion could occur.
II. The solutions are simple and practical.
   A. Stop building nuclear plants.
   B. Dismantle existing nuclear plants.
   C. Devote resources to the development of alternative energy sources.

TEMPORAL PATTERN

Organizing the major issues on the basis of some temporal (time) relationship is another popular organizational pattern. Generally, when this pattern is used the speech is organized into two or three major parts, beginning with the past and working up to the present or the future, or beginning with the present or the future and working back to the past. There are, of course, various ways in which a temporal pattern may be actualized. You might, for example, divide up the major events of your topic and consider each as it occurs or occurred in time. A speech on the development of speech and language in the child might be organized in a temporal pattern and would be divided something like this:

I. Babbling stage
II. Lallation stage
III. Echolalic stage
IV. Communication stage

Here each of the events is considered in temporal sequence beginning with the earliest stage and working up to the final stage—in this case the stage of true communication.

Most historical topics lend themselves to organization by temporal patterning. The events leading up to the Civil War, the steps toward a college education, the history of writing, and the like will all be appropriate for temporal patterning. Time patterns would also be particularly appropriate in describing the essential steps in a multistep process in which temporal order is especially important. The steps involved in making interpersonal contact with another person might look something like this:

I. Spot the person you want to make contact with.
II. Make eye contact.
III. Give some positive nonverbal sign.
IV. Make verbal contact.

SPATIAL PATTERN

Similar to temporal patterning is patterning that organizes the main points of a speech on the basis of space. Instead of organizing events or main points according to a temporal pattern, you organize them on the basis of spatial (space) relationships. Physical objects generally fit well into organization by spatial patterning. For example, you might give a speech on places to visit in southern Europe and you might go from west to east, considering the countries to visit and, within these countries, the cities. The main headings of such a speech might look something like this:

Touring southern Europe
I. Portugal
II. Spain
III. France
IV. Italy
V. Greece

Similarly, the structure of a hospital, school, skyscraper, or perhaps even of a dinosaur would be appropriately described with a spatial pattern of organization.

The layout for a townhouse—once lived in by "average middle-class individuals" and now afforded only by the rich—would lend itself to spatial description. An outline for a townhouse description might look something like this:

Townhouse layout
  I. The first floor consists of the kitchen and pantry.
 II. The second floor consists of the dining room and parlor.
III. The third floor consists of the master bedroom suite.
IV. The fourth floor consists of the children's bedrooms.
 V. The fifth floor consists of the maid's quarters.

HOW TO . . . Title Your Speech

In some ways the title of a speech is a kind of frill. In other ways the title may effectively gain the interest of the audience and, perhaps, stimulate them to listen. Although there are numerous exceptions, generally titles for public speeches should be relatively short, engage the attention and interest of the potential listeners, and be integral to the speech.

1 Short titles are usually easier to remember than are long titles. Titles of top television shows, movies, books, and record albums are all usually short to be easily recalled. A title that is easily held in memory will serve to recall the entire speech or at least some of your main points and, perhaps, your general and specific purpose.

2 A speech title should gain the interest of the potential audience. Again, notice the titles of the most popular movies—all of them seem to invite the audience to ask a question about them and to discover more. They seem to pique the listeners' interests but do not satisfy them completely. This is the technique used in titling many self-help books. *How to Be Your Own Best Friend, How to Win an Argument, How to Read a Person Like a Book,* and numerous others all seem to invite readers to find out how to achieve these important goals.

3 A speech title should be integral to the speech. This is obvious and yet bears mentioning because so often titles are created solely to arouse interest without any concern for the main thrust of the speech. Generally, it is best to be concerned with this issue first. Develop a title that bears some relationship to the major purpose of the speech, then rework it so that it may be easily remembered and arouses interest. Do not mislead the potential audience to expect something they are not going to get.

One last suggestion: title the speech after you have finished the entire speech. The title—like the frosting on the cake—goes on last.

CAUSE–EFFECT/EFFECT–CAUSE PATTERN

Similar to the problem-solution pattern of organization is the cause-effect or effect-cause pattern. Here you divide the speech into two major sections, causes and effects. For example, a speech on the reasons for highway accidents or birth defects might yield to a cause-effect pattern, where you first consider, say, the causes of highway accidents or birth defects and then some of the effects—the number of deaths, the number of accidents, and so on.

A speech on high blood pressure, designed to spell out some of the causes and effects, might look like this:

I. The causes of high blood pressure
   A. High salt intake
   B. Excess weight
   C. Anxiety
II. The three major effects of high blood pressure
   A. Nervousness
   B. Increased heart rate
   C. Shortness of breath

STRUCTURE–FUNCTION PATTERN

In many cases you may want to focus on the structural (how it's constructed) and functional (what it does) aspects of, say, an organization or a living organism. Depending on the specifics of the topic, on the audience, and on the purpose of the speech, you might cover first the structural aspects and second the functional aspects. Or, you might cover each part and under each part consider its structure and then its function. For example, if you wished to give a speech explaining the sensory systems used in sending and in receiving messages, you might use either of these two structure-function patterns:

Pattern one
I. There are five sensory systems for sending and receiving messages.
   A. The visual system is structured . . .
   B. The auditory system is structured . . .
   C. The tactile system is structured . . .
   D. The gustatory system is structured . . .
   E. The olfactory system is structured . . .
II. Each of these sensory systems performs different functions.
   A. The visual system's functions . . .
   B. The auditory system's functions . . .
   C. The tactile system's functions . . .
   D. The gustatory system's functions . . .
   E. The olfactory system's functions . . .

Pattern two
  I. The visual system
     A. The structure of the visual system . . .
     B. The function of the visual system . . .
 II. The auditory system
     A. The structure of the auditory system . . .
     B. The function of the auditory system . . .
III. The tactile system
     A. The structure of the tactile system . . .
     B. The function of the tactile system . . .
 IV. The gustatory system
     A. The structure of the gustatory system . . .
     B. The function of the gustatory system . . .
  V. The olfactory system
     A. The structure of the olfactory system . . .
     B. The function of the olfactory system . . .

TOPICAL PATTERN

Perhaps the most popular pattern of organization is the topical pattern, a pattern that organizes the speech into the major topics without attempting to organize them in terms of time or space or into any of the other patterns already considered. This pattern should not be regarded as a catch-all for topics that do not seem to fit into any of the other patterns, but rather should be regarded as one appropriate to the particular topic being considered. For example, the topical pattern is an obvious one for organizing a speech on the powers of the government. Here the divisions are clear:

  I. The legislative branch is controlled by Congress.
 II. The executive branch is controlled by the president.
III. The judicial branch is controlled by the courts.

A speech on the forms of communication would most likely be organized around a topical pattern like this:

Forms of communication
  I. Intrapersonal communication
 II. Interpersonal communication
III. Small group communication
 IV. Public communication
  V. Mass communication

A speech on important cities in the world could be organized into a topical pattern as well as would speeches on problems facing the college graduate, great works of literature, the world's major religions, and the like. Each of these topics would have several subtopics or divisions of approximately equal importance; consequently, a topical pattern seems most appropriate.

In all of these organizational patterns, it is important to keep in mind what was said earlier about covering a limited area in depth rather than a large area superficially. Although the amount of information you cover will depend on the topic, on the length of time you have to speak, on the listeners' capacity to absorb information, and of course on your own ability to communicate, I suggest you not attempt to construct a speech with more than five main points. Actually, two, three, or four would be preferable. A useful principle to remember in this regard is "less is more": If you want to highlight something, the less you have around the better your chances of highlighting become. Thus, if you want to show off a painting, you should hang it alone rather than with three or four others. On job applications people will often make the mistake of including everything imaginable. When this is done the really important items get lost in the clutter. The same is true in a public speech.

THE MOTIVATED SEQUENCE

Developed by Alan H. Monroe in the 1930s and widely used in all sorts of oral and written communications, the *motivated sequence* is a pattern of arranging your information so as to motivate your audience to respond positively to your purpose. In fact, it may be reasonably argued that all effective communications follow this basic pattern whether it is called the motivated sequence or given some other name. There are in the motivated sequence five steps: attention, need, satisfaction, visualization, and action.

1. Attention

In this step you gain the attention of your listeners through any of a variety of methods: a provocative quotation, a little-known fact, some startling statistics, a personal or humorous anecdote, and so on. These methods are identified in more detail in our discussion of the introduction in Unit 11. The important function of this step is to make the audience give you their undivided attention. If you execute this step effectively, your audience should be anxious and ready to hear what you have to say.

2. Need

Here the demonstration that a need exists is the major point. There may be a need to know something, to change some existing beliefs or attitude, or to recognize that some existing institution is creating difficulties and that something must be done. As a result of this step the audience should feel that they need to know something or that some action needs to be taken.

3. Satisfaction

Here you would present the "answer" or the "solution" to satisfying the need that you demonstrated existed in step 2. You want the audience to understand that what you are informing them about or persuading them to do will in fact satisfy the demonstrated need. In other words, after this step the audience should feel that your information or proposal will correctly and effectively satisfy the need.

4. Visualization

Visualization functions to intensify the audience's feelings or beliefs. It takes the audience beyond the present time and place and enables them to imagine the situation as it would be if the need was satisfied as suggested in step 3. This might be done, for example, by showing the positive benefits to be derived if this advocated proposal was put into operation or if your audience understands and remembers the information you convey. Another method would be to show the negative consequences if your plan is not put into operation, then follow this with the benefits to be derived from implementing your plan. Thus, you will demonstrate not only the negative consequences of not taking action, but also the positive benefits of your plan as well.

5. Action

In this step tell the audience members what they should do to ensure that the need demonstrated in step 2 is satisfied as stated in step 3 and as visualized in step 4. Here you would move the audience to vote a particular way, to speak in favor of X or against Y, to attend the next student government meeting, and so on.

Not all speeches will necessarily contain all five steps. For example, informative speeches need only the first three steps but may continue to include the fourth and perhaps even the fifth step. Let us say you wanted to inform your audience about the workings of home computers. Your steps might look something like this:

Attention:	By the time we graduate, there will be more home computers than automobiles.
Need:	Much like it is now impossible to get around without a car, it will be impossible to get around the enormous amount of information without a home computer.
Satisfaction:	Learning a few basic principles of home computers will enable us to process our work more efficiently, in less time, and more enjoyably.
Visualization:	With these basic principles firmly in mind (and a home computer), you'll be able to stay at home and do your library research for your next speech by just punching in the correct code.
Action:	These few principles should be supplemented by further study. Probably the best way to further your study is to enroll in a computer course. Such a course . . . Another useful way is to read the brief paperback, *The Home Computer for the College Student.*

Notice that an informative speech could have stopped after the satisfaction step because the speaker would have accomplished his or her goal of informing the audience about some principles of home computers. But, in some cases, you may feel it helpful to complete the steps to emphasize your point in detail.

In a persuasive speech, on the other hand, you must go at least as far as visualization (if your purpose is limited to strengthening or changing attitudes or beliefs) or to the action step (if you are attempting to motivate behavior).

REMEMBER the most common organizational patterns:

1 **Problem-solution**
2 **Temporal**
3 **Spatial**
4 **Cause-effect**
5 **Structure-function**
6 **Topical**
7 **Motivated sequence**

SOURCES

Organizational patterns for the body of the speech are considered in all of the works cited in the previous unit. Also see James Gibson, *Speech Organization: A Programmed Approach* (San Francisco: Rinehart Press, 1971). For a discussion of strategies and organizational patterns see James C. McCroskey, *An Introduction to Rhetorical Communication*, 4th ed. (Englewood Cliffs, N.J.: Prentice-Hall, 1982). On the effects of organization see, for example, Richard F. Whitman and John H. Timmis, "The Influence of Verbal Organizational Structure and Verbal Organizing Skills on Select Measures of Learning," *Human Communication Research* 1 (Summer 1975):293–301. For the motivated sequence see Douglas Ehninger, Alan H. Monroe, and Bruce E. Gronbeck, *Principles and Types of Speech Communication*, 8th ed. (Glenview, Ill.: Scott, Foresman, 1978).

UNIT 11

Introductions and conclusions

OBJECTIVES

After completing this unit, you should be able to:

1 *identify the three major functions that an introduction to a speech should serve*
2 *explain some of the specific methods by which these general functions may be achieved*
3 *identify three common faults with introductions*
4 *identify the three major functions that a conclusion to a speech should serve*
5 *explain some of the specific methods by which these general functions may be achieved*
6 *identify three common faults with conclusions*

A speech, like a written composition, has a beginning or introduction, a middle or a body, and an end or conclusion. In the previous unit I focused on the body of the speech and detailed a number of ways to organize the body of the speech. In this unit I focus on introductions and conclusions and specify their functions, how best to construct them to fulfill these functions, and some of the common faults to which they are subject.

INTRODUCTIONS

The introduction to a speech, like the first day of a class or the first date, is especially important because it sets the tone for what is to follow. It should put the audience into a receptive frame of mind and build up a positive attitude toward the speech and the speaker.

The introduction to a speech, although obviously delivered first, should be constructed last—only after the entire speech, including the conclusion, has been written. In this way you will be in a position to see the entire speech before you and will be better able to determine those elements that should go into introducing this now completed speech. If the speech were not completed first, you would be constructing an introduction to a speech you were not very sure of. This same advice also pertains to written compositions; the introductions should always be constructed last.

Functions of introductions

Although an introduction may serve many specific functions, three general ones are singled out here.

Gain attention   The introduction should gain the attention of the audience. In a college classroom if a number of students are giving speeches, it is particularly important that the attention of the audience be secured and maintained in the introduction. Similarly, the college teacher needs to secure attention at the beginning of his or her lecture lest the class continue to think thoughts and trade stories of the weekend. Attention may be secured through various means—by stressing the significance and importance of the topic, by using an interesting story, or by citing some little known facts or statistics.

Establish a relationship with the audience The introduction should establish a speaker-audience relationship that is conducive to the achievement of the speech purpose. This relationship is aided if the audience likes the speaker, if they respect the speaker, and if they think the speaker a knowledgeable individual. It is no easy task to instill these attitudes in the audience in the introduction, as can be appreciated. Nevertheless it will aid you greatly if you can somehow get on the proverbial good side of the audience and establish some credibility.

Orient the audience The introduction should orient the audience in some way to what is to follow in the body of the speech. The main points of the speech may be noted here, or a statement of the general conclusion that will be argued, the way in which the material will be presented, or the point of view or approach to be taken.

REMEMBER the three functions of an introduction:
1   **Gain attention**
2   **Establish a relationship with the audience**
3   **Orient the audience**

Examples of introductions

Let me try to make these somewhat abstract guidelines more specific by providing some examples of how other speakers have introduced their speeches.

SEE EXPERIENTIAL VEHICLE 3.2.

As already noted, sometimes securing attention is not a great problem because the audience is waiting for you and has in fact assembled—sometimes even paid an admission fee—to hear you. The entire British Empire, for example, was gathered to hear Edward VIII's address of abdication to marry Wallis Simpson, and all he had to do was to make the audience know that he was finally going to answer their questions.

> At long last I am able to say a few words of my own. I have never wanted to withhold anything, but until now it has not been constitutionally possible for me to speak.

But most speakers cannot count on such an attentive and responsive audience. At times the speaker has to secure the attention of the audience by demonstrating to them the importance and significance of the topic. Spiro

HOW TO . . . Secure and Maintain Audience Attention

Especially in the introduction but throughout the speech as well, it is essential that you secure and maintain the attention of the audience. If their minds wander away from your speech for any significant amount of time, it will be impossible to achieve your purpose. There are numerous and varied devices to help you maintain audience attention. Here are just 10 of them.

1. *Ask a question.* Questions are effective because they are a change from the normal statements but also because they directly involve the audience; they tell the audience that you are talking directly to them and that you care about their responses.

2. *Make reference to the audience members themselves.* This generally makes all members perk up and pay attention because of the possibility that they too will be involved directly. But this is a useful technique also because it demonstrates that you are speaking to this specific audience and that you know them.

3. *Introduce change.* Change seems a universal attention-getter. Changes from a flood of statistics to a personal illustration or from a series of examples to a quotation are most effective attention devices.

4. *Make reference to recent happenings.* Referring to a previous speech, a recent event, or to some prominent person currently making news will help to secure attention because the audience is familiar with this and will attend to see how you are going to approach it.

5. *Be humorous.* A clever (and appropriate) joke or anecdote is always useful in holding attention. But, unless you are a good joke teller and unless the joke is a good one, avoid this method. Nothing is worse than a joke that no one laughs at or a joke that is so stale that audience members finish the joke for you.

6. *Tell a dramatic story.* Much as we are drawn to television soap operas and dramas, so are we drawn to illustrations and stories about people. Perhaps this is true because we can identify with these people or because we would like to be like them or because it makes us feel our condition is not so bad in comparison with the fate of these others. For whatever reason, we seem anxious to listen to dramatic stories.

7. *Use audiovisual aids.* The use of audio and visual materials is particularly valuable because it is new and different and we are universally attracted to the new and different. In using these aids, be sure that they are used effectively. See Unit 14, ''Amplifying Materials in Informative Speeches.''

8. *Vary the intensity of your delivery.* Your voice and bodily action are among the most effective attention-getters you have available. An increase or decrease in loudness, rate, or bodily movement will gain attention, again because it is a change from what the audience has been hearing and seeing.

9. *Relate your supporting material directly to the audience.* In addition to telling them that the rate of unemployment is going to increase (probably too general to relate to), tell them that this means that 4 out of a class of 30 will be out of work for at least one year after graduation and that 6 of them will have at least one parent out of a job by the end of the year. In addition to telling them that budget cuts will hurt education in the state (again, too

Agnew, for example, introduced his speech on television news coverage in the following way.

> Tonight I want to discuss the importance of the television news medium to the American people. No nation depends more on the intelligent judgment of its citizens. No medium has a more profound influence over public opinion. Nowhere in our system are there fewer checks on vast powers. So, nowhere should there be more conscientious responsibility exercised than by the news media. The question is, Are we demanding enough of our television news presentations? And are the men of this medium demanding enough of themselves?

Attention and the establishment of a positive relationship with an audience is frequently secured by using a specific illustration. Here is one such example.

> I'd like to talk about modern economics today. I'm sure many of us are already familiar with that. But for those who are not, I can illustrate the theory with a story: Jed is a part-time farm worker with a flair for applied economics. One day he "borrowed" a country ham from the farmer who employs him . . . without bothering to tell the farmer. He went downtown and sold the ham to the grocer for $27. Then he used $20 of that money to buy $80 worth of food stamps. With the food stamps he bought $48 worth of groceries. He used the remaining $32 worth of food stamps to buy back the ham. Then he returned the ham to the farmer's smokehouse. So the grocer made a profit, the farmer got his ham back, and Jed has $48 worth of groceries plus $7 in cash. If you see no flaw in that process, then you are already familiar with modern economics. (From a speech by Herbert S. Richey, "The Real Cause of Inflation: Government Services.")

Notice how the following introduction establishes this favorable speaker-audience relationship by stressing the deep concern of the speaker and his own studies in the area of ecology.

> For several years I have been deeply concerned about reports of the destruction of our environment as a result of technological recklessness, overpopulation, and a religious and philosophical outlook that gives little consideration to the preservation of nature. My studies in this area of concern have

turned up evidence that I feel compelled to share with you. I welcome this opportunity to do it. (From a speech by A. L. Jones, "A Question of Ecology: The Cries of Wolf.")

Introducing a speech on "The Dimensions of the Oppression of Women," Phyllis Jones Springen explains her own initial reactions to the topic and thus puts herself in the same position as the audience; at the same time she effectively explains the significance of the topic and how she will approach it.

> When I was asked to speak on "The Dimensions of the Oppression of Women," I laughed. "Oppression" is such an ugly word. Our chairman must have been thinking of those Arab countries where women can't vote and where a woman can be forced to marry any man her father selects, but in the United States women are hardly "oppressed." But as I began to do my research, I quit laughing. There exists a tremendous amount of legal and economic discrimination against the American women. Much of it is subtle and, therefore, hard to recognize.

Some common faults with introductions

The introduction is perhaps the most important single part of the speech; your listeners will frequently form an impression of you based on your introduction and will respond to you according to the way in which they felt about the introduction. It is particularly important then that you avoid some of the common faults that many beginning speakers make. Here are just a few.

Don't apologize A common fault—also common to conclusions—is to apologize for *something.* Generally, don't do it. Your inadequacies—whatever they are—will be clear enough to any discerning listener; you do not have to point them out specifically. You do not have to say, "I am not an expert on this topic" or "I didn't do as much reading on it as I should have." And *never* start a speech with "I'm not very good at giving public speeches." In your entire speech, but especially in your introduction, emphasize the positive; highlight what you consider the best.

Don't pretend Another common fault is for speakers to pretend to be what they are not; experts, when they are not; art critics, when they are not; interested in an issue, when they are not. By presenting to the audience what you think they will want to hear, you are preventing them from knowing you as a person and at the same time are denying your own value and worth. Listeners are not stupid; they do not lack insight. They will be able to tell when you are pretending. Be yourself and highlight your positive qualities.

Don't make hollow promises A related fault is to promise to deliver something that you will not in fact deliver. The speaker who promises to tell you how to solve your love life, how to make a fortune in the stock market, or how to be the most popular person on campus and fails to deliver such insight will quickly lose credibility. Many popular self-help books pretend to deliver such instant insight. Unfortunately, you only discover that they do not deliver after you have paid for the book and the author has received royalties.

Don't rely on gimmicks   Another common fault is to use gimmicks that gain attention but are irrelevant to the nature of the speech or inconsistent with the treatment to be given the topic. Thus, for example, to slam a book on the desk, to yell obscenities, or to otherwise jar the audience into attention usually accomplishes this very limited goal. But when such actions are out of place, the audience will see such actions for what they are—gimmicks and tricks that have fooled them into paying attention. Such actions are resented and will set up a negative barrier between speaker and listener.

SEE
EXPERIENTIAL
VEHICLE 3.3.

REMEMBER the four common problems with introductions, so:
1   **Don't apologize**
2   **Don't pretend to be someone you are not**
3   **Don't make promises you will not keep**
4   **Don't use gimmicks that may backfire**

CONCLUSIONS

"A speech," noted Lord Mancroft, "is like a love affair. Any fool can start it, but to end it requires considerable skill." Although I would not agree that any fool can start a speech (or a love affair)—at least not effectively—it does take exceptional skill to end one.

The conclusion is extremely important since it is the part that the audience will in many instances remember most clearly. It is the conclusion that will in many cases determine what image of you is left in the minds of the audience members. Particular attention must, therefore, be devoted to this brief but crucial part of the public speech.

Functions of conclusions

Like the introduction, the conclusion may have many specific functions. Yet, three general ones may be singled out.

Summarize   First, and perhaps the most obvious function, is to summarize the essentials of the speech. This function is particularly important in an informative speech and less so in persuasive speeches or speeches designed to entertain. In informative speeches, however, it is essential that you wrap up in a convenient summary some of the issues you have presented. Eventually, the details that you have spoken of will be forgotten; the conclusion and especially the summary will probably be remembered longer.

Motivate   A second function—most appropriate in persuasive speeches—is motivation. In the conclusion you have the opportunity to give the audience one final push in the direction you wish them to take. Whether it is to buy bonds, vote a particular way, or change an attitude in one way

149   INTRODUCTIONS AND CONCLUSIONS

or another, the conclusion can be used for a final motivation, a final appeal, a final push in the desired direction.

Provide closure   The third function of a conclusion is to provide some kind of closure. Often the summary will accomplish this but in many instances it will not be sufficient. The speech should come to a crisp and definite end and the audience should not be hanging on wondering whether you have finished or whether you will continue after a short pause. Some kind of wrap up, some kind of final statement is helpful in providing this feeling of closure. It is probably best not to say "thank you" or "It was a pleasure addressing you" or some such trite phrase; these are best left implied.

Examples of conclusions

The general functions of conclusions may be clarified by looking at some examples.

SEE EXPERIENTIAL VEHICLE 3.4.

Adlai Stevenson, in speaking of United States Far Eastern policy, concluded his speech by summarizing the point of view and the major thrust of the speech and provided closure by bringing together the various threads of the speech and relating them to the audience.

> Let this be the American mission in the hydrogen age. Let us stop slandering ourselves and appear before the world once more as we really are—as friends, not as masters; as apostles of principle, not of power; in humility, not arrogance; as champions of peace, not as harbingers of war. For our strength lies, not alone in our proving grounds and our stockpiles, but in our ideals, our goals, and their universal appeal to all men who are struggling to breathe free.

Clarence Darrow, in his summation speech in defense of Henry Sweet, a black charged with murder, directed his conclusion at motivating the jury to vote not guilty in a case that drew national and worldwide attention because of the racial issues involved. A vote of not guilty was in fact quickly returned by a jury of 12 white men.

> Gentlemen, what do you think of our duty in this case? I have watched day after day these black, tense faces that have crowded this court. These black faces that now are looking to you twelve whites, feeling that the hopes and fears of a race are in your keeping. This case is about to end, gentlemen. To them, it is life. Not one of their color sits on this jury. Their fate is in the hands of twelve whites. Their eyes are fixed on you, their hearts go out to you, and their hopes hang on your verdict.

> This is all. I ask you, on behalf of this defendant, on behalf of these helpless ones who turn to you, and more than that—on behalf of this great state, and this great city, which must face this problem and face it fairly—I ask you, in the name of progress and of the human race, to return a verdict of not guilty in this case!

In a speech of a very different kind, Adlai Stevenson eulogizes Sir Winston Churchill and in the conclusion summarizes and brings together all the accomplishments of Churchill to remind us of his greatness.

> The great aristocrat, the beloved leader, the profound historian, the gifted painter, the superb politician, the lord of language, the orator, the wit—yes, and the dedicated bricklayer—behind all of them was the man of simple faith, steadfast in defeat, generous in victory, resigned in age, trusting in a loving providence and committing his achievements and his triumphs to a higher power.

REMEMBER that a conclusion should accomplish these three functions:

1 **Summarize**
2 **Motivate**
3 **Provide closure**

Some common faults with conclusions

As with any part of the speech, beginning speakers often fall into various common faults with conclusions. By highlighting them here, you will be alerted to them and perhaps find it easier to avoid them.

Don't apologize Do not apologize for any manifested inadequacies. Actually, apologies are not always ineffective; in the hands of the right person they may help to interject a needed note of modesty. In most cases, however, it is best not to apologize.

Don't introduce new material Do not introduce new material. You may, of course, give new expression to ideas covered in the body of the speech but do not introduce new material in your conclusion. Instead, use your conclusion to reinforce what you have already said in your discussion and to summarize your essential points.

Don't dilute your position Do not dilute the strength of your speech or your arguments. Expression such as "I know this is not that important," "We really don't know enough about inflation to offer any real advice," "This information is probably dated but it was all I could find," or "I tried to secure other information but I didn't have the time" and so on, are ineffective. Expressions such as these serve no useful purpose. Ethically, of course, you do have the obligation to qualify your assertions as warranted by the evidence, but this should be done in the discussion and not in the conclusion.

SEE EXPERIENTIAL VEHICLE 3.5.
Don't drag out the conclusion Don't drag out the conclusion; end crisply and just once. Beginning speakers will often preface each statement of their conclusion with terms that lead the audience to think that this is the last statement. Expressions such as "in summary" or "in conclusion" or "therefore" and similar ones will often lead the audience to expect an ending. When you are ready to end, end. Do not linger at the door.

REMEMBER the common problems with conclusions, so:

1   Don't apologize
2   Don't introduce new material
3   Don't dilute the strength of your position
4   Don't drag out the conclusion

SOURCES

On introductions and conclusions see Douglas Ehninger, Alan H. Monroe, and Bruce E. Gronbeck, *Principles and Types of Speech Communication* (Glenview, Ill.: Scott, Foresman, 1978); Anita Taylor, *Speaking in Public* (Englewood Cliffs, N.J.: Prentice-Hall, 1979); Michael Osborn, *Speaking in Public* (Boston, Mass.: Houghton Mifflin, 1982); and Joe Ayres and Janice Miller, *Effective Public Speaking* (Dubuque, Iowa: Wm. C. Brown, 1983).

The speeches excerpted in this unit may be found in the following works: Edward VIII, "All for Love" and Clarence Darrow, "Defense of Henry Sweet," in *A Treasury of the World's Great Speeches*, Houston Peterson, ed. (New York: Simon and Schuster, 1965); Spiro Agnew, "Television News Coverage," in L. Patrick Devlin, *Contemporary Political Speaking* (Belmont, Calif.: Wadsworth, 1971); Louis Hausman, "Older Americans: A National Resource," *Vital Speeches of the Day* 43 (January 1, 1977); Herbert S. Richey, "The Real Cause of Inflation" *Vital Speeches of the Day* 43 (April 15, 1977); A. L. Jones, "A Question of Ecology," *Vital Speeches of the Day* 38 (April 1, 1972); Phyllis Jones Springen, "The Dimensions of the Oppression of Women," *Vital Speeches of the Day* 37 (February 15, 1971); Adlai Stevenson, "United States Far Eastern Policy" in *The World's Great Speeches*, 2d ed., Lewis Copeland and Lawrence Lamm, eds. (New York: Dover, 1958); Adlai Stevenson, "Eulogy for Winston Churchill," in *Contemporary American Speeches*, 4th ed., Wil A. Linkugel, R. R. Allen, and Richard L. Johannesen, eds. (Dubuque, Iowa: Kendall/Hunt, 1978). This volume was helpful in locating a number of the above examples, namely, the speeches by Springen, Richey, and Jones.

UNIT 12

Outlining the speech

OBJECTIVES

After completing this unit, you should be able to:

1 identify at least two functions that outlines serve
2 identify two major types of outlines
3 identify at least four suggestions concerning the mechanics of outlining

Of all the time you spend preparing your speech, the time spent outlining is among the most important because the outline is a blueprint for your speech—it lays out in clear form the elements of the speech and their relationship to each other. With this speech blueprint in front of you, you can see at a glance all of the elements of organization considered in the previous units—coordination and subordination, the functions of the introduction and conclusion, the relationship of the major propositions to the thesis and purpose, the adequacy of the supporting materials, and so on. And, like a blueprint for a building, the outline will enable you to spot weaknesses that might otherwise have gone undetected.

You should begin outlining at the same time you begin constructing your speech. Do not wait until you have collected all your material, but rather begin outlining as you are collecting material, organizing it, and styling it. In this way you will be able to take best advantage of one of the major functions of outlines—to tell you where change is needed. Begin outlining, then, as soon as you begin the speech construction process—always, of course, with flexibility. The outline should be changed and altered as necessary at each and every stage of the speech construction process.

I examine outlining at this point in the text because you first needed to gain some familiarity with the basics of organization. Here, then, I consider some of the functions that outlines serve, the types of outlines that may be used, and some of the mechanics of outlining. Lastly, I utilize this unit as a kind of summary for the sections dealing with organization, and suggest that you use your outline to check over and review the general principles of speech organization.

FUNCTIONS OF OUTLINES

Obviously, an outline aids in the process of organization. As you outline the speech, you put into clear form the major points of your speech, the major supporting materials, and the transitions. Once these may be easily examined visually, you may see, for example, if your assertions are properly coordinated, if your supporting materials do in fact support the assertions they are intended to support, and so on. If you are using a temporal or a spatial organizational pattern, for example, you can quickly examine the outline and readily see if, in fact, this temporal or spatial progression is clear or in need of further clarification, reordering, or qualification of some sort.

As already noted, speech outlines provide an efficient way for you to assess the strengths and weaknesses of the speech as it is being constructed. So, for example, let us say you are preparing a speech on censorship and your major points concern sex and violence. With your outline you would be able to see at a glance if your supporting materials are adequately and evenly distributed between the two points rather than discover later that all your examples and statistics concern the violence issue with little relating to the sex issue. The outline will tell you that more material has to be collected on the sex issue or that your speech is almost totally devoted to statistical information and that you need some human interest material, and so on. In short, the outline can guide your collection of information.

The outline, when it is constructed from the beginning of the speech preparation process, provides a means for checking the speech as a whole (or at least as much as you have constructed so far). When you work for a long time on a speech and when each part is constructed over a long period of time, it becomes difficult to see "the forest for the trees." The outline enables you to stand back and examine the entire forest.

Outlines aid in the presentation of the speech—perhaps the only function many speakers at first recognize. The outline is often taken to the podium and referred to by the speaker. In fact, if you are speaking extemporaneously—as you should—you will come to use the outline a great deal in the presentation.

TYPES OF OUTLINES

It should be obvious to you by now that outlines may be extremely detailed or extremely general. In fact, the entire speech may be arranged in outline form, that is, with every item of information arranged not in paragraph form (as it might be in speaking from manuscript), but in outline form. At the other extreme, an outline for a speech on, for example, contemporary music might look something like this:

Contemporary music
 I. Rock
 II. Popular

III. Country
IV. Disco

In between these extremes there are an infinite number of gradations of completeness of detail. What is best for one speaker might prove totally inadequate for another, and, of course, what will prove adequate for a speaker on one topic may prove inadequate for that same speaker on a different topic.

Since you are now in a learning environment where the objective is to make you a more proficient public speaker, your instructor may wish to suggest one type of outline over another. And, of course, just as the type of outline will depend on the specific speaker, the type of outline that proves best for instructional purposes will vary with the instructor. I, for example, prefer that students construct rather detailed outlines, but I recognize that this is for instructional purposes and that once students have learned the art of public speaking, they will adjust the outlining procedures to what fits them best.

The more detail you put into the outline, the easier it will be to examine the parts of the speech for all the qualities and characteristics that were discussed in the previous units. Thus, for example, the speech's balance can only be examined in detail if the outline itself is in detail. Similarly, it will be easier to see if one item actually supports another item if they are both clearly written out and can be thought about for a moment or two rather than if only key words are written down or, as in the example given above, if all supporting materials are omitted entirely. Consequently, I would suggest that, at least in the beginning, you outline your speeches in detail and in complete sentences. The usefulness of an instructor's criticism will often depend on the completeness of the outline.

With these factors in mind, then, I would suggest that you do the following, especially in your beginning speeches. Begin constructing the outline as soon as you get the topic clearly in mind. Revise it constantly. Every new idea, every new bit of information will result in some alteration of basic structure. At this point keep the outline brief and perhaps in key words or phrases. Once you feel pretty confident that you are near completion, construct an outline in detail—using complete sentences—and follow the mechanical principles discussed in the next section of this unit. Use this outline to test your organizational structure, following the questions provided at the end of this unit in the section, "How to Evaluate Your Speech Organization: Part Three Checklist." For speaking purposes, however, I would suggest that you reduce this outline to its bare bones. It should consist of key words that will aid you in the presentation of the speech and should easily fit on one side of a 3 × 5 index card. The key word in that advice is *aid*. The outline should *aid* you in the presentation of the speech; it should not be something that you will rely on and read from, thus avoiding direct eye contact with the audience. If the outline is going to aid you in the presentation of the speech, it has to be brief, containing only that information that you will absolutely need for the few minutes that you stand in front of the audience.

SOME MECHANICS OF OUTLINING

Assuming that the outline you will construct for your early speeches will be relatively complete, here are a few guidelines concerning the mechanics—the technical aspects—of outlining.

Use a consistent set of symbols

The following is the standard, accepted sequence of symbols for outlining:

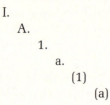

Begin the introduction, the body, and the conclusion with Roman numeral I. That is, each of the three major parts should be treated as a complete unit.

This:

INTRODUCTION
    I. _____
       A. _____
       B. _____
    II. _____

BODY
    I. _____
    II. _____
    III. _____

CONCLUSION
    I. _____
    II. _____

Not This:

INTRODUCTION
    I. _____
    II. _____

BODY
    III. _____

IV. _____
V. _____

CONCLUSION
VI. _____
VII. _____

Use visual aspects to reflect and reinforce the organizational pattern

Obviously, use a proper and clear indentation. This will help to set off visually coordinate and subordinate relationships.

This:

I. Television caters to the lowest possible intelligence.
    A. Situation Comedies
        1. "Benson"
        2. "Three's Company"
        3. "One Day at a Time"
    B. Soap Operas
        1. "As the World Turns"
        2. "General Hospital"
        3. "Young and the Restless"

Not This:

I. Television caters to the lowest possible intelligence.
A. Situation Comedies
1. "One Day At a Time"

Use one discrete idea per symbol

If the outline is to reflect the organizational pattern among the various items of information, use just one discrete idea per symbol. Compound sentences are sure giveaways that you have not limited each item to one single idea. Also, be sure that each item is discrete, that is, that it does not overlap with any other item.

This:

I. Education would be improved if teachers were better trained.
II. Education would be improved if students were better motivated.

Not This:

I. Education might be improved if teachers were better trained and if students were better motivated.

Note that in **This** items I and II are single ideas but in **Not This** they are combined.

This:

I. Teachers are not adequately prepared to teach.
   A. Teacher education programs are inadequate
      1. Support for A
      2. Support for A
   B. In-service programs are inadequate.
      1. Support for B
      2. Support for B

Not This:

I. Teachers are not adequately prepared to teach.
   A. Teacher education programs are inadequate.
   B. Course syllabi are dated.

Note that A and B are discrete in ***This*** but overlap in ***Not This,*** where B is actually a part of A (one of the inadequacies of teacher education programs is that the course syllabi are dated).

Be brief

This injunction applies more to the outline you take to assist you in the presentation of the speech than to the outline you prepare to test for organizational structure. And yet, each should be brief in relation to the entire speech. If the outline is to assist you in seeing all the various parts of the speech in relation to each other, it should be brief enough so that you can see these relationships at a glance.

Use complete declarative sentences

Generally, phrase your ideas in the outline in complete declarative sentences rather than as questions or as phrases. Again, this will further assist you in examining the essential relationships. It is much easier, for example, to see if one item of information supports another if both are phrased in the declarative mode. If one is a question and one is a statement, this will be more difficult.

This:

I. Children should be raised by the state.
   A. All children will be treated equal.
   B. Parents will be released to work.

Not This:

I. Who should raise children?
II. Should the state raise children?
   A. Equality for children
   B. Parents will be released for work.

SEE
EXPERIENTIAL
VEHICLE 3.6. Note that in ***This*** all items are phrased as complete declarative sentences and their relationship is therefore brought out clearly. In ***Not This,*** on the

other hand, a mixture of question, sentence, and phrase obscures the relationship.

REMEMBER to follow these mechanics of outlining:

1. **Use a consistent set of symbols**
2. **Use visual aspects to reflect and reinforce the organizational pattern**
3. **Use one discrete idea per symbol**
4. **Be brief**
5. **Use complete declarative sentences**

A SAMPLE OUTLINE

The following complete outline with side notes, which further clarify its structures and functions, will help you understand and appreciate the various facets of organization and outlining.

Revealing yourself to others

INTRODUCTION

I. If you want to get to know yourself better, reveal yourself to another person: Self-disclose.

   A. This may sound peculiar but it seems to be supported by a great deal of scientific research.

   B. Self-disclosure can lead us to feel better about ourselves but can also lead to lots of problems— loss of friends, of job, and even of self-respect.

   C. Understanding self-disclosure can lead us to make the most effective use of this most important form of communication.

II. I've immersed myself in self-disclosure for the last five years—as student, researcher, and writer—and want to share some insights with you.

   A. As a student I was fortunate to have studied with Professor Jean Civikly of the University of New Mexico and Professor Gary Shulman of Miami University.

   B. As a researcher I conducted over two dozen studies.

Here I try to gain attention by stating what appears to be a contradiction. I could have used a specific instance, a humorous story, an interesting quotation, and various other methods discussed in the "How to" essay in Unit 11. The introductory statement used here has the added advantage in that it introduces the topic immediately.

In these two brief statements I try to emphasize the importance of the topic to the audience to ensure their continued attention and interest.

Note that each statement in the outline is a complete sentence. There are, as explained earlier, other types of outlines (word, phrase, and combination word, phrase, and sentence outlines) which may also be used. You can easily convert this full sentence outline into a phrase or word outline.

Here I establish my connection with the topic and try to answer the inevitable question of the audience: why I am discussing this particular topic. I also attempt to establish my credibility. In this outline I clearly overdo this aspect to emphasize some of the ways in which we may seek to establish credibility. In an actual speech I would have cut this considerably.

Notice that I am assuming that my audience knows the people mentioned; this is why their own credentials are not specified in detail. If the audience were not familiar with such persons, I would have had to give some identifying data.

Notice also the parallel structure (the similarity in phrasing) used in these three examples: As a student . . . , As a researcher . . . , As a writer.

C. As a writer, I spent the last two years, together with Professor Michael Hecht of the University of Southern California, analyzing and synthesizing just about everything known about self-disclosure.

III. In order to understand self-disclosure we need to focus on three aspects.
  A. Self-disclosure is a form of communication in which you reveal information about yourself that is normally kept hidden.
  B. Self-disclosure involves both rewards and problems.
  C. Self-disclosure is influenced by three major factors.

In this section I provide, by explaining to the audience exactly what I will cover in the speech, a rather thorough orientation. For the sake of clarity I state here the three main points that I cover in the body of the speech in the same language. Note also that these three points are repeated in the summary in the conclusion (I A, B, and C). Different language may and often is used. Note, however, that although this repetition is obvious to you reading the speech, it will not necessarily be obvious to the audience. Listeners will not remember the exact wording used and yet such repetition will help them remember your speech.

I also state here the specific purpose of the speech—"to understand self-disclosure." In terms of behavioral objectives to be discussed in Unit 13, the purposes would be stated as follows: After hearing this speech, listeners will be able to: (1) define and explain what self-disclosure is, (2) identify three rewards and three problems of self-disclosure and (3) identify the three major factors that influence self-disclosing communications.

[Let me consider first the definition of self-disclosure.]

The transitions (here indicated in brackets) are stated in rather obvious terms to emphasize their basic structure and function. As explained earlier, with practice you will develop transitional statements with more grace and subtlety. There are additional places where transitions could be used, but I eliminated these lest they clutter the outline and defeat its instructional purpose.

BODY

I. Self-disclosure is a form of communication in which you reveal information about yourself that is normally kept hidden.
  A. Self-disclosure is a type of communication.
    1. Self-disclosure includes overt statements.
      a. An overt confession of infidelity to your lover is self-disclosure.
      b. A letter explaining why you committed a crime is self-disclosure.

This is the first major point of the speech, and here I focus on definitional aspects of self-disclosure. The entire definition is presented in I, and in A, B, and C each element in the definition is explained in more detail.

    2. Self-disclosure includes slips of the tongue and other unintentional communications.
       a. A slip of the tongue in which you reveal that you are really in love with your best friend's spouse is self-disclosure.
       b. An uncontrollable rage in which you tell your boss all the horrible things you've kept inside is self-disclosure.
    3. Self-disclosure is not noncommunication.
       a. Writing personal thoughts in a diary that no one sees is not self-disclosure.
       b. Talking to ourselves when no one over-hears is not self-disclosure.
 B. Self-disclosure involves information about the self not previously known by the listeners.
    1. Telling people something about someone else is not self-disclosure.
       a. Self-disclosure involves the self.
       b. Self-disclosing statements begin with "I."
    2. Telling people what they already know is not self-disclosure.
 C. Self-disclosure involves information normally kept hidden.
    1. Self-disclosure does not involve information that we do not actively keep secret.
    2. Self-disclosure involves only information that we work at to keep hidden, that we expend energy in hiding.

[This then is what self-disclosure is; now let us focus on what self-disclosure may involve.]

Observe how this transition connects what has been discussed with what is to follow.

II. Self-disclosure involves both rewards and problems.
 A. There are three main rewards of self-disclosure.

Notice how this statement clues the listener to expect a two-part division: rewards and problems. Each of these divisions is further broken down to explain the specific rewards and problems that may be derived from self-disclosure.

    1. First, we get to know ourselves better.
       a. Talking about my fear of snakes led me to understand the reasons for such fears.
       b. Results from studies show that persons who disclose have greater self-awareness than do those who do not self-disclose.

Note that here, as in 2 and 3, I provide listeners with guide words ("first," "second," "third") to enable them to keep track of where I am. In the actual speech I might even make this clearer by stating something like "The first reward is that we get to know ourselves better" to emphasize that I am here talking about the *first reward*. Notice that this has the effect of emphasizing that there are other rewards to be discussed and to recall for the listeners that rewards will be followed by a discussion of problems. Again, this may seem overly simplified but, for an audience hearing the speech only once, it will prove helpful.

2. Second, we can deal with our problems better.
    a. Dealing with guilt is a prime example.
    b. Studies conducted by Civikly, Hecht, and
       me show that personal problems are more
       easily managed after self-disclosure.
3. Third, we release a great deal of energy.
    a. It takes energy to keep secrets.
    b. After self-disclosure people feel more re-
       laxed, sleep better, and have a higher en-
       ergy level than before self-disclosure.
B. There are three major dangers of self-disclosure.
    1. First, self-disclosure may involve personal
       problems.
        a. The fear of rejection may be more damaging
           than retaining the secrets.
        b. Self-disclosure may bring to the surface
           problems that you are not psychologically
           ready to deal with.
    2. Second, self-disclosure may involve profes-
       sional problems.
        a. A number of ex-convicts who disclosed
           their criminal records have been fired.
        b. Persons who were treated by psychiatrists
           and who revealed this have had their polit-
           ical careers ruined.
    3. Third, self-disclosure may involve social prob-
       lems.
        a. Peer groups will often withdraw social sup-
           port.
        b. Friends and even relatives may reject you.

> Note again the parallel structure through-
> out the speech outline. Focus, for example, on
> Body II A and B, on Body II B 1, 2, and 3, and
> elsewhere throughout the speech. This parallel
> structure helps clarify significant relationships
> for both the speaker and the listener.

[Self-disclosure, involving both rewards and problems,
does not occur without motivation; rather it is influenced by different factors.]

III. Self-disclosure is influenced by three major factors.
    A. First, self-disclosure is influenced by the commu-
       nication situation.
        1. Self-disclosure is more likely to occur with
           one other person than with large groups.
        2. Self-disclosure is more likely to occur when
           others have self-disclosed.
    B. Second, self-disclosure is influenced by the sex
       of the persons.
        1. Men engage in relatively little self-disclosure.
            a. This is especially true for positive self-dis-
               closures.
            b. This may be due to the conditioning that
               males have undergone.

> In the statement of this last major point it is
> clear that three aspects will be discussed, each
> identified with the guide words "first," "sec-
> ond," and "third."

2. Women engage in greater self-disclosure.
   a. Women reportedly are more concerned with preserving an image.
   b. Women reportedly are more fearful of being hurt.
C. Third, self-disclosure is influenced by the positive-negative quality of the communications.
   1. Positive self-disclosures are more likely to be engaged in than negative self-disclosures.
   2. Negative self-disclosures normally only take place after considerable time has elapsed in a relationship.
   3. Positive self-disclosures may take place with nonintimates but negative self-disclosures usually take place only with intimates.

[These three factors—the communication situation, the sex of the persons, and the positive-negative quality of the communications—are the major ones which influence self-disclosing messages. Let me now summarize in brief some of what we now know about self-disclosure.]

This transition restates the three major points already discussed (serving as an internal summary) and also tells the audience that the conclusion (containing a summary) is next.

CONCLUSION

I. Self-disclosure is a unique form of communication.
   A. Self-disclosure is a form of communication in which you reveal information about yourself that is normally kept hidden.
   B. Rewards and problems await self-disclosure.
   C. Self-disclosure is influenced by such factors as the communication situation, the sex of the persons, and the positive-negative quality of the communication.

Here I provide a summary of the main points in the speech. Notice that these points correspond to the orientation in the Introduction (III, A, B, and C) and to the main points in the Body (I, II, III). Again, the same wording is used to add clarity.

SEE
EXPERIENTIAL
VEHICLE 3.7

II. Self-disclosure is probably our most significant form of communication.
   A. We all engage in it.
   B. It can lead to great advantages and great disadvantages.
   C. By better understanding self-disclosure, we may be in a better position to maximize the advantages and to minimize the disadvantages.

Here I try to accomplish two purposes. First, I try to provide a relatively clear-cut ending to the speech. The last sentence, especially, should make it clear that the speech is finished. The second purpose is to recall the significance of the topic and of the speech. Notice that II C restates the significance of the topic originally provided in the Introduction I.

SOURCES

On outlining see the works cited in the three previous units, particularly those by Ehninger, Monroe, and Gronbeck; Haynes; Amato and Ecroyd; and Gibson. Also see the excellent treatment by Frank J. D'Angelo, *Process and Thought in Composition*, 2d ed. (Cambridge, Mass.: Winthrop, 1980).

HOW TO . . . Evaluate Your Speech Organization: Part Three Checklist

Yes No

■ ■ 1 Is your thesis statement phrased as a complete declarative sentence?

■ ■   Is it clear and specific?

■ ■   Is it limited to one central idea or focus?

■ ■ 2 Has the thesis statement been appropriately used to generate your main ideas?

■ ■   To suggest a suitable organizational pattern?

■ ■   To focus (or not focus) audience attention where you want it?

■ ■ 3 Has your decision to state or not to state your thesis in the actual speech and your phrasing of it been well-reasoned in light of your audience analysis?

■ ■ 4 Are all units of information properly coordinated and subordinated?

■ ■ 5 Are all units of information connected to each other with appropriate transitions?

■ ■ 6 Are there sufficient internal summaries?

■ ■ 7 Is there adequate balance?

■ ■   Among the major parts of the speech (introduction, body, and conclusion)?

■ ■   Among the main points of the speech?

■ ■   Among the forms of supporting material?

■ ■ 8 Is there unity of purpose?

■ ■ 9 Is there coherence-continuity among the parts and items of the speech?

■ ■ 10 Is there appropriate emphasis?

■ ■   Are the more significant points emphasized?

■ ■   Is the use of climax or anticlimax order well reasoned?

■ ■   Is the use of primacy-recency well reasoned?

■ ■ 11 Is the appropriate thought pattern used?

■ ■   Is the thought pattern clear to the audience?

■ ■ 12 Does the introduction gain attention?

■ ■   Does it establish a speaker-listener relationship conducive to the purpose of the speech?

■ ■   Does it orient the audience to what is to follow?

■ ■ 13 Does your introduction avoid the common pitfalls?

■ ■   Apologizing?

■ ■   Pretending to be someone you are not?

■ ■   Making promises you will not keep?

■ ■   Using gimmicks that may backfire?

■ ■ 14 Does the conclusion adequately summarize the main propositions of the speech?

■ ■   Does it motivate your audience?

■ ■   Does it provide closure?

15 Do you in your conclusion avoid the common pitfalls?
   Apologizing?
   Introducing new material?
   Diluting the strength of your position?
   Dragging out the conclusion?
16 Does your outline use a consistent set of symbols?
   Does it use the visual aspect to reflect and reinforce the organizational pattern?
   Does it use one discrete idea per symbol?
   Is it brief?
   Does it use complete declarative sentences?

EXPERIENTIAL VEHICLES FOR PART THREE

3.1 THESIS IDENTIFICATION

Each student should identify the thesis for each of the following works which represent a wide variety of communication forms—movies, novels, plays, short stories, and television shows. After these identifications are made, students should compare their theses with each other in small groups or with the class as a whole. From this brief experience the following should be made clear:

1. The thesis is the central idea—the main assertion—of the communication.
2. Although people will differ somewhat in their statements of the thesis, there should be a fair degree of agreement among those familiar with the work.
3. The identification of the thesis makes the work as a whole more understandable and more meaningful.
4. Any communication work revolves around a central thesis.

SAMPLE COMMUNICATIONS
1. *The Return of the Jedi*
2. *E.T.: The Extra-Terrestrial*
3. *Superman: The Movie* (or *Superman II* or *Superman III*)
4. *1984*
5. *Gone With the Wind*
6. *Valley of the Dolls*
7. *Death of a Salesman*
8. *Our Town*
9. *Hamlet*
10. "The Old Man and the Sea"
11. "The Necklace"
12. "The Lady or the Tiger"
13. "Hill Street Blues"
14. "Love Boat" (identify any episode)
15. Any soap opera (identify any episode)

3.2 ANALYZING INTRODUCTIONS

Read over each of these introductions to various kinds of speeches and identify the functions each of them serves and the means used to achieve these functions.

1   Let us ask ourselves, what is education? Above all things, what is our ideal of a thoroughly liberal education?—of that education which, if we could begin life again, we would give ourselves—of that education which, if we could mould the fates to our own will, we would give our children. Well, I know not what may be your conceptions upon this matter, but I will tell you mine, and I hope I shall find that our views are not very discrepant.
    —Thomas Henry Huxley, "A Liberal Education"

2   There was a South of slavery and secession—that South is dead. There is a South of union and freedom—that South, thank God, is living, breathing, growing every hour. These words, delivered from the immortal lips of Benjamin H. Hill, at Tammany Hall in 1866, true then, and truer now, I shall make my text tonight.
    —Henry W. Grady, "The New South"

3   Mr. President: When the mariner has been tossed for many days in thick weather, and on an unknown sea, he naturally avails himself of the first pause in the storm, the earliest glance of the sun, to take his latitude, and ascertain how far the elements have driven him from his true course. Let us imitate this prudence, and, before we float farther on the waves of this debate, refer to the point from which we departed, that we may at least be able to conjecture where we now are. I ask for the reading of the resolution before the senate.
    —Daniel Webster, "Second Speech on Foote's Resolution— Reply to Hayne"

4   I doubt if any young woman in this University ever approached a tough assignment with more trepidation than this not-so-young woman is experiencing over this assignment. For a commencement address *is* a tough assignment for the most experienced of speakers. But when the speaker is not experienced, when she is not even a speaker, you can, if you'll put yourselves in her quaking shoes, imagine her state of mind. I find myself explaining the familiar panic of that recurrent

nightmare peculiar to actors in which a ghoulish bevy of directors and fellow players are bustling one onto a strange stage shouting "Hurry! Hurry! You're late!" And one has no idea of what one's part is, or for that matter what the play is. And one arrives before the audience completely speechless and, often as not, completely naked. Things are not quite that crucial for I do seem able to speak and I do appear to be clad.
—Cornelia Otis Skinner, "To Maximize One's Life"

3.3 CONSTRUCTING INTRODUCTIONS

Prepare an introduction to one of the topics listed below, making sure that you (1) secure the attention and interest of the audience, (2) orient the audience as to what is to follow, and (3) put the audience into a receptive state. Be prepared to explain the methods you used to accomplish each of these aims.

1 College is not for everyone.
2 It is better never to love than to love and lose.
3 Tenure should be abolished.
4 Maximum sentences should be imposed even for first offenders of the drug laws.
5 All alcoholic beverages should be banned from the campus.
6 Abortion should be declared illegal.
7 Psychotherapy is a waste of time and money.
8 Television should be censored for violence and sex.
9 Euthanasia should be legalized by the federal government.
10 Religion is the hope (opium) of the people.

3.4 ANALYZING CONCLUSIONS

Read over each of these introductions to various kinds of speeches and identify the functions each of them serves and the means used to achieve these functions.

1 If we can stand up to him all Europe may be freed and the life of the world may move forward into broad sunlit uplands; but if we fail, the whole world, including the United States and all that we have known and cared for, will sink into the abyss of a new dark age made more sinister and perhaps more prolonged by the lights of a perverted science.

Let us therefore brace ourselves to our duty and so bear

ourselves that if the British Commonwealth and Empire last for a thousand years, men will still say "This was their finest hour."
—Winston Churchill, "Their Finest Hour"

2   I am endeavoring to show to my countrymen that violent non-cooperation only multiplies evil and that as evil can only be sustained by violence, withdrawal of support of evil requires complete abstention from violence. Nonviolence implies voluntary submission to the penalty for noncooperation with evil. I am here, therefore, to invite and submit cheerfully to the highest penalty that can be inflicted upon me for what in law is a deliberate crime and what appears to me to be the highest duty of a citizen. The only course open to you, the judge, is either to resign your post, and thus dissociate yourself from evil if you feel that the law you are called upon to administer is an evil and that in reality I am innocent, or to inflict on me the severest penalty if you believe that the system and the law you are assigning to administer are good for the people of this country and that my activity is therefore injurious to the public weal.
—Mohandas Gandhi, "Nonviolence"

3   I can conceive of nothing worse than a man-governed world except a woman-governed world—but I can see the combination of the two going forward and making civilization more worthy of the name of civilization based on Christianity, not force. A civilization based on justice and mercy. I feel men have a greater sense of justice and we of mercy. They must borrow our mercy and we must use their justice. We are new brooms; let us see that we sweep the right rooms.
—Lady Astor, "Women and Politics"

4   I am against our participation in this war not only because I hate war, but because I hate fascism and all totalitarianism, and love democracy. I speak not only for myself, but for my Party in summoning my fellow countrymen to demand that our country be kept out of war, not as an end in itself, but as a condition to the fulfillment of all our hopes and dreams for a better life for ourselves and our children, yes, and all the children of this great land. The extraordinary shifts and changes in European alliances should but confirm our resolution to say out of Europe's war, and, ourselves at peace, to seek as occasion permits, the peace of the world.
—Norman Thomas, "America and the War"

3.5 CONSTRUCTING CONCLUSIONS

Prepare a conclusion to a hypothetical speech on one of the topics listed below, making sure that you (1) review the main points of the speech, (2) wrap up the general idea of the speech, and (3) create or reinforce a receptive mood. Be prepared to explain the methods you used to accomplish each of these aims.

1 Undergraduate degree programs should be five-year programs.
2 Proficiency in a foreign language should be required of all college graduates.
3 Children should be raised and educated by the state.
4 All wild-animal killing should be declared illegal.
5 Properties owned by churches and charitable institutions should be taxed in the same way that any other properties are taxed.
6 History is bunk.
7 Suicide and its assistance by others should be legalized.
8 Teachers—at all levels—should be prevented from going on strike.
9 Gambling should be legalized by all states.
10 College athletics should be abolished.

3.6 UNSCRAMBLING AN OUTLINE

This exercise provides you with an opportunity to work actively with the principles of organization and outlining discussed in the previous units. Your task is to unscramble the following 19 statements, from an outline on "Friendship," and fit them into a coherent and logical outline consisting of an introduction, a body, and a conclusion.

1 We develop an acquaintanceship.
2 Friendship is an interpersonal relationship between two persons that is mutually productive, established and maintained through mutual free choice, and characterized by mutual positive regard.
3 We meet.
4 Without friendships we would not be able to function effectively in our daily lives.
5 In order to understand friendships we need to see what a friendship is and its stages of development.
6 Friendship is established and maintained through mutual free choice.

7   Friendship is one of the most important of our interpersonal relationships.
8   Friendship is characterized by mutual positive regard.
9   Friendship is mutually productive.
10 Without friendships our pleasures would not be expanded.
11 We develop an intimate friendship.
12 Friendship is an interpersonal relationship.
13 Without friendships our pain would not be lessened.
14 Friendships develop through various stages.
15 Friendships do not develop full-blown but rather go through various stages—from the initial meeting, through acquaintance, close friendship, to intimate friendship.
16 We develop a casual friendship.
17 By understanding friendship we will be in a better position to develop and maintain productive and enjoyable friendship relationships.
18 Friendship—an interpersonal communication relationship which is mutually productive, established, and maintained through mutual free choice and characterized by mutual positive regard—is one of our most important interpersonal relationships.
19 We develop a close friendship.

3.7 ORGANIZATIONAL ANALYSIS

Select one of the speeches in Appendix D, ''Speeches for Study and Enjoyment,'' and analyze it in terms of organization. Focus on the following:

1   Was the speech characterized by unity of purpose? By coherence? By balance? By emphasis? What specific message elements can you point out to illustrate and support your conclusions?
2   What thought pattern was used? Was this appropriate? Was this effective?
3   What functions did the introduction serve?
4   What functions did the conclusion serve?
5   Did the introduction and the conclusion avoid the common faults identified in these units?
6   Were there adequate transitions and internal summaries?
7   Did the organizational pattern of the speech help in achieving the purposes of the speaker? In what way?

RINGING TONES
INTERNAL
EXTENSION TO EXTENSION
EXTERNAL
OPERATOR/CONSOLE TO EXTENSION
CALL BACK
TYPES OF LINE CARDS
CIRCUIT A
CIRCUIT B
CO/PBX LINE DP
CO/PBX LINE DTMF
CO/PBX LINE DP
CO/PBX LINE DTMF
RINGDOWN TIE LINE
DIAL ICM
ATT LINE
ALL CALL PAGE
SECY HOT LINE
EXECUTIVE ICM
DIAL ICM
ALL CALL PAGE

PART FOUR

TYPES OF PUBLIC SPEAKING

PART FOUR

UNIT 13

General principles of informative speeches

OBJECTIVES

After completing this unit, you should be able to:

1 identify and explain the types of informative speeches
2 explain how purposes may be phrased in terms of behavioral objectives
3 identify and explain at least four principles of information processing

In this unit and in the next we will focus on the informative speech. In this unit our concern is with identifying the various types of informative speeches and with the general principles of information processing that should be observed in all speeches but particularly in speeches concerned with communicating information to an audience.

TYPES AND PURPOSES OF INFORMATIVE SPEECHES

In Unit 2 the purpose of the informative speech was defined and explained in general terms. We now need to elaborate on this aspect of the informative speech. Three levels of purpose are identified: general purpose, specific purpose, and purpose as behavioral objectives. These purposes serve functions similar to the thesis statements discussed at length in Unit 9, "General Principles of Organization"; they guide your selection and organization of supporting materials as well as the language used.

General types and purposes

At the most general level, the informative speech may concentrate on such aspects as description, definition, or demonstration.

Description   In the informative speech of *description* the speaker is concerned with describing a process, a procedure, an event, or an object to the audience. Examples of descriptions are numerous. Speakers may wish to, for example, describe the structure or the function of the brain, the layout of Minneapolis or Nashville, the hierarchy of a corporation or a college, the history of the Vietnam War or of rock 'n roll, the stages a child goes through in learning language, or the stages a manuscript passes through in becoming a book.

Definition   In the informative speech of *definition* the speaker is concerned with defining a term or a system to the audience, explaining how something works or how something may be talked about. It may be a subject new to the audience (What is *psycholinguistics*? What is *constructivism*? What is *dissonance*?) or one familiar to the audience but now being presented in a new and different way. Speakers may wish to, for example, define *love* or *hate*, *realism* or *idealism*, *censorship* or *pornography*. Speakers may compare terms: How do communism and socialism differ? What do Catholics and Protestants believe in common? Speakers may define the implications of various terms: What does it mean to be a "born again Christian"? What does divorce mean to a family? What is a Peace Corps volunteer?

Demonstration Speakers may also wish to demonstrate how something works or how something operates. A process or a procedure may be explained to an audience in speeches of *demonstration*. Speakers may wish to demonstrate how a computer works, how to give mouth-to-mouth resuscitation, how to make sausage, how to dye your hair, how to exercise, how to balance a checkbook, how to dance, how to drive a car, pilot a plane, or navigate a ship, how a heart bypass works, how the body maintains its equilibrium, or how to mix colors.

REMEMBER that informative speeches may focus on a number of different aims, among the most important are:
1 description
2 definition
3 demonstration

Specific purposes

On a somewhat more specific level we might look at the informative speech in terms of the specific items of information (the main points) that you want your audience to understand or learn. For example, one specific purpose might be to inform the audience of the babbling, echolalic, imitative, and true speech stages of language development in the child or of the editing, production, and marketing stages of book production. The four stages in language development would then be developed in four main points in the body of the speech, and the three stages in book production would be developed into three corresponding main points in the body of that speech.

Purposes as behavioral objectives

At a still more specific level we should consider the speech in terms of behavioral objectives, in terms of the behaviors we wish the audience to demonstrate, or what are often called "outcomes." This is the most crucial step in defining the purpose of your speech. You would (1) state the information that the audience will learn from your speech and (2) how the audience will demonstrate this learning in behavioral terms. This may be accomplished in a number of different ways. For example, one purpose stated in behavioral objectives might be phrased as: The audience will be able to state and define the four stages of language development in the child *or* The audience will be able to define the three stages in the book production process. Note that in stating the purpose in this way you are stating not only what you want the audience to learn, but how you will determine whether your purpose has been achieved. If the audience can state and define the four stages in language development, then you have achieved your purpose. If the audience can only state (on the average) two of the four stages, then you have succeeded in accomplishing about half of your purpose. If they cannot do it at all, then you have not achieved your purpose.

Note that you can test the usefulness of your specific behavioral objective by asking yourself if you could readily assess whether or not you have achieved your purpose by examining some behavior of the audience. If you can visualize how you could do this—say, with a simple pencil and paper test in the case of the language development example—then your behavioral objective purpose is probably well stated.

The advantage of stating your purpose in behavioral terms is simple: It provides you with a guideline to test all the information in your speech. Ask yourself whether each piece of information in your speech contributes to your objective. Only those points that contribute to your speech purpose should be retained; all others should be eliminated.

Behavioral objectives in instructional books—such as those prefacing each of the units in this text—are designed to serve similar purposes. The objectives prefacing each of the units in this text are designed to enable you to test yourself—to see if you understand the content of each unit. If you can accomplish the objectives, then you understand the material; if you cannot accomplish the objectives, then you have not sufficiently understood the material and should reread it. In an informative speech situation, objectives may also be used in this way. You may, for example, tell the audience your behavioral objective so that they will be able to determine if they understood your speech or if some clarification or elaboration is needed. It is an excellent learning-teaching technique because it structures the audience feedback in a useful and specific manner.

A summary of the three levels of informative purposes

In summary, then, the three levels of purpose in an informative speech are:

General Purpose: to inform my audience about the functions of a home computer

Specific Purpose: to inform my audience about the functions of the three major parts of a home computer: the central processing unit, the memory, and the input/output system

Purpose as Behavioral Objectives: after hearing my speech the audience will be able to identify and explain the functions of the central processing unit, the memory, and the input/output systems of the home computer

Once you have identified a general idea or subject for your speech, you need to develop it, to analyze it, to identify its major facets. One way of doing this is presented here. The method is simple and derives from the system of topics (called *topoi*) used in the classical rhetorics of Greece and Rome. The method consists of asking a series of questions about your general subject. In the following material, the columns on the left contain seven general questions (Who? What? Why? When? Where? How? and So?) and a series of more specific questions. In the right column I have selected the general subject of "dictionary" and illustrated how *some* of the questions on the left might suggest *some* of the specific aspects of "dictionary." Not all the questions on the left will apply to any given topic, but by asking these general and specific questions about your subject, you should see more clearly how a topic might be divided or analyzed into its significant parts.

WHO?

Who is he or she?
Who is responsible?
Who did it?
To whom was it done?
Who is in favor of (against) this?

Who are the people responsible for making dictionaries?
What is the role of the linguist? the lexicographer? the grammarian?
Who was Noah Webster? Who was Samuel Johnson?

WHAT?

What is it?
What are its parts?
What is it like?
What is it different from?
What does it do?
What are its functions?
What are some examples?
What should we do?
What should we avoid doing?
What does it look like?

What is a dictionary?
What does a dictionary contain?
What are other dictionarylike works? What is a thesaurus?
What are some different types of dictionaries?
What is a dictionary used for?
What is the difference between an abridged and an unabridged dictionary?

Notice that given the specific purpose, there are many behavioral objectives that might be chosen. For example, you may wish to limit the goal to identification (or definition) in which case your purpose would read: After hearing my speech the audience will be able to correctly identify (or define) the three major parts of a home computer: the central processing unit, the memory, and the input/output system. Or, you can attempt a great deal more and state your purpose as follows: After hearing my speech the audience members should be able to correctly use the home computer in storing and retrieving information.

WHY?

Why use it?
Why do it?
Why did it happen?
Why did it not happen?

Why were dictionaries developed?
Why were specialized dictionaries developed?

WHEN?

When did it happen?
When will it occur?
When should it be done?
When did it begin?
When did (will) it end?

When were dictionaries developed?
When should students learn about dictionaries?
When will dictionaries be computerized for everyday use?

WHERE?

Where did it come from?
Where is it going?
Where is it now?

What is the history of the dictionary?
What were early dictionaries like?
What is the state of the art?
What will the dictionary of the future look like?

HOW?

How does it work?
How is it used?
How do you do it?
How do you operate it?
How is it organized?

How do you use a dictionary?
What do you look for in a dictionary?
What questions are better answered by other reference books?

SO?

What does it mean?
What is important about it?
Why should I be concerned with this?
Who cares?
What will it do for me?

Why should I be concerned with dictionaries?
What is the value of a dictionary?
What kind of dictionary should I use?

Select objectives that are manageable in the time you have, taking into consideration the information and abilities already possessed by the audience. To attempt, in a five-minute speech, to inform listeners who have never operated a computer to the point where they could correctly use the system seems absurd. On the other hand, it might be one of a number of suitable goals for an introductory course in computer science.

In subsequent units I will explain other types of speeches, for example, persuasive speeches and special occasion speeches. But it should be clear at this point that no speech is solely an informative speech or a persuasive speech or a special occasion speech. Elements of each type probably exist in all speeches. A lecture on "Achieving Financial Security" will no doubt communicate new information and, hence, be an informative speech. But it will also function to persuade the audience in some ways; it may, for example, motivate them to make certain investments or to save their money and, hence, would be a persuasive speech. Also, the speech may attempt to secure good will for the speaker or to praise the banking industry or Wall Street and, hence, be a special occasion speech. It is best, therefore, to view speeches in terms of primary rather than exclusive purposes.

PRINCIPLES OF INFORMATION PROCESSING

Technically, "information" is something that the receiver does not already know. To tell listeners something they know is not communicating information. A speech devoted to what listeners already know is not an informative speech. In preparing and presenting the informative speech, you need to communicate something new to your receivers. It may be a new way of looking at old things or an old way of looking at new things; it may be a theory not previously heard of or a familiar one not fully understood; it may be devoted to events that the audience may be unaware of or may have misconceptions about. As college students you should need no additional examples of informative speeches since (ideally at least) the lectures you attend are essentially informative speeches; they are speeches designed to tell you something you did not know when you walked into the classroom. The following principles should refine your informative speech-making skills.

Limit the amount of information

There is a limit to the amount of information that a listener can take in at one time. Beginning speakers tend to present a great deal of information and, when they are limited to say five or six minutes, that information is so tightly packed that it is impossible for anyone to understand and retain more than a very small part of it. It is generally best, especially during these beginning efforts, to limit the amount of information that you will communicate and expand, instead, its presentation. Thus, it is better to present two new items of information and explain these with examples, illustrations, descriptions, and the like than to present five new items without this needed amplification.

Stress relevance and usefulness

Information is best attended to and retained when it is perceived as relevant and useful to some need, want, or goal. You may attend to, retain, and internalize the stages in the development of language in children simply because you will be tested on the information and you want to earn a passing or even a high grade. Or, you learn the psychological problems of hearing-impaired children because you will be dealing with these children in your profession. Or, you learn about ways to invest your money because it will help you achieve financial security and independence. The implications should be obvious. If you want the audience to listen to your speech, you must make that information relevant to their needs, wants, or goals. Otherwise, the only feedback you will receive is a look of polite attention. Obviously, this is not enough to satisfy anyone who has spent the time and energy needed to prepare a speech. Throughout the speech, make sure that the audience knows that the information is relevant and useful to them. As the speaker, you may be fully convinced of this but that does not make the audience attend to it; they have to know it and believe it firmly themselves.

Present information in a nonthreatening manner

Information will be listened to more fairly and will be better retained when it is perceived as nonthreatening; alternatively, information will be avoided and resisted when it is perceived as threatening. For example, psychology majors who are intent upon entering clinical psychology will resist information that would inform them of an overabundance of clinical psychologists, the boredom of the work, and the near impossibility of getting into a clinical psychology graduate program. Generally, we seek out information that supports rather than contradicts what we think we already know. Needless to say, this not very admirable quality is often detrimental to intelligent decision making. Yet it is a most common human response.

Present information at the appropriate level

Information is best received and retained when it is presented on an appropriate level. The speaker has to be careful to steer a middle course between being too simple—thus boring or insulting the audience—and being too sophisticated—thus confusing the audience. In this public speaking class, finding the appropriate level should not pose great problems since you and your listeners are probably similar in many ways, and you should be able to tell what level you (and therefore they) would find comfortable. Having mastered an entire body of material and having researched and analyzed it for a period of time, take care not to assume that the material is simple and that the listeners, therefore, will be able to grasp on first hearing what you have taken a week or two to learn.

Relate new information to old

We seem to learn information more easily and retain it longer when it is related in some way to what we already know. This is a procedure we have all followed on numerous occasions. When we want to describe what something looks like or tastes like to someone who has never seen or eaten it, we compare it to something familiar. In explaining the *jicama*, the Mexican potato, we might say, for example, that it looks like a brown-skinned turnip with a white inside and that it tastes something like crispy water chestnuts. As a general rule, then, relate the new to the old, the unfamiliar to the familiar, the unseen to the seen, the untasted to the tasted. In this way the audience will be able to more clearly visualize or somehow perceive what they have never seen or experienced before.

REMEMBER these principles of information processing:
1 Limit the amount of information to be communicated in any one speech
2 Stress the relevance and the usefulness of the information
3 Present information in a nonthreatening manner
4 Present information at the appropriate level
5 Relate new information to old

SOURCES

On types of speeches see Douglas Ehninger, Alan H. Monroe, and Bruce E. Gronbeck, *Principles and Types of Speech Communication*, 8th ed. (Glenview, Ill.: Scott, Foresman, 1978) as well as the references cited in Unit 2. For a general introduction to information processing see Blaine Goss, *Processing Communication* (Belmont, Calif.: Wadsworth, 1982). More advanced treatments are available in, for example, David H. Dodd and Raymond M. White, Jr., *Cognition: Mental Structures and Processes* (Boston: Allyn and Bacon, 1980), and Michael G. Wessells, *Cognitive Psychology* (New York: Harper & Row, 1982).

Amplifying materials in informative speeches

OBJECTIVES

After completing this unit, you should be able to:

1 *explain the nature of examples and illustrations in the speech*
2 *identify the two major tests for examples and illustrations as support*
3 *explain at least three guidelines to follow in effectively using examples and illustrations*
4 *explain the nature of testimony in the speech*
5 *identify the three major tests for testimony as support*
6 *explain at least two guidelines to follow in effectively using testimony*
7 *explain the nature of definition in the speech*
8 *identify the two major tests for definitions as support*
9 *explain at least three guidelines to follow in effectively using definitions*
10 *explain the nature of statistics in the speech*
11 *identify the four major tests for statistics as support*
12 *explain at least three guidelines to follow in effectively using statistics*
13 *explain the nature of audiovisual aids in the speech*
14 *identify the four major tests for audiovisual aids as support*
15 *explain at least three guidelines to follow in effectively using audiovisual aids*

Once you have your specific speech purpose clearly in mind and your main points identified, you need to devote your attention to supporting or amplifying these points. You need to develop each point, each proposition, and each topic so that the audience will understand it more easily. For the informative speech, we will concentrate on materials that amplify, that explain and make vivid. Five such types of amplification are considered in this unit: examples and illustrations, testimony, definitions, statistics, and audiovisual aids. These seem to be the most useful for any speaker but especially for the beginning speaker.

In reviewing each of these forms of amplification, I will explain what these forms are, their major uses or functions, their types and subdivisions, and the tests one would use for examining their usefulness. I approach these discussions, particularly those involving the tests for supporting materials, from the point of view of the speaker, and I advise the speaker to apply the tests before using the various forms of support. However, these tests are also of value to the listener and critic concerned with analyzing and evaluating the speech. All three persons—speaker, listener, and critic—should be concerned with the adequacy of the supporting materials and should apply the various tests suggested here. Lastly, some of the rhetorical issues involved will be explained—the factors that the speaker should take into consideration to ensure that the support works in favor of his or her purpose rather than against it. This same pattern of presentation is followed in Units 16 and 17 where I consider arguments, evidence, and psychological appeals—the types of supporting materials most appropriate to the persuasive speech.

EXAMPLES AND ILLUSTRATIONS

Examples and illustrations are specific instances that are drawn and explained in varying degrees of detail. A relatively brief specific instance is referred to as an *example*; a longer and more detailed example told in narrative or storylike form is referred to as an *illustration*.

Examples and illustrations are particularly useful when you wish to make an abstract concept or idea concrete. For example, it is difficult for the audience to see exactly what you mean by such abstract concepts as "persecution," "denial of freedom," "friendship," and "love" unless you provide specific associations—examples and illustrations—of what you mean. Your examples and illustrations also encourage the listeners to share your pictures of these concepts rather than to fill in their own definition of *love, friendship*, and so on.

Here, for example, Ronald Allen, professor of speech at the University of Wisconsin, uses a number of specific instances to make the relatively abstract—"different kinds of messages using diverse media"—more meaningful and concrete.

> I anticipate that teachers of communication would broaden the focus of language arts study to include a variety of different kinds of messages using diverse media in several communication contexts. A student pondering the expression of love, for example, might study a sonnet by Elizabeth Barrett Browning; Shakespeare's *Romeo and Juliet*; the movie *Love Story*; the historical novel *Nicholas and Alexandra*; the TV program *Mary Hartman, Mary Hartman*; the popular song "A Little Bit More" by Dr. Hook; and his or her own familial and social experiences with the expression of affection. The expression of feelings, like other important communication functions, deserves study from a number of vantage points.

Examples and illustrations also make an idea live—vivid and real—in the minds of the listeners. To talk in general terms about starvation in various parts of the world might have some effect on the listeners. But, very often, one specific example or illustration of a 6-year-old girl who roams the streets eating garbage and being thankful for finding moldy and decaying bread would make the entire idea of starvation more vivid and real. The same is true of many concepts. In explaining friendship, you might tell a story about the way in which a particular friend acted; or, in describing love, the way in which you are loved or love.

Examples and illustrations may be real and factual on the one hand or hypothetical and imagined on the other. Thus, in explaining friendship, you might tell the story of the behavior of an actual friend (and thus have a real or factual example or illustration) or you might formulate a kind of composite of an ideal friend and describe how this person would act in such-and-such a situation (and thus have a hypothetical or imagined example or illustration). Both types are useful; both types are effective.

Testing the example and illustration as support

A couple of questions concerning the use of the example and the illustration are relevant to the speaker (and, as noted earlier, to the listener and critic as well).

1. *Is the example or illustration typical or representative?* Generally, you would want to use an example that is representative of the class of objects that you are speaking about. Training schools that advertise on television frequently show a particularly successful graduate. The advertiser assumes, of course, that the audience will see this example as representative. Perhaps this person is representative. But, I suspect that more often than not representativeness is not achieved or even desired by the advertiser.

At times you may want to draw an example or illustration that is purposefully far-fetched, perhaps for humorous purposes or perhaps to show the inadequacies of an alternative point of view. The important point, I think, is that both the speaker and the audience see the example and the illustration in the same way. If the speaker assumes that the example is typical and logical and the audience that it is a caricature, it will prove ineffective and, in fact, backfire.

2. *Is the example relevant?* Does the example relate directly to the proposition you wish to explain? Beginning speakers, and often even more experienced ones, will have a particularly good story—perhaps a joke—that seems to cry out (in their minds) for retelling and retelling and retelling. At times they will insert this story or illustration in a speech in which it has no place. Although the illustration may be enjoyed and may prove effective, the speech as a whole will suffer. Leave out good but irrelevant examples. Be certain that the example and illustration are not only relevant but that the audience sees the relevance.

When you are using examples to support the validity of a proposition rather than simply to explain it, you should apply the tests explained further in Unit 16 for using the example or specific instance as evidence: (1) Were enough specific instances examined? (2) Were the specific instances examined representative? (3) Were there significant exceptions?

Using the example and illustration effectively

In using the example and illustration, you need to keep in mind that their function is to make vivid and comprehensible those concepts and ideas that might otherwise not be understood.

First of all, examples and illustrations are only useful for explaining a concept; they are not ends in themselves. They should only be as long as necessary to ensure that your purpose is achieved. Details for the sake of details are useless and you will lose the audience's attention.

Second, make the relationship between the proposition or concept and the example or illustration explicit. Remember that this relationship is clear to you because you have constructed the speech. The audience is only going to hear this speech once and, hence, needs to be told explicitly and with no room for misunderstanding that the example or illustration is related in such-and-such a way to the proposition or concept being explained.

Third, make clear the distinction between the real and the hypothetical illustration. Do not try to foist a hypothetical illustration on the audience as a real one; if they recognize it they will resent your attempt to fool them. Statements such as "we could imagine a situation such as . . . ," "I think an ideal friend would . . . ," or simply "A hypothetical illustration of this concept would . . ." make clear that you are in fact using hypothetical illustrations and that you want them understood as such. If the example or illustration is real, again let the audience know this. Such statements as "A situation such as this occurred recently; it involved . . ." or "I have a friend who. . ." or simply "An actual example of this. . ." will help the audience see what you want them to see.

Fourth, in using hypothetical examples and illustrations, take care to make them reasonable and possible. That is, they should not be so bizarre that you lose credibility. Should you wish to denigrate another position or show its unreasonableness in some way, you might construct an absurd example or illustration to show, in turn, how absurd the other position is.

REMEMBER the example should be:
1 typical or representative
2 relevant

And is most effective when:
3 used to explain a concept rather than as an end in itself
4 the relationship between the concept and the example is made explicit
5 the distinction between a real and a hypothetical example is made clear
6 the hypothetical example is itself reasonable and possible

TESTIMONY

In using testimony for amplification you might be concerned with one of two things.

First, you might be concerned with the opinions, beliefs, predictions, or values of some authority or expert. You might, for example, be interested in stating an economist's predictions concerning inflation and depression, an art critic's evaluation of a painting or art movement, a media analyst's opinion of television commercials, and so on. In the following excerpt, for instance, U.S. Congresswoman Shirley Chisholm addresses the Independent Black Women's Caucus of New York City and uses the testimony of noted psychologist Rollo May to bolster her argument that black women must assume political power rather than wait for it to be given to them.

> As Rollo May has put it:
>
>> Power cannot, strictly speaking, be given to another, for then the recipient still owes it to the giver. It must in some sense be assumed, taken, asserted, for unless it can be held against opposition, it is not power and will never be experienced as real on the part of the recipient.
>
>> And those of us in this room know all too well that whatever is given to us is almost always a trap.

Second, you might be interested in an individual as a witness (in the broad sense) to some event or situation. You might, for example, be concerned with the individual who saw a particular accident, with the person who spent two years in a maximum-security prison, in the person who underwent a particular operation, in the Trappist monk who lived for 10 years under a vow of total silence, and so on.

Testimony may be presented to the audience in the form of direct quotations or in the form of paraphrase where you, the speaker, put into your own words what the expert or witness said. Quotations are often useful but at times they become cumbersome; often they are not directly related to the point you are trying to make and their relevance at times gets lost. If the quotation is in technical language that members of the audience will not understand, it then becomes necessary to interject definitions as you go along. Unless the quotation is relatively short, reasonably comprehensible to the audience, and directly related to the point you are trying to make, use your own words, noting that the ideas, the predictions, the evaluations, and whatever are borrowed from your authority or source.

Testing testimony as support

As a speaker concerned with using testimony for amplification (and as a listener or critic concerned with analyzing testimony), you should ask the following questions.

1. *Is the testimony presented fairly?* In using the testimony of others, present it fairly. If there are qualifications made by the expert, these must be included in the speech. You should not extract bits and pieces that best support your argument and imply that these ideas belong to such-and-such an authority. If the ideas of an authority are presented, they should be presented as that authority would want them presented.

2. *Is the person an authority on this subject?* Authorities, especially today, reign over very small territories. Doctors, professors, and lawyers— to name just a few authorities—are actually experts on very small bodies of

knowledge. A doctor may be an expert on the thyroid gland but may know relatively little about skin, about muscles, and about blood. A university professor of history might know a great deal about the Renaissance but no more than a high school history teacher or a college history major about American history. When an authority is used, be certain that the person is in fact an authority *on the specific subject.*

3. *Is the person unbiased?* This question should be asked of both expert and witness accounts. All people are biased in some ways, and you must discover if there are any biases in the sources being cited. The real estate salesperson who tells you to "Buy! Buy! Buy!" and the diamond seller who tells you "Diamonds—the best investment in the world" obviously have something to gain and are biased. To the degree that the source is biased, you should suspect the validity and usefulness of the testimony. This does not mean that normally biased sources cannot provide unbiased testimony; surely they can. It is merely to say that once a bias has been detected, be on the lookout for how this bias *might* figure in this particular bit of testimony.

Using testimony effectively

In using testimony you should stress the competence of the person, whether that person is an expert or a witness. To cite the predictions of a world famous economist of whom your particular audience has never heard will mean little unless you first explain in so many words that "this prediction emanates from the world's leading economist who has successfully predicted all major financial trends over the past 20 years." Now the audience will be prepared to lend credence to what this person says. Similarly, you need to establish the competence of a witness. Consider the statement "My friend told me that in prison drugs are so easy to get that all you have to do is pay the guard and you'll get whatever you want." Stated in this way, the audience might or might not give credence to this statement. On the other hand, if you preface this by noting that your friend was a guard in the state prison for 10 years or that your friend was an inmate for several years, the audience would have some basis for believing what your friend said. In short, establish that the witness has in fact witnessed what he or she claims to have witnessed.

Stress the unbiased nature of the testimony. If the audience perceives the testimony to be biased—whether or not it is in reality—it will have little effect. It is your job, as the speaker, not only to check out the biases of a witness so that you may present accurate information, but also to make the audience see that the testimony is in fact unbiased.

As with all supporting materials, you should stress the recency of the statement to the audience. To say, for example, "General Bailey has noted that the United States has over twice the military power of the Soviet Union" is meaningless if the general's statement is not recent. The recency of testimony in all cases is important and must be stressed to the audience.

HOW TO . . . Tell a Fact from an Inference

We can make statements about the world that we observe, and we can make statements about what we have not observed. In form or structure these statements are similar and could not be distinguished from each other by any grammatical analysis. For example, we can say, "She is wearing a blue jacket," as well as, "He is harboring an illogical hatred." If we diagrammed these sentences, they would yield identical structures, and yet we know quite clearly that they are very different types of statements. In the first one we can observe the jacket and the blue color. But how do we observe "illogical hatred"? Obviously, this is not a descriptive statement but an *inferential statement*—a statement that we make not solely on the basis of what we observe but on the basis of what we observe plus our own conclusions.

There is no problem with making inferential statements; we must make them if we are to talk about much that is meaningful to us. The problem arises when we act as if those inferential statements are factual statements.

Some of the essential differences between factual and inferential statements are summarized in the following table.

Differences Between Factual and Inferential Statements

Factual Statements	Inferential Statements
1. may be made only after observation	1. may be made at any time
2. are limited to what has been observed	2. go beyond what has been observed
3. may be made only by the observer	3. may be made by anyone
4. may only be about the past or the present	4. may be about any time—past, present, or future
5. approach certainty	5. involve varying degrees of probability
6. are subject to verifiable standards	6. are not subject to verifiable standards

Distinguishing between these two types of statements does not imply that one type is better than the other. We need both types of statements; both are useful, both important. Inferential statements, however, need to be accompanied by tentativeness. We need to recognize that such statements may prove to be wrong, and we should be aware of that possibility. Inferential statements should leave open the possibility of other alternatives. If, for example, we treat the statement, "The United States should enforce the blockade," as if it were a factual statement, we eliminate the possibility of other alternatives. When making inferential statements we should be psychologically prepared to be proven wrong so that we will be less hurt if and when we are shown to be incorrect.

"Twelve generals interviewed during the last month and reported in this week's *New York Times* . . ." will be much more effective than the undated and possibly out-of-date testimony so often heard in speeches.

REMEMBER that testimony should be:
1   presented fairly
2   authoritative on the specific subject
3   unbiased

And is most effective when:
4   the competence of the authority is stressed
5   the unbiased nature of the testimony is stressed

DEFINITION

Definitions are useful as amplifying material when you are attempting to explain difficult or unfamiliar concepts or when you wish to make a concept more vivid or forceful. Hugh Walpole, for example, in his classic *Semantics: The Nature of Words and Their Meanings,* considers 25 ways in which a concept may be defined: by behavior ("a scientist is one who . . ."), by sex ("A rooster is the male of the domestic fowl"), by part relations ("A hand is part of the arm"), and so on. I note here some of the modes of definition most useful to you as a speaker attempting to support a point.

One is to define a term by its etymology. For example, in attempting to define the word *communication* you might note that it comes from the Latin *communis* meaning "common"; in "communicating" you seek to establish a commonness, a sameness, a similarity with another individual. And *woman* comes from the Anglo-Saxon *wifman,* which meant literally a "wife man" where the word *man* was applied to both sexes. Through phonetic change *wifman* became *woman.* Most of the larger dictionaries and, of course, etymological dictionaries will help you determine etymological definitions.

You may also define a term by authority. You might, for example, define *lateral thinking* by authority and say that Edward deBono, who developed lateral thinking in 1966, has noted that "lateral thinking involves moving sideways to look at things in a different way. Instead of fixing on one particular approach and then working forward from that the lateral thinker tries to find other approaches." Or you might use the authority of cynic and satirist Ambrose Bierce and define *love* as nothing but "a temporary insanity curable by marriage" and *friendship* as "a ship big enough to carry two in fair weather, but only one in foul."

An operational definition is perhaps the most important method of definition. Here you define a concept by indicating the operations one would go through in constructing the object. Thus, for example, to operationally define a chocolate cake you would provide the recipe. The operational definition of stuttering would include an account of how the act of stuttering is performed and by what procedures stuttering might be observed.

You might also define a term by noting what that term is not, that is, defining by negation. "A wife," you might say, "is not a cook, a cleaning person, a baby sitter, a seamstress, a sex partner. A wife is. . . ." "A teacher," you might say, "is not someone who tells you what you should know but rather one who. . . ."

You might also define a term by direct symbolization, that is, by showing the actual thing or, if that is not possible, by showing some picture or model of it. This, as can be appreciated, is perhaps the best method for defining observables but would obviously not work with abstract concepts, such as friendship and love, or things that are impossible to perceive, such as molecules, infrared rays, and so on.

Earl G. Graves, in his speech "Leadership Challenges in the Private Sector," uses a number of these modes to define the ingredients of leadership. Notice also in this excerpt how Graves establishes his own credibility with references to his acquaintance with Robert Kennedy and Martin Luther King.

What makes a real leader? Is it a tremendous amount of personal energy? Ambition? Experience? The skill of communication with, as some would say, manipulation of others? Brains? Hard work? Is the best motivated executive the one most likely to succeed? What about charisma? Does it come at birth? Is it forged through adversity?

We all know leaders by their definition are people who move others. But what makes a leader? Power alone? Great amounts of money? The opportunity of influencing public opinion? Or is it a combination of all these factors and forces within a person?

I have had the rare and good fortune in my life to have been personally touched and moved by men whose lives rewrote our definitions of leadership in this generation. As an administrative assistant to the late Senator Robert Kennedy and a friend of the Rev. Martin Luther King, Jr.—the American whose leadership and courage gave each of you the opportunity which brings us together this evening—I have seen, felt and followed the intensity of genius and faith; compassion and conviction which moved millions and changed the course of history.

Every human being is so different, yet I can say that the common gift shared by King and Kennedy is the same gift which my father gave me when I was growing up. The gift which has motivated every great leader in history is simply the all-out pursuit of excellence.

That is the foundation of leadership which each of you possesses. The measure of success you achieve in your careers will reflect how much excellence you gain in your lives.

Testing definitions as support

In using definitions the following questions should prove useful.

1. *Does the definition clarify and add to the understanding of the audience?* If the purpose of the definition is to clarify, then it must do just that. This would be too obvious to mention except for the fact that so many

speakers, perhaps for want of something to say, define terms that do not need extended definitions or use definitions that do not clarify, and that, in fact, complicate an already complex concept.

2. *Is your authority credible and known to your audience?* When you use an authority to help define a term, the audience should know who the authority is and should be told the reason for the individual's expertise.

Using definitions effectively

Don't overuse definitions. The object of amplification is to ensure clarity— not to demonstrate intellectual achievement. Often beginning speakers, say when giving a speech on love, will find so many great and clever definitions of love that instead of selecting the one or two that best support the point being made, present all eight or nine. The effect is that the main proposition and the one or two definitions that were most relevant are lost in the verbiage of all the others, so don't overdo it.

Second, be careful not to define a concept with terms that are more difficult than the concept being defined. Again, remember that the object is clarity not obfuscation!

Third, the audience will find it helpful, in your definition of a concept, if you go from the known to the unknown. Start with what the audience knows and work up to what is new or unfamiliar. If, for example, you wish to explain the concept of *phonemics* (with which your audience is totally unfamiliar) and the specific idea you wish to get across is that each phoneme stands for a unique sound, you might begin by noting that much as the alphabet contains letters corresponding to the unique units of the written language, phonemics contains sounds corresponding to the unique units of the spoken language. In this way, you will build on what the audience already knows, a procedure that is useful, if not essential, to all learning.

Fourth, as noted, when you are defining by authority be sure that the authority is known to the audience and that her or his credibility is high. If your authority is not known or if this person's credibility is not high, you should spend some time establishing both familiarity and credibility. If you do not, there is little point in using an "authority"—in fact, from the point of view of the audience, you will not have used an "authority."

REMEMBER, when using definitions as support, they should be:
1   clear and add to the understanding of the audience
2   authoritative

And are most effective when:
3   they are not overused
4   simple and familiar terms are used
5   the unknown is defined in terms of the known
6   the competence of the authority (if one is used) is stressed

STATISTICS

Statistics are summary numbers. Statistics are an organized set of numbers that help us to see at a glance the trends or other important characteristics of an otherwise complex set of numbers. For a teacher to read off 50 grades on the last examination for you to see where you stand would not help since it would be difficult for you to grasp where exactly your score fell in relation to the others in your class. In such cases, statistical information is much more helpful. Particularly helpful for the speaker are the measures of central tendency, measures of correlation, and measures of difference.

Measures of central tendency tell you the general pattern of a group of numbers. The *mean* is the arithmetic average of a set of numbers—for example, the mean grade on the midterm was 89, the mean expenditure on personal-grooming items is $40 per year, the mean income for scientists is $24,000, and so on. The *median* is the middle score; 50 percent of the cases fall above the median and 50 percent of the cases fall below it. For example, if the median score on the midterm was 78, it would mean that half the class scored higher than 78 and half scored lower. Lastly, the *mode* is the most frequently occurring score; it is the single score that most people received. If the mode of the midterm was 85 it would mean that more students received 85 than any other single score.

Measures of correlation tell you how closely two or more things are related. You might say, for example, that there is a high correlation between smoking and lung cancer or between poverty and crime or between psychological insight and suicide. It is important that you recognize that high correlations do not mean causation. The fact that two things vary together (that is, are highly correlated) does not mean that one causes the other. They may both be caused by some third factor, for example.

Measures of difference tell you the extent to which scores differ from some hypothetical average or from each other. For example, the *range* tells us how far apart the lowest score is from the highest score. The range is simply computed by subtracting the lowest from the highest score. If the lowest score on the midterm was 76 and the highest was 99, the range would be 23 points. Generally, a high range indicates great diversity whereas a low range indicates great similarity.

Percentiles are useful for specifying the percentage of scores that fall below a particular score. For example, if you scored 700 on the College Entrance Examination Board test, you were approximately in the ninety-seventh percentile. This means that 97 percent of those taking the test scored lower than 700. Generally, the twenty-fifth, fiftieth, and seventy-fifth percentiles (also called, respectively, the first, second, and third quartiles) are distinguished. The second quartile, or fiftieth percentile, is also the median since exactly half the scores are above and half are below.

Naturally, to compute your own statistics you will need a course or two in statistics. As a speaker you will also need to know how to use the statistics you encounter.

In the following two excerpts the speakers use summary figures—here, measures of central tendency—to make their assertions more vivid and more meaningful. Ernest L. Boyer, U.S. Commissioner of Education, uses the arithmetic mean to demonstrate that children are avid television viewers.

> *Young children—2 to 5 years old—now watch television over 4 hours every day, nearly 30 hours a week. That's more than 1500 hours every year. And by the time a youngster enters first grade he or she has had 6000 hours of television viewing.*

To stress the prevalence of emotional problems and suicide among college students, Patricia Ann Hayes, a student, uses statistics effectively.

> *Dr. Dana Farnsworth, a leading expert in the field of student mental health, lists some rather ominous nationwide statistics for colleges. He stresses that of each 10,000 students 1000 will have emotional conflicts severe enough to warrant professional help, 300–400 will have feelings of depression deep enough to impair efficiency, 5–10 will attempt suicide, and 1–3 will succeed in taking his own life. If these statistics are true, my university should encounter 15–45 suicide attempts of which 3–6 will be successful.*

Testing statistics as support

In using statistics you should ask the following questions.

1. *Were the statistics based on a large enough sample?* The size of the sample is always important and this is one reason why few advertisers will ever report the size of their sample. You might be told that four out of five nutritionists surveyed chose Blotto milk, but you are not told how large the entire sample was. If they merely tested groups of five until they found one group where four would endorse Blotto, you would not put much confidence in those statistics. The sample must be large enough so that you can expect that if another group were selected, the results would be the same as those reported in the statistics. Enough nutritionists should have been surveyed so that if you went out and selected five at random, four would endorse Blotto.

2. *Was the sample a fair representation of the entire population?* If you wish to make inferences about an entire class of people, you must sample the group fairly and include representatives of all subgroups. Thus, it would not be fair to make inferences about the attitudes of college professors on the importance of communication if you only surveyed communication professors. Nor, however, would it be fair if you only surveyed professors of science, or of the arts, and so on.

3. *Was the statistic based on recent sampling?* This is particularly important since things change so rapidly. To report mean income, church attendance, or smoking statistics without ensuring recency would be meaningless.

4. *Were the statistics collected and analyzed by an unbiased source?* Remember our advertisers! They are intent on selling a product; they make

their living that way. When they say "four out of five," you need to ask who collected the data and who analyzed it?

Using statistics effectively

Keep in mind that the audience will ask essentially the same questions that a good researcher would ask in analyzing statistics; you, as a speaker, must answer these implied questions. Thus, stress the unbiased nature of the source who collected and analyzed the statistics, the representativeness of the sample, and the recency of the statistical collections and computations.

Further, you must make the statistics clear to an audience that will hear the figures only once. Consequently, figures should be rounded off so they are easy to comprehend and retain. To say that the median income of workers in this city is $12,347 may be accurate but it would be better to say that it is "around $12,300" or even "a bit more than $12,000."

SEE EXPERIENTIAL VEHICLE 4.1.

When using numbers of any kind it is essential that they be made meaningful to the audience. To say, for example, that the largest office buildings are the twin towers of the World Trade Center and that there is a total of 4,370,000 square feet of rental space does not mean very much until it is made to live in the minds—and particularly in the experiences—of the audience. To say, for example, that the Sears Tower in Chicago is 1559 feet tall does not visualize its height. But to say that this is equivalent to the length of more than four football fields makes the height of the building a bit clearer.

Lastly, make explicit the connection between the statistics and what they show. To say, for example, that college professors make an average of $18,000 per year needs to be related specifically and explicitly to the proposition that teachers' salaries should be raised or lowered—depending on your point of view.

REMEMBER that statistics should be:
1   based on a large enough sample
2   based on a representative sample
3   based on recent sampling
4   collected and analyzed by unbiased sources

And are most effective when:
5   the unbiased nature of the statistics is stressed
6   the statistics are made clear to the audience
7   the statistics are made meaningful to the audience
8   the connection between the statistics and what they show is made clear

AUDIOVISUAL AIDS

Audiovisual aids are one of the most powerful means of amplification. To aid comprehension and to make ideas vivid and easier to remember, few forms of amplifying material serve as well as the audiovisual aid. A few of the more popular and useful are identified here.

The actual object   If you are speaking on the care and feeding of elephants, it would be difficult to bring the actual thing to class. On the other hand, if you were talking about the workings of a computer or a lie detector or certain kinds of tropical fish, it might be quite possible to use these as visual aids. As a general rule (to which there are probably many exceptions), the best audiovisual aid is the object itself; bring it to your speech if you possibly can.

Models   Models—replicas of the actual object—are particularly useful when attempting to explain complex structures such as the hearing mechanism, the vocal apparatus, the brain, and the like. These models help to clarify for the audience the size of the various structures, their position, and how they interface with each other.

The chalkboard   The chalkboard is particularly useful because of its ease of use and general availability. All classrooms have such a board and you have all seen them used by teachers with greater or lesser effect; in some way, you have all had some "experience" with them. The chalkboard may be effectively used to record key terms or important definitions or even to outline the main structure of your speech.

Transparent and opaque projections   Serving a purpose similar to the chalkboard are transparent and opaque projections. Most communication departments have such projectors readily available. At some point in your public speaking class, you should master their use since they are extremely helpful for giving any type of oral presentation. A *transparency* is made from any carbon imprint (pencil, xerox, or typing done with a carbon ribbon) and then projected onto the wall or a screen, making a relatively small image large enough to be seen from all parts of the room. This is most useful for outlines that are complex and for which you do not wish to take up a great deal of time writing on the board. Another advantage is that you can write on the transparencies while you are speaking—circle important items, underline key terms, and draw important connections among terms. Opaque projectors serve a similar function but use the actual page or photograph rather than a specially made transparency. Perhaps the greatest advantage of such projections is that they can be presented to the audience and then removed from sight by just flicking the light switch.

In using transparencies or opaque projections, do not clutter them up with too much material. Use the transparency to highlight a few of the most essential points. Depending on your specific purpose, you may find it helpful to disclose what is contained on the transparency gradually rather than all at once. A piece of lightweight cardboard works well to cover the item; this enables you to disclose each point just as you wish the audience to attend to it. If you put too much information on a transparency or allow the audience to see too much of it too early, it will be difficult for you to focus their attention where you want it. So limit the information—project only that information that you want the audience to focus on at that time.

Some projectors generate a great deal of noise, so you may have to adjust your speech volume to combat this extra noise. If you are particularly ambitious, you may want to enclose your transparencies in cardboard frames. The frames can then be labeled, perhaps with notes on how you wish to discuss the transparency. This will make them easier to incorporate throughout the speech. You can add color by using transparencies of different colors and also by using grease pencils or marking pens in a variety of colors. In selecting the marking pens, make certain that they will project clear images and not resist the plastic surface; not all marking pens are effective. Be careful, in using color, not to do such an elaborate job that your audience begins to focus on the artwork and ignores your message. Like everything else in a speech, the color should contribute to your basic purpose.

Handouts As a teacher I probably make more use of handouts than of any other audiovisual aid. They are helpful in explaining complex material and also in providing the audience members with a permanent record, to which they may refer at some later time, of what went on during the lecture. Thus, in discussing the theories and research bearing on how we comprehend and remember sentences, for example, I distribute the same sentences used in the lecture so that the students may annotate these and not waste time copying down 100 to 200 sample sentences. Handouts are also useful for presenting complex information that you want your audience to refer to throughout your speech. Handouts have the disadvantage that if they are extremely interesting or contain information not yet conveyed in your speech, the audience members may peruse them when you would rather they devote their attention to what you are saying.

Charts, graphs, and diagrams These "graphics" are most useful in conveying a variety of types of information. Organizational charts show clearly how an organization is structured and the relationships among the individuals. Flow charts are excellent for illustrating various processes such as the production of a widget from solid disc to completed, polished, and packaged widget. Bar graphs and line graphs are most useful for showing differences among elements over time. In every communication textbook, and this one is no exception, there is at least one diagram of the communication process. Hopefully it clarifies the elements involved and the relationships among them. As a speaker your diagrams would serve similar functions.

Maps Maps are useful for showing not only the obvious geographical elements but for showing changes throughout history, population density, immigration patterns, economic conditions, the location of various resources, and hundreds of other issues you may wish to develop in your speeches.

People Oddly enough people can function quite effectively as "audiovisual aids." To demonstrate the muscles of the body, for example, a well-built weight lifter is an ideal visual aid. Also, to demonstrate different voice patterns, skin complexions, or hairstyles, people are most appropriate. Aside from the obvious assistance they will provide in demonstrating their muscles or voice qualities, they almost invariably help you to secure and maintain the attention and interest of the audience.

Slides Slides are useful for showing various scenes or graphics that you simply cannot describe in words. The great advantages of slides are their visual appeal (and hence their attention-getting value) and their ease of preparation and use. Again, most departments of communication have slide projectors so availability should not cause any difficulty. When planning to use slides, allow yourself sufficient time for shooting, developing, and organizing them. To plan a speech utilizing slides only to find that on the day you are scheduled to speak, the slides are still at the processing lab is not a pleasant prospect, so plan ahead.

Films, filmstrips, and videotapes At one time the film media would have been difficult for most student speakers to use. Today they are readily available and their use in amplifying a lecture should be clear to you. I use a variety of films to illustrate some of the breakdowns in interpersonal communication, the techniques for and the progress made in teaching animals to communicate, and various other topics. Filmstrips are also useful because they enable you to regulate timing more closely. Thus, if during a lecture there are a number of questions, you can easily stop the filmstrip to address these issues whereas with a film it is a bit more cumbersome. Although it is a great deal to undertake, you might consider making your own videotape to illustrate your talk. But remember, a bad film is a bad audiovisual aid and it detracts rather than adds to the effectiveness of your speech.

Pictures Assuming that you do not have films or slides, the next best visual aid is a picture. There are, however, many hazards involved in using this type of aid, so I hesitate to recommend its use. If the picture is large enough for all members of the audience to see clearly (say, poster size), if it clearly illustrates what you want to illustrate, and if it is mounted on cardboard, then use it. Otherwise, do not. Do not pass pictures around the room; this only functions to draw attention away from what you are saying. Listeners are looking for the pictures to get to them and will invariably miss a great deal of your speech in the interim.

Records and tapes To deliver a speech about music and not provide the audience with samples would seem strange and very likely the audience's attention would be diverted from what you are saying to why you have not provided the actual music. But records and tapes can be useful for many other types of speeches as well. A speech on advertising would be greatly helped, for example, by having actual samples of advertising as it is played on radio or television. A tape of such examples would go a long way

FIGURE 14.1

Growth of the cable television industry in the United States as of January of each year. (*Source:* Warren K. Agee, Phillip H. Ault, Edwin Emery, *Introduction to Mass Communications,* 6th ed. New York: Harper & Row, 1979, p. 280.)

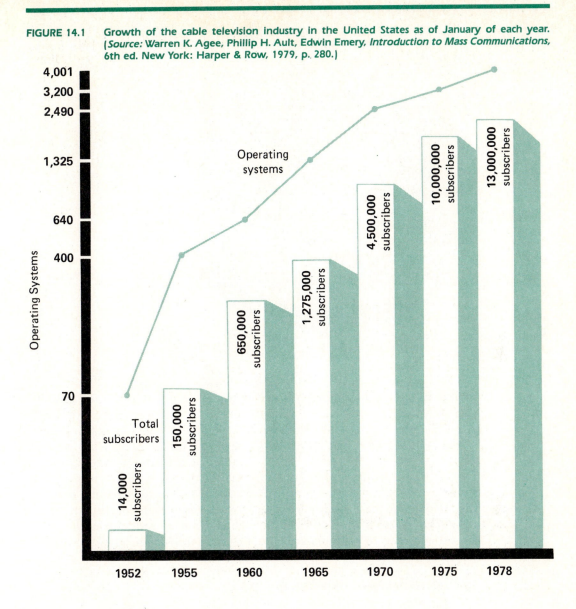

to help clarify exactly what you are talking about and would also serve to break up the oral presentation most effectively.

Figures 14.1–14.4 are varied examples of visual aids. All were professionally prepared, but your own visual aids do not need to be this professional. Nevertheless, it is a good idea to make your visuals of as high a

FIGURE 14.2 Frequency of crimes against the person, property, and public order. (*Source:* N. J. Demerath, III, and Gerald Marwell, *Sociology Perspectives and Applications,* New York: Harper & Row, 1976, p. 293.)

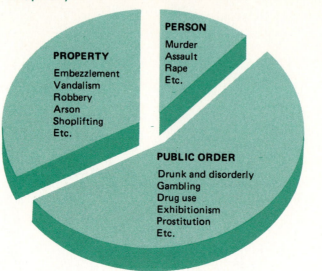

quality as your verbal presentation. Notice that visual aids are particularly well-suited for presenting information in which various figures are compared. Figures 14.1 and 14.2 are excellent illustrations of some of the ways in which information may be visually presented. Visual aids are also useful for presenting complicated relationships among different structures or functions as in, for example, the organizational chart of an advertising agency (Figure 14.3). Here your audience will be able to see at a glance the numerous components that make up the agency and their relationships to each other. The locations of the endocrine glands in males and females are well illustrated in the very simple sketch of the male and female bodies in Figure 14.4.

Testing audiovisual aids as support

In using audiovisual aids ask yourself the following questions.

1. *Is the aid relevant?* It may be attractive, well-designed, easy to read, and possess all the features one could hope for in an audiovisual aid, but if it is not relevant to the topic, it would be better left at home.

2. *Does the aid reinforce the message?* Throughout this book, it has been emphasized that all the messages being sent to the listeners should reinforce each other. The same is true of audiovisual aids. They must reinforce both verbal and nonverbal messages. Audiovisual aids are not some-

FIGURE 14.3　The structure of an advertising agency. (*Source: Warren K. Agee, Phillip H. Ault, and Edwin Emery.* Introduction to Mass Communications, *6th ed., New York: Harper & Row, 1979, p. 36.)*

ADVERTISING AGENCY ORGANIZATION CHART

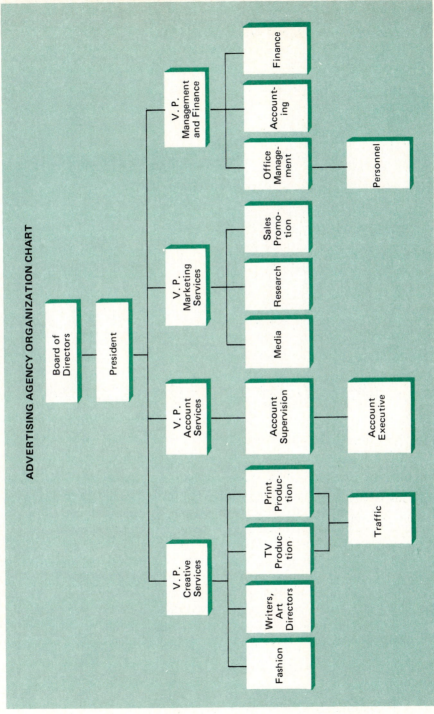

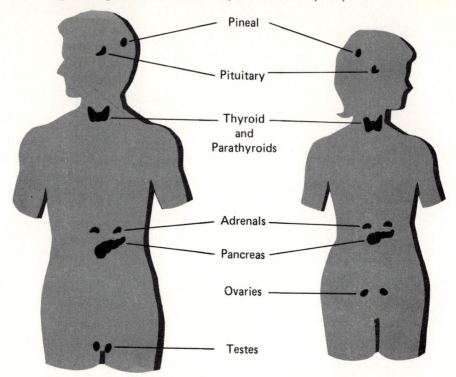

thing apart from the speech; they are an integral part of the speech as a whole.

3. *Is the message conveyed by the aid evident?* If it is not clear, it obviously serves no purpose. In fact, it will significantly detract from the effect of the speech since the listeners will devote attention to trying to decipher what the aid conveys and lose part of what you are saying in the speech. Two guidelines should govern clarity: First, it should be legible; it should be easy to read. Second, it should be simple enough to comprehend without great difficulty. You don't want listeners spending inordinate amounts of time trying to see where time is indicated, or what the different colors mean, or what the double arrows mean. Whatever is important should be explained in the speech and the aid should clarify and add vividness to your speech.

4. *Is the aid appealing?* Audiovisual aids, like people, work best when they are appealing. Sloppy, poorly designed, and dirty visual aids will detract from the purpose they are intended to serve. Visual aids should be

attractive enough to engage the attention of the audience, being careful, however, not to make the aid so attractive that it engages the attention of the audience to the point of distraction. The well-developed almost nude body may be effective in selling underwear, but such gimmicks probably detract if your object is to explain the profit-and-loss statement of Exxon.

Using audiovisual aids effectively

SEE EXPERIENTIAL VEHICLE 4.2.

In using audiovisual aids keep the following points in mind. First, use the aid only when it is relevant. Show it when you want the audience to concentrate on it and then remove it. If you are using the chalkboard, write the terms or draw the diagrams when you want the audience to see them and then erase them. If you do not remove the visual, the audience's attention may remain focused on the board when you want to go on to something else.

Second, when you are using a number of audiovisual aids, be familiar with their order and subject matter. This seems obvious, yet it is one of those simple principles that is so often violated. In classrooms, for example, teachers will refer to diagrams and to maps prefacing their remarks with statements such as "now what was this supposed to illustrate" or "I can't seem to find the Amazon River."

Third, when using visual aids, test them prior to the speech. Be certain that they can be easily seen from all parts of the room. Ask someone to react to them so that you can get a fresh and unbiased perspective. If you are using a phonograph, make sure the electricity works for your equipment. If using films, make sure the shades can be pulled down and that the room can be made dark enough for projection.

Fourth, decide exactly how and when you want to use the aids. Rehearse the speech with the audiovisual aids incorporated into the presentation. Practice the actual motions. If you are going to use a chart, how will you use it? Will it stand by itself? Will you tape it to the board? Will you ask another student to hold it? Will you hold it yourself?

Fifth, and most important, do not talk to your visual aid. Talk with your audience at all times. Know your aids so well that you can point to what you want to point to, without breaking eye contact with your audience.

Although these may seem like picky little issues, when neglected they can cause major difficulties and render an otherwise effective and well-constructed speech a total failure. At the same time, with just a little time and effort devoted to these details, audiovisual aids can add greatly to the effectiveness and informativeness of your public speeches.

REMEMBER, when using audiovisual aids as support, they should be:
1 **relevant to the task at hand**
2 **reinforcing of the message**
3 **clear and self-evident**
4 **appealing**

And are most effective when:

5   used only if they will enhance the speech
6   you are especially familiar with them
7   you have previously tested them
8   you have rehearsed the entire speech using the audiovisual aids
9   they do not hinder speaker-audience contact

SOURCES

On amplification see, for example, Douglas Ehninger, Alan H. Monroe, and Bruce E. Gronbeck, *Principles and Types of Speech Communication,* 8th ed. (Glenview, Ill.: Scott, Foresman, 1978), and Donald C. Bryant and Karl R. Wallace, *Fundamentals of Public Speaking,* 5th ed. (Englewood Cliffs, N.J.: Prentice-Hall, 1976). The speeches cited in this unit include: Ronald Allen, "Do You Really Want to Know Why Johnny Can't Write or Read, or Speak or Listen," *Vital Speeches of the Day* 43 (December 15, 1976):148–150; Earl G. Graves, "Leadership Challenges in the Private Sector," *Vital Speeches of the Day* 44 (March 15, 1978):337; Shirley Chisholm, "Vote for the Individual, Not the Political Party," *Vital Speeches of the Day* 44 (August 15, 1978):670–671; Ernest L. Boyer, "Communication: Message Senders and Receivers," *Vital Speeches of the Day* 44 (March 15, 1978):334–337; Patricia Ann Hayes, "Madame Butterfly and the Collegian," *Winning Orations, 1967* (Detroit, Mich.: The Interstate Oratorical Association, 1967), pp. 7–10, reprinted in *Contemporary American Speeches,* 2d ed., Wil A. Linkugel, R. R. Allen, and Richard L. Johannesen, eds. (Belmont, Calif.: Wadsworth, 1969), pp. 262–266.

UNIT 15

General principles of persuasive speeches

OBJECTIVES

After completing this unit, you should be able to:

1 *identify and explain the types of persuasive speeches*
2 *explain how persuasive speech purposes may be phrased as behavioral objectives*
3 *identify and explain at least four principles of persuasion*

The persuasive speech will be the focus in this unit and the following two. In this unit the concern is with identifying the several types of persuasive speeches and with the general principles of persuasion. These principles are applicable to all forms of communication interaction but are especially significant in speeches designed to persuade.

TYPES AND PURPOSES OF PERSUASIVE SPEECHES

The vast majority of speeches are designed to persuade the listener. The speeches of politicians, advertisers, and religious leaders are perhaps the clearest examples of persuasive speeches. But—as will be made clear throughout this entire book—persuasion is all around us, all of the time.

General types and purposes

At the most general level we may distinguish between (1) speeches that attempt to move or change the audience's attitudes in the direction being advocated and (2) speeches that attempt to get the audience to behave in a certain way.

Attitude change   We may think of an attitude as a tendency or predisposition to behave in a certain way. Thus, if we have a favorable attitude toward chemistry, we would be more apt to elect chemistry courses, to read about chemistry, to talk about chemistry, and to conduct chemistry experiments. If we have an unfavorable attitude toward chemistry, we would avoid chemistry courses, not read about chemistry, and so on. If we have a negative attitude toward Venusians, we would resist their moving into our neighborhoods, attending our schools, and marrying our children. "Attitude" is a hypothetical construct—it is a psychological fiction created to simplify our explanations of behaviors and behavioral tendencies. We cannot observe a person's negative attitude in the same way that we can observe a person's aggressive behaviors. Instead, we infer the existence of certain attitudes from observing the individual's behaviors. If, for example, an individual speaks against censorship, reads everything that criticizes censorship, and writes articles denouncing censorship, we infer that this person has a negative attitude toward censorship. We have not observed the "negative attitude," rather, we have observed behaviors that we attribute to the negative attitude.

In persuasion, then, we are concerned with moving attitudes in a predetermined direction. Thus, we may wish to make an audience already hostile to the legalization of marijuana even more hostile, or we may attempt to convert them to favor legalization. As can be appreciated from this example, the goals may range widely in terms of ease of accomplishment. Whereas it is relatively easy to strengthen an audience's existing attitude, it is relatively difficult to totally reverse it.

Behavior change   Although we talk frequently about attitude and attitude change, we are ultimately concerned with behavior—specifically with changes in behavior. We assume that if we change attitudes, we will have changed perhaps not the actual behaviors but at least the likelihood or probability of certain behaviors. The persuasive speech addressed to motivating a behavior change may focus on just about any behavior imaginable—to vote in the next election, to vote for Senator Smith, to give money to the Community Chest, to buy a ticket to the football game, to move to California, to change jobs, to take a particular course in college, to major in economics, to buy a particular car or motorcycle or home, to date a particular individual, and so on. Both attitude and behavior changes—as these examples should illustrate—come in all types, varying from the relatively insignificant to the change of major importance.

Some theorists label the process of changing attitudes and changing behaviors differently and talk of changing attitudes as *conviction* and changing behaviors as *persuasion*. Others talk of changing attitudes as *persuasion* and changing behaviors as *actuation*. In this book the term *persuasion* will be used to designate either type of situation, largely because changes in attitude cannot logically be separated from changes in behaviors.

Specific purposes

On a somewhat more specific level, we must specify what we want our audience to accept in our attempt to change either their attitudes or their behaviors. Thus, if our general purpose is to persuade our audience to enroll in a course in astrology, then our specific purpose might be to convince the audience that a course in astrology is enjoyable, easy, and relevant to their present and future needs. These three points (enjoyment, ease, and relevance) would then be developed as the three main issues in the speech. If your general purpose is to get your audience to try computer dating, your specific purpose might be to convince them that computer dating is an easy way to meet another person, is inexpensive, and is socially rewarding. In this speech the three elements of ease, inexpensiveness, and social reward would then be developed.

Purposes as behavioral objectives

Like in the speech to inform, we may, in the speech to persuade, formulate specific purposes in terms of behavioral objectives—behaviors we wish the audience to manifest as a result of the speech. You could determine, for example, that you want the audience to announce their preference that Senator Smith be reelected, that they will argue in favor of Puerto Rico becoming the fifty-first state, and so on. Or you could rely on written methods of indicating change and state, for example, that the audience will change their opinions in favor of Senator Smith on a shift-of-opinion ballot or that in a mock election they would vote for Senator Smith.

Of course, you might also focus on the specific behaviors that you wish the audience to demonstrate. For example, you might state that the audience should buy a savings bond, read a particular book, buy a Honda, donate money to the Heart Fund, or watch a particular television show or film.

As in the informative speech, you can test the usefulness of your behavioral objective purpose by asking yourself if you would be able to tell—from observing the audience's behavior or reactions—if you have achieved your purpose. Further, you can use your behavioral objective purpose as a reference point against which all other parts of the speech may be checked. Every bit of supporting material you use should further the attainment of the behavioral objective. If something does not advance the objective in some way, then it should not be used.

A summary of the three levels of persuasive purposes

In summary, then, the three levels of purpose in a persuasive speech are:

General Purpose: to persuade my audience that Elizabeth Grey should be elected senior class president

Specific Purpose: to persuade my audience that Elizabeth Grey should be elected senior class president because she is reliable, conscientious, and knowledgeable about school politics

Purpose as Behavioral Objectives: after hearing my speech, the audience will vote for Elizabeth Grey for senior class president

There are a wide variety of behavioral objectives that might be chosen once you have clearly determined your specific purpose. A more limited behavioral objective than the one stated above might be: After hearing my speech, the audience members will be more positive toward the candidacy of Elizabeth Grey than they were before the speech, as measured by a shift-of-opinion ballot. Or you might select a much more difficult goal such as: After hearing my speech, the audience members will each contribute at least 10 hours of their time to campaigning for Elizabeth Grey's election as senior class president. In phrasing your behavioral objectives be certain to select ones that are manageable in the time you have available and that you take into consideration the attitudes and opinions that the audience already holds. Thus, for example, if your audience is already in favor of Grey's election, then your purpose to get them to actually vote for her seems manageable. On the other hand, if they are initially opposed to her election, then a goal to totally reverse them in one short speech may be unrealistic; perhaps you should content yourself with stimulating a more positive attitude toward her election than they had before hearing your speech.

REMEMBER that persuasive speeches may focus on:
1 **influencing attitudes, opinions, values, and beliefs**
2 **motivating behaviors**

PRINCIPLES OF PERSUASION

Thousands of articles and books—crammed with theories, descriptions, observations, and experimental tests—have been written about persuasion. Offered here is only a very small sampling of the principles of persuasion with the objective of getting you started on your first speeches. Throughout the rest of the text you will encounter additional principles—based largely on the results of experimental studies and careful observations—as needed.

The credibility principle

A speaker will be more persuasive if she or he is perceived as credible by the audience. This means that the audience should perceive the speaker as being competent or knowledgeable, of good character, and charismatic or dynamic. If you project these characteristics, you will have a much greater chance of being believed than if you are seen not to possess them. You know this is true from your own experience; there are certain people that you believe and others that you do not believe, and that these decisions to believe or not to believe exist apart from any consideration of what is being said. This concept of credibility was discussed at length in Unit 4, "Public Speaking Ethics and Credibility."

The attractiveness principle

A speaker will be more persuasive if he or she is perceived as attractive and well-liked. This is a crucial characteristic that many persuasion texts omit entirely, perhaps for fear of offending. But this principle emerges from both the scientific study and the casual observation of persuasion with amazing consistency and cannot be avoided. The more attractive (physically and in personality) the speaker, the better the chance of being successful in persuasion. This does not mean that you have to look like Victoria Principal or Billy Dee Williams but it does mean that physical and personality attractiveness—as perceived by the audience—are helpful components of the persuasion transaction. The obvious implication is that any speaker who wishes to effectively persuade an audience should give some attention to his or her own attractiveness.

The selective exposure principle

Audiences will generally follow the "law of selective exposure." It has at least two parts: (1) that listeners will actively seek out information that supports their opinions, beliefs, values, decisions, behaviors, and the like and (2) that listeners will actively avoid information that contradicts their existing opinions, beliefs, attitudes, values, behaviors, and so on. There are a few qualifications to this "law" that are interesting to note. For example, if a person is very sure of himself or herself (that is, very sure that the opinions and attitudes held are logical, valid, and productive), then this person might not bother to seek out the support of others or may not actively avoid nonsupportive messages. Selective exposure is exercised most often when confidence in one's opinions and beliefs is weak.

This principle of selective exposure suggests a number of implications for the speaker. For example, if you are attempting to persuade an audience that holds very different attitudes from your own, you should anticipate selective exposure operating and proceed inductively; that is, hold back on your main purpose until they have assimilated some of your evidence and argument and only then relate it to your main (and initially contrary) proposition. If you were to present them with your thesis first, they might just tune you out without giving your position a fair hearing. Another implication is that you must be thoroughly knowledgeable about the attitudes of your audience if you are to succeed in making the necessary adjustments and adaptations. Still another implication is that if you, as a speaker, have been successful in weakening the confidence of the listeners in their initial position, they will seek out other sources of information to restore that confidence. In many instances they will seek out the very information that will contradict what you have been persuading them to accept. Thus, at the end of your speech, it may appear that you have been successful. But you may find that the additional information exposure subsequent to the speech convinces the listeners even more of their initial position than before you began speaking. In this instance it is necessary to reinforce your point of view repeatedly—like advertisers do—or to somehow make the audience feel comfortable with their new attitudes and beliefs. In our discussion of "A Question of Balance" in Unit 17, specific suggestions are offered for dealing with this complex situation.

The audience participation principle

Persuasion is greatest when the audience participates actively. In experimental tests, for example, the same speech is delivered to different audiences. The attitudes of one audience are measured before and after the speech, the difference being a measure of the speech's effectiveness. The attitudes of another group are measured before and after the speech, but they are also asked, for example, to paraphrase or summarize the various arguments of the speaker. It is consistently found that those listeners who participated actively (as in paraphrasing or summarizing) were more persuaded than those who passively received the message. Demagogues and propagandists who succeed in arousing huge crowds often have the crowds chant slogans, repeat catch phrases, and otherwise participate actively in the persuasive experience.

The inoculation principle

The principle of inoculation may be explained with the biological analogy on which it is based. Suppose you lived in a germ-free environment. Upon leaving this germ-free environment and upon exposure to germs, you would be particularly susceptible to infection because your body has not built up an immunity—it has no resistance. Resistance, the ability to fight off germs, might be achieved by the body, if not naturally, through some form of inoculation. You would, for example, be injected with a weakened dose of the germ so that your body begins the fight by building up antibodies that create an "immunity" to this type of infection. Your body, then, because of its production of antibodies, is able to fight off even powerful doses of this germ.

The situation in persuasion is similar to this biological process. Some of our attitudes and beliefs have existed in a "germ-free" environment, in an environment in which these attitudes and beliefs have never been attacked or challenged. For example, many of us have lived in an environment in which the values of a democratic form of government, the importance of education, and the traditional family structure have not been challenged. Consequently, we have not been "immunized" against attacks on these values and beliefs. We have no counterarguments (antibodies) prepared to fight off these attacks on our beliefs. So, if someone were to come along with strong arguments against these beliefs, we might be easily persuaded.

Contrast these "germ-free" beliefs with issues that have been attacked and for which we have a ready arsenal of counterarguments: Our attitudes on the draft, nuclear weapons, college athletics, and thousands of other issues have been challenged in the press, on television, and in our interpersonal interactions. As a result of this exposure, we have counterarguments ready for any attacks on our beliefs concerning these issues. We have been inoculated and immunized against attacks should someone attempt to change our attitudes or beliefs.

The major implications of the inoculation principle for persuasion should be clear. First, if you are addressing an inoculated audience you must take into consideration the fact that they have a ready arsenal of counterarguments to fight your persuasive assault. Be prepared, therefore, to achieve only small gains; don't try to totally reverse the beliefs of a well-inoculated audience.

Second, if you are trying to persuade an uninoculated audience, your task is much simpler in that you do not have to penetrate a fully developed immunization shield. You also must recognize that even when an audience has not immunized itself, they take certain beliefs to be self-evident and may well tune out any attacks on such cherished beliefs or values. Again, proceed slowly and be content with small gains. Further, an inductive approach would suit your purposes better here. Attacking cherished beliefs directly will create impenetrable resistance; instead, build your case by first presenting your arguments and evidence and gradually work up to your conclusion.

Third, if you are attempting to strengthen an audience's belief, give them the antibodies they will need if ever under attack. Consider raising counterarguments to this belief and then demolishing them. Much like the injection of a small amount of a germ will enable the body to build an immunization system, presenting counterarguments and then refuting them will enable the listeners to effectively immunize themselves against future attacks on these values and beliefs. This procedure has been found to confer greater and longer-lasting resistance to strong attacks than by merely providing the audience with an arsenal of supporting arguments.

The motivational principle

Listeners are best persuaded when your propositions are positively linked to their motives—their desires, wants, wishes, and needs. You will be persuasive to the extent that you can relate the attitudes and behaviors you wish the audience to exhibit with such motives as status, financial gain, affection, love, friendship, sex, attraction, self-esteem, individuality, independence, competition, and so on. This issue of motivation is so important that it is covered in depth in Unit 17 "Motivating Behavior in Persuasive Speeches."

The magnitude of change principle

One of the most obvious principles of persuasion and yet one which many speakers totally ignore is this: the greater and more important the change desired by the speaker, the more difficult its achievement will be. The reason for this is simple enough: We normally demand a greater number of reasons and lots more evidence before we make important decisions—career changes, moving our families to another state, or investing our life savings in certain stocks. On the other hand, we may be more easily persuaded (and demand less evidence) on relatively minor issues—whether to take "History of Television" rather than "History of Film," or to give to the United Heart Fund instead of the American Heart Fund.

Generally, people change gradually, in small degrees over a long period of time. And although there are cases of sudden conversions, this general principle seems to be valid more often than not. Persuasion, therefore, is most effective when it strives for small changes and works over a considerable period of time. Persuasion that attempts to convince the audience to radically change their attitudes or to engage in behaviors to which they are initially opposed will frequently backfire on the speaker. During this type of situation, the audience will frequently tune out the speaker, closing its ears to even the best and most logical arguments.

REMEMBER these principles of persuasion:
1   The credibility principle
2   The attractiveness principle

3   The selective exposure principle
4   The audience participation principle
5   The inoculation principle
6   The motivational principle
7   The magnitude of change principle

SOURCES

There are numerous and excellent works on persuasive speaking that will prove useful to you. Some new techniques are covered briefly in Gerald R. Miller and Michael Burgoon, *New Techniques of Persuasion* (New York: Harper & Row, 1973). A review article on inoculation by William J. McGuire, who has done most of the theorizing and research on this principle, may be found in "Inducing Resistance to Persuasion: Some Contemporary Approaches," in Leonard Berkowitz, ed., *Advances in Experimental Social Psychology*, vol. I (New York: Academic Press, 1964), pp. 191–229. A comprehensive overview is provided by Mary John Smith, *Persuasion and Human Action: A Review and Critique of Social Influence Theories* (Belmont, Calif.: Wadsworth, 1982). A useful work on persuasive speaking is Joseph A. Ilardo, *Speaking Persuasively* (New York: Macmillan, 1981). Additional works on persuasion are also referenced in the "Sources" for Units 16 and 17.

Developing arguments for persuasive speeches

OBJECTIVES

After completing this unit, you should be able to:

1 *explain the nature of argument in public speaking*
2 *identify the three general tests for reasoning*
3 *explain the nature of literal and figurative analogies as forms of reasoning*
4 *identify the two major tests for reasoning from analogy and at least two guidelines to follow in effectively using reasoning from analogy*
5 *explain the nature of cause-effect reasoning*
6 *identify the three major tests for reasoning from causes and effects and at least two guidelines to follow in effectively using reasoning from causes and effects*
7 *explain the nature of reasoning by sign*
8 *explain the major test for reasoning from sign and at least two guidelines to follow in effectively using reasoning by sign*
9 *explain the nature of reasoning from specific instances to a generalization and from a generalization to a specific instance*
10 *identify the three major tests for reasoning from a specific instance to a generalization and at least two guidelines to follow in effectively using specific instances*
11 *identify the two major tests for reasoning from a generalization to a specific instance and at least two guidelines to follow in effectively using reasoning from general principles to specific instances*

In this excerpt from Sir Arthur Conan Doyle's *The Adventures of Sherlock Holmes*, Holmes is speaking to Dr. Watson:

> "How do I know that you have been getting yourself very wet lately, and that you have a most clumsy and careless servant girl?"
>
> "My dear Holmes," said I, "this is too much. . . . It is true that I had a country walk on Thursday and came home in a dreadful mess; but as I have changed my clothes, I can't imagine how you deduce it. As to Mary Jones, she is incorrigible, and my wife has given her notice; but there again I fail to see how you work it out."
>
> He chuckled to himself and rubbed his long nervous hands together. "It is simplicity itself," said he; "my eyes tell me that on the inside of your left shoe, just where the firelight strikes it, the leather is scored by six almost parallel cuts. Obviously they have been caused by someone who has very carelessly scraped round the edges of the sole in order to remove

crusted mud from it. Hence, you see, my double deduction that you had been out in vile weather, and that you had a particularly malignant boots-licking specimen of the London Slavey."

On the basis of various bits and pieces of "evidence," Holmes has drawn a "conclusion."

The evidence together with the conclusion constitute an argument—the substance of this unit. More specifically, this unit continues the discussion of supporting materials, this time focusing on materials that prove or attempt to prove the validity of a proposition or conclusion. First, we will explore the general nature of argument and reasoning and some general tests of evidence, then focus on the major types of argument: analogy, cause-and-effect, sign, and specific instance.

ARGUMENT, REASONING, AND SUPPORT

By "argument" I do not mean a disagreement or a dispute but rather a reason or series of reasons, that lead to or support a conclusion. *Evidence* together with the *conclusion* that the evidence supports equal an argument. By "reasoning" I mean the process of formulating conclusions on the basis of evidence.

When you argue a point in a public speech or attempt to demonstrate the usefulness of a particular way of looking at something or postulate some general principle, you are attempting to prove something to the listeners. That is, your function is a rhetorical one in the sense that you hope to prove the proposition, not in any objective sense but rather in the minds of the listeners. In the vast majority of cases that you would deal with as a public speaker, the issues cannot be proven in any objective sense. Rather, you seek, as a speaker, to establish the probability of your conclusions in the minds of the listeners. Thus, the process is in part a *logical* one of demonstrating the postulated relationship, and also a *psychological* one of convincing or persuading the listeners to accept the conclusions as you have drawn them. Throughout this discussion this dual function should be kept in mind.

What is said here is applicable to the speaker in constructing the speech, to the listener in receiving and responding to the speech, and to the speech critic or analyst in analyzing and evaluating the speech. A poorly reasoned argument, inadequate evidence, and stereotypical thinking, for example, must be avoided by the speaker, recognized and responded to by the listener, and negatively evaluated by the critic.

Before getting to the specific forms of argument or reasoning, some general tests of support applicable to all forms of argument should be stated. These general tests (and, in fact, all the tests of adequacy) are stated as questions so that you may use them to evaluate various sources of evidence and thus more easily test the adequacy of your argument and the validity of the information you use to support your argument.

Is the support recent?

We live in a world of rapid change; what was true 10 years ago is not necessarily true today. Economic strategies that worked for your parents will not necessarily work for you. Whereas, for example, your parents saved money and avoided getting into debt, in times of inflation many economists advise us not to save but to spend and to borrow as much money as possible. As the world changes so must our strategies for coping with it. And what is true of economic examples is also true of other areas. No area, in fact, is immune to change. Therefore, it is particularly important that your supporting materials be as recent as possible. Recency alone, obviously, does not make an effective argument. Yet, other things being equal, the more recent the evidence and support the better.

Is there corroborative support?

Very few conditions in this world are simple; most relationships, most issues are complex. Consequently, in reasoning about any issue, you should support the proposition from different areas, sources, and perspectives. For example, in advocating that you take such-and-such a course of study, your evidence should come not only from educational authorities attesting to, say, the value of the program, but also from government statistics, from industrial economic forecasts, and so on. That is, in supporting a thesis, evidence and argument should be gathered from numerous and diverse sources all pointing to the same conclusion. This will not only help the speaker convince listeners that the conclusion is valid, but will add generally to speaker credibility.

Are the sources unbiased?

We each see the world through our own individual filters; we do not see the world objectively, but instead we see it through our prejudices, our biases, our preconceptions, our stereotypes, and so on. Others see the world through their filters; no one is objective.

Consequently, in evaluating evidence you should establish how biased the sources are and in what direction they are biased. You would not treat a tobacco company report on the connection between smoking and lung cancer with the same credibility as a report by some impartial medical research institute. You should question research conducted and disseminated by any special interest group. We listen every day to commercials on television reporting research results that invariably support the superiority of one product (ours) over another (theirs). Although we may say that such research reports do not influence us, advertisers know they are effective enough to continue financing them. In short, as a speaker and as a listener, you have to be particularly careful to recognize bias in your sources. It is always legitimate to ask, then, To what extent might this source be biased? Might this source have a special interest that leads her or him to offer the evidence being offered?

1   recent
2   corroborated by other evidence
3   unbiased

REASONING FROM ANALOGY

In reasoning from analogy, you compare like things and conclude that since they are alike in so many respects they are also alike in some heretofore unknown or unexamined respect. Analogies may be literal or figurative. In a *literal analogy* the items being compared are from the same class—cars, people, countries, cities, or whatever. For example, in a literal analogy we might argue that (1) New York, Philadelphia, London, and Paris are like Los Angeles in all essential respects—they are all large in area, have a few million people, have a central inner city, and so on; (2) these cities have all profited from low-cost subway transportation; (3) therefore, Los Angeles would also profit from the construction of a subway system. Here, then, we have taken a number of like items belonging to the same class (large cities), have pointed out a number of similarities (area, population), and have then reasoned that the similarity would also apply to the unexamined item (the subway system).

In a *figurative analogy*, the items compared are from different classes. These analogies are more useful for amplification than for reasoning. A figurative analogy might compare, for example, professors with birds: We would note that, as birds are free to roam all over the world, professors need to be free to roam all over the intellectual universe—admittedly a somewhat absurd analogy.

In a speech, "The Vital Need for Technology and Jobs," Thomas A. Vanderslice, vice-president and group executive of General Electric Company, used a most effective figurative analogy, comparing the human body with the country, to stress the importance of research and improvement.

> I am told that Casey Stengel, on reaching one of his supernumerary birthdays, was asked,—looking back on his long life in baseball, what would he have done differently.
>
> The "Old Perfesser" thought a bit, and said: "If I'd known I was going to live so long, I'd have taken better care of myself."
>
> My remarks today are dedicated to the proposition that this country, and our form of government, will be around for a while yet, and we'd better take good care of what we have.

As this example illustrates, the figurative analogy only creates an image, it does not prove anything. Its main purpose is to clarify and it is particularly useful when you wish to make a complex process or relationship clearly understandable to the audience.

Testing reasoning from analogy

In testing the adequacy of an analogy—here of literal analogies—two general questions need to be asked.

1. Are the two cases being compared alike in essential respects? In the example of the subway system in the various large cities, one significant and essential difference was not noted: The population of Los Angeles covers a wider geographical area than the other cities and is not as centralized, as, say, New York or Philadelphia. Consequently, the subway would have to cover an area much greater than it would have to cover in other cities. Construction costs and operating expenses would be greater and high fares would jeopardize its low-cost transportation function.

2. Do the differences make a difference? In any analysis, regardless of how literal it is, the items being compared will be different. No two things are the same; every item is unique. But in reasoning with analogies you need to ask if the differences make a difference. Obviously, not all differences make a fundamental difference. The geographical spread of the various cities, however, is a substantial difference as far as subways are concerned.

Using reasoning from analogy effectively

In using analogies stress the numerous and significant similarities between the items being compared and minimize the differences between them. If the audience knows that there are differences, but you do not squarely confront these differences, your argument is going to prove ineffective. The listeners will be wondering, "But what about the difference in . . .?" Instead of increasing effectiveness, you will only have succeeded in diminishing it.

REMEMBER in using analogies to:
1   use cases that are alike in essential respects
2   use cases in which the differences do not make a significant difference

And are most effective when:
3   similarities are stressed
4   differences are minimized
5   differences are confronted squarely

REASONING FROM CAUSES AND EFFECTS

In reasoning from causes and effects, you may go in either of two directions. You may reason from cause to effect (from observed cause to unobserved effect) or from effect to cause (from observed effect to unobserved cause).

Causal reasoning would go something like this. You would argue, for example, that X results from Y; and since X is undesirable, Y should be eliminated. With actual events substituted, you would have something like this: Cancer (X) results from smoking (Y); and since cancer is bad, smoking should be eliminated. Alternatively, of course, you might argue that X results from Y; and since X is desirable, Y should be encouraged. For example, general self-confidence (X) results from positively reinforcing experiences (Y); therefore, to encourage the development of self-confidence, foster positively reinforcing experiences.

Testing reasoning from causes and effects

In testing reasoning from cause to effect or from effect to cause, ask the following questions.

1. Might other causes be producing the observed effect? For example, if you observe a particular effect (say, high crime or student apathy) you need to ask if causes other than the one you are postulating might be producing these effects. Thus, you might postulate that poverty leads to high crime, but there might be other factors actually causing the high crime rate. Or poverty might be one cause, but it might not be the most important cause. Consequently, you have to explore the possibility of other causes producing the observed effects.

2. Is the causation in the direction postulated? If two things occur together, it is often difficult to determine which is the cause and which is the effect. For example, a lack of interpersonal intimacy and a lack of self-confidence often seem to go together. The person who lacks self-confidence seldom has intimate relationships with others. But which is the cause and which is the effect? It might be that the lack of intimacy creates or "causes" low self-confidence, but it may also be that low self-confidence leads to or "causes" a lack of intimacy. Of course, it might also be that some other previously unexamined cause (a history of negative criticism, gross ugliness, obvious stupidity) might be producing both the lack of intimacy and the low self-confidence.

3. Is there evidence for a causal rather than merely a time-sequence relationship? Two things might vary together, but they may not be related in a cause-effect relationship. One often cited and particularly vivid example is the cock crowing and the sun rising. The cock crows and the sun comes up, but no one would argue that the cock's crowing causes the sun to rise. Divorce frequently results after repeated instances of infidelity, but infidelity itself may not be the cause of the divorce rate. Rather, some other factor may be leading to both infidelity and divorce. Thus, even though infidelity may precede divorce, it may not be the cause of it. When you assume that a temporal relationship implies a causal relationship, you are committing a fallacy of reasoning called *post hoc ergo propter hoc* ("after this, because of this").

Using cause-effect reasoning effectively

In reasoning from causes and effects, stress the causal connection, pointing out (1) that other causes are not significant and may for all practical purposes be ruled out, (2) that the causal connection is in the direction postulated, that is, that the cause is indeed the cause and the effect is the effect, and (3) that the evidence points to a causal connection—that the relationship is not merely related in time.

Further, depending on the specific purpose of the speech, the audience needs to be made to realize that this causal connection can be altered to their advantage. It may be strengthened if the effect is desirable or broken if the effect is undesirable.

REMEMBER, in reasoning from causes and effects, make certain that:
1   other causes are not producing the observed effect
2   the causation is in the direction postulated
3   there is evidence for a causal rather than simply a temporal relationship

And is most effective when:
4   the speaker stresses that other possible causes may be ruled out, that the causation is indeed in the postulated direction, and that the relationship is indeed a causal one

REASONING FROM SIGN

About 5 years ago I went to my doctor because of some minor skin irritation. Instead of looking at my skin the doctor focused on my throat, noticed that it was enlarged, felt around a bit, and began asking me a number of questions. Did I tire easily? Yes. Did I drink lots of liquid? Yes. Did I always feel thirsty? Yes. Did I eat a great deal without gaining any weight? Yes. She then had me stretch out my hand and try to hold it steady. I couldn't do it. Lastly, she took a close look at my eyes and asked if I noticed that they had expanded. I hadn't been aware of it but when it was pointed out I could see that my eyes had expanded a great deal. All of these indicators were signs of a particular illness.

Based on these signs, she made the preliminary diagnosis that I had a hyperthyroid condition. The results from blood and other tests confirmed the preliminary diagnosis. I was promptly treated and the thyroid condition was corrected. Medical diagnosis is a good example of reasoning by sign. The general procedure is relatively simple. If a sign and an object, event, or condition are repeatedly or frequently paired, the presence of the *sign* is taken as evidence or proof of the presence of the object, event, or condition. Thus, the tiredness, the extreme thirst, the overeating, and so on, were taken as signs of hyperthyroidism since they frequently accompany the condition. When these signs (or symptoms) disappeared after treatment with radioactive iodine, it was taken as a sign that the thyroid disease had been arrested. Further tests confirmed this as well.

The same general kind of reasoning is used in legal matters to determine guilt or innocence. Recall any of a hundred television or film dramas.

Someone is killed. The detective-hero looks for signs of guilt. A motive, a history of violence, an inability to account for the time during which the murder took place are signs which together are taken as support for the conclusion that "Higgins" did it. In Agatha Christie's *Witness for the Prosecution*, Leonard Vole is accused of murdering a wealthy widow. It looks as if he will be convicted until his wife, Christine, is made to take the stand as a witness for the prosecution. During her testimony it is "discovered" that she was trying to have him convicted for the murder to serve her own ends. When this is discovered, it is taken as a sign of Leonard's innocence and he is acquitted. Soon after the trial is over we learn that Christine merely played the role of the unfaithful wife to establish Leonard's innocence. Her real motive was to provide signs that would be taken as evidence of Leonard's innocence.

SEE
EXPERIENTIAL
VEHICLE 4.3.

More mundane but perhaps more meaningful instances of reasoning by sign occur every day. The teacher looks at the class and sees two students in the back reading the newspaper, three students staring out the window, four students engaged in private conversation, one asleep. Any teacher would reason from these signs that the class was not very interested in the lecture. In a disco or bar or party, if someone asks you to dance and buys you a drink, engages you in conversation, and stares longingly into your eyes, you would normally take these as signs that this individual is interested in you and would like to pursue the relationship beyond this initial point.

Testing reasoning from sign

In reasoning from sign there are a number of questions that should be asked.

1. Do the signs necessitate the conclusion drawn? Given the extreme thirst, the overeating, and the like, how certain may one be of the "hyperthyroid" conclusion? With most medical and legal matters we can never be absolutely certain, but we can be certain beyond reasonable doubt.

2. Are there other signs that point to the same conclusion? In the thyroid example, the extreme thirst could have been brought on by any number of factors. Similarly, the swollen throat and the overeating could have been attributed to other causes. Yet, taken together they seemed to point quite clearly to only one reasonable diagnosis that was later confirmed with additional and more sophisticated signs in the form of blood tests and thyroid scans. Generally, the more signs that point toward the conclusion, the more confidence you can have that it is valid.

3. Are there contradictory signs? That is, are there signs pointing toward contradictory conclusions? If, for example, "Higgins" had a motive and a history of violence (signs that would support the conclusion that Higgins was the murderer), but if Higgins also had an alibi for the time of the murder (a sign pointing to the conclusion of innocence), the conclusion of guilt would have to be reconsidered or discarded.

Using reasoning from signs effectively

In reasoning from sign, stress the certainty of the connection between the sign and the conclusion. Make the audience see that given these signs, no other conclusion is at all likely—that for all practical purposes, all other conclusions are ruled out. This is generally the procedure followed in law. The guilt of an individual must be established not conclusively but beyond all *reasonable* doubt. The audience should be made to see that your conclusion drawn from sign is the best—the most reasonable—conclusion possible.

Make the connection between the signs and the conclusions obvious to the audience. If you, as a speaker, know of the connection between, say, enlarged eyes and hyperthyroidism, this does not mean that the audience knows it. State explicitly that enlarged eyes can only be produced by hyperthyroidism and that, therefore, the sign (enlarged eyes) can lead to only one reasonable conclusion (hyperthyroidism).

As with other forms of reasoning, try to answer the anticipated objections of your audience to your line of reasoning. For example, let us say that you are trying to argue that women are discriminated against in jobs in higher education. Among the signs you might use are that there are few women at the higher ranks of associate and full professor; that few women are chairpersons, deans, or presidents; and that few women serve on important committees that determine college policy, tenure, and promotion. One frequently raised objection to this line of reasoning is that few women go into higher education; hence, the counterargument goes, there would naturally be fewer women in these higher positions. You should anticipate a rebuttal such as this and in your argument point out that the figures for women are *disproportionately* lower—that the percentage of women in these higher positions is significantly lower than would be expected on the basis of pure chance.

REMEMBER, in reasoning from sign, that:
1   the signs should support the conclusion you have drawn
2   other signs point in the same direction
3   contradictory signs should be accounted for

And is most effective when:
4   the certainty of the connection between the sign and the conclusion is stressed and is made obvious
5   the major counterarguments that the audience is likely to raise are answered

REASONING FROM SPECIFIC INSTANCES AND GENERALIZATIONS

In reasoning from specific instances, you examine several specific instances and then conclude something about the whole. Thus, you taste one piece of spaghetti as it is cooking and conclude something about the whole—that it needs, for example, to cook a bit more. With spaghetti, there is little danger in this kind of reasoning; the worse that can happen is that a pound of spaghetti will be served overcooked or undercooked. Consider, however, the same process when you examine (or meet and interact with) several members of a particular racial or religious group and on that basis conclude something about the entire class.

Reasoning from specific instances is particularly useful when you want to develop a general principle or conclusion but cannot examine the whole. You sample a few communication courses and conclude something about communication courses in general; you visit several Scandinavian cities and conclude something about the whole of Scandinavia. This same general process operates in dealing with one person. You see, for example, a particular person in several situations and conclude something about the person's behavior in general. You date a person a few times, or maybe even for a period of several months, and on that basis draw a general conclusion about the suitability of that person as a spouse.

Technically, you may also argue in the other direction—namely, from a general principle to some specific instance. That is, you begin with some general statement or axiom that is accepted as true by the audience and argue that since something is true of the entire class, it must also be true of the specific instance, which is a member of that class.

Reasoning from general principles—which is actually more a way of presenting your argument than a type of reasoning or argument—is useful when you wish to argue or demonstrate that some unexamined instance has certain characteristics. The general principle and an unexamined item's membership in that class are noted and the conclusion is drawn that, therefore, the item also possesses the qualities possessed by the whole. For example, listeners may all accept the notion that Martians are lazy, uncooperative, and dull-witted. This is the general principle or axiom that is accepted. The argument would then apply this general principle to a specific instance, for example, "Obviously we should not hire Delta X since we do not want a lazy, uncooperative, stupid colleague."

Note in this excerpt from Ken Lonnquist's speech, "Ghosts," how he argues against abortion from the general principle that one does not have control over the body of another. Notice also the effective use of the analogy with the slave master.

> We say that it is our right to control our bodies, and this is true. But there is a distinction that needs to be made, and that distinction is this:
> Preventing a pregnancy is controlling a body—controlling your body. But preventing the continuance of a human life that is not your own is murder.
> If you attempt to control the body of another in that fashion, you become as a slave master was—controlling the lives and the bodies of his slaves—chopping off their feet when they ran away, or murdering them if it pleased him. This was not his right; it is not our right.

Testing reasoning from specific instances to a generalization

You should apply a number of tests in reasoning from specific instances.

1. Were enough specific instances examined? Obviously there will be a limit to the number of specific instances you can examine; your time, energy, and resources are limited. And yet, it is important that enough instances be examined to justify your conclusion. Exactly what is enough will vary from one situation to another. You cannot spend three days in a foreign country and conclude something about the entire country; you cannot interact with three Ethniquians and conclude something about all Ethniquians. Two general guidelines might prove helpful in determining how much is enough. First, the larger the group you wish covered by your conclusion, the greater the number of specific instances you must examine. Second, the greater the diversity of items in the class, the more specific instances you will have to examine. If you wish to draw conclusions about a class of 75 million Martians, you will have to examine a considerable number of Martians before drawing any valid conclusions. On the other hand, if you are attempting to draw a conclusion about a bushel of 100 apples, sampling a few would seem sufficient.

Some classes or groups of items are relatively homogeneous whereas others are more heterogeneous; this will influence how many specific instances constitute a sufficient number. The spaghetti in the boiling water are all about the same; thus, sampling one usually tells you something about all the others. On the other hand, communication courses are probably very different from each other and to draw a conclusion about the entire group of communication courses will require a considerably larger sample.

2. Were the specific instances examined representative? Specific instances must be representative. If you wish to draw conclusions about the entire class, you must examine specific instances coming from all areas or subclasses within the major class. Thus, you could not draw conclusions about New Yorkers from merely examining persons living in Sutton Place or Murray Hill or Gramercy Park—three of the more sophisticated and expensive sections of the city. Rather, you would have to sample instances from all important areas of the city—the expensive sections, the ghettos, the residents of one-family houses and the residents of high-rise co-ops, and so on. Similarly, if you wanted to draw conclusions about the student body of your school, you could not simply examine communication majors or physics majors or art majors. Rather, you would have to examine a representative sample. When students attempt to survey other students, they will often select one area of the college and there take a "random" sample. However, you know that the students who are found in the library are not the same as those found in the smaller rooms of the student union or in the cafeteria or in the gym. To take a representative sample you might have to examine, for example, persons at each of these significantly different locations or perhaps use some kind of random sampling procedure from, say, the registrar's list of students. The important point to see here is that if you wish to draw conclusions about the whole, all significant parts of the whole must be examined in some way.

3. Are there significant exceptions?   When you examine specific instances and attempt to draw a conclusion about the whole, you must take into consideration the exceptions. Thus, if you examine a number of Venusians and discover that 70 percent have I.Q.'s of less than 80, you might be tempted to draw the conclusion that Venusians are stupid. But what about the 30 percent who have I.Q.'s of over 140? These are significant exceptions that must be taken into account when drawing your conclusion and would necessitate qualifying your conclusion in significant ways. Exactly how many exceptions will constitute "significant exceptions" is not easy to determine and will certainly vary from one situation to another.

SEE EXPERIENTIAL VEHICLE 4.4.

As a speaker, you have an obligation to your listeners to disclose significant exceptions. To hide these would be dishonest and also usually ineffective from a persuasive point of view because, more often than not, the audience either has heard or will hear of these exceptions. If you have not mentioned them, they will become suspicious of your all-around honesty, and your credibility will quickly decline.

Needless to say, advertisers are notorious in covering up significant exceptions. Thus, to have an advertiser say that "9 out of 10 dentists recommend Blippo" seems very convincing until you begin asking about the other groups of 10 examined where only 2 or 3 recommended Blippo toothpaste. Furthermore, while we are on this topic, it is instructive to note that "9 out of 10 dentists recommend . . ." will often depend on the question asked of the dentists. Whether the question is "Would you recommend Blippo over all other toothpastes?" or "Would you recommend Blippo instead of just plain water?" will naturally influence the responses. Seldom, however, are the actual questions asked provided listeners.

REMEMBER, in reasoning from specific instances to generalizations, that:
1   a valid number of specific instances must be examined
2   the specific instances examined must be representative of the whole
3   the significant exceptions must be accounted for

And is most effective when:
4   the sufficient sampling and representativeness are stressed
5   the exceptions are taken into consideration and accounted for to the satisfaction of the audience

Testing reasoning from a generalization to specific instances

In testing reasoning from general principles to specific instances two major tests should be applied.

1. Is the general principle true or at least probably true?   Obviously, if the general principle is not true, it would be useless to attempt to apply it to any specific instance. In most instances you cannot know if a general principle is true simply because you cannot examine all instances of the class. You will note, of course, that if you examine all instances of the class, there is no reason to use this form of reasoning since you have, in effect, examined the instance to which you wish to apply the general principle. For example, if you examine all the apples in the bushel, there is no reason to formulate the general conclusion that all the apples are rotten and to say that, therefore, one particular apple is rotten. In examining all the apples you will have examined the specific apple. Consequently, what we are really dealing with is a general principle that seems to be "usually" and "probably" true. Thus, our conclusions about any specific instance will also only be "usually" or "probably" true.

2. Is the unknown or unexamined item clearly a specific member of the class? If you want to draw a conclusion about a particular Atlantan and want to reason that this person is assertive because all Atlantans are assertive, you have to be certain that this person is in fact a member of the class of Atlantans.

HOW TO . . . Analyze an Argument: The Toulmin Model

One of the most insightful ways to analyze an argument is to lay it out according to a model developed by Stephen Toulmin, a British philosopher and logician—whether it is your own that you are contemplating using in your speech or one used by someone else. In Toulmin's model there are three essential parts and an additional three parts that may be used depending on the argument and the audience. The three essential parts are claim, data, and warrant.

The *claim* is the conclusion you wish the audience to accept; it is the proposition you want the audience to believe is true or justified or right. For example: *Tuition will be increased.*

The *data* are the facts and opinions, the evidence, used to support your claim. For example: *The college has recently incurred vast additional expenses.*

The *warrant* is the connection leading from the data to the claim. The warrant is the principle or the reason why the data justify (or warrant) the claim. For example: *Tuition has been in the past and is likely to continue to be the principle means by which the college pays its expenses.*

In addition to these three elements (which are essential to all arguments), there are three other optional elements that may or may not be present depending on the type of argument advanced and the nature of the audience to be persuaded.

The *backing* is the support for the warrant—the supporting material that backs up the principle or reason expressed in the warrant. Backing is especially important if the warrant is not accepted or believed by the audience.

For example: *Over the last 40 years, each time the college incurred large expenses, it raised tuition.*

The *qualifier* is the degree to which the claim is asserted; it is an attempt to modify the strength or certainty of the claim. The qualifier is used only when the claim is presented with less than total certainty. For example: *probably.*

The *reservation* (or rebuttal) specifies those situations under which the claim might not be true. For example: *unless the college manages to secure private donations from friends and alumni.*

Usually these six parts of an argument are laid out in diagrammatic form to further illustrate the important relationships. A diagram of the example given here is presented below.

SEE
EXPERIENTIAL
VEHICLE 4.5.

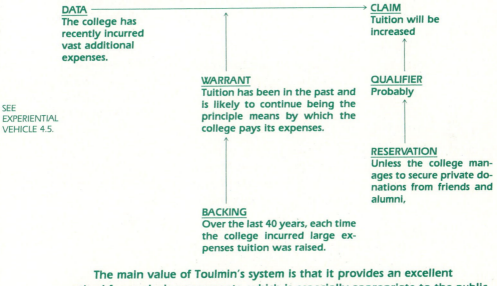

DATA
The college has recently incurred vast additional expenses.

CLAIM
Tuition will be increased

WARRANT
Tuition has been in the past and is likely to continue being the principle means by which the college pays its expenses.

QUALIFIER
Probably

RESERVATION
Unless the college manages to secure private donations from friends and alumni,

BACKING
Over the last 40 years, each time the college incurred large expenses tuition was raised.

The main value of Toulmin's system is that it provides an excellent method for analyzing arguments, which is especially appropriate to the public speaking situation. The following questions may help to further enable you to analyze the validity and possible effectiveness of your arguments:

1 Are the data sufficient to justify the claim? What additional data are needed?
2 Is the claim properly (logically) qualified? Is the claim presented with too much certainty?
3 Is the warrant adequate to justify the claim on the basis of the data? Does the audience accept the warrant or will it need backing? What other warrants might be utilized?
4 Is the backing sufficient for accepting the warrant? Will the audience accept the backing? What further support for the warrant might be used?
5 Are the essential reservations stated? What other reservations might the audience think of that should be included here?

Using specific instances and generalization effectively

In reasoning from specific instances to general principles, you should stress in your speech that your specific instances are sufficient in number to warrant the conclusion you are drawing, that the specific instances are in fact representative of the whole, that your sample was not drawn disproportionately from one subgroup, and that there was an absence of significant exceptions. That is, you will be more convincing if you can answer the questions that an intelligent and critical listener will ask of your evidence.

In reasoning from general principles to specific instances you should make certain that the general principle is accepted by the audience. If it is not accepted, if it is not believed to be true, any attempt to use it as evidence concerning a specific instance will be doomed to failure. To say, "We all know that . . ." or "You and I believe that . . ." does not mean that the audience "knows that . . ." or "believes that . . . ." Considerable audience analysis must be conducted prior to using this type of argument. Clearly, the general principle must be accepted *before* you attempt to use it as a basis for a conclusion about an unexamined specific instance. If some members do not accept the principle, you must either use a different form of reasoning or spend some time convincing the audience of the truth of the principle. Similarly, as a speaker, you should stress that the specific instance clearly falls into the class covered by the general principle.

REMEMBER, in reasoning from a generalization to a specific instance, that:
1   the general principle should be true or at least probably true
2   the unknown or unexamined instance should be clearly a specific instance that falls under this generalization

And is most effective when:
3   the general principle is accepted by the audience

SOURCES

Most public speaking texts fail to do justice to argument and evidence in speech making; it is best to consult works in argumentation and logic. I would recommend the following: Craig R. Smith and David M. Hunsaker, *The Bases of Arguments: Ideas in Conflict* (Indianapolis: Bobbs-Merrill, 1972); Abne M. Eisenberg and Joseph A. Ilardo, *Argument: A Guide to Formal and Informal Debate*, 2d ed. (Englewood Cliffs, N.J.: Prentice-Hall, 1980); Douglas Ehninger and Wayne Brockriede, *Decision by Debate*, 2d ed. (New York: Harper & Row, 1978); Nicholas Capaldi, *The Art of Deception* (Buffalo, N.Y.: Prometheus Books, 1971); and Michael A. Gilbert, *How to Win an Argument* (New York: McGraw-Hill, 1979). Perhaps the best single source is Stephen Toulmin, Richard Rieke, and Allan Janik, *An Introduction to Reasoning* (New York: Macmillan, 1979).

Full texts of the speeches cited may be found in Thomas A. Vanderslice, "The Vital Need for Technology and Jobs," *Vital Speeches of the Day* 43 (December 15, 1976):150–154 and Ken Lonnquist, "Ghosts" in *Contemporary American Speeches*, 4th ed., Wil A. Linkugel, R. R. Allen, and Richard L. Johannesen, eds. (Dubuque, Iowa: Kendall/Hunt, 1978), pp. 176–181.

UNIT 17

Motivating behavior in persuasive speeches

OBJECTIVES

After completing this unit, you should be able to:

1 *explain the role of psychological appeals in motivating behavior*
2 *explain Maslow's hierarchy of motives*
3 *identify at least three principles of motivation and explain their relevance to the public speaking transaction*
4 *explain the operation of at least eight motivational appeals*
5 *explain the concept of psychological balance and its relevance to motivational appeals*

Persuasion is a most complex process. What persuades one person may have no effect on another. What persuades one person to vote for censorship may persuade another to campaign vigorously for the removal of all restrictions on free communication. What persuades one person to act immediately may persuade another to act two months or even two years later. There are differences and variations in all aspects and dimensions of persuasion.

Amid all these variations, it seems universally agreed that psychological appeals—the appeals to one's needs, desires, and wants—are the most powerful. Because of their importance, this entire unit is devoted to explicating the role of psychological appeals in public speaking. Specifically, four major issues are considered: First, the nature of psychological appeals; second, using theory and research in the psychology of motivation, a set of four principles and corollaries of motivation will be applied to public speaking; third, specific motivational appeals and how these may be used in public speaking; fourth, the theory of balance as it relates to persuasion through motivational appeals.

PSYCHOLOGICAL APPEALS

Psychological appeals are those appeals that are directed at an individual's needs, wants, desires, wishes, and so on. Although psychological appeals are never totally separate from rational appeals—appeals that are directed to one's reasoning and logic—they are considered separately here. We are primarily concerned here with motives, with those forces that energize or move or motivate a person to develop, change, or strengthen particular attitudes or ways of behaving. For example, one motive might be the desire for status; this motive might then move the individual to develop certain attitudes about appropriate and inappropriate occupations, the importance or unimportance of saving and investing money, and so on. It may move this person to behave in certain ways—to buy Gucci shoes, a Rolex watch, and a Tiffany diamond. It should be clear from these examples that this same status motive may motivate different persons in different ways. Thus, the status motive may lead one person to enter the poorly paid but respected occupation of nursing and another to enter the well-paid but often disparaged real estate or diamond business.

One of the most useful and insightful analyses of motives is Abraham Maslow's fivefold classification, reproduced in Figure 17.1. One of the as-

FIGURE 17.1   Maslow's "hierarchy of needs." (*Source:* Based on Abraham Maslow, *Motivation and Personality,* New York: Harper & Row, 1970.)

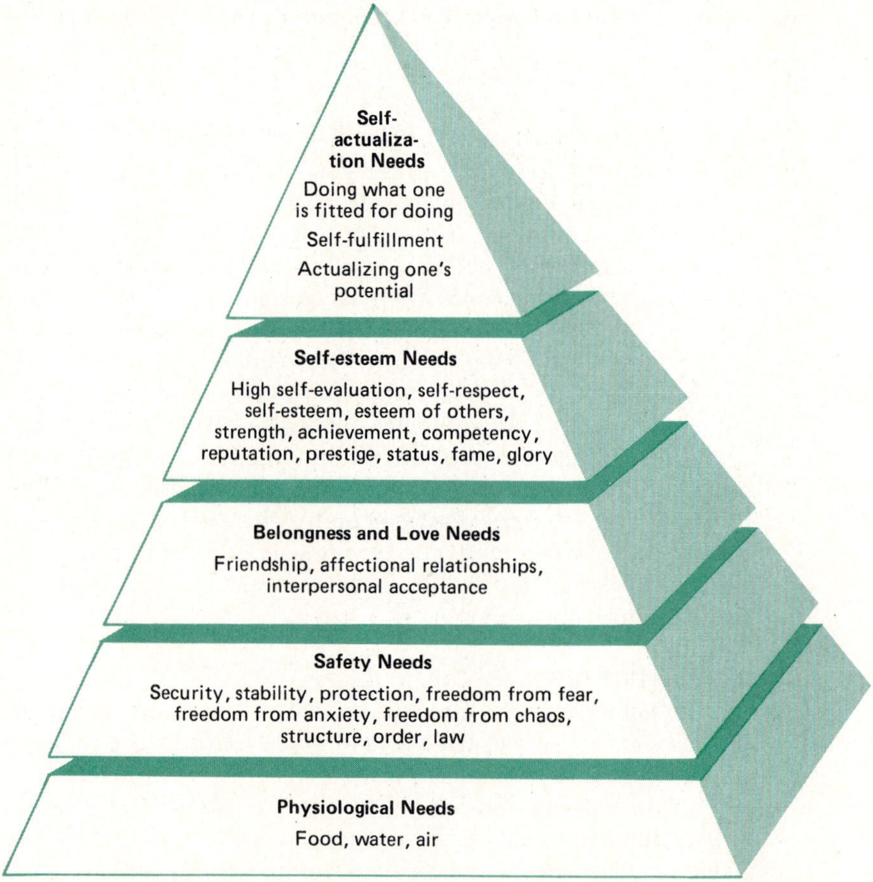

Self-actualization Needs
Doing what one is fitted for doing
Self-fulfillment
Actualizing one's potential

Self-esteem Needs
High self-evaluation, self-respect, self-esteem, esteem of others, strength, achievement, competency, reputation, prestige, status, fame, glory

Belongness and Love Needs
Friendship, affectional relationships, interpersonal acceptance

Safety Needs
Security, stability, protection, freedom from fear, freedom from anxiety, freedom from chaos, structure, order, law

Physiological Needs
Food, water, air

sumptions here is that people seek to fulfill the need at the lowest level first and only then the need at the next higher level. Thus, for example, people do not concern themselves with the need for security or freedom from fear if they are starving (that is, if their food need has not been fulfilled). Similarly, they would not be concerned with friendship or affectional relationships if their need for protection and security has not been fulfilled. I have appropriated the insights of Maslow—as well as of various other theorists and researchers—in the development of the principles of motivation that follow.

PRINCIPLES OF MOTIVATION

If you are to apply motivational appeals effectively to persuasion and in fact to all forms of public speaking, you will need to understand some basics of motivation and the ways in which motives operate. Here I attempt to cover some general principles of motivation as they relate to the public speaking process in general and to persuasion in particular. These principles should prove useful in understanding motivation, in applying motivational appeals in your public speeches, and in listening to and evaluating the speeches of others.

Before looking at these principles, recognize that motives are not illogical or irrational. Many theorists in persuasion assume that motives are the illogical side of discourse and behavior; they are not. They may, for convenience, be compared to and separated from arguments and evidence, but they are clearly not illogical. Rather, they are better thought of as "alogical" or "arational," that is neither logical nor illogical, neither rational nor irrational. In appeals to needs and desires you are not appealing to the individual's "animal nature"—whatever that may be. Rather, you are appealing to some very human dimensions—one's needs, desires, and wants. In fact, most of the motivational appeals discussed here are absent in animals.

Also, recognize that people frequently do not tell the truth about their motivations. Sometimes this lack of truth is due not to any intent to lie or mislead but to a lack of understanding of the significant relationships and patterns. At other times it is due to subconscious processes, such as rationalization. People may not want to think that they have done something out of selfish motive: People tell themselves (and believe) that they gave money to the charity collection in the office because they wanted to help the starving children, not because it was the boss's favorite charity and the boss was standing right behind them as they dug into their wallets. Sometimes, of course, people choose to lie; they do not want others to know why they have behaved in certain ways.

In attempting to connect motives and behaviors, you should question the flood of altruism that seems to break loose when people are asked their motives for various behaviors.

Motives differ

Motives are neither static nor do they operate in the same way with different people. Motives differ from one time to another and from one person to another.

Time differences   Motives change with time. Motives that are crucial to you at this time in your life and that motivate a great deal of your current thinking and behavior may not be operative in 10 or even 2 years. They may fade and others may take their place. Now, for example, attractiveness may be one of the more dominant motives in your life; you have a strong need to be thought attractive by your peers. Later in life this motive may be replaced by, for example, the desire for security, for financial independence, for power, or for fame. And, of course, the strength of the various motives changes. Whereas certain motives may be extremely strong now, they may play only secondary roles in later life.

Some motives may become functionally autonomous. Consider, for example, the poor person who has throughout life scrimped and saved. Now, however, the individual becomes wealthy—through saving, inheritance, or luck. Even though wealthy, the individual still saves and still scrimps as before. The saving behavior which was at one time motivated by real and present motives—the need to survive, perhaps—is now self-motivating. A frequently encountered example is the professor who writes and conducts research to gain tenure and promotion, but when tenure and the full professorship do come, the writing and the research do not stop. They have in many cases become self-motivating—they have become an integral part of this individual. Frequently, of course, different motives take over. Where, for example, at one time it was the desire for job security that motivated the research, now it may be a desire for increased status—to see one's name in print—or for the influence that writing may enable one to achieve.

People differences   Motives function differently with different people. This is simply a specific application of the general principle: People are different. No two people are the same. Consequently, different people will respond differently to the very same motive. Further, different motives in different people may lead to the same behavior. Thus, three persons may choose to become college professors—one because of its security, one because of its relative freedom, and one because of its status. The resultant behavior in all three cases is essentially the same but the motivational histories are very different.

Because of this you need to rely not on the appeal to one motive but on appeals to a number of different motives that acknowledge the differences among people.

Motives are ordered

Not all motives are of equal intensity—some are particularly powerful and exert a strong influence on behavior. Others are less powerful and may influence behavior only slightly. Further, motives may be ordered in terms of their degree of generality or specificity.

Strong and weak motives   Motives exist in varying degrees of intensity. Some motives are strong, others are weak, and the vast majority are somewhere in between. To complicate matters a bit more, the intensity of the various motives will vary from one time to another and from one communication situation to another. Motivational intensity may be measured in various ways. For example, you may examine the choices that people make and infer that these choices are indicative of how strongly they are motivated by a certain issue. Imagine yourself being offered two jobs; one job offers a high degree of security but little money whereas the other offers little security but big money. The choice that you make may then be used to infer the relative strength of the security and the financial-gain motives. Another indicator of motivational intensity is the degree of punishment you will endure to gain the desired goal. How much abuse will you take to realize a particular desire? How much ridicule will you take from peers before dropping plans to date or marry a particular individual? How much punishment will James Bond take before he capitulates and gives Dr. No or Goldfinger what they want?

Since motives vary in intensity and strength, they vary in the influence they have on the individual. It is obvious that people will be influenced more by motives that are strong and less by motives that are weak. But determining which motives the audience holds strongly and which are weak is not easy; in fact, it may well be one of the most difficult tasks you face as a speaker and persuader. And yet if you are to identify those motives that will strongly influence the audience, you must focus on those that are especially potent, otherwise time will be wasted on motives ineffective in influencing behavior.

Maslow's hierarchy revisited   The notion of an ordered hierarchy of motives comes from the work of Abraham Maslow mentioned earlier. You will recall that in this system certain needs have to be satisfied before other needs can motivate behavior (Figure 17.1). Thus, for example, the physiological needs for food and drink and for safety have to be satisfied—at least to some extent—before others, such as affection or self-actualization, can function. Thus, the speaker must ascertain what needs of the audience have been satisfied and, therefore, what needs might be stimulated. In most college classrooms, for example, you may assume that the two lowest levels—physiological needs and safety needs—have been reasonably fulfilled. In many students, however, the third level (love needs) is not fulfilled, and propositions may be linked to these with great effectiveness. Thus, to assure the audience that what you are saying will enable them to achieve more productive interpersonal relationships or greater peer acceptance will go a long way to securing their attention and receptiveness.

If Maslow's concept of the hierarchical ordering of motives is correct, it would be of little value to appeal to the self-esteem needs if the belonging and love needs are not satisfied: these latter needs have to be satisfied before the higher level self-esteem (and self-actualization) need can motivate behavior.

Another implication is that satisfied needs cannot be further motivated. If the safety need of an individual is satisfied, that individual will not be motivated to seek further satisfaction of this need.

General and specific motives   Motives are general classes of needs, desires, wants, and the like. For example, the achievement motive may include a host of specifics which, when taken together, make up and define achievement for this specific individual. People are not motivated by appeals to abstract and general motives but rather to specific aspects or manifestations of these motives—a simple fact that most works in public speaking and persuasion fail to make clear. Thus, to appeal to status—defined in abstract and general terms—does nothing or at best very little to motivate specific attitudes and behaviors. Rather, you need to appeal to, for example, the desire to be recognized by others on the street, having a job that is respected by family and peers, having a home in an exclusive part of town, going to Europe on the QEII and returning on the Concorde, and so on. That is, you need to operationalize the general motive to a specific motive; generally, the more specific, the more effective the appeal. Consider, for example, the difference between the teacher's appeal to read this book because it will help to make you an educated person versus the appeal to read this book because it will help you to pass this course or the next test.

Motives interact

Motives rarely operate in isolation; usually a collection of motives operate together. Sometimes these motives operate in the same direction, all influencing behavior in the same way. At other times, motives conflict with one another, each stimulating behavior in somewhat different directions.

Motives in concert   Motives that affect behavior are usually multifaceted. Isolated motives—if such things exist—rarely (if ever) lead to behavior or attitude change. Rather, motives operate in packages, each reinforcing the other. In cases where a number of motives may influence behavior in the same direction (that is, where they operate in concert), the speaker should appeal to a number of motives rather than limiting the speech to just one. For example, if you want an audience to contribute money to space research, appeal to a variety of motives—loyalty to one's country, safety, curiosity, achievement, and the like. Of course, concentrate your energies on those motives that seem the most influential.

Motives in conflict   It would be convenient if all our motives energized us in the same direction and for the attainment of the same goal. But that is not the case, and that is why we experience conflicts. The major types of motivational conflicts that have been identified (and which you will remember from elementary psychology) are the approach-approach, approach-avoidance, and avoidance-avoidance conflicts. In the *approach-approach conflict* there are two desirable but mutually exclusive alternatives. You are motivated to approach both but can have only one. For example, you may be offered two excellent jobs: one may offer glamour and the other may offer security; you want both but can have only one. Or, you might want to take two excellent communication courses, but they meet at the same time and you can take only one. In the *approach-avoidance conflict* you have one alternative that is both desirable and undesirable. One motive leads you to approach it and one motives leads you to avoid it. Exercise is a common example: One motive (good health or an attractive body) may lead you to approach the exercise but one motive (physical discomfort) may lead you to avoid it. Or, the motive to lose weight, stay on your diet, and remain physically attractive may lead you to say no to the chocolate cake, but the motive to enjoy yourself may lead you to say yes. In the *avoidance-avoidance situation* there are two alternatives, both undesirable but one of which must be chosen. Thus, to get to San Antonio from New York there are two major alternatives—flying (fear may motivate you to avoid this alternative) and train or bus (time loss and physical discomfort may motivate you to avoid this alternative). And yet you have to get to San Antonio; one alternative has to be chosen. Or, you might have to choose between giving up your ski weekend to write a term paper or failing the course—two unpleasant alternatives but one of which must be chosen.

Motives operate in complex ways

The ways in which motives interact with attitudes and behaviors are not simple and not easy for any speaker to predict. For example, we cannot examine motivation and draw definite conclusions about attitudes and behaviors, nor can we examine attitudes and behaviors and draw definite conclusions about motives. Two corollaries related to motive complexity are noted here.

No one-to-one correspondence
There is no one-to-one correspondence between motive on the one hand and attitude and behavior on the other. You cannot look at various attitudes and behaviors, for example, and conclude with any degree of certainty what the individual's motives are—although psychiatrists have been attempting to do just this for the last hundred years or so with, it seems, random success. Conversely, we cannot examine motivation and conclude that, therefore, such-and-such behaviors or attitudes will be manifested. The relationship between attitudes and behavior on the one hand and motivations on the other do not allow a simple cause-effect explanation; such an explanation is totally inadequate for complex, mutually dependent relationships.

The implication of this for the speaker is that any attempt to reason from motive to behavior or from behavior to motive must be done in terms of probabilities, not certainties. You will have to make educated guesses as to what motives will work with which audiences and stimulate what behaviors. The more you know about your specific audience, the better these guesses are likely to be.

No simple equation Motivation does not guarantee action. A person may be motivated to engage in a specific bit of behavior and yet may not engage in the behavior. It is important to recognize therefore that there are factors other than motives operating here. Such behavior may not be emitted because it is inhibited due to some fear or anxiety. Behavior that is socially unacceptable is clearly and frequently of this type. You may be motivated to pick your nose or scratch various parts of your body but you control yourself because such behaviors are not socially acceptable. Similarly, you may be motivated to speak out against the KKK but may be inhibited because of fear that some harm may come to you. Frequently people may be motivated to behave in a certain way but will restrict the behavior to various contexts—for example, in private or when with selected close friends.

You may succeed in motivating an audience to engage in some behavior even though there is no evidence that the behavior is in fact emitted or going to be emitted in the future. This, as can be appreciated, poses special problems for the critic who wishes to evaluate the effectiveness of the speech and yet cannot find any evidence for the speaker's success.

REMEMBER the following principles of motivation:
1 **Motives differ from one time to another and from one person to another.**
2 **Motives are ordered, varying in intensity and in generality.**
3 **Motives interact, sometimes in concert and sometimes in conflict.**
4 **Motives operate in complex ways:**
   a. **There is no one-to-one correspondence between motive and attitudes/behaviors, and**
   b. **Motivation does not guarantee behavior**

MOTIVATIONAL APPEALS

In employing motivational appeals, you might address many specific motives. Naturally each audience will be a bit different and motives that are appropriately appealed to in one situation might be inappropriate or ineffective in another. You will always have to exercise judgment and taste. Here are just a few of the motives to which appeals may be made.

Altruism

Altruism, some would argue, does not exist. All our motives are selfish, they would say. And perhaps they are right. Any action, any belief, any attitude can usually be traced to a motive that might be regarded as selfish—to greed, to sensory pleasure, to personal power. But it is equally true that most of us want to believe that our motives are altruistic, at least sometimes. We want to do what we consider the right thing; we want to help others; we want to contribute to worthy causes. We want to help the weak, to feed the hungry, and to cure the sick. The fact that we might derive some kind of selfish pleasure from these actions does not militate against our viewing them as being motivated in part at least, by altruism. Appeals to altruism are most effective when done with moderation. If they are not moderate, they will seem unrealistic and totally out of touch with the way real people think in a world that is practical and difficult to survive in.

Fear

We are motivated in great part by a desire to escape from fear. We fear the loss of all those things that we desire; we fear the loss of money, of family, of friends, of love, of attractiveness, of health, of job, and, in fact, just about everything we now have and value. We fear punishment, rejection, failure. We also fear the unknown, the uncertain, the unpredictable.

The use of fear in persuasion has been studied extensively, and the results seem to indicate that moderate amounts of fear probably work best. With low levels of fear, the audience is not motivated sufficiently to act, and with high levels of fear they become too frightened to consider the speech at all and simply tune the speaker out.

A good example of the use of fear in persuasion can be seen in the American Express traveler's checks commercial where you are led to believe that if you lose traveler's checks other than American Express they will not be refunded. It was interesting to watch the counteradvertisements that First National City Bank launched protesting this American Express commercial. The later American Express commercials have Karl Malden add that refunds are made by other companies but that most persons prefer American Express. Nevertheless, the fear tactic remains in the main part of the commercial.

SEE
EXPERIENTIAL
VEHICLE 4.6.

The other side of fear is safety. We all have a need for safety. Maslow put safety at the second level, just above the satisfaction of the physiological need for food and drink. We want to feel protected, to be free of fear. Sometimes the safety motive is seen in the individual's desire for order, structure, and organization. We fear what is unknown, and order and structure make things predictable and, hence, safe.

Individuality and conformity

These two conflicting motives are discussed together because they are opposite sides of the same coin and often operate simultaneously—each pulling in a different direction and each functioning to lessen the effects of the other. Clearly, we have a need for uniqueness, for individuality; we want to stand out from the crowd; we want to be special. The fear of many people is to be lost in the crowd, to be indistinguishable from everyone else. And yet, we also want to conform, to be one of the crowd, to be "in." We want to be like those we admire and respect. Consider, for example, the way we dress, the way we talk, even the way we think and act. In large part we do what we do because we desire to conform to some standard or, perhaps,

HOW TO . . . Avoid Being Taken In

In *The Fine Art of Propaganda,* prepared for the Institute for Propaganda Analysis by Alfred McClung Lee and Elizabeth Briant Lee, seven propaganda devices are identified—seven ways in which the propagandist (the unethical persuader) attempts to gain our compliance without logic or evidence. These are devices we should be able to identify and not allow ourselves to be taken in by them.

1. NAME CALLING

Here the propagandist gives an idea, a group of people, or a political idelogy a bad name ("Communist," "Nazi") and in this way attempts to make us condemn the idea without analyzing the argument and evidence.

2. GLITTERING GENERALITY

This is the opposite of name calling. Here the propagandist attempts to gain our acceptance of some idea by associating it with things we value highly ("democracy," "Americanism"). By using "virtue words," the propagandist attempts to get us to ignore the evidence and simply approve of the idea.

3. TRANSFER

Here the propagandist associates his or her idea with something we respect (in order to gain our approval) or with something we detest (in order to gain our rejection).

4. TESTIMONIAL

This device involves using the authority of some person to gain our approval (if we respect the person) or our rejection (if we do not respect the person). This is the technique of advertisers who use testimonials of famous and well-liked people to get us to buy everything from toothpaste to cereal to designer jeans.

5. PLAIN FOLKS

With this propaganda device, the speaker identifies himself or herself and their propositions with the audience. The speaker and the proposition are good—the "reasoning" goes—because they are one of the people, just "plain folks" like the rest of us.

6. CARD STACKING

The persuader here selects only the evidence and arguments that build a case (even falsifies evidence and distorts the facts). Although there was a deliberate attempt to distort the available evidence or to select only that which would fit the speaker's conclusions, the "evidence" is presented as being a fair and unbiased representation.

wish to imitate some person we admire. Successful motivation, then, would consist of making the audience members see themselves standing out from the crowd but never as "outsiders," only as individuals who have a unique identification but who are nevertheless closely identified with the positively evaluated groups.

Power, control, and influence

We all want power, control, and influence. First, we want power over ourselves; we want to be in control of our own destinies, our own fate. We want to be responsible for our own successes and, to a lesser extent, for our own failures. As Emerson put it, "Can anything be so elegant as to have few wants, and to serve them one's self?"

We also want control over other persons. We want to be influential. We want to be opinion leaders. We want others to come to us for advice, for guidance, for instructions. (I think this is why the role of teacher is so appealing to so many people.) Similarly, we want to have control over events and things in the world; we want to control our environment. Practically every communication book designed for the popular market (that is, a non-textbook) emphasizes how the knowledge of communication will enable you to achieve power and control and influence—whether in sales, in work, or in love. Listeners will be motivated when they can see their power, control, and influence increase as a result of their learning what the speaker has to say or believing or acting as the speaker suggests.

Self-esteem and approval

"In his private heart," wrote Mark Twain, "no man much respects himself." And perhaps because of this, we all seem to have a powerful need to have a positive self-image, to see ourselves in the best possible light. We want to see ourselves as self-confident, as worthy and contributing human beings. Inspirational speeches, speeches of the "you are the greatest" type, never seem to lack receptive and suggestive audiences.

Self-esteem is, at least in part, attained through gaining the approval of others. We all want approval. College students, it seems, are especially concerned with peer approval, but you also want approval from your family, from your teachers, elders, and even children. Somehow the approval of others makes us feel positive about ourselves. If we are approved of by others, we assume that we must be deserving of such approval. Also, however, approval from others ensures our attainment of a number of related goals. For example, if we have peer approval, we probably also have influence. If we have approval, we will likely have some status. In relating your propositions to the audience's desire for approval avoid being too blatant and obvious. Few people want to be told that they need or desire approval. Many prefer to think that approval is fine but that one should not actively seek it. In most cases, it seems, the verbalization and the actual feeling differ considerably.

Love and affiliation

We are motivated to love and be loved. We want to be assured that someone (preferably lots of people) loves us. At the same time we want to be assured that we are capable of loving in return. As college students, many of you have probably not considered the possibility that you may not be loved or that you may not love in return. But some will not experience love. Love, it seems, is not for everyone and for some this causes no great problem— they are able to channel their energies into other areas and, in many cases, succeed extremely well, perhaps because their energies were more concentrated on, say, teaching or medicine or making money. For most persons, however, love and the pursuit of it occupy a considerable amount of time and energy. To the extent that you can teach your audience how to be loved and how to love, you will have not only an attentive but a most grateful audience.

We also want affiliation—friendship and companionship. We have a desire to be a part of a group despite our equally potent desire for independence and individuality. Notice that the advertisements for discos, singles bars, and dating services, and so on, will emphasize the need for affiliation, for companionship. On this basis alone they successfully gain the attention, interest, and participation of hundreds of thousands. Again, such affiliation seems to assure us that we are in fact worthy creatures. If we have friends and companions, surely we are people of some merit. In a survey of high school seniors entering college in the fall of 1979, "strong friendships" was rated as "extremely important" by 69 percent of the 17,000 students surveyed. "A good marriage and family life"—another example of an affiliative need—was the only life goal ranked higher than strong friendships; it was listed as "extremely important" by 79 percent of those surveyed. Further, when these students were asked what factors would contribute to future job satisfaction, 57 percent noted that a "chance to make friends" was "very important."

Achievement

We want to achieve in whatever we do. As students you want to be successful students; as a teacher and writer I too want to be successful. We want to achieve as friends, as parents, as lovers. This is why we read books and listen to speeches that purport to tell us how to be better achievers. Although achievement is, in part, a personal matter, we also want others to recognize our achievements as real and valuable. "Being successful in my work" was noted as "extremely important" by 63 percent of entering college students. In using the achievement motive, speakers should be explicit in stating how their speech, their ideas, and their recommendations will contribute to the listeners' achievements. If you tell the listeners how they can learn to increase their potential, earn better grades, secure more prestigious jobs, and become more popular with friends, you will have a highly motivated audience.

Financial gain

"Money," said George Bernard Shaw, "is the most important thing in the world. It represents health, strength, honor, generosity, and beauty as conspicuously as the want of it represents illness, weakness, disgrace, meanness, and ugliness. Not the least of its virtues is that it destroys base people as certainly as it fortifies and dignifies noble people." To some extent I suspect we are all motivated by the desire for financial gain—for what it can buy, for what it can do. We may be concerned with buying necessities, luxuries, or perhaps most importantly time—time to do the things we all want to do and not be tied to the pedestrian and the mundane, like ironing, washing, typing, painting, and so on. Advertisers know this motive well and will frequently get persons interested in their messages by using such key words as SALE, 50% OFF, SAVE NOW, and the like. All of these are appeals to the desire for money. Today, many students are choosing their majors and, in fact, their careers based on the money they promise. Accounting currently enjoys unprecedented popularity on college campuses largely because it offers a reasonably good opportunity for a well-paid job. English, history, and philosophy, on the other hand, are currently experiencing a severe decline. Clearly, this up-and-down pattern is related in large part to the job market and to potential salaries. Concern for lower taxes, for higher salaries, for fringe benefits are all related to the money motive. Show the audience that what you are saying or advocating will make them money and they will listen with considerable interest, much as they read the current get-rich-quick books that are flooding the bookstores.

Status

One motive that accounts for a great deal of our behavior—too much, some would argue—is our desire for status. In our society status is mainly measured by an individual's occupation and wealth. Often job and money are positively related; at other times they are not. Nevertheless, in most estimates of status, the two are significant. But we might mention other kinds of status. For example, there is that status that comes from competence on the athletic field, from excelling in the classroom, or from superiority on the dance floor. To be most effective, link your propositions with your specific audience's desire for status. Beginning college students give considerable attention to their future jobs but rank interest and the utilization of skills and abilities as more important than other qualities we normally think of as being part of status. For example, in a recent survey, 17,000 students were asked what would make for future job satisfaction. Of those qualities listed as "very important," 93 percent noted "interesting to do" and 74 percent noted "uses skills and abilities." On the side normally considered as qualities of status, a "chance to earn a good deal of money" was noted by 47 percent, "a job most people look up to, respect" by 37 percent, and "high status, prestige" by 36 percent. I suspect that these percentages change considerably with age, giving greater importance to status in the form of financial gain and societal approval.

Self-actualization

According to Abraham Maslow the self-actualization motive does not influence attitudes and behaviors until just about all other needs are satisfied. And since these other needs are very rarely all satisfied, the time spent appealing to self-actualization might better be spent on other motives. And yet, I suspect that regardless of how satisfied or unsatisfied our other desires are, we all have in some part a desire to self-actualize, a desire to become what we feel we are fit for. If we see ourselves as poets, we must write poetry; if we see ourselves as singers, we must sing; if we see ourselves as teachers, we must teach. Even if we do not pursue these as occupations, we nevertheless have a desire to write poetry, to sing, or to teach—even if only in our imaginations. A speech that appeals to self-actualization then, would probably be one that encouraged the listeners to strive for their highest ideals.

REMEMBER the usefulness of the following motives:
1 altruism
2 fear
3 individuality and conformity
4 power, control, and influence
5 self-esteem and approval
6 love and affiliation
7 achievement
8 financial gain
9 status
10 self-actualization

A QUESTION OF BALANCE

Balance theory, also referred to as consistency and homeostasis, offers another approach to motivation. The assumptions of balance theory are simple and intuitively satisfying. The general assumption of all balance theories is that there is a universal tendency to maintain balance. *Balance* might be defined as a state of psychological comfort in which your attitudes (and the objects and persons about which you have attitudes) are related as you would want them to be or as you would psychologically expect them to be. The alternative, *imbalance*, would then be defined as a state of psychological discomfort in which the attitudes and attitude objects are related in ways that are undesirable and psychologically unexpected. Let me make these two states more specific, and the intuitive appeal of this approach will become clear. If you love someone, you expect that person to love you in return. If that love is returned, you are in a state of balance. But if that love is not returned, you are in a state of imbalance or psychological discomfort. You expect your best friend to dislike your worst enemy. If this is the case, you are in a state of psychological harmony or balance. If, on the other hand, your friend likes your enemy, you are in a state of psychological discomfort or imbalance.

Three balanced states   The following three situations are representative of balanced states:

1   Well-liked Professor Schmedley favors positively evaluated marijuana reforms laws *(P + P)*.
2   Disliked Senator Millstone favors negatively evaluated capital punishment *(N + N)*.
3   Well-liked M. M. Birdfood dislikes the disliked W. W. Bigtoe *(P − N)* and vice versa *(N − P)*.

In the first example two positively evaluated objects (denoted by P) relate positively ("favors" denoted by +). You expect two positively evaluated objects to be positively connected. You expect two of your friends, for example, to like each other: P + P. In the second example, two negatively evaluated objects connect positively ("favors"). You expect two negatively evaluated objects to attract, to like each other. You expect two negatively evaluated objects (denoted by N), say two of your enemies, to like each other: N + N. In the third example a positively evaluated object relates negatively ("dislikes" denoted by −) to a negatively evaluated object. You expect a positively and a negatively evaluated object to be disconnected (or negatively related). You expect your friend to dislike your enemy: P − N.

Three unbalanced states   The following three situations represent states of imbalance or psychological discomfort. In such cases, individuals will be motivated to change their attitudes in order to restore balance.

1′   Well-liked Professor Schmedley argues against positively evaluated marijuana reform laws *(P − P)*.

2' Disliked Senator Millstone argues against negatively evaluated capital punishment $(N - N)$.

3' Well-liked M. M. Birdfood likes disliked W. W. Bigtoe $(P + N)$ and vice versa $(N + P)$.

In the first example, two positives are negatively related. Since you expect two positives to be positively related (as in the case of two friends liking each other), you are psychologically uncomfortable in this situation. In the second example, two negatives are negatively related. Since you expect two negatives to be positively related (as in the case of your two enemies liking each other), you are in a state of psychological discomfort. In the third example, a positive and a negative are positively related. Since you expect a positive and a negative to be negatively related (as in the case of expecting your friend to dislike your enemy), you are in a state of imbalance.

The motivation to restore balance

A state of imbalance creates motivation to change attitudes. Consider the three imbalanced situations. In the first you might restore psychological comfort by changing your attitudes toward Professor Schmedley or toward marijuana reform laws. Or you might even change your perception of the connection between the two positively evaluated objects and say, for example, that the good professor objects publicly but privately favors such laws. Any one of these changes would produce a balanced state. Note, however, that two changes would only produce another imbalanced state. For example, if you changed your attitude toward both the professor and the reform laws you would have two negatives negatively connected, $N - N$, another imbalanced state.

In the second example you might change your negative evaluation of the senator to a positive one or your negative attitude toward capital punishment to a positive one, or you might perceive the negative connection between the two as somehow not being accurate and come to believe that there is really a positive connection between these two negative objects.

In the third example you can change your evaluation of either one of the elements (either toward Birdfood or toward Bigtoe) or, as in the previous examples, question the connection between the two attitude objects.

Implications for persuasion

Balance theory has a number of significant implications for the public speaker attempting to persuade an audience.

Imbalance as motivation   A person is only motivated to change attitudes and behaviors when she or he is in a state of imbalance. When a person is in a state of balance there is no motivation to change; all is comfortable (just as the satiated individual does not seek food). You will succeed in changing the attitudes of the audience only to the extent that you create a state of imbalance or psychological discomfort and show them that acceptance of your propositions will restore balance or psychological harmony.

Audience analysis as prerequisite   You must thoroughly know the audience's attitudes and the connections they perceive among various attitude objects. It would be impossible to use the credibility of, say, Senator Milktoast without first knowing what attitudes the audience holds toward the senator. Thorough audience analysis must precede any attempt to utilize the principles of balance to motivate attitude and behavior change.

Creating associations   You have two basic alternatives to gain acceptance for a proposition or point of view. First, you could associate the proposition positively with some positively evaluated source. That is, you could create a positive bond between an already positively evaluated source and your proposition. Thus, this pattern would be in a state of balance if your proposition were positively evaluated: $P + P$. A second alternative is to associate negatively your proposition with some negatively evaluated source. For example, you would create a negative bond between an already negative source and your proposition, that is, that the senator dislikes your proposition. This pattern would be in a state of balance if your proposition were positively evaluated: $N - P$.

If, on the other hand, you are arguing against a particular proposition or point of view, that is, if you want to create a negative attitude toward a certain issue, you again have two alternatives. First, you might create a positive bond between an already negatively evaluated source and your proposition, leading to a state of balance if your issue is negatively evaluated: $N + N$. Second, you might create a negative bond between an already positive source and the issue you wish the audience to feel negatively about. This too would create a balanced state: $P - N$.

You probably utilize these very principles every day when you attempt to persuade someone to think or behave in a certain way. Consider, for example, trying to convince a friend to take a particular course with you. Although the specifics might differ from one person to another and from one situation to another, the general pattern would probably be to create a positive connection between this course and some other positively evaluated attitude objects. You might say, for example, that other students rated the course as excellent; this would produce a balanced state if the course were evaluated positively as well: other students (P) rated highly $(+)$ this course (P). If you want someone to stay away from a particular person, for example, you might attempt to create a positive connection between this person and some negatively evaluated object—for example, you might argue that this individual has been responsible for the mistreatment of numerous animals or has been "bad-mouthing" you and your friends. Such an argument would positively connect a negative (mistreatment of animals) with this particular person. The pattern would be in a state of balance if this person were negatively evaluated $(N + N)$.

Restoring balance   If you create imbalance in the minds of the audience, you should seek to provide specific and immediate restoration of balance through the acceptance of your proposition or thesis. The reason you create imbalance in the minds of the audience is so that they will seek balance restoration from you and your proposition. Some years ago, for example, people were frightened about atomic attacks, radiation, and the like. They were put into a state of imbalance; they and their families (P) were positively associated with attack and radiation (all N). The balance restorer was the bomb shelter which functioned to change the positive connection to a negative one. We and our families would not be connected to radiation; the resultant pattern was a balanced one: $P - N$.

SEE
EXPERIENTIAL
VEHICLE 4.7.

We see this same principle operate today in all aspects of persuasion. We are told, for example, that our energy resources are being depleted and that we will in effect soon be positively connected to all sorts of negative consequences. The pattern is that we (P) will be positively related ($+$) to the negatives of high costs of energy and the lack of available energy and, hence, the lack of comfort in the heat and the cold (all N). Clearly this is a case of psychological discomfort ($P + N$). The balance restorer is to save energy. In this way the positive connection to all these negatives will be eliminated or changed to a negative ($P - N$). In fact, you could probably find this basic pattern in every effective persuasive speech, regardless of the specific topic, the audience to which it was addressed, when the speech was constructed, or whether or not the speaker consciously understood anything about motivation.

REMEMBER the role of the theory of balance for the persuasive speaker:

1   People are only motivated to change their attitudes and behaviors when they are in a state of imbalance.

2   In order to utilize the insights of balance theory in persuasion, you must be familiar with the audience's attitudes and the connections they perceive among attitude objects.

3   In order to gain acceptance, two general procedures may be followed:
   a. associate your proposition with positively valued objects, or
   b. disassociate your proposition from negatively valued objects.

4   In order to create a negative attitude, two general procedures may be followed:
   a. create a positive relationship between an already negatively evaluated object and your proposition, or
   b. create a negative relationship between an already positive object and the proposition you wish the audience to evaluate negatively.

5   When imbalance is created in the minds of the audience, the effective speaker provides specific and immediate restoration of balance through the acceptance of his or her proposition.

SOURCES

For psychological appeals, works on persuasion will help more than most public speaking textbooks. Patricia Niles Middlebrook, *Social Psychology and Modern Life* (New York: Knopf, 1974) covers motivational appeals most thoroughly and provides an excellent summary of research. For the system proposed by Abraham Maslow, see his *Motivation and Personality* (New York: Harper & Row, 1970). Herbert Simons provides a useful summary and analysis of motivational theories in his "Psychological Theories of Persuasion," *Quarterly Journal of Speech* 57 (December 1971):383–392. Wayne N. Thompson, *The Process of Persuasion: Principles and Readings* (New York: Harper & Row, 1975) reprints some seminal works on motivation and persuasion and provides a useful analysis of these and current research. For the study on student values see Jerald G. Bachman and Lloyd D. Johnston, "The Freshmen, 1979," *Psychology Today* 13 (September 1979);79–87. An excellent up-to-date overview of theories and research in persuasion is provided by Stephen W. Littlejohn, *Theories of Human Communication*, 2d ed. (Belmont, Calif.: Wadsworth, 1983), pp. 133–158. For a more detailed presentation see Mary John Smith, *Persuasion and Human Action* (Belmont, Calif.: Wadsworth, 1982).

UNIT 18

Special types of speeches

OBJECTIVES

After completing this unit, you should be able to:

1 *explain the nature and purpose of the speech of introduction*
2 *explain at least three principles to follow and three pitfalls to avoid in the speech of introduction*
3 *explain the nature and purpose of the speech of presentation or acceptance*
4 *explain at least three principles to follow and three pitfalls to avoid in speeches of presentation and acceptance*
5 *explain the nature and purpose of the speech to secure good will*
6 *explain at least two principles to follow and two pitfalls to avoid in the speech to secure good will*
7 *explain the nature and purpose of the speech of tribute*
8 *explain at least two principles to follow and two pitfalls to avoid in the speech of tribute*

Thus far informative and persuasive speeches have been emphasized. These are clearly the most common and the most important in our culture and in our time. But there are other speeches that are traditionally grouped as "special occasion" or "ceremonial" speeches. These are, in part, speeches of information and, in part, speeches of persuasion. They are reviewed separately largely because their purposes are a bit more limited in scope. Writers identify and classify these speeches in different ways: as speeches of introduction, courtesy, tribute, good will, nomination, self-justification, and entertainment. I will identify and explain what are, for our purposes, the four main types of special occasion speeches: (1) the speech of introduction, whether of a speaker or of a general topic area as in a symposium; (2) the speech of presentation or acceptance; (3) the speech designed to create good will, which includes not only the securing of good will for others (for example, institutions, companies, professions, and the like) but also for the securing of good will for oneself—what some writers have called the speech of self-justification; and (4) the speech of tribute, for example, the eulogy, the farewell, the dedication, and the commemoration. We will review, for each of these types, first its nature and purpose, second, some principles to follow in the construction and presentation of the speech, and third, some pitfalls or common faults to be avoided.

THE SPEECH OF INTRODUCTION

Nature and purpose

The speech of introduction is usually designed to introduce another speaker or to introduce a general topic area and a series of speakers. Often, for example, before a speaker addresses an audience another speaker sets the stage by introducing both the speaker and the general topic that will be addressed. At conventions, where a series of speakers address an audience, a speech of introduction might introduce the general topic on which the speakers will focus and perhaps provide connecting links among the several presentations.

The general purpose of the speech of introduction is to gain the attention and to arouse the interest of the audience for the speaker and the topic. It should pave the way for favorable and attentive listening. It should seek to establish an atmosphere conducive to achieving this particular speech purpose.

The speech of introduction is basically informative and follows the general patterns already laid down for the informative speech. The main difference is that instead of concentrating on the issues or dimensions of an area or topic from your point of view, you focus on the topic in the way the main speaker would approach it.

Principles to follow

In the speech of introduction, these four general principles should be followed.

Establish the significance of the speech Perhaps the major concern of the speaker introducing another speaker is to establish the importance, relevance, and timeliness of the impending speech to this specific audience, thereby gaining the audience's attention and interest in the main speaker.

Establish relevant connections In the speech of introduction you should establish a connection or a relationship among the essential elements in the public speaking act. At a minimum these would include connections among the speaker, the topic, and the audience. That is, you should answer the implicit questions of the audience: Why listen to this speaker on this topic? Why is this speaker appropriate to speak on this topic? What do we (the audience) have to do with this speaker and this speech topic? If you can satisfactorily answer such questions, you will have done your job of establishing a ready and receptive audience for the speaker.

Stress the speaker's credibility Make a special effort to establish the main speaker's credibility. The speech of introduction is the ideal opportunity to present those accomplishments of the speaker that the speaker could not mention with modesty. A review of the factors or dimensions of credibility (see Unit 4, "Public Speaking Ethics and Credibility") should prove useful in suggesting how to establish the speaker's credibility. The most general guideline to use here is to try to answer the audience's question: What is there about this speaker that has earned her or him the right to speak on this topic, to this audience? In answering this question, you will inevitably establish the speaker's credibility.

Be consistent with the main speech   The speech of introduction should be consistent in style and manner with the major speech. To introduce a speaker on terminal diseases in a humorous and flippant style would clearly be inappropriate. Conversely, to introduce a humorist in a somber and formal style would be equally inappropriate. In judging style and manner, predict the tone that the main speech will take. As you answer an invitation with the same degree of formality with which it is extended, you introduce a speaker with the same degree of formality that will prevail during the actual speech. This is only fair—the speaker should not need to eradicate an inappropriate atmosphere created by the speech of introduction. To ensure that your speech of introduction will be appropriate in style and tone, question the speaker prior to the engagement. In fact, it is always desirable to ask the speaker if there is anything that should or should not be mentioned in the speech of introduction. It is not only courteous but will also prove helpful and effective. Much as the speech of introduction should be consistent in tone with the main speech, it should also be appropriate to you as a person. If, for example, you are introducing a humorist but are yourself not very good at being funny, do not try to be—nothing is worse than an inept comedian. Just be yourself, adopt a relatively neutral manner, and let Bob Hope get his own laughs.

Pitfalls to avoid

Here are a few of the more common faults or pitfalls that speakers encounter when they introduce another speaker. These pitfalls should be easier to avoid once they have been identified and reviewed here.

Don't air your own views   Don't use this occasion as a forum to air your own views. If your function is to introduce the speaker, introduce the speaker—not your own views, theories, assumptions, and differences.

Don't cover the speaker's topic   Don't cover the substance of the topic or what the speaker will discuss. Sometimes the person giving the speech of introduction gets carried away because of their own interest in the topic and constructs a speech that only incidentally introduces the speaker and primarily discusses the topic on which the main speaker is planning to speak. Clever stories, jokes, startling statistics, or historical analogies, which are often effective in speeches of introduction, will prove a liability if this material was to be used by the speaker. It is not uncommon to find a speaker without an introduction or a conclusion because the material was used in the speech of introduction. If you have any doubts, check with the speaker well in advance of the actual speech. In this way you will avoid duplicating and embarrassing the speaker and yourself.

Don't oversell the speaker   Speakers giving introductions have a tendency to oversell the speaker, the topic, or both. The speech of introduction should be complimentary but should not create an image impossible to live up to. To say, for example, that "Morso Osrom is not only the world's greatest living expert on baldness but a most fascinating, interesting, and humorous speaker as well" only adds difficulties to the speaker's task. It would be better to let the speaker demonstrate his or her own communicative abilities. The same is true for the topic. To say that "this is the most important topic today" or "without the information given here we are sure to die paupers" will only encumber the speaker by setting unrealistic expectations for the audience.

SEE
EXPERIENTIAL
VEHICLE 4.8
Be brief   Remember that the audience has come to hear the main speaker and that your function is simply to introduce the speaker. In actual practice speeches of introduction vary considerably in length—from "Ladies and Gentlemen, the President" to pages and pages. You will have to judge how long is long enough. If the main speech is to be brief—say, 10 or 20 minutes—your speech of introduction should be no longer than 1 or 2 minutes. If, on the other hand, the main speech is to be at least an hour long and your speech of introduction is also commendatory, then it might last 5 or 10 minutes or even longer. In all cases, however, keep clearly in mind that the audience has come to hear the main speaker, not you. It might help to visualize yourself as a member of the audience listening to your own speech of introduction. How much would you want to hear?

REMEMBER, in the speech of introduction, to:
1   establish a connection or relationship among speaker, topic, and audience
2   establish the speaker's credibility
3   be consistent in style and manner with the major speech

And to avoid:
4   using the occasion to air your own views
5   covering what the speaker intends to discuss
6   overselling the speaker
7   taking too much time

THE SPEECH OF PRESENTATION OR ACCEPTANCE

Nature and purpose

Speeches of presentation and speeches of acceptance are considered together because they frequently occur together or very close to each other in time, and because the same general principles seem to govern both types of speeches.

The speech of presentation is designed (1) to place the award or honor in some kind of context and, at the same time, (2) to give the award a little extra air of dignity or status. Speeches of presentation may be of various types and may focus on rewarding a colleague for an important accomplishment (Teacher of the Year) or recognizing a particularly impressive performance (Academy Award winner); it may honor an employee's service to a company or a student's outstanding grades and athletic abilities.

The speech of acceptance is the counterpart to this honoring ceremony. Here the recipient accepts the award and also attempts to place the award in some kind of context. At times the presentation and the acceptance speeches are rather informal and amount to a simple "You really deserve this" and an equally simple and direct "Thank you." At other times, as, for example, in the presentation and acceptance of the Nobel Prize, the speeches are formal and are prepared in great detail and with great care. These speeches are frequently reprinted in newspapers and books throughout the world. Somewhere in between these two extremes lies the average speeches of presentation and acceptance.

Principles to follow

In the speech of presentation there are two main principles to follow.

State the reason for the presentation   As the presenter you should make clear to the audience why this particular award is being given to this particular person. If the scholarship is being awarded for the best athlete of the year, then say so. If the gold watch is being awarded for 30 years of faithful service, say this.

State the importance of the award   The audience (as well as the group authorizing or sponsoring the award) will no doubt want to hear something of the importance of the award. You can relay this in a number of different ways. For example, you might refer to the previous recipients (assuming they are well known to the audience), the status of the award (assuming that it is a prestigious award), its influence on previous recipients, and so on.

Three general principles should be considered in preparing and presenting your speech of acceptance.

Thank those who selected you for the award   Thank the people responsible for sponsoring and awarding you the award—the Academy members, the board of directors, the student body, your fellow teammates, and so on.

Acknowledge others who helped   Much as an author will thank those persons who helped her or him in the writing of a particular book (see, for example, the acknowledgments in the Preface of this book), the award recipient should thank those instrumental in achieving the award. In thanking such people, be specific without boring the audience. It is not necessary to detail exactly what each person contributed but it is interesting to the audience to learn, for example, that Pat Tarrington gave you your first role in a soap opera or that Chris Willis convinced you to play the role in this film that led to an Academy Award.

Convey your feelings   Put the award into a personal perspective. Tell the audience what the award means to you right now and perhaps what it will mean to you in the future. Allow the audience a personal closeness to you that they might not have experienced otherwise.

Pitfalls to avoid

Speeches of presentation and acceptance have similar pitfalls that you will want to avoid.

Don't miscalculate the importance of the award   While you should neither underestimate nor overestimate the importance or significance of an award, it seems that most speakers err in the direction of exaggeration. When this is done the presenter, the recipient, and the entire situation can appear ludicrous. Be realistic. A good guideline to follow is to ask yourself what this award will mean next year or 5 years from now to these very same people. Will they remember it? Will it have exerted a significant influence on their lives? Will the local or national newspapers report it? Is it a likely item for a television spot? Obviously, the more questions you answer "yes," the less likelihood of your exaggerating. The more "no" answers, the more reserved you need to be.

Don't be long-winded   Few people want to hear long speeches of presentation or acceptance. Normally, these awards are given at dinners or at some other festive functions and people are generally anxious to get on with other activities—eating, playing ball, or whatever. Of course, if there are many awards to be given out on this same occasion, then you have added reason to be especially brief. We see this very common-sense principle violated yearly on the Academy Awards show. Generally, the length of the speech should be proportional to the importance of the award. Awards of lesser importance should be presented and accepted with short speeches; awards of greater significance may be presented and accepted with longer speeches. Be especially careful when acknowledging those who helped you. Do not include everyone you have ever known. Select the most significant ones and identify these. Everyone knows that there were others who influenced you, so it is unnecessary to state the obvious: "And there are many others too numerous to mention who helped me achieve this wonderful award."

Don't talk in platitudes and clichés   Platitudes and clichés abound in speeches of presentation and acceptance. Be especially careful not to include expressions that will lead your audience to think that this is a canned presentation and that the entire ceremony is perfunctory. Obvious examples to avoid are: "This speaker is so well known that no introduction is nec-

SEE
EXPERIENTIAL
VEHICLE 4.9.

A cliché is an overused phrase that has lost its novelty, its vitality, and part of its meaning and that calls attention to itself because of its overuse—it is an expression you will want to avoid in your speeches. Here is a sampling of clichés to be avoided.

The whole ball of wax
By hook or by crook
In this day and age
Sweet as sugar
Happy as a lark
Busy as a bee
Tall, dark, and handsome
Tell it like it is
Black as coal
Free as a bird
In the pink
No sooner said than done
Tried and true
The grass is always greener
Cool as a cucumber
With bated breath
Pretty as a picture
Last but not least
Work like a dog
Right as rain
To all intents and purposes
Quick as a flash
Hard as a rock
It goes without saying
Few and far between
No sooner said than done
From the ridiculous to the sublime

essary'' or ''I really don't deserve this award'' or ''There is no one more deserving of this award than this year's recipient.'' If you wish to express these same sentiments, word them so that they do not appear so trite that the audience focuses attention on the style of your speech rather than on its content.

REMEMBER, in the speeches of presentation and acceptance, to:
1   state the reason for the presentation
2   state the importance of the award being presented

3 express thanks to those who gave you the award
4 acknowledge others who helped you achieve the award
5 indicate the meaning of the award to you

And to avoid:
6 overestimating or underestimating the importance of the award
7 giving too long a speech
8 talking in platitudes and clichés

THE SPEECH TO SECURE GOOD WILL

Nature and purpose

The speech to secure good will is a most peculiar hybrid; it is part information and part persuasion and it is difficult to determine where information ends and persuasion begins. In fact, the strength of the good will speech often depends upon the extent to which the information and the persuasion function are blurred in the minds of the audience.

On the surface, the speech to secure good will functions to inform the audience about a product, company, profession, institution, way of life, or person. (When this "person" is the speaker, we often refer to this as a speech of self-justification.) Beneath this surface, however, lies a more persuasive purpose: to heighten the image of a person, product, or company—to create a more positive attitude toward this person or thing. Many speeches of good will—all such speeches, some would argue—have a still further persuasive purpose: to get the audience to ultimately change their behavior toward the person or company. That is, such a speech functions to create good will but invariably also functions to alter behavior; the securing of good will and the changing of behavior are not, in reality, separable.

Speeches of good will abound. Consider, for example, IBM's television advertising. They do not attempt to sell computers or to get the audience to buy IBM stock—at least not directly. Instead, their advertising time provides you with information on the company—on its research, on its contributions to making life easier, on its recent advances in communication and information storage and retrieval. On the surface, the speech is one of information; IBM is informing the audience about the workings of the company. But the purpose does not end there. Another purpose is to get us to feel more positively about IBM, to develop a more positive image of the company. Still another purpose would be to get us to change our behaviors toward that company—for example, to buy an IBM typewriter (even though typewriters might never have been mentioned in the advertisement), to purchase stock in the company (look at their research and their recent advances), and perhaps to select an IBM computer over others (again, not mentioned specifically).

A good example of the speech to secure good will is the advertisement for Gannett which appears on the opposite page. Notice that in this ad there is nothing that tells you to buy the product or to advertise in it; it focuses instead on associating Gannett with positive values. From reading this we clearly feel more positively about Gannett.

A variant of the speech to secure good will is the speech of self-justification, where the speaker seeks to justify his or her actions to the audience. Political figures do this constantly. Richard Nixon's "Checkers Speech," his Cambodia-bombing speeches, and, of course, his Watergate speeches are clear examples of self-justification. Edward Kennedy's Chapaquiddick speech, in which he attempted to justify what happened when Mary Jo Kopechne drowned, is another example.

Whenever there is a significant loss of credibility, the speaker will be called upon to offer a speech of self-justification. As any political leader's image goes down, the frequency of the self-justifying speeches goes up.

Principles to follow

In attempting to secure good will, whether for some other individual or group of persons or for yourself, the following principles should prove helpful. Remember that the audience very likely wants to entertain positive feelings because they are easier to deal with and are more pleasant. Your main function then is to give the audience reason to feel good will toward you or your company, profession, and so on.

Demonstrate the contributions that deserve good will   Most importantly, demonstrate to the audience how they may specifically benefit from this company, product, person, and so on or, at least (in the speech of self-justification), how they have not been hurt or not hurt willfully. Often this is accomplished very obliquely. When IBM demonstrates that they have accomplished a great deal through research, they also stress implicitly and sometimes more directly that these developments make it easier to function in business or in the home. General Electric's "Progress is our most important product" is designed to secure good will and to demonstrate to the audience that the company has specifically benefited the audience—with more free time, less hard labor, and more accessible and inexpensive entertainment.

Stress uniqueness   In a world dominated by competition, the speech to secure good will must stress the uniqueness of the specific company, person, profession, and so on. It should be clearly distinguished from all others. Otherwise, any good will you secure will be spread over the entire field. IBM clearly distinguishes itself from all competitors, and A&P does not advertise the value of supermarkets in general but of A&P in particular.

Establish credibility   Speeches to secure good will must also establish credibility, thereby securing good will for the individual or commodity. To do so, concentrate on those dimensions of credibility discussed earlier. Demonstrate that the subject is competent, of good intention, of high moral

THE DOORS OF INJUSTICE

SENECA FALLS, New York—In 1976, an ex-policeman disappeared while fishing on Seneca Lake in Upstate New York. Two men were arrested and accused of his murder, even though the body was never found.

Carol Ritter, court reporter for Gannett Rochester Newspapers, went to cover the pretrial hearing for the accused.

When she arrived at the courtroom, Ritter and other reporters were barred from the hearing on the pretext that the accused would not be able to get a fair trial if the pretrial hearing was covered by the press.

The Gannett Rochester Newspapers strongly disagreed and challenged the judge's right to close the doors of justice to the people, including the press. They took that challenge to the Supreme Court of the United States.

Gannett believes no judge should have the right to shut the people and their free press out of such pretrial hearings, where an overwhelming majority of criminal prosecutions are resolved.

Can you imagine up to 90 percent of all court cases being settled in secret? Gannett could not. But on July 2, 1979, the Supreme Court ruled it could happen.

Gannett protests vigorously this abridgment of the First Amendment. Not only has the Court limited journalists' access to gathering and reporting the news for the public, but it has also trampled on the peo-ple's freedom to know, the cornerstone of our rights as a free people in a free society.

The freedoms of the First Amendment must be cherished, not shackled.

At Gannett, we have a commitment to freedom in every business we're in, whether it's newspaper, TV, radio, outdoor advertising or public opinion research.

And so from Burlington to Boise, from Fort Myers to Fort Wayne, every Gannett newspaper, every TV and radio station is free to express its own opinions, free to serve the best interests of its own community in its own way.

Gannett

A World Of Different Voices
Where Freedom Speaks

character, and so on. Who could not have good will toward such an individual, product, or business?

Pitfalls to avoid

The following are three faults found in many speeches designed to secure good will. Try actively to avoid them.

Don't be obvious   An ineffective good will speech is an obvious advertisement, an effective one is not—that is their main distinction. The effective good will speech looks, on the surface, very much like an objective informative speech; it will not appear to ask for good will, except on close analysis.

SEE
EXPERIENTIAL
VEHICLE 4.10.

Don't plead for good will   This admonition is especially appropriate in the speech of self-justification. Criers may achieve some goals, but in the long run they seem to lose out; few people want to go along with someone who appears weak. If you attempt to justify some action, justify it with logic and reason; do not beg for good will, demonstrate that it is due you. This may sound a bit like Madison Avenue, but there is no intention to mislead or to misrepresent facts. Nor is it to say that attempts to gain sympathy through various emotional means are unethical or ineffective. Rather, it is to suggest that most audiences are composed of reasonable people who prefer to act out of logic, who recognize that not everyone is perfect, and who are ready to establish or reestablish good will toward an individual.

Don't overdo it   Lastly, do not overdo it. Overkill is ineffective. You will turn off your audience rather than secure their good will. It is helpful in this respect to remember that your perspective and the perspective of your audience are very difficult. Your acquaintance with the product or company or profession may fully convince you of its greatness, but your audience does not have that acquaintance and, consequently, will not appreciate too many superlatives.

REMEMBER, in the speech to secure good will, to:

1   stress the benefits the audience members may derive from this product, person, or company
2   stress the uniqueness of this product, person, or company
3   establish your credibility and the credibility of the subject

And to avoid:

4   being obvious in your attempts to secure good will
5   pleading for good will
6   overdoing the superlatives

THE SPEECH OF TRIBUTE

Nature and purpose

The speech of tribute encompasses a wide variety of speeches. All, however, are designed to pay some kind of tribute to a person or event. They include:

the eulogy, designed to praise the dead; the farewell; the dedication; the commendation, praising some living person; and the commemoration of some particular event or happening.

The general purpose of the speech of tribute is to inform the audience of some accomplishment or of the importance of some event. It should also heighten the audience's awareness of the occasion, accomplishment, or person; strengthen or create positive attitudes; and make the audience more appreciative than they are at present. On the surface, then, the purpose is informative, but below the surface, it is persuasive.

Principles to follow

In the speech of tribute, these three principles should prove effective.

Involve the audience The speaker should attempt to involve the audience in some way. This is not always easy—some tributes seem to just involve the individual being praised and some abstraction such as history, posterity, or culture. It is the speaker's job here to make this history, posterity, or culture apply in specifics to the audience. That is, if a eulogy is given, the meaning and accomplishments of the individual being eulogized should be related to the specific audience. The audience members would rightly ask, "What did this person's life mean to me?" The speaker should answer this in some way. When an award is presented, stress the meaning for the audience members of the award or of the person's accomplishment.

State the reason for the tribute In addition, although this should not be your primary concern, you should give the audience some idea of why you are making this tribute. Oftentimes it is obvious; the teacher praises the student, the president congratulates the employee, the student eulogizes the teacher, and so on. The connections in these cases are obvious and when they are, they should not be belabored. But when they are not obvious to the audience, then some mention should be made of why you are the person giving this tribute.

Be consistent with the occasion The speaker should construct and present a speech that is consistent with the specific occasion. This does not mean that all eulogies must be somber or that all sports award presentations must be frivolous but only that the speech should not contradict the basic mood of the occasion.

Pitfalls to avoid

Avoid the following major problems in speeches of tribute.

Don't praise yourself Much as the speaker giving an introduction to another speaker should not use the time to air his or her own views, the speaker paying tribute to another should not deliver a tribute to oneself. You may wish to state, in a relatively objective manner why you are the chosen speaker, but it is not necessary to detail your own awards or accomplishments in paying tribute to someone else.

Don't go overboard   The speech of tribute records the positive and the speaker should indeed be positive. But don't go overboard and overplay the specific accomplishments of an individual, which is ineffective and dishonest. The person's accomplishments should be stated in proportion to the actual accomplishments. With some eulogies it is difficult to recognize the real person for all the unrealistic and undeserved (and dishonest) praise.

Don't qualify negatively   Do not qualify negatively; qualify positively. There are ways of qualifying what you want to say without appearing negative and in speeches of tribute this is especially important. Thus, the same information is communicated in each of the following two statements:

1   Although Franco Columbo is not the world's greatest bodybuilder, he is one of the top ten.
2   Franco Columbo is one of the top ten bodybuilders in the world.

SEE EXPERIENTIAL VEHICLE 4.11. Both statements say essentially the same thing but only the second one is really positive; the first is positive with a negative tone. Be particularly careful of terms such as *but, however, although, even though,* and so on because they may qualify the accomplishments of an individual in a negative rather than a positive manner. This admonition to qualify positively rather than negatively would seem obvious, and yet I have frequently heard students and teachers make such statements as "Although this paper was not the best I've seen, it was one of the best" or "Your speech was really effective but there were a number which were better." Would it not be just as easy (even easier) to say "This was one of the best papers I have seen" or "This speech was one of the most effective I have heard"?

REMEMBER, in the speech of tribute, to:
1   involve the audience in some way
2   state the reason for the tribute
3   deliver a speech that is consistent with the occasion

And to avoid:
4   using the time to praise yourself
5   praising the individual disproportionately
6   qualifying negatively

SOURCES

Most thorough public speaking textbooks discuss the speech for the special occasion. Perhaps the best single source for this type of speech is Clark S. Carlile, *Project Text for Public Speaking,* 4th ed. (New York: Harper & Row, 1981). Also excellent is Douglas Ehninger, Alan H. Monroe, and Bruce E. Gronbeck, *Principles and Types of Speech Communication,* 8th ed. (Glenview, Ill.: Scott, Foresman, 1978); Glenn R. Capp, G. Richard Capp, Jr., and Carol C. Capp, *Basic Oral Communication,* 3d ed. (Englewood Cliffs, N.J.: Prentice-Hall, 1981); and Donald C. Bryant, Karl R. Wallace, and Michael C. McGee, *Oral Communication: A Short Course in Speaking,* 5th ed. (Englewood Cliffs, N.J.: Prentice-Hall, 1982). Brief, popular, and sound discussions of a variety of special occasion speeches may be found in Leon Fletcher, *How to Speak Like a Pro* (New York: Ballantine, 1983).

HOW TO . . . Evaluate Your Purpose and Supporting Materials: Part Four Checklist

Yes No

☑ ☑ 1 Is the speech purpose appropriate to the speech situation?

☑ ☐ 2 Is the speech purpose phrased in specific terms, for example, in terms of behavioral objectives?

3 Did you follow the principles of information processing?:

☑ ☑   Did you limit the amount of information?

☑ ☑   Stress the relevance and usefulness of the information?

☑ ☑   Present information in a nonthreatening manner?

☑ ☑   Present information at the appropriate audience level?

☑ ☑   Relate new information to old?

☑ ☑ 4 Have you amplified your ideas with appropriate examples and illustrations?

☑ ☑   Testimony?

☑ ☑   Definitions?

☑ ☑   Statistics?

☑ ☑   Audiovisual aids?

5 Did you follow the principles of persuasion?:

☑ ☑   The credibility principle?

☑ ☑   The attractiveness principle?

☑ ☑   The selective exposure principle?

☑ ☑   The audience participation principle?

☑ ☑   The inoculation principle?

☑ ☑   The motivational principle?

☑ ☑   The magnitude of change principle?

☑ ☑ 6 Is your evidence recent?

☑ ☑   Is it corroborated by additional support?

☑ ☑   Is it based on unbiased sources?

☑ ☑ 7 Does your reasoning from analogy meet the tests of adequacy?

☑ ☑ 8 Does your reasoning from causes and effects meet the tests of adequacy?

☑ ☑ 9 Does your reasoning from sign meet the tests of adequacy?

☑ ☑ 10 Does your reasoning from specific instances and generalizations meet the tests of adequacy?

☑ ☑ 11 Is your evidence and argument presented effectively?

☑ ☑ 12 Have you made effective use of such motivational appeals as altruism; fear; individuality and conformity; power, control and influence; self-esteem and approval; love and affiliation; achievement; financial gain; self-actualization; and status?

☑ ☑ 13 Did your speech of introduction establish a relationship among speaker, topic, and audience?

☑ ☑   Did it establish your credibility?

☑ ☑   Did it maintain a consistency in style and manner with the major speech?

Yes	No	
■	■	Did it avoid using the occasion to air your own views?
■	■	Did it duplicate the main speaker's intended topic?
■	■	Did it avoid overselling the speaker?
■	■	Did it take up too much time?
■	■	14 Did your speech of tribute involve the audience?
■	■	Did it state the reason for the tribute?
■	■	Did it maintain a consistency with the occasion?
■	■	Did you avoid praising yourself?
■	■	Did you praise the individual out of proportion?
■	■	Did you qualify the tribute positively?
		15 Did your speech to secure good will give the audience reasons
■	■	to think positively?
■	■	Did it stress the uniqueness of this person or product?
		Did it establish your own credibility and the credibility of the
■	■	person?
■	■	Did you avoid being too obvious in securing good will?
■	■	Did you avoid pleading for good will?
■	■	Did you avoid generally overdoing the good will pitch?

EXPERIENTIAL VEHICLES FOR PART FOUR

4.1 AMPLIFICATION

Here are presented some rather bland, uninteresting statements. Select one of them and amplify it using at least three different methods of amplification. Identify each method used. Since the purpose of this exercise is to provide you with greater insight into forms and methods of amplification, you may, for this exercise, manufacture, fabricate, or otherwise invent facts, figures, illustrations, examples, and the like. In fact, it may prove even more beneficial if you went to extremes in constructing these forms of support.

1 Significant social and political contributions have been made by college students.
2 The Sears Tower in Chicago is the world's tallest building.
3 Dr. Kirk is a model professor.
4 My grandparents left me a fortune in their will.
5 The college I just visited seems ideal.
6 The writer of this article is a real authority.
7 I knew I was marrying into money as soon as I walked into the house.
8 Considering what that individual did, punishment to the fullest extent of the law would be mild.
9 The fortune teller told us good news.
10 The athlete lived an interesting life.

4.2 THE WELL-AMPLIFIED INFORMATIVE SPEECH

Prepare and present to the class an informative speech, approximately five minutes in length, in which you utilize at least three different forms of amplification and at least two different audiovisual aids. The topics may be drawn from those presented in Unit 2 or from those speech stimuli presented in Appendix C.

I wrote the following speech to illustrate the fallacies of reasoning discussed in Stuart Chase's excellent *Guide to Straight Thinking*. Read over this speech and try to identify as many reasoning fallacies as you can. It is not necessary that you know the technical names for these various fallacies; the important point is that you can identify when propositions or points of view are poorly or illogically supported and why they are poorly supported.

THE HONOR SYSTEM: AN EVIL IN DISGUISE

Yesterday the proposal to institute the honor system at Blake College was submitted and next week we are to vote on whether the proposal is to be accepted or rejected. Although everyone of us present knows quite well that the system would never work, let me give you a few reasons.

We've all had at least one course in philosophy, and we know that Plato, one of the most perceptive philosophers of all time, stresses repeatedly in the *Republic* the need for the teacher to exert vigilant control over the student. But Plato is not the only great mind to perceive this truism. Numerous other philosophers have repeated the same view—Isocrates, Cicero, and Quintilian are just a few of them.

Let us look for a moment at who is advocating the adoption of this system. Professors Morgan and Burnside are the system's two outstanding spokespersons. Both have been up before the board for subversive activities and we all know that Professor Morgan was denied tenure at Carlson College only a few years ago. Moreover, numerous communist schools have such a system and I for one do not wish to follow their practice. The next thing you know the cafeteria and book store will be organized under this system. And who could resist such temptation?

Now, our opposition says that we are being unprogressive. Yet they have repeatedly refused to appropriate enough money for new labs and equipment for the Physics and Chemistry Departments.

The honor system may work at some schools but not in others. Blake College is simply one where it will not work. The honor system is like a paste necklace—it looks good from a distance but when you get up close you can see how worthless it really is.

Last year this system was tried at Davidson College and it didn't work. If it couldn't work at Davidson then it surely won't work here at Blake. In fact, during the year the honor system was used at Davidson six students were expelled and four married couples were divorced.

spends more time with the kids than with Pat and frequently goes out after work with people from the office. Often, Chris has told me, they sit for hours without saying one word to each other.

4.5 MODELING AND ANALYZING AN ARGUMENT

This exercise is designed to provide you with an opportunity to work with the concepts of Toulmin's model of argument. Each student should select one of the ''claims'' listed below and construct and diagram an argument using Toulmin's system. Include all six parts of the argument: claim, data, warrant, backing, qualifier, and reservation. After each person has constructed and diagrammed one argument, the papers should be collected, randomized, and redistributed so that each student has a diagrammed argument developed by someone else. In groups of five or six (or with the class as a whole), each student should analyze the argument, evaluating its validity and its potential rhetorical effectiveness for an audience composed of students from your class. The five questions presented earlier may prove helpful.

CLAIMS

1 Senator Smiley should be reelected.
2 College football should be abolished.
3 Everyone has ESP.

4.6 CONSTRUCTING MOTIVATIONAL APPEALS

The *New York Post* (September 17, 1979, p. 19) reported that according to ''exhaustive studies,'' the 10 greatest sources of fear, in order of importance, are:

1 Fear of losing money or not making enough; 80 percent noted this financial fear.
2 Fear of losing their jobs; 74 percent noted this.
3 Fear of ill health; 69 percent cited fear of real or imaginary ailments.
4 Fear of negative personal appearance; 59 percent feared that their personal appearance might handicap their chances for success.
5 Fear of political developments; 56 percent cited the fear of taxes and various government trends.

6   Fear of incompatibility; 44 percent feared marital difficulties and general incompatibility.
7   Fear of lack of self-confidence; 40 percent feared not having enough self-confidence.
8   Fear of religious confusion; 37 percent worried about what they should believe in terms of religious and philosophical convictions.
9   Fear of sexual matters; 34 percent worried about sexual temptations or transgressions.
10 Fear of trouble with relatives; 33 percent feared difficulties with relatives.

Select one of the specific purposes and audiences noted below and develop a motivational appeal based on one or more of these fears. After constructing these appeals share the results of your labors with others, either in small groups or in the class as a whole. In your discussion you may wish to consider some or all of the following questions.

1   Why did you select the specific motivational appeal(s) you did?
2   Why did you assume that this (these) appeal(s) would prove effective with the topic and the audience selected?
3   How effective do you think such an appeal would be if actually presented to such an audience?
4   Might some of the appeals backfire and stimulate resentment in the audience? Why might such resentment develop? What precautions might be taken by the speaker to prevent such resentment from developing?
5   What are the ethical implications of using these motivational appeals?
6   What appeals to fear might prove more effective than the 10 noted here?
7   Where in the speech do you think you would place this (these) appeal(s)? In the beginning? Middle? End? Why?

PURPOSES

1   Marijuana should (not) be made legal for all those over 18 years of age.
2   Cigarette smoking should (not) be banned in all public places.
3   Capital punishment should (not) be law in all states.
4   Social Security benefits should be increased (decreased) by at least one-third.
5   Retirement should (not) be mandatory at age 65 for all government employees.

6   Police personnel should (not) be permitted to strike.
7   National health insurance should (not) be instituted.
8   Athletic scholarships should (not) be abolished.
9   Property taxes should be lowered (increased) by 50 percent.
10   Required courses in college should (not) be abolished.
11   Teachers should (not) be paid according to performance rather than (but according to) seniority, degrees earned, or publications.
12   Divorce should (not) be granted immediately when the parties request it.

AUDIENCES

1   Senior citizens of Metropolis
2   Senior Club of DeWitt Clinton High School
3   Small Business Operators Club of Accord
4   American Society of Young Dentists
5   Council for Better Housing
6   Veterans of Vietnam
7   Los Angeles Society of Interior Designers
8   Catholic Women's Council
9   National Council of Black Artists
10   Parent-Teachers Association of New Orleans Elementary Schools
11   Midwestern Council of Physical Education Instructors
12   Society for the Rehabilitation of Ex-Offenders

4.7 MOTIVATIONAL ANALYSIS AND THE SPEECH

This exercise focuses on the use of motivational appeal in a public speech. The general purpose of this experience is to provide you with an opportunity to gain greater insight into the structure and function of motivational appeals.

Select one of the speeches in Appendix D, "Speeches for Study and Enjoyment," and explain to the class in an informal talk of about five minutes the operation of psychological appeals in the speech.

The following questions may help to provide some structure for your analysis.

1   What is the primary audience for this speech? Is there a secondary audience? What specific message elements lead you to your conclusions?

2   What is the primary purpose of the speech? Is there a second-
    ary or tertiary purpose? What specific message elements lead
    you to your conclusion?
3   What motivational appeals did the speaker use? Altruism?
    Safety? Fear? Individuality and conformity? Power/control/in-
    fluence? Self-esteem? Affiliation? Love? Freedom? Achieve-
    ment? Curiosity? Approval? Financial gain? Self-actualization?
    Status?
4   Did the speaker make any attempt to create an imbalance and
    to restore balance? Explain.

4.8 THE SPEECH OF INTRODUCTION

Prepare a speech of introduction approximately two minutes in length.
For this experience you may assume that the speaker you introduce will
speak on any topic you wish. Do, however, assume a topic appropriate
to the speaker and to your audience—your class. You may wish to select
your introduction from one of the following suggestions:

1   Introduce a historical figure to the class.
2   Introduce a favorite or famous teacher.
3   Introduce a contemporary religious, political, or social leader.
4   Prepare a speech of introduction that someone might give to
    introduce you to your class.
5   Introduce your favorite author—alive or dead.
6   Introduce a famous media (film, television, radio, recording)
    personality—alive or dead.
7   Introduce a famous sports figure.

4.9 SPEECHES OF PRESENTATION AND ACCEPTANCE

Pairs of students should be formed. One student should serve as the
presenter and one as the recipient of a particular award or honor. The
two students can select a situation from the list presented below or
make one up themselves. The presenter should prepare and present a
two-minute speech in which she or he presents one of the awards to
the other student. The recipient should prepare and present a two-
minute speech of acceptance.

The situations noted below are purposely stated in rather general terms. The two students should specify in greater detail how they will define the nature and purpose of the award.

1   Full scholarship to college
2   Academy Award for best performance
3   Gold watch for service to the company
4   Athlete of the Year
5   Miss or Mr. America
6   Medal for bravery
7   $5 million for the college library
8   Award to the graduating senior with the highest grade point average
9   Award to the Mayor of Goatsville for greatest improvement in educational services
10 Book award
11 Mother (Father) of the Year award
12 Honorary Ph.D. in communcation for outstanding contributions to the art and practice of effective communication
13 "Rocky" award for greatest improvement
14 Award for outstanding achievement in architecture
15 Best-dressed student at the college
16 Congeniality award
17 Award for raising a prize hog
18 Award for a gold record
19 Man (Woman) of the Year
20 Award for outstanding contributions to the organization

4.10 THE SPEECH TO SECURE GOOD WILL

Prepare a speech approximately three to five minutes in length in which you attempt to secure the good will of your audience toward one of the following:

1   your college (here visualize your audience as high school seniors)
2   a particular profession or way of life (for example, teaching, religious life, nursing, law, medicine, bricklaying, truck driving)
3   this course (here visualize your audience as college students who have not yet taken this course)
4   the policies of a particular foreign country now in the news
5   a specific multinational corporation

1 Prepare a speech approximately three to five minutes in length in which you *welcome* one of the following persons to your college:

   a. a political official
   b. movie star
   c. a scientist
   d. an astonaut
   e. a visitor from another planet
   f. a famous athlete
   g   an author
   h. a criminal
   i. a millionaire
   j. a comedian

2 Prepare a *eulogy* approximately three to five minutes in length. Even if you select a person who has been dead for some time, the eulogy should be placed in the present. Focus on the contributions of this person to the present time and the present audience.

3 Prepare a speech approximately two minutes in length in which you make a *presentation*. Some suggestions are to present:

   a. a scholarship to a fellow student
   b. an Academy Award
   c. a Grammy
   d. an award to a favorite teacher of the year
   e. an award to an employee who is just retiring after 50 years of service to the company
   f. an award to Miss or Mr. Bodybuilder
   g. a substantial financial gift to a specific charity
   h. an award to one of your parents for Parent of the Year
   i. an award to a scientist for a recent and significant discovery or invention
   j. an award for Student of the Year

PART FIVE

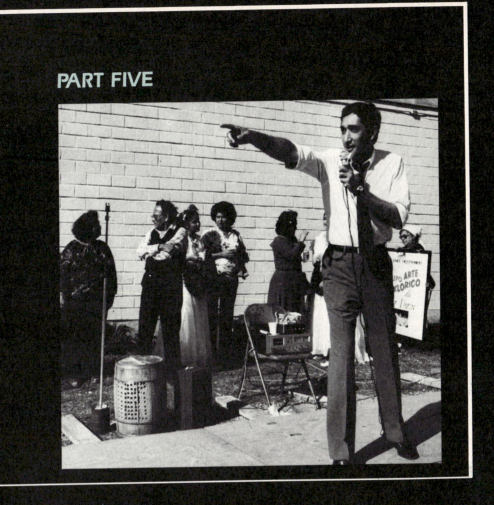

STYLE AND THE PUBLIC SPEECH

PART FIVE

UNIT 19

General principles of style

OBJECTIVES

After completing this unit, you should be able to:

1 *define and explain the principles of* abstraction, objectivity, *and* intensity *as they apply to language*
2 *define* denotation *and* connotation
3 *explain the major differences between oral and written style, as produced and as received*
4 *define and explain the characteristics of clarity, appropriateness, and interest as they relate to an effective public speaking style*
5 *identify at least three functions of humor in public speaking*
6 *explain at least four guidelines that should be applied in using humor in public speaking*

Style in public speaking refers to the words that you select to communicate your thoughts and the ways in which these words are arranged into phrases and sentences and, in turn, to the ways in which these phrases and sentences are arranged into longer units. Your selection and arrangement of words, phrases, and sentences are crucial factors in determining the success or failure of a public speech. Great ideas phrased in uninteresting or difficult to understand language will have little effect on the audience or may even have detrimental effects.

Four topics are the focus of this unit. First, how language works and the three general principles of language (abstraction, objectivity, and intensity) are explained so that you can get a better idea of how language operates and how it is best manipulated to serve your purposes. Second, the nature of oral style is considered and is distinguished from the style of the written composition or essay. Third, three general characteristics of effective public speaking style (clarity, appropriateness, and interest) are explained. Fourth, the role of humor and the guidelines for its effective use in public speaking are considered. Unit 20 offers even more specific suggestions for making the style of your public speeches more effective.

HOW LANGUAGE WORKS

Language is perhaps the most complex variable involved in the entire public speaking process and is the one that has led to the most research and theorizing. Entire courses are devoted to language (psycholinguistics, sociolinguistics, for example) and, in fact, an entire academic discipline (linguistics) concentrates exclusively on language. Here those general principles of language most applicable to public speaking are considered: abstraction, objectivity, and intensity. These three principles need to be kept clearly in mind throughout your attempt to style your speech.

Language varies in abstraction

Abstraction refers to the level of language being used and ranges from extremely specific or concrete terminology to extremely general or abstract. Consider, for example, the following list of terms:

Art
Literature
Russian literature
Russian novel
The Brothers Karamazov

At the top there is the general or abstract "art" which includes all of the other items on the list as well as various other items—Flemish painting, abstractionism, film, and so on. "Literature" is somewhat more specific, more concrete. It includes all of the items below it as well as various other items such as novels, English poetry, and biography, but it excludes all art that is not literature. "Russian literature" is again more specific than "literature" and would exclude everything that is not Russian. "Russian novel" further limits "Russian literature" to the genre of novels, excluding poetry, drama, and biography. *The Brothers Karamazov* specifies concretely the one item to which reference is being made.

SEE
EXPERIENTIAL
VEHICLE 5.1.
In selecting words and phrases in styling your speech, chose words from a wide range of abstraction. At times, a general term may suit your needs best whereas at other times a more specific term may serve better. Generally, however, the specific term seems the better choice. Notice that the more general term—say, "art"—conjures up a number of different images. One person in the audience may focus on painting, another on sculpture, another on architecture, and still another on literature. To some "literature" may bring to mind poetry; to others, the novels of Henry James; to others, French plays, and so on. Notice that as you get more specific—less abstract—you guide the images that will come to the minds of the audience members. Generally, you should find that this is the more desirable and effective course of action when you want to increase their understanding or move them to act or change their attitudes.

Language varies in objectivity

The best way to explain how language varies in terms of objectivity is to introduce two new terms: *denotation* and *connotation*.

Denotation The *denotative* meaning of a term is its objective meaning, its dictionary meaning. This is sometimes referred to as its *referential* meaning—that is, it points to specific references. Thus, the denotation of the word *book* is, for example, the actual book, a collection of written pages bound together between two covers. The denotative meaning of *dog* is a four-legged canine. The denotative meaning of *to kiss* is, according to the *Random House Dictionary*, "to touch or press with the lips slightly pursed in token of greeting, affection, reverence, etc." The denotative meaning for *neighbor*, again according to the *Random House Dictionary*, is "a person who lives near another; a person or thing that is near another."

Connotation The *connotative* meaning, however, is quite different. The connotative meaning is our affective, our emotional meaning for the term. The word *book* may signify boredom or excitement, or it may recall the novel we have yet to read or perhaps this textbook that you are reading right now. Connotatively *dog* may mean friendliness, warmth, and affection. *To kiss* may, connotatively, mean warmth, good feeling, and happiness, and *neighbor* may signify security, camaraderie, nosiness.

Using denotative-connotative meanings All words (other than *function* words such as prepositions, conjunctions, and articles) have both denotative and connotative meaning. The relevance of this to you, as a public speaker, is considerable. Seldom do listeners misunderstand the denotative meaning of a term. Even if you are forced to use a term with which the audience is not familiar, you can define it, give a few examples, and thus ensure that it is clearly understood. Similarly, arguments seldom center on denotation. Rather, misunderstandings almost invariably center on connotative meaning. A speaker may, for example, use the term *neighbor*—to stick with a previous example—and may wish to communicate security and friendliness but to some of the audience the term may connote unwanted intrusions, sneakiness, and general nosiness. Speaker and audience may clearly agree that denotatively *neighbor* means one who lives near another; what they disagree on and what consequently leads to the misunderstanding is the connotation of the term.

Consider such terms as *politician, jock, lady, police, sex, religion, professor,* and *education*. I'm sure you can easily appreciate the varied connotative meanings that an audience may have for these terms. Once you acknowledge that your connotative meaning for a term is not necessarily the same as that of your audience, you should become more careful in selecting words to convey your intended meaning and not something entirely different—even contradictory.

The connotative meaning, then, varies on what might be called an *evaluative* dimension. The connotative meaning you have for a term may be seen in terms of how positive or how negative it is. For example, *politicians* may to some people mean "poorly paid public servants who take all sorts of abuse from the people they are looking out for" and thus be highly positive. To others it may mean "crooked, money-grubbing individuals who live off the taxpayer's money and look out only for what good they can do for themselves" and thus be extremely negative. As a speaker, you need to consider the audience's evaluation of various key terms before using them in a speech. When you are a part of the audience, as in a public speaking class, you already know (generally at least) how the other members feel about particular terms. But when you address an audience very different from yourself, this prior investigation becomes crucial. When there is any doubt, you would be well advised to select another word or to qualify the word in some way to make clear exactly what you wish to communicate.

Language varies in intensity

Much as you can raise your voice in terms of intensity, you can also phrase your ideas with different degrees of stylistic intensity. You can, for example, refer to an action by an individual as "failing to support our position" or as "stabbing us in the back." You can say that a new proposal will "endanger our goals" or "destroy us completely." You can refer to a child's behavior as "playful," "creative," or "destructive" and describe that child as "pretty" or as "beautiful." The point here is that language may be varied to express different degrees of intensity—from mild through neutral to extremely intense.

A specific example of the influence of intensity of language should convince you that words must be carefully chosen if they are to have the desired effect, and that intensity is one of the language variables that must be considered in selecting your words. In one study subjects were individually shown the same film of two cars crashing into each other. The difference was in the words used to describe the "crash." After viewing the film the subjects were asked to estimate how fast the two cars were going when they "smashed," "collided," "bumped," "hit," or "contacted." As expected the estimated speeds differed depending upon the single word used to describe the accident. The results are presented in Table 19.1. Note for example that the difference between "smashed" and "contacted" resulted in a difference of nine miles in estimated speed and the difference between "smashed" and "hit" resulted in a difference of almost seven miles in estimated speed.

TABLE 19.1 Language intensity and perception

Descriptive Word	Mean Estimated Speed
Smashed	40.8
Collided	39.3
Bumped	38.1
Hit	34.0
Contacted	31.8

Perhaps even more interesting than these differences is the finding that when the groups who saw the film in which the cars were described as having "hit" or "smashed" were retested and asked if there was any broken glass, differences again emerged. Although there was no broken glass in the actual film, 14 percent of those who saw the film described with the word "hit" reported the presence of broken glass while 32 percent of those who saw the film described with "smash" reported seeing broken glass. As the results of this study show (and those of numerous others might have been included as well), the intensity of the language used influences the meaning of what is "seen" and what is "remembered." The intensity of the language used should depend on the specific purpose you wish to achieve. That is, considerations of clarity should be paramount. Another consideration should be the audience's viewpoint. For example, if your audience is in favor of Martians being admitted to the motorcycle club and you, as a speaker, are against their admission, you should be careful not to use language that is too intensively negative toward Martians lest the audience disagree right at the start and not listen to your arguments.

SEE EXPERIENTIAL VEHICLE 5.2.

REMEMBER that language varies in:
1 **abstraction**
2 **objectivity**
3 **intensity**

ORAL STYLE

It may be stated as a preface that there is such a quality as "oral style," a quality of spoken language that clearly differentiates it from written language. You do not speak as you write. The words and grammatical constructions you use differ depending on whether you are speaking or writing. The major reason for this difference is that you compose speech instantly; you select your words and construct your sentences as you think your thoughts with very little time in between the thought and the utterance. When you write, however, you compose your thoughts after considerable reflection and even then often rewrite and edit as you go along. Another reason for the difference (and this one from the point of view of the listener) is that the listener hears a speech only once and therefore it must be made instantly intelligible. The reader can reread an essay, look up an unfamiliar word, and otherwise spend a great deal of time understanding the meaning of the written communication. The listener, however, is forced to move at the pace of the speaker. Temporary attention lapses may force the reader to reread a sentence or paragraph but such lapses can never be made up by the listener.

Thus, the two forms of communication differ in the way in which they are produced and in the way in which they are received. These differences lead speakers and writers to compose differently. At the same time, the differences in reception demand that speakers and writers employ different

One of the best ways to add color—novelty, style, distinction—to your speech is to make use of the figures of speech and stylistic devices that have been a part of rhetoric since ancient times. Here are a few of the many figures of speech you might attempt to use in your speech along with a general guide to pronunciation.

Alliteration (ă lĭt′ er ā′ shŭn) repetition of the same initial sound in two or more words; "fifty famous flavors."

Antithesis (an tith′ i sis) presentation of contrary ideas in parallel form: "wealth makes the marriage; want of it makes the divorce."

Climax (klī′ maks) the arrangement of individual phrases or sentences in ascending order of forcefulness: "as a child he lied; as a youth he stole; as a man he killed."

Hyperbole (hī pur′ bə lē) the use of extreme exaggeration: "your obedient and humble servant" or "I'm so hungry I could eat a cow."

Irony (ī′ rə nē) the use of a word or sentence whose literal meaning is the opposite of that which is intended: a teacher handing back failing examinations might say (using irony), "So pleased to see how many of you studied so hard."

Metaphor (met′ ə fôr) the comparison of two unlike things: "She's a lion when she wakes up" or "he's a real bulldozer."

Metonymy (mi ton′ ə mē) the substitution of a name for a title with which it is closely associated: "City Hall issued the following news release" where *City Hall* is used instead of *the mayor* or *the city council;* or "She will suffer the wrath of the crown" where *crown* is used instead of *king* or *government.*

Personification (pər son ə fə kā′ shən) the attribution of human characteristics to inanimate objects: "this room cries for activity" or "my car is tired and wants a drink."

Rhetorical question (ri tôr′ i kəl) the use of a question to make a statement or to produce some desired effect rather than to secure an answer since the answer to the question is usually obvious: "Do you want to be popular?" or "Do you want to get well?"

Simile (sim′ ə lē) the comparison of two unlike objects by using the words *like* or *as:* "He takes charge like a bull" or "The teacher is as gentle as a lamb."

rules or principles to guide them in composing messages for their particular mode of expression and reception.

On a purely descriptive level, spoken language differs from written language in a number of important ways. Generally, spoken language consists of shorter, simpler, and more familiar words than the written language. There is a great deal more qualification in speech than in writing. For example, speakers will make greater use of such expressions as *although, however, perhaps, to me,* and so on. Writers probably edit out such expressions before it is published. Spoken language also contains a greater number of self-reference terms (terms that refer to the speaker himself or herself) and a greater number of "allness" terms (for example, *all, none, every, always, never*). Spoken language is also significantly less abstract than written language; spoken language contains more finite verbs and less abstract nouns (two major ingredients in abstraction) than does written language.

In large part, this spoken style needs to be retained in the public speech. But since the public speech is composed much like a written essay—with considerable thought and deliberation and much editing and restyling—special consideration must be given to retain and polish the style that seems most appropriate to the spoken mode and that is most effective in communicating meaning to listeners.

The specific suggestions presented in the following unit are designed to guide you in styling a speech that will retain the best of the oral style while maintaining comprehension and persuasion.

REMEMBER that compared to written style, oral style is characterized by:
1   **shorter, simpler, and more familiar words**
2   **greater qualification**
3   **more self-reference terms**
4   **more allness terms**
5   **fewer abstract terms**

GENERAL CHARACTERISTICS OF EFFECTIVE PUBLIC SPEAKING STYLE

The style of a public speech—regardless of the specific audience, the specific speaker, or the specific topic—may be guided by the following three principles or characteristics of effective style. These characteristics are *clarity*, *appropriateness*, and *interest*. Here they are defined and their relevance to public speaking is explained. In the next unit specific guidelines are presented to assist you in achieving these qualities.

Clarity

At one time—before the widespread use of audio recorders and before the wide dissemination of public speeches in newspapers and specialized pamphlets—it was argued that the speech is heard but once and consequently must be instantly intelligible. Unlike the written essay that can be read and reread, the public speech is heard and it is gone; if the audience cannot understand it the first time around, it is simply lost. Consequently, clarity and simplicity of style were the most important and significant stylistic features.

Clarity of expression is not to be misinterpreted to mean oversimplicity or as a directive to phrase your thoughts in one-syllable words and three-word sentences. Clarity here means that quality of language that aids the listener in understanding the speaker's thought; that quality that reduces ambiguity and the possibility of misunderstanding; that quality that recognizes the inevitable difference between speaker and listener and yet facilitates mutual understanding and even empathy. Clarity is perhaps the most important characteristic of style so your first concern should be with making the message clear—with taking special care to assure that what is being explained or argued cannot be misinterpreted.

Appropriateness

The style of a speech must be appropriate to you as a speaker, to your audience, to the occasion, and to the speech topic.

The speaker   Some people seem comfortable using certain language but when others try to use the very same language, they appear ridiculous. Some people can swear and cuss and it all seems natural and appropriate, yet another's use of the exact same language would make us cringe or laugh. The college professor may use three- and four-syllable words to explain a simple concept and we see this as appropriate; but for the stereotyped cab driver or construction worker to use the same words somehow seems foolish. So, perhaps the first rule of appropriateness is to use the language with which you are comfortable. Do not try to use language that is appropriate to your professor or to your butcher or to your mother. Use the language that feels appropriate to you. Cultivate it, to be sure. Refine it. Polish it. But always make sure that you are comfortable with it.

The audience   Language must also be appropriate to the audience. Perhaps most obviously, it should be appropriate to their level of understanding. The professor who speaks to a group of first-year students as if addressing an academic convention of PhD's is clearly violating this very simple rule. If the topic is one which is unfamiliar to your particular audience, you will have to explain many of the terms, give numerous examples, and perhaps ask frequently, "Is this clear?" Appropriateness to an audience also refers to such considerations as the use of taboo or forbidden words and euphemisms—expressions that are "polite" substitutions for terms that might be considered "inappropriate." With some audiences some. words may be regarded as taboo whereas with other audiences they may be considered everyday expressions. Similarly, some audiences would be insulted by the use of euphemistic expressions. In classroom speeches this generally poses no great problem; because you are a part of the audience you are similar to the others and so probably have a good feel for what is and what is not considered appropriate. But you may not know other audiences as well and will have to be careful not to use terms that they find offensive, derogatory, or insulting.

The occasion   Language must also be appropriate to the occasion. It would be wise to keep in mind that certain occasions require different language. Some occasions are more solemn than others and so require a bit more reverence and perhaps a bit more formality. Other occasions are more casual and so allow for a more relaxed and conversational type of style. Should the style not be appropriate to the occasion, it will draw attention to itself and the audience will focus on the way in which you are saying something rather than on the substance of your speech.

The speech topic   Lastly, style must be appropriate to the speech topic. Some topics—death, for example—may demand a style that would be inappropriate for football, for example. This does not mean that topics are in and of themselves solemn or light, formal or informal; only that the topic of your speech and particularly the way in which you want to approach the topic should influence the way in which you phrase your ideas.

Interest

All public speaking principles, and language is no exception, should function to make the public speech interesting to the audience. If it does not interest them and does not hold their attention, it is not going to have the desired effect. Our minds wander easily and at the least provocation. We know this from attempting to listen to other speakers, whether they be fellow students, teachers, politicians, or religious leaders. When a speech does not interest us our minds wander—we begin to think about what we will do this afternoon, about an enjoyable experience, or about an upcoming examination or paper that is due next week. What we need to realize, emotionally as well as intellectually, is that other people respond to us in this very same way. When we fail to hold their attention, their minds will wander and we will simply be tuned out. Consequently, we need to devote considerable attention to making our speech as interesting as possible.

REMEMBER that an effective public speaking style is:
1   clear
2   appropriate to the speaker, audience, occasion, and topic
3   interesting

THE HUMOROUS STYLE

Humor in a public speech serves a number of important functions. In a speech that is long and somber, humor serves to break up the mood, lighten the tone, and, at times, may serve as a creative and useful transition. Humor is excellent support material and frequently enables the speaker to effectively emphasize a point, crystallize an idea, or rebut an opposing argument. Humor frequently helps to establish the credibility of the speaker; we tend to believe people who have a sense of humor more than those who do not. Humor serves well to gain attention and to maintain interest and, in this capacity, is particularly useful in speech introductions. Humor also makes it easier for listeners to recall what the speaker has said.

Some of you are probably excellent humorists; you can look at a situation, find the humor in it, and convey this humor to an audience easily and clearly. Others of you are probably ineffective humorists. In between these extremes lie most of us. All of us, however, could probably improve the humor in our communications.

One obvious way to secure humorous materials is to create it yourself. Out of your own experiences, your observations of others, and of the world generally, you could construct humorous anecdotes, jokes, and stories. This procedure, if you have tried it, is difficult at best and demands a wit and a perspective on life that, unfortunately, not all of us possess. Another way to secure humorous material is to adapt the material of others to your own needs and to the needs of the specific public speech. In addition to live and media performances, there are many excellent written sources for such material. A glance through any large bookstore or library will unearth many helpful (and entertaining) works.

Guidelines in using humor

For humor to be effective in a public speech, it should be relevant, brief, spontaneous, tasteful, and appropriate.

Relevance   Like any other type of supporting material, the humorous anecdote or story must be germane to your topic and to your specific speech purpose. If it is not, don't use it. If you must go to exceptional lengths to make the story "fit" or if you have to seriously distort the humor or the proposition it is intended to support, then your material cannot be relevant.

Brevity   Humor in public speaking seems to work best when it is brief. If it occupies too great a portion of the speech (or if there are too many such humorous episodes), the audience may question the seriousness with which you are approaching your topic. Humor in special occasion speeches, however, may logically occupy a greater percentage of the entire speech than in most informative or persuasive speeches.

Spontaneity   Humor is best achieved when it is communicated spontaneously. If humor appears studied or too well practiced, it may lose its effectiveness. In telling a humorous anecdote, for example, always keep your eyes on the audience and never on your notes. At the same time that humor should appear spontaneous, you should recognize the difficulty of "getting a laugh," so test your humor on your friends or family first to gauge their reactions and improve your delivery.

Don't telegraph your humorous material by long prefaces or by telling the audience that you are going to tell a funny story—invariably the story turns out to be a bore. Let the humor of the story speak for itself.

Try also to develop a spontaneous retort just in case your humorous story turns out to be a dud. Don't look surprised, hurt, or as though you've lost control of yourself and your material. Instead develop a clever response. Johnny Carson is a master of these rejoinders, which are often a great deal more humorous than even his best jokes.

Tastefulness   Humor should be tasteful. Reject vulgar and off-color expressions; coarseness is never a substitute for wit. Avoid poking fun at any group, race, religion, nationality, sex, sexual minority, occupation, or age group. Ethnic jokes, so popular today, should be especially avoided; they have no place in a public speech. At the same time, be careful of telling jokes at your own expense, of poking too much fun at yourself. Although we are often our own best foils, in a public speaking situation poking fun at ourselves could damage our credibility—the audience might see us as a clown rather than a responsible advocate.

Generally, sarcasm and ridicule are best avoided. It is rarely humorous and it is often difficult to predict how an audience will respond. Its members may well wonder when the sarcasm or ridicule will be directed at them.

Appropriateness Like all forms of support, humor should be appropriate to you as the speaker as well as to the audience and the occasion. Tell jokes in your own style—not in the style of Phyllis Diller or Woody Allen. Invest time in developing a style that is your own and with which you are comfortable. Kitchen humor, jokes about babies, or anecdotes about the single's scene are not likely to prove effective with a group of retired teamsters. The topic of the joke, as well as its implications, should be relevant and appropriate to all of the elements in the public speaking experience.

REMEMBER that humor in a public speech is most effective when it is:
1   **relevant**
2   **brief**
3   **spontaneous**
4   **tasteful**
5   **appropriate**

SOURCES

For language and style see, for example, the readings in my *Language: Concepts and Processes* (Englewood Cliffs, N.J.: Prentice-Hall, 1973), and a recent linguistics text such as Adrian Akmajian, Richard A. Demers, and Robert M. Harnish, *Linguistics: An Introduction to Language and Communication* (Cambridge, Mass.: M.I.T. Press, 1979). The view of style presented here is more fully developed in my "Style and Stylistics: An Attempt at Definition," *Quarterly Journal of Speech* 53 (1967):248–255. The study on the influence of language intensity on perception was conducted by E. F. Loftus and J. C. Palmer, "Reconstruction of Automobile Destruction: An Example of the Interaction between Language and Memory," *Journal of Verbal Learning and Verbal Behavior* 13 (1974):585–589. For humor see Charles Gruner, *Understanding Laughter: The Workings of Wit and Humor* (Chicago: Nelson-Hall, 1978) and Norman N. Holland, *Laughing: A Psychology of Humor* (Ithaca, N.Y.: Cornell Univ. Press, 1982). An excellent overview of language is provided by J. Dan Rothwell, *Telling It Like It Isn't* (Englewood Cliffs, N.J.: Prentice-Hall, 1982).

UNIT 20

Effective style in public speaking

OBJECTIVES

After completing this unit, you should be able to:

1 *identify at least six stylistic guidelines*
2 *explain the importance of memory in public speaking*
3 *explain the sleeper effect*
4 *explain selectivity in remembering*
5 *explain at least four principles that the speaker might use to ensure that the audience remembers the speech*
6 *explain the nature of mnemonic devices in public speaking*

Now that the general language principles and the general criteria for style in the public speech are understood, the obvious and relevant question is: How can you apply this knowledge to improve your speech style? What suggestions can be offered that would enable you to style your speech so that it is clear, appropriate, and interesting?

This question is addressed in two parts. First, some specific guidelines to help you style your speech more effectively are considered. Second, the relationship between style and memory is considered, and some of the ways you can style your speech are suggested to make it more easily remembered.

STYLISTIC GUIDELINES

In styling your speech your two major goals should be to make your message clear and to maintain the interest of your audience throughout the speech. To achieve this clarity and to maintain interest (1) use simple terms and sentence patterns; (2) vary the levels of abstraction; (3) use guide phrases; (4) use repetition, restatement, and internal summaries; (5) personalize your language; (6) use moderate rather than extreme language; (7) use familiar terms; and (8) be sure that your language does not offend any members of your audience.

Simple terms and sentence patterns

Because a speech in normal circumstances is only heard once, it is not possible for members of the audience to look up an unfamiliar word or unwind complicated sentence patterns in order to get at the meaning you wish to convey. On the other hand, overly simplified language can turn off the audience and lead them to think that you have nothing of value to communicate. Even more important is that you should never "talk down" to the audience; condescension impedes communication. Simple language and grammatical constructions result in immediate comprehension but will not insult the audience. Generally, simple, active, declarative sentences are preferred to the more complex, passive sentences because these forms are easier to understand and grasp with just one exposure. It has been found, for example, that active sentences ("The dog caught the ball") are easier to comprehend than passive sentences ("The ball was caught by the dog"). Affirmatives ("The circle follows the square") are easier to understand than negatives ("The square doesn't follow the circle"). With questions, nontags ("Does the circle follow the square?") are easier to comprehend than tag questions ("The circle follows the square, doesn't it?"). The "tag" is the short phrase that asks for agreement: doesn't it? didn't he? wasn't it? It is interesting to note that women use a significantly greater number of tag questions than men—it is one of the ways in which women frequently dilute the strength of their messages.

Levels of abstraction

Most people seem to prefer a mixture of the abstract and the concrete, the specific and the general. By mixing these levels of abstraction you communicate in a much clearer, a more interesting, and a more meaningful fashion. By mixing the levels of abstraction you can more actively involve the audience in your speech. If a speech concentrates solely on low-level abstractions, that is, on concrete terms and sentences, the audience will probably become bored. Similarly, if you only talk in terms of high-order abstractions, using highly abstract and all-inclusive terms, the audience will again become bored.

Active words and sentence patterns

In all forms of communication, active words and sentence patterns are to be preferred over more passive words and patterns. When styling your speech, use language that makes your people and even your objects move. To say "The elephant was chased by the mouse" or "The lawyer was thrown out of court by the judge" is to phrase your ideas in the passive mode, a relatively static and unmoving state. To say, on the other hand, "The mouse chased the elephant" and "The judge threw the lawyer out of court" creates the feeling of movement, of activity. Similarly, in selecting individual words, select words that convey activity. Instead of saying "The students are here," it would be more effective to replace the relatively inactive *are* with *arrived* or *barged in* or whatever term best suits your meaning. "The old couple went up the street" conveys little action, but we get a much clearer image of movement when we hear "The old couple struggled up the street" or "The old couple raced up the street." We can say "Cut flowers don't look as good as flowers in the garden" or one can say, as did Malcolm de Chazal, "The flower in the vase still smiles, but no longer laughs." We can say "Ideas cannot be confined" or, as did Prince Metternich, "It is useless to close the gates against ideas; they overleap them."

Guide phrases

Listening attentively to a public speech is difficult work and consequently you should assist the audience in any way you can. One of the most effective ways is to use frequent transitional phrases that provide a kind of bridge between one set of ideas and another or between one piece of evidence and another. Phrases such as "Now that we have seen how . . . , let us consider how . . . ," will help to keep the audience on the right track. Even terms such as *first, second, and also, although,* and *however* help the audience to better follow your thought patterns. Much like transitions, markers will help audience comprehension. You should make frequent use of marker terms that will provide signposts to the audience. Numbers and letters are perhaps the most obvious examples, but phrases such as "The second argument is . . ." or "The last example I want to provide . . ." help to focus the audience's thinking on the kind of outline you are using.

Repetition, restatement, and internal summaries

Much like transitions and marker phrases help to keep the audience on the same track with you, repetition (repeating something in exactly the same way), restatement (rephrasing an idea or statement), and internal summaries (summaries or reviews of subsections of the speech) all help the listeners to better follow what you are saying. Many speakers hesitate to include such stylistic elements because they feel it makes the speech seem simple and elementary. But some speakers feel this way because they are so familiar with the speech that to them it is elementary. The listeners, however, who will hear the speech but once, will surely appreciate these aids to comprehension.

All this is not to imply that tautologies are therefore to be welcomed in the public speech. (A *tautology* is a needlessly redundant expression, an expression that says the same thing twice.) Here are a few of the more common examples: *absolutely sure, actual truth, again reiterate, cash money, clearly unambiguous, crazy maniac, I myself personally, most unique, new innovation, personal opinion, recline back, overexaggerate,* and *written down.* Avoid these and similar expressions.

Personalized language

Although public speaking is a relatively formal kind of performance, it seems to help if some personalization can be introduced. This is perhaps most clearly seen in the college lecture situation where the teachers who seem to really reach their students are the ones who personalize their courses and lectures, who introduce some of themselves into the discussions. The same is true in public speaking even if you will only face this audience once.

The best guide to what is personalized language is to focus on the language of everyday conversation and note its characteristics. This is invariably personalized language. It makes frequent use of personal pronouns, *I, you, he, she*; it makes use of contractions, simple sentences, and short phrases; it makes use of repetition and restatement. It avoids long, complex, and passive sentences. It avoids the use of the pronoun *one* or phrases such as *the speaker, the former/the latter* (which are difficult to retrace), and, in general, those expressions that are more popular and more expected in the language of written prose than in the language of everyday communication. This is not to say that the language of a public speech should be common or trite. Quite the contrary! The language of the speech should be as polished as the language of the written essay, but it should be conversational in tone and direct in reference.

Moderation

Extremism in style is generally best avoided. Specifically, extremism in the use of what are called "allness" terms is generally misleading. The use of such terms as *all, every, none, always, never*, and the like are seldom descriptive of reality. You can seldom know *all* or *every* of anything and so it is best to more accurately reflect reality with terms that are less extreme but more descriptive. *Some, seldom, often, rarely*, and the like are generally more descriptive of reality and are to be preferred, especially in public speaking where listeners are not afforded the luxury of asking for clarification on such terms.

SEE EXPERIENTIAL VEHICLE 5.3.

Another type of extremism to avoid is what is called "polarization" or "either/or" language. *Polarization* refers to the tendency to divide the world, its objects, and its people into two classes, two extremes—the bad and the good, the ugly and the beautiful, the rich and the poor. Extremes represent a small portion of the real world; the vast majority of people, objects, and events fall in between these extremes. And yet many speakers persist in categorizing people as "for us" or "against us," "liberal" or "conservative," "pro-*X*" or "con-*X*." One reason for this tendency is that our language provides an abundant source of easy-to-use labels for the extremes. For example, it is easier to think and to communicate about someone as "rich" or "poor," as "healthy" or "sick," or as "sane" or "insane," than to qualify such statements with *somewhat, moderately, fairly*. A recent letter to the editor of a New York newspaper posed a perfect two-valued argument: "If the Russians are our friends, why are we arming ourselves to the teeth? If the Russians are our enemies, why are we selling them 25 million tons of grain?" At first glance this type of expression sounds logical. Upon closer inspection it becomes clear that our relations with Russia and the Russian people are much more complex than a simple "friend" or "enemy" dichotomy allows.

As both a speaker and a listener, you should immediately begin to ask questions when anything even moderately complex is divided into only two categories. Coins do have two sides but almost everything else has many sides, not just two. Do not fall into the trap of responding to such obviously either/or questions as "Are you for us or against us?" "Are you liberal or conservative?" "Are you in favor of it or against it?" Recognize that you may be in favor of certain aspects and against other aspects of the very same proposal. You may be liberal on certain issues and conservative on others or, more likely, vary in "liberalness" and "conservativeness" on different issues.

Familiar terms

As a beginning public speaker, you may fall into a pattern of using terms that are jargon within the subject matter being discussed but which are unfamiliar to the audience. And while this usage often gives the audience the impression that you may be something of an expert on the topic, it also creates a number of negative impressions. One impression is that you are putting yourself above the audience, and this is generally resented. Another impression is that you really do not care to communicate but are more concerned with the subject of the speech than with the audience, and this too is generally resented. But perhaps the most significant implication is that it prevents clear and accurate communication and often draws the audience's attention to the words used rather than focus on the subject. If the audience has to pause to ask itself what a *chiropteran* is, then it has less time to devote to understanding what you are attempting to communicate.

A preference for the familiar should not be taken as a license to use timeworn clichés. Expressions such as "green with envy," "to be in hot water," "pretty as a picture," "the writing on the wall," "the whole ball of wax," and numerous others communicate nothing or very little. At the same time they have the effect of drawing attention to themselves and giving the audience the impression that you are unimaginative and uncreative and therefore must resort to these clichés.

Another common error that speakers make is to assume that the initials for various organizations or objects are known to the audience when, in fact, they may be totally unfamiliar. Most audiences know the meaning of UN, NOW, KKK, and NAACP, but many do not know, for example, the meaning of ASEAN, OAU, WIPO, IMCO, EFTA, OAS, OECD, and numerous others. If such initials are to be used, identify what they stand for early in the speech.

Nonoffensive language

The sexist aspect of language has only recently become the center of a great deal of interest. Basically, the masculine pronoun or professions designated by masculine names should not be used generically, nor should the term *man* be used to refer to human beings. Many, of course, will disagree with this and yet with a bit of reflection you can easily see why these constructions should be avoided. Why should a hypothetical doctor, dentist, or lawyer be referred to with masculine pronouns and references? Similarly why should the hypothetical individual be called *he*? That this is traditional and convenient are not satisfactory answers although these seem the only arguments ever used. It is probably best to use *he and she* or *person* instead of just *he* or *man*. Similarly, terms such as *chairman* should be replaced by *chairperson*. In a similar vein, terms that were at one time used to refer to a woman in a specific position (normally originating from a masculine term) should be avoided; for example, *poetess, Negress, Jewess, heroine, actress*, and the like.

SEE EXPERIENTIAL VEHICLE 5.4.

I single out sexism in language primarily because it is a rule that is so easy to follow but so often abused, and because women have for so long been given second-class status that it is clearly time to change. However, women are not the only group that you, as a public speaker, may offend in your use of language. There are many others. No one has the right to insult or to denigrate others because of their sex, race, sexual preference, religion, or nationality. In one textbook, for example, the author, in attempting to make the point that jokes are often made at the expense of some minority group, quotes a joke that puts down a particular national group. He thus makes his point but does so at the expense of an entire group of persons. I have often witnessed teachers who, in attempting to be funny, will put down gay men and lesbians without any recognition that in their class there are a number of gay men and lesbians. In another communication book, the authors ask the reader to talk with a black person and try to see how this person sees the world. This may have seemed a reasonable enough suggestion to the authors, but they should have realized that they were assuming that all readers were white. There was, in that simple suggestion, the clear presumption that the readers were white, just as so much writing assumes maleness as the norm.

REMEMBER these stylistic guidelines:

1　Use simple terms and sentence patterns.
2　Vary the levels of abstraction.
3　Use active words and sentence patterns.
4　Use guide phrases.
5　Make frequent use of repetition and restatement.
6　Personalize your language.
7　Use moderation in language.
8　Use familiar terms.
9　Use language that will not offend audience members.

STYLE AND MEMORY

In the early development of the art of public speaking, the topic of memory occupied a significant place. In the classical view of rhetoric or public speaking there were five major divisions or "canons": (1) the finding of arguments (invention), (2) the organization and strategy of arrangement (disposition), (3) the language and style of the speech (elocution), (4) the delivery of the speech (pronunciation), and (5) the memory of the speech (*memoria*). Essentially, this topic of memory was treated from the point of view of the speaker learning the speech. That is, *memoria* was concerned with the techniques for memorizing the speech. Throughout the development of public speaking, this concern became less and less important until it was finally dropped from most texts on public speaking. Interestingly enough, while memory was dropped from public speaking books, it became of great interest and concern to the general public and, in fact, a number of recent best sellers have been devoted to memory and its improvement. *The Memory Book,* by Harry Lorayne and Jerry Lucas, for example, was a number one best seller throughout the country, and numerous others have sold hundreds of thousands of copies—attesting to the popular concern with memory improvement. It seems widely recognized that success in business, in social affairs, and especially in education is greatly dependent upon the ability to remember—whether it be names, faces, facts, ideas, applications, or whatever.

Nature and importance of memory in public speaking

The main purpose here is to suggest how you, as a public speaker, might better aid the *listener* in remembering your speech. That is, if your function is to communicate information and argument to a listener, surely part of your function is to ensure that this material is retained over a long period of time. And that is memory.

The sleeper effect   Research has shown, for example, that there is a tendency to disassociate the source from the message after a period of time. For example, you might hear that the student body president thinks that required courses in college lead to a high failure rate and a totally elective system leads to a high percentage of students graduating. Or you might hear a fellow student argue against abstractionism in art because it debases the human spirit. At some later time you may find that you remember the messages, but have forgotten the sources. Thus, you can easily recall the connection between required courses and failure rate and between abstractionism and the debasing of the human spirit, but in each case you forgot where you heard that information. As these examples illustrate, the initial sources of the information are crucial and in one sense tell you the degree of confidence you can have in the arguments and conclusions. But because of the tendency to disassociate source and message, you lose this vital piece of information. This disassociation of source and message and the later recall of (and even agreement with) the message is often referred to as the "sleeper effect." The sequence of events might go something like this;

1   A low credibility source argues that X is Y.

2   You disbelieve the argument and even "forget it" because of your low opinion of the source.

3   At a later date, you yourself argue that X is Y, forgetting that the argument originally came from this source of such low credibility.

This, essentially, is the sleeper effect; the argument that X is Y was "sleeping."

Selective remembering   A further reason for treating memory in public speaking is selective remembering; you remember things as you want to remember them. People often distort a message so that it fits into the structure they want it to fit. There is a tendency in most persons to remember in ways that are convenient, ego-protecting, and nonpunishing. This very same selectivity in memory is seen in forgetting. Charles Darwin, who was a meticulous researcher, would take great effort to write down everything he found that might prove contradictory to his theories since he knew it would be particularly easy to forget such informaton. Nietzsche, the German philosopher in *Beyond Good and Evil*, put this idea more poetically: " 'I did that,' says my memory. 'I could not have done that,' says my pride, and remains inexorable. Eventually—the memory yields." The point is simple: People remember what they want to remember and forget what they want to forget. You therefore need to be particularly vigilant lest you find that you not only remember and forget according to your preferences, but that you fail to remember material that may be unpleasant but essential for you to retain.

There is a tendency to omit, alter, and add details when you "remember" things. With a better knowledge of how memory works, you will be in a better position to control your memory. That is, you can direct your memory or you can let your memory direct you; the former seems clearly preferable whether you are functioning primarily as a speaker or as a listener.

Aiding the listener's memory

There is much that you, as a speaker, can do to assist the listener in remembering the speech. Although memory books do not deal with this issue, a great deal of insight can be derived from experimental research on memory and information processing. Here are a few of the major techniques that you might use to ensure that your speech will be remembered by the audience. It should be noted that all of these techniques have found experimental support in cleverly and carefully designed research.

Interest and relevance   The first and most important principle you can follow in aiding the memory of the listener is to make your speech interesting and relevant. This should be intuitively obvious; you learn easier and remember better that which is interesting and relevant to your own life. The reasons for this are simple: you give this type of material much greater attention; you allow yourself fewer lapses in attention. Almost automatically you relate this new information to your own life and to previously known information. This association of the new with the old helps you to retain and internalize the information. Another reason is that you think more about material that you find interesting and relevant and, consequently, engage in what is generally called "active rehearsal"—a process that aids all kinds of memorization significantly. You would have little trouble remembering the address for a job interview that promises you $1000 per week to start (nor would you easily forget the amount of money being offered), but you would have difficulty learning a complex set of numbers if they bore no relevance to your immediate life.

Association   In order to introduce the second principle, first read the following passage and try to remember as much of it as you can.

> With hocked gems financing him, our hero bravely defied all scornful laughter that tried to prevent his scheme. "Your eyes deceive," he had said. "An egg, not a table, correctly typifies this unexplored planet." Now three sturdy sisters sought proof. Forging along, sometimes through calm vastness, yet more often over turbulent peaks and valleys, days became weeks as many doubters spread fearful rumors about the edge. At last, from nowhere welcome winged creatures appeared signifying momentous success.

Now write down as much of the paragraph as you can remember without looking back. Do this now.

If you respond as do my own students, it should be difficult for you to remember very much of the paragraph. Most of it passed right out of what is called "short-term" memory into forgetfulness; most of the material in the passage was probably never "long-term" memory. If you were asked why you had trouble remembering the passage, you would probably say that it was difficult to remember because it did not make sense. And you would be correct; it was difficult because it did not make sense. Now, however, reread the paragraph with the following title in mind: "Christopher Columbus Discovering America." Again write down as much as you can remember. Do this now before reading any further. Unless I miss my guess, your memory should have been much better this time. Even if you were reading this for the first time, if you had been given the title, you would have been able to retain a great deal simply because the title made sense out of what initially seemed like nonsense.

This little exercise, then, illustrates a second important principle of memory: in attempting to get anyone to remember anything, you should try to *associate* it with what is already known. We all know the story of Columbus and by associating this paragraph with that familiar story it was easier to remember.

The principle of association is essential to the speaker either learning material to present to the audience or attempting to foster the learning of the material by the audience. If a new theory you are discussing resembles an old theory that the audience is familiar with, mention this and then point out its differences. If feedback in human communication works like the feedback system in a thermostat (with which the audience is already familiar), make mention of that.

Meaningfulness Tying the new to the old is one of the best ways to assist the learning of new material. In the example of the Columbus passage, the title assisted the remembering of the passage because it made it meaningful. For example, you realized that the "three sturdy sisters" were the ships Columbus sailed; that the "calm vastness" and the "turbulent peaks and valleys" were the ocean; what "the edge" referred to; and so on. That is, the title made meaningful and concrete what was previously meaningless and abstract. The third principle is, then, that whatever you want someone to remember must be made *meaningful*. Students in my psycholinguistics classes will often be tempted to write down exactly what I say on the theory that they will memorize it and be able to use it on an examination. The problem comes of course when I reword or rephrase some concepts or theory—then they are lost. The reason they are lost is that they did not get the meaning of the message; they merely wrote down the words, and words without meaning are extremely difficult to internalize and pass on to long-term memory.

Organization or patterning A fourth principle that is widely recognized for its usefulness in aiding memory is that of *organization* or *patterning*. Things are much more easily remembered if they are presented in some kind of pattern, if they are organized in some way. It has been shown experimentally, for example, that when college students were asked to memorize a list of words shown to them one at a time they had great difficulty. One group, however, was told that they should attempt to organize the words in terms of the alphabet, that each word began with a different letter and that in recalling the list they should go through the alphabet, recalling first the *A* word, then the *B* word, and so on. As would be expected, the group so instructed did significantly better than the group not given this clue. That is, by providing subjects with some pattern, some organizational scheme to fit the information into, their memory was aided greatly. Use this insight and likewise assist the listeners to remember what you say in the speech.

The patterns of organization considered in the discussion of organization and outlining (Units 9 to 12) were designed to present the listeners with patterns they could easily remember. Time sequences and spatial sequences, for example, are obvious examples of using known organizational patterns to assist memory. As a speaker, you should be careful when the main points of the speech do not fit into some clearly marked organizational pattern. If they do not, special care must be taken to ensure that they are remembered. Try repetition and restatement, a summary visual aid of the main points, some slides presenting the main ideas, or arguments.

One of the most widely used systems is the *mnemonic device*. Mnemosyne was the Greek goddess of memory from whose name comes *mnemonic*. For example, if I were to ask how many days there are in November, you might go through the mnemonic rhyme, "Thirty days has September, April, June, and November."

A useful mnemonic device is the *mediated associate*. The spelling distinction between *angle* and *angel* may be remembered by recalling that the sequence *el* goes up physically as do angels. And you may remember that *abscissa* refers to the horizontal axis and that *ordinate* refers to the vertical axis by remembering that in uttering the words *abscissa* and *ordinate* your lips imitate the direction of the axis; thus, in saying the *a* of *abscissa* your mouth forms a horizontal line whereas in forming the *o* of *ordinate* your mouth makes a vertical line.

I can still remember the 12 cranial nerves from college physiology because of the sentence "On old Olympus towering top a fine and gentle vision stands high," which reminds me of the first letter of each of the cranial nerves. Similarly, I can still remember the seven primary colors red, orange, yellow, green, blue, indigo, and violet by the name Roy G. Biv. As can be appreciated from these few examples, this technique can get very corny and you have to be careful in using these devices to apply a judicious mixture of subtlety and directness—always a most difficult combination but one that you will cultivate with experience in public speaking.

SEE
EXPERIENTIAL
VEHICLE 5.5.

Focusing   The fifth principle for enhancing the memory—perhaps the most obvious and the most intuitively satisfying—is *focusing*. In any speech, there are several crucial items that you may want the audience to remember. Regardless of how long the speech is, in summary form it can be reduced to a few principles. The same is true of most college lectures. Most of the time is spent on illustrations, examples, definitions, and the like. The essential points that the instructor wishes to get across in an hour lecture can usually be summarized very briefly. Yet, speakers are notorious for neglecting to tell the audience what they should concentrate on. The speaker assumes the audience knows what they should retain; the teacher also thinks the student will recognize the essential points of the lecture. But this is often not the case. Many remember the interesting illustrations or the examples and fail to remember what the illustrations were meant to illustrate and what the examples were examples of. As a public speaker, you should take pains to ensure that the listeners are clear on the essential points to remember. It is your obligation to focus the listeners' attention on the essentials of the speech. If you wish the listeners to retain the five major techniques used to help an audience remember, it is your responsibility to make certain that the listeners remember. The best way for you to focus the listeners' attention is simply to say, "I want you to focus on five points that I will make in this speech: (1) . . ." and to repeat at least once again but preferably two or three times these very same points. With experience and a greater facility in the art of public speaking, you will be able to do this with just the right combination of subtlety and directness.

REMEMBER, the following principles of style and memory will make your speech easier to remember:

1   interest and relevance
2   association
3   meaningfulness
4   organization or patterning
5   focusing

SOURCES

Style is most thoroughly covered in Jane Blankenship, *A Sense of Style: An Introduction to Style for the Public Speaker* (Belmont, Calif.: Dickenson, 1968).

For the stylistic suggestions I relied heavily on the findings of experimental research as far as was possible, particularly on my "Some Psycholinguistic Aspects of Active and Passive Sentences," *Quarterly Journal of Speech* 55 (December 1969):401–406; "Comprehension Factors in Oral and Written Discourse of Skilled Communicators," *Communication Monographs* 32 (June 1965):124–128; and Jane Blankenship and Herman G. Stelzner, eds., "Relative Ease in Comprehending Yes/No Questions," in *Rhetoric and Communication* (Urbana: University of Illinois Press, 1976), pp. 143–154. Also see Herbert Clark, "The Power of Positive Speaking," *Psychology Today* 8 (September 1974):102, 108–111. Although the language of the speech differs significantly from the language of the written composition, many of the suggestions for clarity are similar and, consequently, the more numerous works on written style may be consulted. I would recommend the classic William Strunk, Jr., and E. B. White, *The Elements of Style,* 3d ed. (New York: Macmillan, 1979), and Michael Lipman and Russell Joyner, *How to Write Clearly: Guidelines and Exercises for Clear Writing* (San Francisco: International Society for General Semantics, 1979). For a review of the literature on some of the ways in which language varies see James J. Bradac, John Waite Bowers, and John A. Courtright, "Three Language Variables in Communication Research: Intensity, Immediacy, and Diversity," *Human Communication Research* 5 (Spring 1979): 256–269. On some of the changes in sexist language see Barbara Bate, "Nonsexist Language Use in Transition," *Journal of Communication* 28 (Winter 1978): 139–149.

The suggestions for aiding memory were derived in large part from psychological and psycholinguistic studies on memory and comprehension. The "Columbus" study was conducted by D. J. Dooling and R. Lachman, "Effects of Comprehension on Retention of Prose," *Journal of Experimental Psychology* 88 (1971):216–222. The best available summary of research on language, memory, and comprehension is provided by Herbert H. Clark and Eve V. Clark, *Psychology and Language: An Introduction to Psycholinguistics* (New York: Harcourt Brace Jovanovich, 1977). A more abbreviated summary is provided by Dan I. Slobin, *Psycholinguistics,* 2d ed. (Glenview, Ill.: Scott, Foresman, 1979). Two of the many such books currently available that are not research oriented but contain a great deal of useful insight for the public speaker are James D. Weinland, *How to Improve Your Memory* (New York: Barnes & Noble, 1957), and Harry Lorayne and Jerry Lucas, *The Memory Book* (New York: Ballantine Books, 1974). A more sophisticated consideration of memory is provided by Ulric Neisser, *Memory Observed: Remembering in Natural Contexts* (San Francisco, Calif.: W. H. Freeman, 1982).

HOW TO . . . Evaluate Your Speech Style: Part Five Checklist

Yes No

- ☐ ☐ 1 Is the language of the speech clear?
- ☐ ☐ 2 Is the language of your speech appropriate to you as the speaker?
- ☐ ☐ To your audience?
- ☐ ☐ To the occasion?
- ☐ ☐ To the speech topic?
- ☐ ☐ 3 Is the language interesting?
- ☐ ☐ 4 Is the language simple rather than complex?
- ☐ ☐ Are the terms and sentence patterns easy to understand?
- ☐ ☐ 5 Are the levels of abstraction varied?
- ☐ ☐ 6 Are guide phrases (transitions and marker terms) used in sufficient number?
- ☐ ☐ 7 Are repetition, restatement, and internal summaries used appropriately?
- ☐ ☐ 8 Is the language used personalized?
- ☐ ☐ 9 Is the language used characterized by moderation: are "allness" and "polarized" expressions avoided?
- ☐ ☐ 10 Are familiar rather than unfamiliar terms used?
- ☐ ☐ Are clichés avoided?
- ☐ ☐ 11 Is the language nonoffensive? Are any terms that may prove offensive to any person or groups of persons eliminated?
- ☐ ☐ 12 Does the style of the speech aid the listener's memory?:
- ☐ ☐ Does the language help to make the speech interesting and relevant to the audience?
- ☐ ☐ Is the principle of association used effectively?
- ☐ ☐ Does the style help to make new and complex material meaningful to the audience?
- ☐ ☐ Is the principle of organization or patterning used to aid the listener's memory?
- ☐ ☐ Is focusing used to fix the audience's attention on certain key issues?

EXPERIENTIAL VEHICLES FOR PART FIVE

5.1 ABSTRACTION IN LANGUAGE

This exercise is designed to enable you to become better acquainted with the notion of abstraction in language. For each of the following terms, supply one that is more concrete (that is, less abstract): *professor, holiday, animal, criminal, college, academic subject, actress, film, food, game.*

After you have provided a less abstract term for each of these stimulus words, provide a term that is more abstract than the stimulus word.

Examine each set of three words. You should be able to see from even a cursory examination that the more concrete terms create images much more easily and clearly than do the more abstract terms.

5.2 QUALIFICATION AND QUANTIFICATION IN LANGUAGE

Read each of the following sentences and respond to the questions with specific numbers.

1 His mother is tall. How tall is she?
2 My geography instructor, Mr. Higgins, is fat. How fat is he?
3 That novel was a best seller last year. How many copies did it sell?
4 For a physician, he doesn't make much money. How much did he make last year?
5 She watches a lot of television. How many hours per week does she watch?
6 College professors put in a lot of time preparing for a new course. How many hours would go into the preparation of a new course—from beginning to prepare the course syllabus to the preparation of the final lecture?
7 Her father is very old. How old is her father?

8 The student is a fast reader. How many words per minute can the student read?

9 He talks very slowly. How many words does he speak per minute?

10 The van Gogh painting was sold at auction for a record price. How much did it sell for?

Share your responses with others. From these responses it should be clear that general descriptions (old, tall, fat) are perceived differently by different people. If you want to create the same meaning (or at least similar meanings) in the minds of your many listeners, it is essential to be specific.

5.3 POLARIZATION

Below are presented 10 stimulus words. Read down the list and for each term write the opposite term in Column 2. Do this now before reading any further.

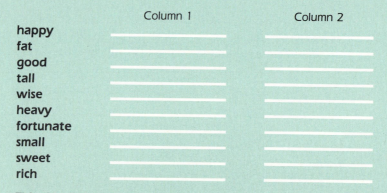

	Column 1	Column 2
happy		
fat		
good		
tall		
wise		
heavy		
fortunate		
small		
sweet		
rich		

This should have taken a very short time. There should have been little difficulty in thinking of these opposites. The terms should be relatively short and appear with great frequency in our language. Also, if you compare your responses with those of other students, you should find that there is great agreement. In more technical language there should be great intersubject agreement. Further, if you were asked to perform this same task a week or a month from now, your responses then should prove similar to the responses you just gave. That is, there is high intrasubject agreement.

The next step in this experience is to visualize each of the 10 pairs of terms as a continuum with the terms representing the two extremes. Next, respond to each continuum with a term that describes the middle group. Write these middle terms in Column 1. For example, respond to the first continuum with a term that describes the middle group between *happy* and *sad,* and so on. Do this now for all ten pairs before reading any further.

Compared to the opposite responses given in Column 2, these should have taken a good deal longer to think of and the phraseology used should be considerably longer. The terms or phrases used are probably not of such high frequency as the opposite terms filled in earlier. If you compare these responses to those of other students, you will find less intersubject agreement, and if you compared these responses with responses taken at a later time, you will find that there is less agreement (less intrasubject agreement) than with the opposites.

What implications does this experience have for the tendency to polarize? Be as specific as possible.

5.4 STYLE ANALYSIS

Select one of the speeches in Appendix D, "Speeches for Study and Enjoyment," and analyze it for style. Specifically, focus on the following:

1 Clarity of style. Is the speech clear? In what specific ways did the speaker achieve (not achieve) clarity?
2 Appropriateness of style. Is the style appropriate to the speaker, audience, occasion, and topic? On what specific stylistic cues do you base your conclusions?
3 Stylistic interest. Is the style interesting? What specific devices did the speaker use to make the speech style interesting?
4 Simplicity of style. Is the style simple? Complex? What factors make for simplicity? Complexity?
5 Abstraction. Does the speaker vary the levels of abstraction used or is the speech presented on one level?
6 Active words and sentence patterns. Are the words and sentence patterns used active? Do they convey activity and movement rather than a static and passive state?
7 Guide phrases. Are sufficient guide phrases used to aid the listener-reader in understanding the speech? Identify specific guide phrases.
8 Repetition, restatement, and internal summaries. How are repetition, restatement, and internal summaries used? Are they used effectively or ineffectively?
9 Personalization of style. Is the style used personal? How is such personalization (or lack of it) achieved?

10 Imagery. Did the speaker create images for the listener-reader? In what specific ways?

11 Familiarity of terminology. Are familiar (rather than special-ized) terms used? Did the speaker make use of clichés? Can you identify specific clichés?

12 Nonoffensiveness of language. Did the speaker use language that might offend any group? Can you identify specific in-stances?

5.5 MEMORY ANALYSIS

Select one of the speeches in Appendix D, "Speeches for Study and Enjoyment," and analyze it for devices that might aid the memory of the listeners-readers. Specifically, focus on such issues as the following:

1 Is the speech interesting and relevant to the listeners-readers? In what ways?

2 Is new information associated with what the audience already knows? How is this achieved?

3 Is the new material made meaningful to the audience? How is this achieved?

4 Does the organization or patterning of the speech assist in re-membering the speech?

5 Did the speaker use the principles of focusing to aid audience memory for the speech?

PART SIX

DELIVERY IN PUBLIC SPEAKING

General principles of delivery

OBJECTIVES

After completing this unit, you should be able to:

1 *explain the question of standards in regard to delivery*
2 *explain at least five general principles of delivery*
3 *explain the general functions of delivery*
4 *define the four general methods of delivery:* impromptu, manuscript, memorized, *and* extemporaneous
5 *identify the major advantages and disadvantages of the impromptu method of delivery*
6 *identify the major advantages and disadvantages of the manuscript method of delivery*
7 *identify the major advantages and disadvantages of the memorized method of delivery*
8 *identify the major advantages and disadvantages of the extemporaneous method of delivery*
9 *explain at least three general guidelines for using notes*

Perhaps the aspect of public speaking that creates the most anxiety is delivery. Few student speakers will worry very much about organization or about audience analysis or about style, but most worry about delivery. This, unfortunately, makes delivery seem the most important aspect of public speaking. It is not. And yet, its importance cannot be denied. It clearly influences the effectiveness of the speech and, consequently, is a variable we must consider.

To begin with, don't chew gum; don't pick your nose. Don't open your speech with "I hate to give speeches." Don't scratch your head. Don't keep your eyes focused on your notes. Don't wear dark sunglasses. Don't kick the lecturn. Don't keep your hands in your pockets. Don't play with your hair. Obvious? They certainly are. And yet I have seen student speakers (and even more experienced speakers) do every one of these. And when questioned and brought to their attention, I have had them look incredulously at me, as if to say, "Does it matter?" Yes, it matters. It matters a great deal.

But the main purpose of this unit is not to catalog the behaviors of ineffective speakers—it is to consider some of the general principles and methods that govern effectiveness in delivery so that each speaker can adapt them to her or his own personality. In the last unit voice and bodily action will be the topic and more specific suggestions for effective delivery will be offered.

No one method of delivery is better than any other. What method works best will depend on numerous factors, in fact, on all the variables covered in this text. To be sure, there are patterns to be preferred but the preference must be based not on arbitrary standards but on legitimate considerations of effectiveness. The standards for delivery must be grounded in effectiveness. The purpose of the voice and of the bodily movement is to add effectiveness to the speech itself.

CHARACTERISTICS OF EFFECTIVE DELIVERY

There are a number of qualities that make the delivery of a speech effective. These are general characteristics not limited or restricted to one style of bodily action or to one pattern of speech; rather, they apply to all aspects and forms of delivery. Delivery seems most effective when it possesses the following characteristics.

Delivery is natural

Nothing seems to be more justly resented by an audience than phoniness—speakers pretending to be something they are not. Listeners want to see and hear speakers who appear natural. An audience is more inclined to believe someone when they feel that person is speaking with natural and genuine feelings. Remember, speaking is an art and art should conceal its artfulness.

Another relevant aspect of naturalness is that your delivery should not call attention to itself; it should appear so natural that it is hardly noticed. When voice or bodily action are so prominent that they are distracting, the audience concentrates on the delivery and their attention is lost from the speech.

Delivery reinforces the message

Effective delivery gives emphasis to what you, as a speaker, wish emphasized. A story of starvation told in the lilting tone of voice reminiscent of a stereotyped 16-year-old will not emphasize what needs to be emphasized. Voice and bodily movement must reinforce the content, the point of view, and the general perspective of the speech.

Effective delivery aids instant intelligibility. Your main objective is to make your ideas understandable to an audience. Delivery either helps or hinders comprehension. A low voice you strain to hear, sharp decrease in volume at the ends of sentences, slurred diction—all obviously hinder comprehension. Since messages are also communicated facially, wearing sunglasses during a speech will also impair intelligibility. The same principle is true for avoiding eye contact in general by looking out of the window, at the floor, or at notes.

Delivery is appropriate

This concept of appropriateness covers a great deal of territory. Surely the delivery must be appropriate to you as a speaker; you cannot assume the delivery mannerisms of another individual without creating some incongruity, some inconsistency. The vocal and the bodily dimension of communication must be your own. This is not to say that your style cannot be improved, but only that you must recognize that your delivery style is yours and any attempt at improvement must consider you as an individual.

Delivery must also be appropriate to the audience, the occasion, and the subject matter of the speech. Delivery that is appropriate to a speech designed to entertain a group of refrigerator salespersons in Des Moines may not be appropriate in a speech designed to persuade a group of college students to enlist in the navy. Delivery must be consistent with all the other variables in the public speaking situation; to the extent that it is not, it will call attention to itself as well as violate the appropriateness principle.

Delivery is comfortable

Effective delivery is comfortable to the speaker. Usually this principle is phrased in the negative: Delivery is ineffective when it causes the speaker discomfort. Unnatural vocal quality or pitch level may cause physical discomfort and perhaps damage the vocal mechanism. Thus, if you have a normally high-pitched voice but force yourself to speak in deep resonant tones, you will soon be visiting a throat specialist. Strained delivery may also cause psychological discomfort. I suspect that the audience most often notes this discomfort and the speech is less well received than it might be.

Delivery is varied

Listening to a speech is hard work. It is not easy to sit quietly and absorb a great deal of information. You know this is true from listening to lectures; it isn't always pleasant. Flexible and varied delivery relieves this difficulty. A monotone would surely put the audience to sleep; similarly, a motionless body behind a podium hardly keeps the audience alert. Not surprisingly, a delivery without flexibility also deadens the speaker; it is almost as if the speaker gets caught up in the monotony and forgets that he or she is attempting to communicate information to an audience.

If you think of your thoughts and what you want to convey to the audience and if you stay relatively loose, you will find that your delivery will vary appropriately with what you are saying and that it will almost effortlessly reinforce what you want to emphasize.

REMEMBER that effective delivery:
1   is natural
2   reinforces the message
3   is appropriate
4   is comfortable
5   is varied

Throughout our discussions of public speaking we noted that everything about you communicates; you simply cannot prevent yourself from sending messages to others and the way in which you dress is no exception. In fact, your attire will figure significantly in the way your credibility is assessed, the extent to which you will be given attention, and your general effectiveness in persuasion and in communicating information. Unfortunately, there are no universal rules that can be followed for all situations. Rather, only some general guidelines can be offered; these should be modified and tailored for you and each unique situation.

1. AVOID EXTREMES AND NOISEMAKERS

Don't allow the clothing you wear to dominate the situation. Your clothes should not steal the attention of the audience away from what you are saying. This is particularly important for those who are prone to wear a great deal of jewelry. Too much of anything will divert audience attention from your message to your appearance—the speech must remain your principle concern.

2. DRESS COMFORTABLY

Clothes that permit ease of movement should be preferred. If you are a size 34 don't try to fit into a 32 on the theory that you need to look your best. If you're a 34 your best will be presented in a 34. Clothes that make you look pinched in around the middle merely succeed in making you look pinched in around the middle—a simple and obvious fact that many people don't seem to realize.

You should also dress so that you are psychologically comfortable. If you feel psychologically uncomfortable in your new grey pin-striped suit, don't wear it to give your speech; wear the old brown one. A speaker's psychological discomfort is easily perceived by sensitive listeners and often makes them become uncomfortable as well. Dress so that you feel good about yourself. Similarly, delivering a public speech is not the time to dress your sexiest. Tight jeans and sweaters and shirts open to the navel may be appropriate for some situations but public speaking is not one of them. The reason is obvious: these clothes deliberately draw attention to your physical self and away from your message.

3. DRESS APPROPRIATELY

Your clothing should be appropriate to the occasion, the topic, the other speakers (if you are one of several), and to the audience. Generally, the more serious a topic, the more formal should be your dress; the more formal the audience the more formal your dress, and so on. Delivering a speech in jeans and a sweatshirt might be appropriate for an informal audience at camp when speaking on football or archery, but would probably be inappropriate when speaking to an audience of physicians on the importance of psychological training. If we had to formulate a general rule of appropriateness in dress, I think it would be this: dress a level above the level of the audience.

METHODS OF DELIVERY

Speakers vary widely in their methods of delivery. Some speak "off-the-cuff," with no apparent preparation; others read their speeches from manuscript. Some memorize their speeches word for word; others construct a detailed outline and actualize the speech itself at the moment of delivery. Four general methods of delivery may be distinguished: impromptu, manuscript, memorized, and extemporaneous. Each has advantages and disadvantages.

The impromptu method of delivery

The impromptu method of delivery involves speaking without any specific preparation for the speech. You and the topic meet for the first time and immediately the speech begins. One procedure used in the training of public speakers is to have speech topics written on index cards which are placed face down on a table. A member of the class is chosen by some random procedure, selects a card, reads the topic, and immediately (or perhaps after a few seconds to collect some thoughts) begins talking for a specified amount of time. This is impromptu speaking in the raw.

On some occasions impromptu speaking cannot be avoided. In a classroom, after someone has spoken, you might be asked to comment on the speaker and the speech you just heard and, in effect, give an impromptu speech of evaluation. In asking or answering questions in an interview situation you are giving impromptu speeches, albeit extremely short ones. At meetings, persons with particular expertise are often called upon to give an impromptu comment on various issues. Impromptu speaking, when it cannot be avoided, as in these few examples, is greatly aided by cultivating public speaking ability in general. The more proficient a speaker you are, the better you will be able to function impromptu. The training for impromptu speaking would be the same as for any public speaker. When impromptu speaking is used as a training device to focus on certain aspects of, say, bodily action or voice or on the mechanics of introducing or concluding a speech, it has a place in public speaking training. But impromptu speeches should not be designed to replace or substitute for speeches developed after thorough preparation and rehearsal—there is no comparison.

Advantages If used properly, the impromptu experience has some merit. Its greatest advantage in a classroom situation is that there is very little pressure for excellence or in fact for anything approaching the standards necessary if you had the time to research, prepare, and polish your speech. Hence it is often a useful introductory exercise.

SEE EXPERIENTIAL VEHICLE 6.1.

Another use of the impromptu speech is in consciousness-raising groups. Here a group of people gather, a topic is selected by the members of the group, and through some random procedure an individual is selected to begin speaking. Each person has a specified amount of time, say 10 minutes, for his or her speech. After the first person has spoken, the next person in a clockwise direction speaks and so on until each person in the group has spoken. The basic idea of these consciousness-raising groups—and they vary somewhat in their rules and formats—is for the members to discuss their feelings and to learn about them from their own verbalizations and the talks of the other members. In this type of situation, the impromptu speech is particularly valuable.

Disadvantages Perhaps the major disadvantage of the impromptu speech is that it focuses on appearances. The aim is often to *appear* to give an effective and well-thought-out speech. Another disadvantage is that it does not permit attention to research, style, and to organizational matters. Because of this inadequacy, the audience is likely to get bored. This in turn will make you, the speaker, feel all the more awkward and uncomfortable.

The manuscript method of delivery

In the manuscript method the entire written speech is read to the audience. The process is most time consuming and laborious, but necessary for some occasions. For example, where exact timing and wording is required, the manuscript method is the safest to use. It might be disastrous if a political leader did not speak from manuscript on sensitive issues. An ambiguous word, phrase, or sentence that proved insulting, belligerent, or conciliatory could cause serious problems. With a manuscript speech, an in-depth analysis of style, content, organization, and all other elements of the speech can be undertaken. In fact, the great advantage of the manuscript speech is that an entire staff of speech experts and advisers can review it and offer suggestions as to potential problems, how to resolve them, and so on. Manuscript delivery allows you to say exactly—*word for word*—what you and perhaps a host of speech writers and advisers wish to say.

Advantages With a manuscript speech, the major advantage is that timing can be precisely controlled. This is particularly important when delivering a recorded speech (on television, for example); it does not help to have your great conclusion cut off so that the fifty-ninth rerun of "The Odd Couple" can go on as scheduled. There is no danger of forgetting, no danger of being unable to find the right word. Everything is there for you on paper; consequently, a great deal of anxiety is removed, especially for the beginning speaker. Another advantage is that you can distribute copies of it and are less likely to be misquoted.

Disadvantages There are also disadvantages with manuscript delivery. Perhaps the most obvious is that it takes a great deal of time to write out a speech word for word. This is more of a problem for the beginning speaker than it is for the more accomplished speaker who has had experience and learned to compose quickly. But for the beginning speaker, it can represent numerous extra hours of unrewarding work.

Another disadvantage is that it is difficult to read a speech and sound natural and nonmechanical. Reading material from the printed page with liveliness, naturalness, and spontaneity is itself a skill difficult to achieve without considerable practice. Audiences do not like speeches to be read;

they prefer that speakers speak with them. Consequently, it is more difficult to please and ultimately inform or persuade an audience when reading from manuscript.

Reading a manuscript makes it difficult to take in and respond to feedback from your listeners. With a manuscript you are committed to the speech word for word. What happens when you see on the faces of your audience that your last point was not understood? To stop and amplify would cause a number of problems. More than likely, you would be forced to go on and ignore these feedback signs.

When the manuscript is on a stationary lectern, as it most often is, it is impossible to move around. You are forced to stay in one place; the speech controls your movement or, rather, your lack of movement. If you are in a room the size of most college classrooms, you would probably want to move around at least a bit. With the manuscript speech you are, for the most part, prevented from moving. You might of course take the speech in your hand and move about, but this is awkward without considerable practice.

The memorized method of delivery

Like the manuscript method, the memorized method is used when exact timing and exact wording is crucial—in politically sensitive cases, in cases where media impose severe restrictions. The memorized method involves writing out the speech word for word and committing it to memory. The speech is then usually "acted out."

Advantages The memorized method allows you to devote careful attention to style. Like the manuscript speech, the exact word, phrase, or sentence may be carefully reviewed and any potential problems eliminated. One of the reasons the memorized delivery is popular is that it possesses all the advantages of the manuscript method but allows you freedom to move about and to otherwise concentrate on delivery.

Disadvantages The great disadvantage is the danger of forgetting. Generally, in the way that speeches are learned, each sentence hangs on the previous one and cues the recall of the following one. When one sentence is forgotten it is likely that the entire speech will be forgotten. And when this danger is coupled with the natural nervousness that accompanies the beginning speaker's efforts, it seems a most inadequate method of delivery to select.

The memorized method is even more time consuming than the manuscript method since it involves additional time for memorization. When you recognize that you may easily forget the speech, even after spending hours memorizing it, it hardly seems worth the effort.

The memorized method does not allow for ease in adjusting to feedback. In fact, there is less opportunity to adjust to listener feedback than in the manuscript method. And if you are not going to adjust to feedback, the main advantage of face-to-face contact is eliminated.

Lastly, it should be noted that unless you are an accomplished actor, it will be difficult—if not impossible—to sound natural reciting a memorized speech.

The extemporaneous method of delivery

Extemporaneous delivery involves thorough preparation, a commitment to memory of the main ideas and the order in which they will appear, and perhaps a commitment to memory of the first and last few sentences of the speech. There is, however, no commitment to exact wording.

Advantages   The extemporaneous method is useful in most speaking situations when exact timing and wording are not required. Good lecturing by college teachers uses the extemporaneous method; they have prepared thoroughly, have the organization clearly in mind, and know what they want to say and in what order they want to say it. But they have given no commitment to exact wording.

This method allows for great flexibility to feedback. Should a point need clarification, you can elaborate on it when it will be most effective. With this method it is easy to be natural because you are being yourself. It is the method that comes closest to conversation or, as some theorists have put it, enlarged conversation. With the extemporaneous method, you may move about and interact with the audience.

Disadvantages   Although the extemporaneous method is clearly to be preferred, especially in the public speaking classroom situation, it too has some disadvantages. The major disadvantage is that you may stumble and grope for words. If the speech has been rehearsed a number of times, however, this is not likely to happen. Another disadvantage is that the precise attention to style that you can give the speech in the manuscript and memorized methods cannot be given here. And yet, this disadvantage too can be circumvented by memorizing those phrases you want to say exactly. There is nothing in the extemporaneous method that would preclude your committing to memory selected phrases, sentences, or quotations.

Guidelines for speaking extemporaneously   Having stated a clear preference for the extemporaneous method I do suggest that you memorize three parts of such a speech: (1) your opening lines, perhaps the first two or three sentences; (2) the main ideas in the order in which they will be presented; and (3) your closing lines, perhaps the last two or three sentences of the speech. As you grow in sophistication, you may choose to memorize certain phrases that you feel are particularly felicitous and noteworthy, but for now these three should be the only memorized parts of the speech. I suggest that you memorize these for two reasons. First, the opening and closing lines should be memorized so that you can focus complete attention on the audience and best feel the interaction with them. Memorizing these parts will put you more at ease. You will feel more in control of the situation, once you know exactly what you will say in opening and in closing the speech. Second, memorize the main ideas in order so that you will feel in control of the speech and the speech-making situation and will not have to refer to notes when making your main points. After all, if you expect your audience to remember these points, surely you should remember them as well.

All four methods have something to recommend them. The impromptu method is useful in training certain aspects of public speaking; the manuscript and memorized methods are especially useful when exact timing and wording are essential; and the extemporaneous is most useful when naturalness, responsiveness to feedback, and general flexibility are important. Generally, it is suggested that you concentrate on the extemporaneous method of delivery. At the same time try to acquire some familiarity with the other methods in case you have to employ them.

REMEMBER the four basic methods of delivery:
1 impromptu
2 manuscript
3 memorized
4 extemporaneous

A NOTE ON NOTES

For speeches it may be helpful to use notes. A few simple guidelines may help you avoid some of the common errors made in using notes.

First, and most important, keep your notes to a minimum. Although your instructor may wish to advise you differently, as a general rule the fewer notes you take with you the better off you will be. The difficulty, as you will discover, is not in learning the speech. The difficult part, and the reason why so many speakers bring notes with them, is that they want to avoid the face-to-face interaction required. But with experience, you should find this face-to-face interaction the best part of the public speaking experience. Do not bring with you the entire speech outline; there may be too much of a temptation to rely on it and hence prevent you from speaking directly to the audience. Instead, compose a brief outline, using only key words, and bring this to the lectern with you. One side of a 3 × 5 index card should be sufficient for most speeches. This will relieve anxiety over the possibility of your forgetting your speech but will not be extensive enough to prevent meaningful speaker-audience interaction.

Second, know your notes intimately. Rehearse at least twice with the same notes that you will take with you to the speaker's stand.

Third, use your notes with "open subtlety." Do not make them more obvious than necessary, but at the same time don't try to hide them from the audience. On the one hand, do not gesture with your notes and, on the other, do not turn away from the audience to steal a glance at them either. Use them openly and honestly but gracefully, with "open subtlety."

Fourth, do not allow your notes to prevent you from speaking directly to your audience. When referring to your notes, pause to read what has to be read, then regain eye contact with the audience and continue your speech. Do not read from your notes, just take cues from them. The one exception to this is an extensive quotation or complex set of statistics that must of necessity be read. Then, almost immediately, resume direct eye contact with the audience.

SOURCES

On delivery in general see Wayne N. Thompson, *Responsible and Effective Communication* (Boston: Houghton Mifflin, 1978) and Robert C. Jeffrey and Owen Peterson, *Speech: A Text with Adapted Readings*, 3d ed. (New York: Harper & Row, 1980). On methods of delivery see also Douglas Ehninger, Alan H. Monroe, and Bruce E. Gronbeck, *Principles and Types of Speech Communication*, 8th ed. (Glenview, Ill.: Scott, Foresman, 1978). On the relative importance of verbal and nonverbal messages see, for example, Timothy G. Hegstrom, "Message Impact: What Percentage is Nonverbal?," *Western Journal of Speech Communication* 43 (Spring 1979): 134–142.

For the discussion on using notes I relied heavily on the excellent treatment by James C. McCroskey, *An Introduction to Rhetorical Communication*, 4th ed. (Englewood Cliffs, N.J.: Prentice-Hall, 1982). I was influenced to include the impromptu speaking experience after hearing Benjamin Sevitch's "The Impromptu Speaking Assignment," paper delivered at the Eastern Basic Course Directors Conference, Bridgeport, Connecticut (October 16, 1982).

UNIT 22

Nonverbal communication: Voice and bodily action

OBJECTIVES

After completing this unit, you should be able to:

1 *define* volume *and identify the major problems of volume in public speaking*
2 *define* rate *and identify its major problems in public speaking*
3 *define* pitch *and identify its major problems in public speaking*
4 *define* quality *and identify its major problems in public speaking*
5 *identify the major functions of eye contact*
6 *explain the role of facial expressions in public speaking*
7 *explain the general principles of appearance of the public speaker*
8 *explain the role of gestures in public speaking*
9 *explain the guidelines that the public speaker should follow in regard to movement*
10 *define* proxemics *and explain its role in public speaking*

FOUR CHARACTERISTICS OF VOICE

Generally, four dimensions or aspects of the voice may be distinguished: *volume, rate, pitch,* and *quality.* Your manipulation of these will enable you to control your voice to greatest advantage.

Volume

Volume refers to the relative intensity of the voice. Loudness, which is often equated with volume, refers to the perception of that relative intensity. In an adequately controlled voice, volume will vary according to the distance between speaker and listener, the amount of competing noise, the acoustics of the room, and the emphasis which the speaker wishes to give a particular concept or idea.

Influences on volume Obviously the distance you are from the listener will influence the volume of your voice and the subsequent loudness perception by the listener. Speakers who have never spoken before an audience or who have given only a few speeches will often project inappropriate volume. You should probably solicit the assistance of a friend and see if you can be heard comfortably. If not you can increase or decrease the volume until the loudness seems appropriate. You should remember, however, that sound travels better in an empty room and adjust accordingly.

The amount of competing noise will also determine what is and what is not an appropriate volume. In a noisy situation you must increase your volume. Technically this is referred to as the signal-to-noise ratio—the relationship between the intensity of the signal and the noise. Generally, speech needs to be approximately 10 decibels (a technical measure of sound intensity) higher than noise if it is to be heard without great interference. Fortunately, through experience with noisy environments, you almost automatically monitor and adjust appropriately the signal-to-noise ratio. But keep in mind that noise will always be present in any communication situation and that volume is one defense against its effects.

The acoustics of the room influence volume although most speakers do not understand acoustics sufficiently to modify their volume accordingly. Suffice it to say here that when the room is crowded—with people, with heavy drapes, or with lots of furniture, the volume will have to be increased because these items will absorb the sound waves and leave that much less for listeners to receive. In an empty room, the sound will travel without such hindrances.

Volume should be varied in order to give certain ideas and concepts emphasis. To speak at the same volume—even if it is a most powerful volume—will not distinguish your main from your lesser points. Ideas are generally emphasized when they are uttered in a volume different—either higher or lower—from the preceding statements.

Problems with volume   The problems with volume are easy to identify though they are difficult to recognize in ourselves. One obvious problem is an overly soft voice. When speakers speak so low that listeners have to strain to hear, the speaker will soon tire since this requires a great expenditure of energy. On the other hand, an overly loud voice will prove disturbing because it intrudes on our psychological space more than we are willing to tolerate. It feels as if someone is sitting too close or is leaning all over us. An overly loud voice is especially disturbing if the voice is also unpleasant.

Perhaps the most common problem is that speakers—particularly the extremely nervous—do not vary vocal volume enough. But an equally important problem is a volume pattern that, although varied, varies in a pattern that—after a very short time—becomes totally predictable.

Fading away at the ends of sentences is particularly disturbing. Here the speaker uses a volume that is appropriate, but he or she ends sentences (particularly long sentences) with the last few words delivered in an extremely low and often garbled manner. This becomes so unnerving that the audience will almost surely tune out the speaker. You need to be particularly careful when finishing sentences; they must be heard by the audience at an appropriate volume.

Not all problems of volume can be readily improved. For example, some volume difficulties may be caused by deep-seated problems requiring professional help. For example, inadequate volume brought about by extreme shyness or self-consciousness or some sense of personal inadequacy will not be solved by a course in public speaking. These issues might be identified here, but professional help may be needed. Hearing loss also creates volume difficulties. The hearing-impaired often speak at a volume that seems totally inappropriate to others. This is usually excessive volume, but there are also hearing losses that lead to an inappropriately low speaking volume.

Rate

Rate refers to the speed with which you speak and is normally measured in the number of words or syllables spoken per unit of time, usually per minute. Approximately 160 to 170 words per minute seems average for speaking as well as for reading aloud.

Influences on rate   Rate is dependent upon a number of a factors. Time considerations will often motivate rate variation. When there is little time and much to say, you may rush and speak at a rate that is abnormally fast for you as well as for most listeners. The content of the speech will often influence the rate at which you speak. Serious material usually is spoken at a slower rate than humorous material; poetry varies a great deal but seems, on the average, to be spoken at a slower rate than prose. Sportscasters seem to speak most rapidly, perhaps attempting to echo the quick pace of the game they are reporting—as if they are reporting as the game is being played. A news analyst, on the other hand, will vary his or her pace depending on the story. The death of a beloved personality almost invariably calls for a slow and measured pace whereas the opening of a new disco or film might require a faster pace. When the listening conditions and the acoustics are good, the rate may be a little more rapid because attention is not lost because of noise. But when the conditions are poor, the rate must compensate for this and be slower.

Problems with rate   The problems of rate are speaking too fast or too slow, with too little variation or too predictable a pattern, or with inappropriate pauses. If you talk too fast you deprive your listeners of sufficient time to comprehend, digest, think about, and perhaps internalize what you are saying. If the rate is extreme, the listeners will simply not be willing to spend the time and energy needed to understand the speech.

A rate that is too slow allows the listeners' minds to wander to more personal matters, to more immediate matters—to their recent date, to their next examination, and to a host of matters totally unrelated to the speech. As a speaker, you have to be careful not to bore the audience and yet not give them information at a pace that is too rapid to absorb. You have to strike a happy medium—a pace that engages the listeners and allows them time for reflection without boring them.

Like volume, rate variations may be underutilized or totally absent. If you speak at the same rate throughout the entire speech, you are not making use of one of your most important vocal characteristics. Rate variations should be used to add emphasis and variety—to call a listener's attention to certain points. If you speak of the dull routine of an assembly line worker in a pace that is rapid and varied, and of the wonder of a circus with a pace that is the same throughout with absolutely no variation, you are clearly misusing this most important vocal dimension. Again, if you are conscious of what you are saying and if you are interested in communicating with an audience, your rate variations should flow naturally and effectively.

Too predictable a rate pattern is sometimes as bad as no variation at all. If the audience can predict—consciously or unconsciously—your rate pattern, clearly you are in a vocal rut and are not communicating ideas but words that have been memorized or are printed on paper.

Inappropriate pauses are a major problem, especially among beginning speakers. Pauses should be used for effect at various points in the speech. For example, pauses should separate the major parts of the speech—the introduction, body, and conclusion. Similarly, pauses should separate the main points in an argument and, in general, should separate one idea from another. Much as you use a period and a capital letter to separate one sentence from another, you use pauses to separate one assertion in the speech from another. Remember that the listeners do not have a printed text in front of them and, consequently, do not see paragraph divisions, headings in boldface type, italics, and all sorts of typographical devices designed to separate and highlight various ideas. In large part the function of these divisions in type are served by pauses in a speech.

As you should use pauses to give your speech the emphasis and divisions it needs, you should avoid pauses that are distracting. Psycholinguists refer to these as "filled pauses"—the *ers*, *ehs*, *ahs*, and the like. These pauses are for the most part unproductive and ineffective and give the audience the impression that you are not quite sure of what to say. If you need time to think of a particular word or to recall the next argument, simply pause with no vocalization at all. The *er*, *eh*, and *ah* do not help memory, they distract the audience, and they contribute negatively to your credibility.

Pitch

Pitch refers to the relative highness or lowness of the voice as perceived by the listener. More technically, pitch is created by the rate at which your vocal folds vibrate. If they vibrate rapidly, the voice is perceived as having a high pitch; if they vibrate slowly the voice is perceived as having a low pitch.

Influences on pitch The frequency of vibration is a function of the length of the vocal cords, their thickness, and their tension as they vibrate. The longer, thicker, and more relaxed the vocal cords are, the lower the pitch will be; the shorter, thinner, and more tense the cords are, the higher the pitch. Men have vocal cords that are normally longer, thicker, and less tense than women's and, consequently, the pitch of men's voices is characteristically lower than that of women.

In addition to anatomical features, tension affects pitch. Thus, extreme tension—often parodied in comedy—results in an abnormally high pitch. Persons who are normally or frequently tense will often speak at a pitch that is higher than "normal" for their anatomical structures. Persons who are frequently down, may speak at a pitch level that is lower than normal for their anatomical structures. However, you can also vary the tension of the vocal folds by simply singing the musical scale; as you go up in pitch, you tense your vocal folds, and as you go down in pitch, you relax them.

Pitch changes often signal changes in the meanings of many sentences, the most obvious being the difference between a statement and a question. Thus, the difference between the declarative sentence, "So this is the creep you want me to meet" and the question "So this is the creep you want me to meet?" is inflection or pitch. This, of course, is obvious. But note also that, depending upon where the inflectional change is put, the meaning of the sentence changes drastically. Consider the following sentences, where the higher pitch is symbolized by italics:

1   Is **this** the creep you want me to meet?
2   Is this the **creep** you want me to meet?
3   Is this the creep you want **me** to meet?
4   Is this the creep you want me to **meet**?

They are all questions but note that they all differ.

Problems with pitch   The obvious problems of pitch are pitch levels that are too high, too low, and too patterned. Neither of the first two problems are common in speakers with otherwise normal voices. If you sense that you are speaking at a pitch level that is too high or too low, you should probably speak with your instructor and have the matter looked into.

A pitch pattern that is too predictable or monotonous may be corrected with some practice. Pitch changes should come naturally from the sense of what is being said. Normally you do not have to wonder whether the last sentence was a statement or a question; it is signaled in the words used as well as in the pitch. Similarly, since each sentence is somewhat different from every other sentence there should be a normal variation—a variation that results not from some predetermined pattern but rather from the meanings you wish to convey to the audience.

Quality

The fourth characteristic, quality, is unlike volume, rate, and pitch in that it does not have a clear physiological dimension and cannot be measured as the others. Rather, *quality* is a general characteristic of the voice that refers to a variety of factors by which one voice is distinguished from another. Quality is used to refer to such characteristics as nasality/denasality, breathiness, and hoarseness, as well as a number of other factors.

Nasality/denasality   Excessive nasality means that you speak through your nose—a quality that most persons find unattractive and difficult to listen to. If you put your hand under your nose and you can feel the air being expelled, it is a good bet that you have too much nasality. In English there are only a few sounds that are normally made with nasal resonance—m, n, and ng. Some speakers, however, pronounced many of the sounds with extreme nasal resonance. Becoming conscious of the difference in nasal and nonnasal (or oral) resonance, will often enable you to make the correction almost automatically. The opposite side of the problem is denasality—a condition that at times is often confused with nasality, but is actually, its opposite; it is the absence of nasality. You can easily experience this by holding your nose as you speak; you will sound as if you have a bad cold. Again, it is an unpleasant voice to listen to. An unusual degree of tenseness often produces denasality; once the speaker learns to relax, some of this denasality will be eliminated.

If you have excessive nasality or denasality and it is evidenced in formal as well as informal, tense as well as relaxed encounters, you should consult a physician to explore the possibility of a deviated septum or some other physiological problem.

SEE
EXPERIENTIAL
VEHICLE 6.2.

Breathiness   Another problem of quality is breathiness. To appreciate the meaning of this concept, say a few sentences aloud normally and then speak these same sentences in a whisper. In both situations hold your hand in front of your mouth. You will no doubt find that the whispered sentences produced a great deal more breath than the normally spoken sentences. In some people, however, the excessive breathiness characteristic of whispering also characterizes normal speaking. This problem is caused when the vocal folds are not brought together and excessive air escapes while speaking.

Sometimes speakers will assume breathiness on the assumption that this is sexy. Marilyn Monroe and contemporary imitators did a great deal to make the breathy voice popular. Although this type of voice may be attractive in certain situations and in moderation, it frequently results in fatigue because it takes a great deal of energy to speak for any length of time with a breathy voice. In the extreme, using excessive breath may swell and "thicken" the vocal cords and require professional help to correct.

Hoarseness   A third problem is hoarseness, a condition you are probably familiar with from having had a sore throat. It appears as a huskiness, a noise-filled voice. When the tissues of the vocal mechanism get swollen—as they do when infected—the vocal folds are not able to vibrate as smoothly as they normally do. The result is hoarseness. In men, it is mistaken as a sign of roughness, masculinity, and general toughness. Gangsters are traditionally pictured in the media with hoarse voices.

Perhaps the major difficulty with hoarseness is impaired intelligibility. A hoarse voice also tires fast; frequent rest periods are necessary and long discourses, such as public speeches, are exhausting.

REMEMBER the four major dimensions of the voice:

1 volume
2 rate
3 quality
4 pitch

BODILY ACTION

The use of the body is obviously an integral instrument in the public speaking transaction. You speak with your body as well as with your mouth. The total effect of the speech is determined not only by what you say but by the way you present it—by the movements, gestures, and facial expressions. You really know this from your own interpersonal interactions; you develop certain attitudes and feelings about others not only on the basis of what they say, but also on the basis of how they look and what they do with their bodies. And of course, they make these judgments about you as well. The same is true in public speaking.

Following are the six dimensions of bodily action that have relevance to the public speaking situation: eye contact, facial expression, appearance, gestures, movement, and proxemics. Each of these is discussed as to its nature, the major problems associated with it, and the ways in which it may be used to increase your effectiveness as a public speaker.

Eye contact

Perhaps the most important single aspect of bodily communication is eye contact. In interpersonal communication, more information is communicated through eye contact than through any other means. Although the influence of eye contact is somewhat less in public speaking, it is always significant.

You know, again from your interpersonal interactions, that you trust information coming from eyes more than you trust information coming from the mouth. If you are to secure the trust of the audience, you will have to demonstrate this through eye contact as well as through other means.

The two major problems with eye contact are insufficient eye contact and eye contact that is not spread fairly over the entire audience. If you do not maintain enough eye contact, you will appear distant, unconcerned, and less trustworthy than you would if you looked directly at the audience. Audience feedback will be impossible to secure without eye contact.

Some speakers will focus on selected portions of the room or even on selected supportive listeners without realizing that they are ignoring the rest of the audience. They seem to feel that they are maintaining eye contact and that that is sufficient—an assumption often made without conscious awareness. You should attempt eye contact with the entire audience—to involve all the listeners in the public speaking transaction and to otherwise communicate equally with the members on the left and on the right, in both the back and the front.

Facial expression

Facial expressions are particularly important in communicating emotions. Nonverbal researchers refer to these as *affect displays*. These are the facial expressions that show emotional meaning; they are the expressions demonstrating anger and fear, boredom and excitement, doubt and fear, and a host of other emotions that most persons display quite naturally.

Affect displays are displayed quite naturally even when you may not wish to display them. Affect displays have a way of creeping out without the speaker wanting them to. These are the facial movements that give you away—that betray your boredom even though you say you are interested, that tell the person you are with that you are tired even though you protest that you are wide awake. If you attempt to convince an audience of a proposition you are not interested in or in favor of, you will often be betrayed by these facial movements.

The art of the actor is to display such facial expressions and emotions when not feeling them personally. And I have no doubt that there are numerous politicians who have been trained to convey emotional feelings that are often antithetical to what they are really feeling. I think this is especially obvious when politicians address numerous different groups and essentially tell management what it wants to hear and labor what it wants to hear; the rich are told one thing and the poor are told another, and so on. The effective (though not necessarily ethical) politician is the one who can make all audiences believe that what is being said is what is being felt. This is largely, though not exclusively, accomplished through facial expressions.

Gestures

When bodily action in public speaking situations is discussed, the role of gestures—movements of the arms and hands—seem to come to mind most readily. The role of gestures in the communication process has been studied throughout the last decade in considerable depth. Part of this research and theory has been devoted to a classification of the various types of movements. Most gestures would fall into the class of nonverbal behaviors called *illustrators*, those behaviors that quite literally illustrate the verbal messages. For example, in saying "Come here," there will be movements of the head, of the hands and arms, and of the entire body that motion the listener in your direction. Your body as well as your verbal messages say "Come here."

The best bodily action is that which is spontaneous and natural to the speaker, to the audience, and to the speech. If you are relaxed and comfortable with yourself and with the audience, natural bodily action will be generated without any conscious and studied attention to it. This seems the most reasonable approach in guiding your behavior.

Movement

Movement refers here to the gross bodily movements. It generally helps to move around a bit; it keeps the audience and you more alert. Naturally, this is impossible when speaking from a stationary microphone or when movement is otherwise restricted. And yet you can give the illusion of movement by stepping back or forward or flexing the upper torso so that it appears that you are moving a great deal more than you in fact are.

Three problems to be avoided are too little, too much, and too patterned movement. With too little movement, you may appear strapped to the podium, perhaps even afraid of the audience, perhaps not interested in the situation enough to involve yourself fully. With too much movement, the audience begins to concentrate on the movement itself, wondering where you will wind up next. With too patterned movement—as with all nonverbal aspects—the audience becomes bored; too steady and predictable a rhythm becomes tiring very quickly. The audience will often view you as nonspontaneous and uninvolved.

You may use gross movements with considerable effect to emphasize transitions and to emphasize the introduction of a new and important assertion. Thus, when making a transition, you might take a step forward to signal that something new is coming; similarly, this type of movement may signal the introduction of an important assumption, bit of evidence, or closely reasoned argument.

Proxemics

Proxemics refers to that area of nonverbal communication concerned with space. It encompasses such areas as the space you require or expect or demand while interacting with others—some need a great deal of space while others prefer to interact at close range. The way in which you lay out space in your home, the possessiveness you have to various territories, the use of space to signal status relationships (the larger, higher up, and closer the office to the boss, the higher the individual's status), and even the ways in which cities and towns are constructed all represent proxemic communications.

In public speaking the space between you and the listeners and among the listeners themselves is often a crucial factor. If you stand too close to the audience, they might feel uncomfortable, as if being looked over too closely and as if their personal space is being violated. If you stand too far away from the audience, you might be perceived as uninvolved, uninterested, and uncomfortable with the entire public speaking transaction. These perceptions of too close and too far by the audience may in reality involve distances that are actually extremely small. Thus, if you are in front of the class in a normal classroom, you might have perhaps six feet to utilize. A foot back or a foot forward might well give the impression of too far or too close.

SEE EXPERIENTIAL VEHICLE 6.3.

I have often witnessed large classrooms holding perhaps 20 or 30 students spread out over the 200 or 300 seats available. For a speaker to speak effectively with such a group would seem to me most difficult. In this situation you would be wise to pause and to simply ask the audience to come together. With some kind of physical closeness you will be much better able to maintain appropriate eye contact, accurately read audience feedback, and help the audience to feel some kind of unity with you and with each other, which will almost always help you achieve your purpose.

REMEMBER these general guidelines to effective use of bodily action in public speaking:

1 **Maintain eye contact with your entire audience.**
2 **Think and feel what you are saying and allow your facial expressions to convey these feelings.**
3 **Gesture naturally—neither too much nor too little.**
4 **Move around a bit, avoiding too little, too much, and too patterned movement.**
5 **Position yourself neither too close nor too far away from your audience and try to keep audience members relatively close to each other.**

A DELIVERY IMPROVEMENT PROGRAM

Throughout the discussion of voice and bodily action, it should have been apparent that delivery is a most complex dimension of public speaking. Guidelines were presented throughout the discussions for the improvement of both of these aspects of delivery. Here a general improvement program is suggested that should be of value in dealing with long-term improvements.

1. First, seek feedback from someone whose opinion and insight you respect. Your public speaking instructor may be a logical choice but someone majoring in communication or in speech pathology (for the vocal dimensions) might also be appropriate. Get an honest and thorough appraisal of both your voice and your bodily action.

2. Second, learn to hear and see and feel the differences between effective and ineffective patterns. Learn to hear, for example, the patterned nature of your pitch or your overly loud volume; a tape or cassette recorder would be most helpful. Learn to feel your rigid posture or your lack of arm and hand gestures. Once you have perceived these differences, concentrate on acquiring more effective patterns. Practice a few minutes each day. Avoid becoming overly conscious of any source of ineffectiveness; just try to increase your awareness of it and work on one problem at a time. Do not try to change all your patterns at once.

3. Seek additional feedback on the changes. Make certain that the patterns you are practicing and that you hear, see, and feel as more effective

are also perceived by others as more effective. Remember that you hear yourself through air transmission as well as through bone conduction. Others hear you only through air transmission, so what you hear and what others hear will be different. Similarly, there are great differences between what we can see and feel in regard to our own bodily action and what others can see and feel.

4. For voice improvement, consult a book for practice exercises and for additional information on the nature of volume, rate, pitch, and quality (see the suggestions under "Sources").

5. If any of these difficulties persist see a professional. For voice problems see a speech clinician. Most campuses have some kind of speech clinic and you can easily avail yourself of their services. For bodily action difficulties talk with your public speaking instructor.

You should also seek professional help if you are psychologically uncomfortable with any aspect of your voice or your bodily action. It may be that all you have to do is to hear yourself or see yourself on a videotape—as others see and hear you—to convince yourself that you sound and look fine. But regardless of what is causing this discomfort, if you are uncomfortable do something about it. In a college community, there is more of such assistance available to you at no cost than you will ever experience again. Make use of it.

SOURCES

On voice see Joseph A. DeVito, Jill Giattino, and T. D. Schon, *Articulation and Voice: Effective Communication* (Indianapolis: Bobbs-Merrill, 1975); Mardel Ogilvie and Norma S. Rees, *Communication Skills: Voice and Pronunciation* (New York: McGraw-Hill, 1969); and Robert King and Eleanor DiMichael, *Articulation and Voice: Improving Oral Communication* (New York: Macmillan, 1978).

For any substantial insight into nonverbal communication, see the specialized works in this area. I would particularly recommend the following: Mark Knapp, *Nonverbal Communication in Human Interaction*, 2d ed. (New York: Holt, Rinehart and Winston, 1978); Dale G. Leathers, *Nonverbal Communication Systems* (Boston: Allyn & Bacon, 1976); and Lawrence Rosenfeld and Jean Civikly, *With Words Unspoken* (New York: Holt, Rinehart and Winston, 1976). On sex differences in nonverbal communication see Robert Rosenthal and Bella M. DePaulo, "Expectations, Discrepancies, and Courtesies in Nonverbal Communication," *Western Journal of Speech Communication* 43 (Spring 1979): 76–95; Marianne LaFrance and Clara Mayo, "A Review of Nonverbal Behaviors in Women and Men," *Western Journal of Speech Communication* 43 (Spring 1979): 96–107; and Loretta A. Malandro and Larry Barker, *Nonverbal Communication* (Reading, Mass.: Addison-Wesley, 1983).

HOW TO . . . Evaluate Speech Delivery: Part Six Checklist

Yes No

■ ■   1 Does your delivery seem natural rather than call attention to itself and detract from your message?

■ ■   2 Does your delivery reinforce and give emphasis to your message?

■ ■   3 Is your delivery style appropriate to you as a person?

■ ■   To your audience?

■ ■   To the occasion?

■ ■   To the subject matter?

■ ■   4 Do you feel (and appear to be) comfortable with your style of delivery?

■ ■   5 Is your delivery flexible and varied?

■ ■   6 Does your delivery aid audience understanding?

■ ■   7 Is your method of delivery (impromptu, manuscript, memorized, or extemporaneous) appropriate to you as the speaker?

■ ■   To your audience?

■ ■   To the occasion?

■ ■   8 Is your volume loud enough for all to hear but not so loud as to be distracting?

■ ■   Is it varied rather than kept at one steady (boring) intensity?

■ ■   9 Is your rate neither too fast nor too slow?

■ ■   Is it varied rather than unvaried?

■ ■   10 Is your pitch varied to communicate the nuances you wish to convey?

■ ■   11 Is your voice without excessive nasality or denasality?

■ ■   Breathiness?

■ ■   Hoarseness?

■ ■   12 Do you maintain appropriate eye contact with the entire audience?

■ ■   13 Do your facial gestures reinforce your verbal messages?

■ ■   14 Is your attire appropriate to the public speaking situation?

■ ■   Are extreme and potentially distracting clothes avoided?

■ ■   15 Do your gestures and bodily movements reinforce rather than contradict your verbal messages?

■ ■   Are "studied" and artificial gestures avoided?

■ ■   16 Are you speaking at an appropriate distance from your audience—neither too far nor too close?

EXPERIENTIAL VEHICLES FOR PART SIX

As an exercise in delivery, the following experience may prove useful. Students should be given three index cards each. Each student should write an impromptu speech topic on each of the cards. The cards should be collected and placed face down on a table. A speaker is chosen through some random process and selects two cards, reads the topics, selects one of them and takes approximately one minute to prepare a two- to three-minute impromptu speech.

A few guidelines may prove helpful.

1   Do not apologize. Everyone will have difficulty with this assignment so there is no need to emphasize any problems you may have.

2   Do not express verbally or nonverbally any displeasure or any negative responses to the experience, the topic, the audience, or even to oneself. Approach the entire task with a positive attitude and a positive appearance. It will help make the experience a more enjoyable one for both you and for your audience.

3   When you select the topic, jot down two or three subtopics that you will cover and perhaps two or three bits of supporting material that you will use in amplifying these two or three subtopics.

4   Develop your conclusion. It will probably be best to use a simple summary conclusion in which you restate your main topic and the subordinate topics that you discussed.

5   Develop an introduction. Here it will probably be best to simply identify your topic and orient the audience by telling them the two or three subtopics that you will cover.

The topics to be used for impromptu speaking should be familiar but not clichés. They should be worthwhile and substantive, not trivial. They should be neither too simplistic nor too complex. Here are some sample topics that may be used in lieu of the procedure suggested above:

1. The values of a college education.
2. What makes someone attractive?
3. How to meet another person.
4. What is love?
5. What is friendship?
6. How to resolve conflict.
7. How to communicate with your family.
8. What is success?
9. What makes a person happy?
10. Places to visit.
11. Things to do.
12. An ideal day.
13. An ideal relationship.
14. An ideal occupation.
15. An ideal lover.
16. An unusual pet.
17. Tough decisions.
18. My favorite movie.
19. My favorite television show.
20. My favorite sport.
21. My favorite meal.
22. My favorite character from literature.
23. Unusual pastimes.
24. An important moment from history.
25. A current national concern.
26. My hero.
27. What I hate most.
28. The type of person I dislike.
29. What to do on a Saturday night.
30. How not to be a good student.
31. How to survive in college.
32. How to say "I love you."
33. How to hurt someone you love.
34. Body language.
35. Contemporary music.

In this exercise a subject recites the alphabet attempting to communicate each of the following emotions:

anger
fear
happiness
jealousy
love
nervousness
pride
sadness
satisfaction
sympathy

The subject may begin the alphabet at any point and may omit and repeat sounds, but the subject may use only the names of the letters of the alphabet to communicate these feelings.

The subject should first number the emotions in random order so that he or she will have a set order to follow which is not known to the audience, whose task it will be to guess the emotions expressed.

As a variation, have the subject go through the entire list of emotions: once facing the audience and employing any nonverbal signals desired and once with his or her back to the audience without employing any additional signals. Are there differences in the number of correct guesses depending on which method is used?

For Discussion and Response

1   What are some of the differences between sending/receiving "emotional meaning" and "logical meaning"?

2   Davitz and Davitz found the number of correct identifications for these emotions to be as follows: anger (156), nervousness (130), sadness (118), happiness (104), sympathy (93), satisfaction (75), love (60), fear (60), jealousy (69), and pride (50). Do these figures correspond to those obtained in class? What conclusions would you draw relevant to the relative ease/difficulty of expressing the several emotions?

[1] This exercise is based on J. R. Davitz and L. J. Davitz, "The Communication of Feelings by Content-Free Speech," *Journal of Communication* 9(1959):6–13.

3   Do you think there is a positive relationship between sending and receiving abilities in situations such as this? Is the person adept at sending the emotions also adept at receiving them? Explain.
4   What variables might influence sending ability? Receiving ability?
5   What personality factors seem relevant to the sending and receiving of emotions?

6.3 NONVERBAL COMMUNICATION

Groups of 8 to 12 persons should be formed. Through some random procedure, each group is divided into two sections or subgroups. (Throw slips of paper, half with *A* written on them and half with *B* written on them, into a box and have each person draw out a piece to determine what subgroup he or she will be in.)

The entire group should watch the same half-hour television show—to be selected by the entire group. Situation comedies or dramas where you have some familiarity with the characters but not with the plot would work best (avoid *TV Guide* summaries for this exercise). Soap operas would be inappropriate since you would have to know too much about the plot to analyze it; on the other hand, if you know about the plot, nothing of significance would probably happen in any half-hour show.

One-half of the group (say, the *A*'s) should watch the show *without* any sound; the other half (the *B*'s) should watch the show normally. After viewing the show, the entire group should get together. Those students who viewed the show without sound should attempt to summarize the plot. The *B*'s should not interrupt or correct the *A*'s as they are attempting to reconstruct the plot. This nonintervention will be most difficult but it is essential.

After the summary or reconstruction of the plot by the soundless group, the other half should attempt to specify the ways in which the reconstruction was inaccurate and the possible reasons for it. After the basic plot has been accurately summarized by the *B*'s—this time assisted by the *A*'s—the entire group should consider some or all of the following issues:

1   What gross bodily movements are used to communicate?
2   What messages did facial expressions communicate?
3   What did the eyes communicate?
4   How were hand gestures used and what did they communicate?

5   What messages did clothing and general appearance communicate?
6   How was space used to communicate? What are some of its messages?
7   Was touch used to communicate? What messages did it communicate?
8   What types of messages were most helpful in deciphering the plot?
9   What conclusions are you willing to draw concerning the relative contribution of sound and bodily movements in communication?

APPENDIX A

Asking and answering questions

In many public speaking situations there is a question-and-answer session during which the audience is invited to ask questions of the speaker, usually for a specified amount of time. In some instances, the chairperson will recognize audience members who then address their questions to the speaker. In other cases, the speaker acknowledges the audience members and answers their questions in turn.

The question-and-answer session is not appropriate in all public speaking situations. Certainly, such a session would be out of place after a eulogy, the presentation of an award, or a welcoming speech. Generally, question-and-answer sessions are appropriate following informative and persuasive speeches. The major purposes of such sessions are (1) to further exploration of the issues raised in the speech and (2) to provide the audience an opportunity to pursue issues and ideas raised in the speech.

In practice such sessions also serve to provide the audience members with an opportunity to state their reactions to the speech and express some of their own views on the ideas presented and to provide the speaker with additional opportunities to inform or to persuade the audience. As a learning device, the question-and-answer period serves important learning-teaching functions. It provides the speaker with the challenge to think quickly and organize thoughts with a minimum amount of preparation time. It also provides the speaker with useful feedback on audience reactions.

As with all principles of public speaking, those of asking and answering questions must be adjusted to the specific situation and individual involved. Nevertheless, some general guidelines may be presented.

ASKING QUESTIONS

Ask questions you really want answered

Do not ask questions just because you think they might be clever or make you look good to the audience or to the boss or teacher. Similarly, do not ask questions for which you can easily and quickly find the answer yourself. This merely uses up valuable time that might be better used seeking answers to questions that cannot be readily located and that are somehow more integral to this particular public speaking encounter.

Help the speaker to understand your question

Remember that after a person has delivered a public speech, it is frequently difficult to recover composure and effectively listen to questions, sometimes very intricate questions. Therefore, help the speaker by phrasing your questions in different ways or perhaps by giving an example of what you mean.

Be supportive of the speaker

Phrase your questions in a friendly style, in a manner that communicates a genuine desire to secure information or explore relevant issues. Do not ask questions in a way that might appear to attack the speaker. Little is gained when the style of questions and answers is that of attack and counterattack.

Do not use the question period to give a speech

The question period is designed to provide the audience with an opportunity to seek additional information and not to allow selected members of the audience an opportunity to give speeches of rebuttal. If you have a point of view very different from the speaker and wish to give a speech in refutation, then try to arrange a rebuttal speech. Don't use the question period for this purpose.

Avoid loaded questions

To force the speaker into giving you the answer you want is manipulation. This is unfair to both the speaker and the audience and serves no useful purpose. Generally, this has the effect of increasing defensiveness on the part of the speaker who will often respond with a counterattack. The result is a conflict instead of a search for information and understanding.

State your entire question at once

If your question is in two parts, state them both and let the speaker divide them in his or her responses. Say, for example, "I wonder if you are against the plan to increase tuition and, if so, where you would get the added funds that are needed?" This type of question then allows the speaker the opportunity to elaborate with specific reference to your concerns.

ANSWERING QUESTIONS

Each speaker will naturally handle questions in a manner that is unique and consistent with his or her personality and speaking style. Nevertheless, a few guidelines may be suggested for effectively dealing with questions from the audience.

Clarify the question

As obvious as this suggestion may sound, it is one that is frequently ignored by even the most professional speakers. If there is the slightest doubt in your mind that you may not understand the question, ask the person to repeat it or say something like, "As I understand the question, you're asking me to explain my position on the entire educational tax package." In this way the questioner has an opportunity to correct any misinterpretation. There is little sense in answering a question that has not been asked.

Do not fabricate answers

If you are asked a question for which you do not have the answer, then simply admit it. Audiences will know when you are bluffing; to bluff an answer is insulting to the audience and at the same time will destroy your credibility. A simple "I'm sorry but I don't know the answer to that question" or "I don't have the figures here but I can find them out for you" or "I'm not certain but I seem to recall that . . . , but I will check on that to make sure" will be most appreciated. In this way the audience sees that you are being honest with them and not attempting to deceive them—something everyone universally resists and rejects.

Repeat the question

Most students are well aware of the problem created when teachers respond to a question without repeating it. Often the result is that you have to sit through a lengthy answer to a question you never heard. Such explanations are difficult (at best) to process and relate to the appropriate issues or topics. Repeating the question has two very specific benefits. First, it will ensure that you understand the question. Second, it will ensure that the other members of the audience have heard it and will therefore be able to follow your response.

Respond clearly and directly

The question period should not be used to give another speech. Specific questions demand specific answers—short and to the point. Some questions—those that ask for opinions or projections, for example—may require more lengthy responses. Relatively speaking, however, answers should be brief. Even if the question is phrased as a yes/no question, elaborate at least a bit—perhaps stating the reasons or the evidence that leads you to your conclusion. The questioner will probably feel cheated if given too brief an answer.

Don't engage in private dialogues

Some questioners expect to have a dialogue with the speaker, responding to each of the speaker's responses and expecting the speaker to respond to each of these, with the result that the time is used up by this one questioner. Try to avoid this development. For example, tell the questioner that you will see her or him later and discuss this aspect of the topic further, or say that you want to respond to some other questions first and if there is time you will elaborate on these other issues. Sometimes it may be necessary to be more direct and say something like "I'm afraid we're spending too much time on this topic and that if we continue a lot of other questions will go unanswered." Then simply acknowledge another questioner. Be careful, however, not to do this if you sense the audience wants this line of questioning pursued. If you do, it may appear that you are trying to avoid answering this line of questioning and that you are sidestepping certain topics or issues.

Be supportive of the questioner

The audience is likely to identify more with the questioner from their ranks than with you, the speaker. If you treat a questioner abruptly or negatively in some way, this will often be seen as addressed to the entire audience. I'm sure you can recall a number of teachers who have done this and in the process alienated the entire class. Also, realize that the questioner is serving a most important function for you. He or she is in effect telling you that this question is something the audience is concerned with and is giving you an opportunity to deal with it. In a sense the questioner is providing you with insight into the concerns of the audience—something that had you had the time and the knowledge, you would have discovered in your audience analysis. Furthermore, this is an excellent opportunity for you to build your credibility. Remember that the audience is continually revising its opinion of you. An effective speech and a high credibility perception during the speech may all be erased by inept handling of one question. So, be supportive. Thank the speaker (verbally or perhaps with some nonverbal expression of acknowledgment) and perhaps even comment that the question is a most valuable one (assuming that it is). This will not only tell the audience that you respect them but it will encourage others to ask questions which, again, gives you the opportunity to further your speech purpose, whether it is to inform or to persuade. Comments such as, "That question is irrelevant" or "I won't waste my time with that type of question" may be appropriate on rare occasions—as when the questioner is heckling or when the questioner makes some sexist or racial attacks. As a general rule, assume that the questioner is sincere and thoughtful in asking the question. Rarely will you lose anything by being courteous and polite.

Break complex questions into parts

If you do break up a question into its component parts, let the audience know what you are doing. Say, for example, "There are two parts to this question: the first part asks what I would do about tuition and the second asks what my opponent would do. Let me answer each part in turn."

Asking and answering questions effectively is a unique and difficult skill to master. Yet with experience and a careful eye on the questions and answers of others, you should be able to sharpen your skills considerably.

The small group encounter

We are all members of various small groups. The famly is the most obvious example, but we also function as members of a team, class, a collection of friends, and so on. Some of our most personally satisfying and productive communications take place within the small group context.

In this section we examine the small group encounter: three types of small groups (the problem-solving, idea-generation, and learning groups), and some guidelines for both members and leaders to follow in small group communication encounters.

A *small group* is a collection of individuals, few enough in number so that all members may communicate with relative ease as both senders and receivers, and who are related to each other by some common purpose and with some degree of organization or structure among them. These several characteristics of the small group will be further clarified as we consider each of the three major types of small group situations.

TYPES OF SMALL GROUPS

Each of three major types (the problem-solving group, the idea-generaton group, and the educational or learning group) is discussed according to its general nature and the procedures that members would follow in participating in such groups.

The problem-solving group

Perhaps the type of group most familiar to us when we think of small group communication is the probem-solving group—a group of individuals meeting to solve a particular problem or to at least reach a decision that may be a preface to the solution.

In a problem-solving discussion it is useful to identify approximately eight steps that should be followed. These steps are designed to make problem-solving more efficient and more effective. Although some of the initial steps may at first seem unnecessary and there may be a temptation to short-circuit this process, it has been found repeatedly that this does not in fact save time; rather it wastes time in the long run. These steps to be followed are:

1. Define the problem In many instances the nature of the problem is clearly specified, and everyone in the group knows exactly what the problem is, for example, what color the new soap package should be or what the name for the new candy bar should be. In other instances, however, the problem may be vague, and it remains for the group to define it in concrete, unambiguous, specific terms. The problem should also be limited in some way so that it identifies a manageable area for discussion. Thus, for example, the general problem may be poor campus communications. But such a vague and general topic is difficult to tackle in a problem-solving discussion, and so it is helpful to specify the problem clearly for purposes of this discussion. Generally, it is best to define the problem as an open-ended question ("How can we improve the student newspaper?") rather than as a statement ("The student newspaper needs to be improved") or a yes/no question ("Does the student newspaper need improvement?"). The open-ended question allows for greater freedom of exploration and does not restrict the ways in which the problem may be approached. Further, the statement of the problem should not suggest possible solutions, as would, for example, "How can faculty supervision improve the student newspaper?" Here we are stating that faculty supervision is the solution to the problem of improving the student newspaper rather than leaving the solutions open for discussants to identify and evaluate.

2. Identify the significance of the problem In many groups all the participants will be aware of the importance or significance of the problem. In other groups it may be helpful for the significance of the problem to be stressed. Sometimes the importance of an issue is recognized only in the abstract, and it may be helpful for its importance to be made more concrete. Sometimes it is recognized that the problem is important for others, and it remains to be pointed out how the problem affects the members of the group themselves. Group members need to be aware of what the implications of the problem are, how this problem may lead to other problems, in what ways this problem blocks goals that group members value, how this problem impinges on the lives of group members, and so on. The more important the problem is perceived to be by the group members, the more importance they will give to the problem-solving process and the more energy they will be willing to expend in dealing with the problem.

3. Analyze the problem In the analysis of the problem the group members seek to identify the ramifications of the problem. Given a general problem, we seek in this analysis stage to identify its particular dimensions. Although there are no prescribed questions to ask of all problems, appropriate questions (for most problems) seem to revolve around the following issues: (1) *Duration*. How long has the problem existed? Is it likely that it will continue to exist in the future? What is the predicted course of the problem? For example, will it grow or lessen in influence? (2) *Causes*. What are the major causes of the problem? How certain may we be that these are the actual causes? (3) *Effects*. What are the effects of the problem? How significant are these effects? Who is affected by this problem? How significantly are they affected by the problem? Is this problem causing other problems? How important are these other problems?

Applied to our newspaper example, the specific questions we might ask in the analysis stage might look something like this. Under "duration" we might ask, How long has there been a problem with the student newspaper? Will the problem continue in the future? Does it look as though it will grow or lessen in importance? Under "causes" we might ask, What seems to be causing the newspaper problem? Are there specific people (an editor, a faculty adviser, for example) who might be causing the problem? Are there specific policies (editorial, advertising, design) that might be causing the problem? How sure are we that these "causes" are the actual or real causes of the problem? Under "effects" we might ask, What effects is this problem producing? How significant are these effects? Who is affected—students? alumni? faculty? Are there people within or outside the college community who are not benefiting as they should from the student newspaper?

4. Establish criteria for evaluating the solutions Before any solutions are proposed, the group members should identify the standards that will be employed in evaluating the possible solutions, the criteria that will be used in selecting one solution over another. This is a particularly difficult aspect of problem solving but an essential one. Generally two types of criteria need to be considered. First, there are the practical criteria—for example, that the solutions must not increase the budget (assuming that there is a limited amount of money to be spent on the newspaper); the size of the newspaper cannot be increased (if this is tied to the budget); the number of issues per semester may not be increased. The solution must be such that it enables the staff of the paper to be drawn from all volunteers regardless of their qualifications, must lead to an increase in the number of advertisers, the readership must increase by at least 10 percent, and so on. Second, there are the value criteria, and these clearly are much more difficult to identify and to determine. These might include, for example, that the newspaper must be a learning experience for all those who work on the paper or that it must reflect the attitudes of the board of trustees, of the faculty, or of the students.

After the solutions are identified (step 5), the members go back to these standards to make certain that the new solution does meet these criteria.

5. Identify possible solutions At this brainstorming stage the members attempt to identify as many solutions as possible. It is best to focus on quantity rather than quality. Try to identify as many solutions as possible. Brainstorming may be particularly useful at this point. *Brainstorming* is a technique for literally bombarding a problem and generating as many ideas or solutions as possible. In this case such solutions might include incorporating reviews of faculty publications; student evaluations of specific courses; reviews of restaurants in the campus area; outlines for new courses; student, faculty, and administration profiles; and employment information.

6. Evaluate solutions After all the solutions have been proposed, the members go back and evaluate each of them according to the criteria for evaluating solutions established in step 4. For example, to what extent does incorporating reviews of area restaurants meet the criteria for evaluating solutions? Would it increase the budget? Would it lead to an increase in advertising revenue? Each solution should be matched against the criteria for evaluating solutions.

7. Select the best solution(s) At this stage the best solution or solutions are selected and put into operation. Thus, for example, we might incorporate in the next issues reviews of faculty publications and outlines for new courses, assuming that these two possible solutions best met the criteria for evaluating solutions.

8. Test selected solutions After we put the solution(s) into operation, we attempt to test their effectiveness. We might, for example, poll the students in terms of their responses to the new newspaper, or we might examine the number of copies purchased (if the students buy individual copies), or we might analyze the advertising revenue or determine whether the readership did increase 10 percent.

If these solutions prove ineffective, then it is necessary to go back to one of the previous stages and go through part of the process again. Often this takes the form of selecting other solutions to test, but it may involve going further back to, for example, a reanalysis of the problem, an identification of other solutions, or a restatement of criteria.

These eight steps may seem at first to be rather rigidly prescribed, but for beginning problem-solving discussions it would probably not be a bad idea to follow the pattern with some precision. When discussants become more adept at the problem-solving process, the steps may be approached with greater flexibility, where participants go back and forth and may skip a step and come back to it after a normally later step has been covered. Even with such flexibility, however, the problem-solving process is generally fairly clearly prescribed. In contrast, the structure for the idea-generation discussion, to be considered next, is fairly loose.

The idea-generation group

Many small groups exist solely for the purpose of generating ideas, whether they are involved in advertising, politics, education, or, in fact, any field where ideas are needed, and that would include all fields. Although members may get together and simply generate ideas, a formula is usually followed, particularly that formula called *brainstorming*. In this system the group members meet in two periods: the first is the brainstorming period proper and the second is the evaluation period. The procedure is relatively simple. A problem is selected that is amenable to many possible solutions or ideas. Group members are informed of the problem to be brainstormed before the actual session so that some prior thinking on the topic is done. When the group meets, each person contributes as many ideas as he or she can think of. Ideas should be recorded either in writing or on tape. During this idea-generating session four general rules are followed:

1. **No negative criticism is allowed**   All ideas are treated in exactly the same way; they are written down by a secretary. They are not evaluated in this phase, nor are they even discussed. Any negative criticism—whether verbal or nonverbal—is itself criticized by either the leader or the members.

2. **Quantity is desired**   The assumption made here is that the more ideas the better; somewhere in a large pile of ideas will be one or two good ones that may be used. The more ideas generated, the more effective the brainstorming session.

3. **Combinations and extensions are desired**   While we may not criticize a particular idea, we may extend it or combine it in some way. The value of a particular idea, it should be noted, may well be in the way it stimulates another member to combine or extend it.

4. **Freewheeling is wanted**   By this is meant that the wilder the idea the better. Here the assumption is that it is easier and generally more profitable to tone an idea down rather than to spice it up. A wild idea can easily be tempered, but it is not as easy to elaborate on a simple or conservative idea.

After all the ideas are generated, a period that takes no longer than 15 or 20 minutes, the entire list of ideas is evaluated, and the ones that are unworkable are thrown out while the ones that show promise are retained and evaluated. Here, of course, negative criticism is allowed.

The educational or learning group

In educational or learning groups the purpose is to acquire new information or skill through a mutual sharing of knowledge or insight. At times one person, say a teacher, will have the information, and the group exists simply as a means for disseminating the information the teacher possesses. But this function is just as well, if not more effectively, served by a lecture. In most small group learning situations all members have something to teach and something to learn, and the members pool their knowledge to the mutual benefit of all.

In the educational or learning group, members may follow a variety of discussion patterns. For example, a historical topic might be developed chronologically, with the discussion progressing from the past into the present and perhaps predicting the future. Issues in developmental psychology—for example, language development in the child or physical maturity—might also be discussed chronologically. Many topics lend themselves to spatial development, where the discussion follows a left-to-right or a north-to-south pattern—for example, the development of the United States might take a spatial pattern going from east to west or a chronological pattern going from 1776 to the present. Other suitable patterns, depending on the nature of the topic and the needs of the discussants, might be developed in terms of causes and effects, problems and solutions, structures and functions.

Perhaps the most popular pattern is the topical pattern, in which the main topic is divided into its subdivisions without regard for time or space considerations, for example. A group might discuss the functions of the legal profession by itemizing each of the major functions and discussing these without regard for any additional system of ordering. The structure of a corporation might also be considered in terms of its major divisions. As can be appreciated, each of these two topics may be further systematized by, say, ordering the functions of the legal profession in terms of importance or complexity and ordering the major structures of the corporation in terms of decision-making power.

These patterns, it should be noted, are essentially the same patterns that we consider under the structures of public speaking; they are actually patterns for organizing all sorts of communications.

What is most important for the discussants and the leader to recognize is that some pattern, some prearranged agenda, must be developed if the discussion is to progress productively and if each of the major topics is to be given adequate time.

GUIDELINES FOR SMALL GROUP MEMBERS

Here are several guidelines that will help make the participation of members in small group communication both more effective and more enjoyable.

Be group-oriented

Perhaps the most general and the most important suggestion to keep in mind is that in the small group communication situation, you are a member of a group, a member of some larger whole. Your participation is of value to the extent that it advances the goals of the group with effectiveness and with member satisfaction. Your responsibility is toward the group rather than to any one individual or yourself. The effective participant is one who cooperates with others to achieve some mutually satisfying goal. In the small group situation your task is to pool your talents, knowledge, and insight so that a solution may be arrived at that is more effective than a solution that could have been reached by any one individual.

Part of this group orientation involves a recognition that each person in the group is of value and is equal to every other person. Therefore, in making a comment or advancing a proposal, do so with a clear understanding that there are a number of people in the group who should be addressed equally. This simple suggestion is often violated, especially in groups where there is a powerful leader or perhaps where there is one lone but vocal dissenter. In these groups it often happens that members address their comments to these individuals rather than to the group as a whole in an attempt to impress the leader or to convince or silence the dissenter. This type of behavior spirals—an increased focus on the leader or on the dissenter leads to a further increased focus on the leader or the dissenter, which in turn leads to a still further increased focus, and so on.

The receiving end of this issue is that members should be responsive to the comments of all members and, in fact, should facilitate the contributions of all members rather than being responsive to only those members they like or those they wish to impress. All members have the potential for making valuable contributions, and it is unfair to give any member less than full attention. Further, indicate your responsiveness verbally and nonverbally. Make the person know—with what you say and what you do with your body—that you are listening, understanding, and taking into consideration what he or she is saying.

This call for group orientation is not to be taken as a suggestion for abandoning one's individuality or giving up one's personal values or beliefs for the sake of the group. This is clearly an undesirable extreme but one seen frequently in many contemporary cults and small groups. Individuality with a group orientation is what is advocated here.

Center conflict on issues

Conflict in small group communication situations is inevitable. If some form of conflict does not occur, the group is probably irrelevant or the members are so bored they do not care what is going on. Conflict is a natural part of the exchange of ideas; it is not something that should be feared or ignored. Conflict should be recognized as a natural part of the small group communication process, but it should be centered on issues rather than on personalities. Conflict creates problems in small group communication when it is person-centered rather than issue-centered.

When you disagree with what someone has said, make it clear that your disagreement, your conflict, is with the proposal advanced, the solution suggested, the ideas expressed, and not with the person. Similarly, when someone disagrees with what you say, do not take this as a personal attack but rather as an opportunity to discuss issues from an alternative point of view. Often conflict does center on personalities, and when this happens members of the group have a responsibility to redirect that conflict to the significant issues and should try to get the conflicting individuals to see that the goals of the group will be better advanced if the conflict is pursued only insofar as it relates to the issues under consideration.

Be critically open-minded

One of the most detrimental developments in a small group occurs when members come to the group with their minds already made up. When this happens, the small group process degenerates into a series of individual debates, each person arguing for his or her own position. As noted repeatedly, the small group process is a cooperative venture where each member contributes something to the whole and where the resultant decision or solution emerges from the deliberations of all members. Each member therefore should come to the group equipped with relevant information—facts, figures, and ideas that will be useful to the discussion—but should not have decided on the solution or conclusion they will accept. Thus, any solutions or conclusions that are advanced should be done so with tentativeness rather than definiteness. Discussants should be willing to alter their suggestions and revise them in the light of the discussion.

Ensure understanding

Most discussions that fail probably do so because of a lack of understanding. We need to make sure that our ideas and our information are understood by all participants. If something is worth saying, it is worth making sure that it is clearly understood. And so when in doubt, ask the members if what you are saying is clear—not with "Can you understand that bit of complex reasoning?" but rather with "Is that clear?" or "Did I explain that clearly?"

Make sure too that you understand fully the contributions of the other members, especially before you take issue with them. In fact, it is often wise to preface any extended disagreement with some kind of statement such as "As I understand you, you want to exclude Martians from playing on the football team, and if that is correct then I want to say why I think that would be a mistake." Then you would go on to state your objections. In this way you give the other person the opportunity to clarify, deny, or otherwise alter what was said and thus frequently save yourself a long argument and the group's time and energy.

GUIDELINES FOR SMALL GROUP LEADERS

In the relatively formal small group situations such as politicians planning a campaign strategy, advertisers discussing a campaign, or teachers considering educational methods, the leader has a number of specific functions.

These functions are not the exclusive property of the leader; rather they are functions that when performed are performed by a person serving a leadership role. Put differently, it is more important that these functions be served than who serves them. In situations where a specific leader is appointed or exists by virtue of some position or prior agreement, these functions are generally expected to be performed by him or her. It is important to note that leadership functions are performed best when they are performed unobtrusively—when they are performed in a nonobvious, natural manner. Leaders perform six major functions.

Activate the group interaction

In many situations the group needs no encouragement to interact. Certainly this is true of most groups with definite goals and an urgency about their mission. On the other hand, there are many groups which for one reason or another need some prodding, some stimulation to interact. Perhaps the group is newly formed and the members feel a bit uneasy with one another. Here the leader serves an important function by stimulating the members to interact. It is also important to note that this function needs to be served when the individuals of a group are acting as individuals rather than as a group. This is often the case in classroom situations when some members of a class know each other from other classes or perhaps when they graduated from the same high school. These students may stick together and function as subgroups rather than as equal members of the large groups. In this case the leader must do something to make the members recognize that they are part of a group rather than of a subgroup or pair.

Maintain effective interaction throughout

Even after the group is stimulated to group interaction, it is necessary for the leader to see that the members maintain effective interaction throughout the discussion and throughout the membership. Discussions have a way of dragging after the preliminaries are over and before the meat of the problem is addressed. When this happens it is necessary for the leader to again prod the group to effective interaction. Also, interaction is seldom shared by all members equally, but this in itself does not create problems. Problems are created, however, when this disproportionate participation is extreme or when members feel an uneasiness about entering the group interaction.

Keep members on the track

The leader should recognize that most individuals are relatively egocentric and have interests and concerns that are unique to them. Because of this, each individual will tend to wander off the track a bit. It is the leader's task to keep all members on the track—perhaps by asking relevant questions, by interjecting internal summaries as the group goes along, or perhaps by providing suitable transitions so that the relationship between the issue just discussed and the one about to be considered is made clear. In some problem-solving and educational groups a formal agenda may be used to assist in this function.

Ensure member satisfaction

The leader should recognize that all members have different psychological needs and wants and many people enter groups because of these needs and wants. Even though a group may, for example, deal with political issues, the various members may have come together for reasons that are more psychological than political or intellectual. If a group such as this is to be effective, it must not only meet the surface purposes of the group (in this case political) but also the underlying or psychological purposes that motivated many of the members to come together in the first place.

One sure way to ignore these needs is for the leader to insist that the group members do nothing that is not directly related to the surface purposes of the group. Digressions, assuming that they are not extremely frequent or overly long, are significant parts of the small group communication process and should be recognized as such.

Encourage ongoing evaluation and improvement

All groups will encounter obstacles as they attempt to solve a problem, reach a decision, or generate ideas. No group is totally effective. All groups have room for improvement. This, of course, is an obvious statement. What is not so obvious is that it is the responsibility of the group members (encouraged by the leader) to seek out these obstacles and to attempt to improve the process of group interaction. This is an extremely important but an extremely difficult task for any individual or group to undertake. People do not like to confront their shortcomings or be told that they are not functioning as effectively as they might. And yet, if the group is to improve. it must focus some attention on itself, and along with attempting to solve some external problem must attempt to solve its own internal problems as well.

Prepare the group members for the discussion

Groups form gradually and need to be eased into any discussion that is meaningful. It is the function of the leader to prepare the group members for the discussion, and this involves preparing the members for the small group interaction as well as for the discussion of a specific issue or problem.

Diverse members should not be expected to just sit down and discuss a problem without becoming familiar with each other at least superficially. Similarly, if the members are to discuss a specific problem, it is necessary that a proper briefing be introduced. Perhaps materials need to be distributed to group members before the actual discussion, or perhaps members need to be instructed to read certain materials or view a particular film or television show. Whatever the prediscussion preparations, it should be organized and coordinated by the leader.

These are just a few functions generally considered to be the responsibility of the leader. Obviously there are additional tasks of the leader that are unique to each individual situation. These tasks will become apparent as the group interacts and as the members develop greater skill in the process of small group interaction. The few functions presented here should provide some initial guidance in conducting and leading an effective small group discussion.

SOURCES

Introductions to the area of small group communication are plentiful and generally excellent. Useful works include B. Aubrey Fisher, *Small Group Decision Making: Communication and the Group Process*, 2d ed. (New York: McGraw-Hill, 1980), and Alvin A. Goldberg and Carl E. Larson, *Group Communication: Discussion Processes and Applications* (Englewood Cliffs, N.J.: Prentice-Hall, 1975). A number of interesting case studies as well as a thorough overview of small group communications are provided by John F. Cragan and David W. Wright, *Communication in Small Group Discussions: A Case Study Approach* (St. Paul, Minn.: West, 1980). A summary and critique of 114 studies in small group communication are provided by John F. Cragan and David W. Wright, "Small Group Communication Research of the 1970's: A Synthesis and Critique," *Central States Speech Journal* 31 (Fall 1980):197–213. Also see Ernest G. Bormann, "The Paradox and Promise of Small Group Communication Revisited," *Central States Speech Journal* 31 (Fall 1980):214–20 and Samuel L. Becker, "Directions of Small Group Research for the 1980's," *Central States Speech Journal* 31 (Fall 1980):221–24.

On members' and leaders' roles see Kenneth D. Benne and Paul Sheats, "Functional Roles of Group Members," *Journal of Social Issues* 4 (1948):41–49, and Marvin Shaw, *Group Dynamics: The Psychology of Small Group Behavior*, 3d ed. (New York: McGraw-Hill, 1981). Perhaps the single best source on leadership is Cecil A. Gibb's "Leadership," in G. Lindsey and E. Aronson, eds., *The Handbook of Social Psychology*, 2d ed., vol. 4 (Reading, Mass.: Addison-Wesley, 1969), pp. 205–282.

APPENDIX C

Guidelines and stimuli for speech topics

GUIDELINES FOR SPEECH TOPICS

Perhaps the question students in a public speaking class most often ask is, "What will I talk about?" "I'm not interested in international affairs, the Middle East, the Soviet–Chinese conflicts, communism versus capitalism. I'm not interested in social and political problems such as national health insurance, tax rebates, church-state relations, the aged, the poor, sexual discrimination. I'm not interested in local issues such as mass transit, real estate taxes, and rezoning laws." Or perhaps, more accurately, "I am interested in such issues in the sense that I know they're important; I know I should be more knowledgeable about them than I am. But the actual fact is that I am not very interested in such topics nor do I see myself as knowledgeable enough to speak with any degree of authority on these topics." This attitude—with individual variation, of course—is not uncommon; many, if not most, college students feel the same way. This need not lead to despair; all is not lost.

Nevertheless, the question remains: "What do I speak about?" Actually, there are hundreds of things to talk about. Suggestions are to be found everywhere and anywhere, and one of the purposes of this unit is to offer these suggestions. But before offering specific suggestions I want to distinguish, at least in general terms, suitable from unsuitable topics. A suitable speech topic should have the following three characteristics: (1) it should be worthwhile; it should deal with matters of substance; (2) it should be appropriate to speaker, audience, and occasion; and (3) it should be limited in scope and purpose.

Worthwhile

Some topics, I think, are best reserved for the cafeteria, for cocktail parties, and for speaking that is needed to fill in periods of silence. The topics of a public speech, however, need to be *worthwhile*, need to be of significance. Such topics must address issues that have significant implications for the audience. Whether you use Oxydol soap powder, Charmin toilet tissue, or Hanes pantyhose seems, to me at least, to be of no consequence whatsoever. It would all be the same if you used Era, Cottenelle, or L'eggs. What soap powder you use is irrelevant to the average person.

One excellent guideline to determine what is worthwhile, from your audience's point of view, is to look at some of the national and regional polls concerning what people think is important—the significant issues, the urgent problems. For example, a survey conducted by the Roper organization for H. & R. Block in 1978, *The American Public and the Income Tax System*, found that Americans felt the following were the most significant issues (beginning with the most important): controlling inflation, lowering the crime rate, making the tax system fair, improving the educational system, improving the nation's defense capabilities, setting up a program to provide national health insurance for everyone, lowering unemployment, improving and protecting the environment, lowering Social Security taxes, simplifying income tax forms, and improving public transportation.

In a survey conducted by Public Research in 1978, the following issues were considered the major problems confronting our country that the respondents themselves worried about (again, beginning with the most important): inflation, crime and lawlessness, the tax burden of the working American, the rising costs of hospital and health care, unemployment, energy, the condition of older people, the declining quality of education, pollution of air and water, and the condition of blacks and other minorities.

In a survey conducted for *Psychology Today* (September 1981), the personal hopes and fears of Americans were investigated. The following hopes were named (from the most often named to those named by at least 5 percent of the respondents): better or decent standard of living, good health for self, economic stability in general (no inflation), happy family life, peace of mind, emotional maturity, own a house or live in a better one, peace in the world, aspirations for children, good job (congenial work), wealth, employment, good health for family, and to be a normal, decent person. And the greatest personal fears were (again, in descending order): lowered standard of living, ill health for self, war, economic instability in general, inflation, unemployment, ill health of family, and crime.

Another recent study conducted by *Psychology Today* (July 1981) identified the 10-top "hassles and uplifts." The 10 greatest hassles (beginning with the greatest) were: concern about weight; health of a family member; rising prices of common goods, home maintenance; too many things to do; misplacing or losing things; yard work or outside home maintenance; property, investment, or taxes; crime; and physical appearance. The 10 greatest uplifts were: relating well with your spouse or lover; relating well with friends; completing a task; feeling healthy; getting enough sleep; eating out; meeting responsibilities; visiting, phoning, or writing someone; spending time with family; and a pleasing home.

Naturally all audiences are different; yet, such surveys are useful starting points for giving you some insight into what others think is important and, hence, what they should be interested in listening to.

Appropriate

The second criterion, *appropriateness*, is a somewhat more complex notion. To be suitable a speech must be appropriate to the speaker, to the audience, and to the occasion.

Appropriate to the speaker
Appropriateness to the speaker is always difficult to determine, largely because it is difficult to see ourselves from the point of view of the audience. Nevertheless, we have to try. At an obvious level we easily recognize that the sloppy, poorly dressed, and generally unkempt individual should not be speaking on proper grooming; whether or not the individual knows the topic quite well on an intellectual level, we question his or her real understanding of it. At a somewhat less obvious (and therefore more meaningful) level, take the psychology professor who believes in and lectures on the principles of conditioning and its effectiveness in controlling behavior and yet smokes two or three packs of cigarettes a day. This professor is sending contradictory signals: attesting to the effectiveness of conditioning and smoking, which—the evidence tells us—is self-destructive.

Another dimension of appropriateness you should consider is that your topics, now as well as in the future, should interest and be meaningful to you. Do not select a topic merely because it will fulfill the requirements of an assignment—although at times you may be reduced to this. Try to select a topic about which you know something and would like to learn more; you will not only acquire this new knowledge but will discover how to learn more about the topic, for example, the relevant journals, the noted authorities, and so on. Unless you are a most accomplished speaker, your enthusiasm or lack of it will show through during the speech; if you select a topic you are not interested in, you will have an extremely difficult time concealing this from the audience.

Appropriate to the audience   In much the same way that you consider appropriateness from your own vantage point, try to look at it from the point of view of the audience. What are they interested in? What would they like to learn more about? On what topics would they find the time listening to your speech to be well spent? An admittedly obvious point frequently overlooked by beginning speakers is that it is a lot easier to please an audience when you speak on a topic which interests them. To interest them in a totally new topic or in one in which they think they are not interested takes the expertise of a professional. Teachers do this with varying degrees of success every day. For now I would suggest that you take the somewhat easier alternative and concentrate on those topics that your audience is interested in and wishes to learn more about. Speaking in a class situation makes this potentially difficult decision a lot easier since you can assume that your classmates are interested in the same kinds of things you are. In selecting topics, try to play the role of a teacher and ask yourself what topics would benefit the audience. The topic should prove to be intellectually and personally stimulating and satisfying.

Appropriate to the occasion   The occasion also imposes limits and restrictions to be considered in selecting a topic. Time limitations will exclude certain topics because they are too complex. You could not explain generative transformational grammar, psycholinguistics, the sociology of mass media or sex differences in communication in a five-minute speech. Narrow the topic so that certain topics, too broad and inclusive in themselves, may be divided into smaller segments appropriate for relatively short speeches.

While a classroom situation will probably offer few problems created by the "occasion," outside of the classroom the occasion imposes a number of serious restrictions. Some occasions call for humorous subjects that, in other contexts, would be out of place and offensive. Speeches of personal experience may be appropriate in one context but inappropriate in another.

Limited in scope and purpose

Perhaps most important is that a suitable topic of a public speech must be limited in scope and purpose. Probably the major problem with beginning speeches is that they attempt to cover everything in five minutes: the history of Egypt, why our tax structure should be changed, the sociology of film, and the like are clearly too broad and attempt to cover too much. The inevitable result is that nothing specific is covered—everything is touched on but only on the surface. No depth of insight is achieved with a broad topic and all the speaker succeeds in doing is telling the audience what is already known. Invariably the audience feels cheated that it has gained nothing as a result of listening to this speech.

STIMULI FOR SPEECH TOPICS

Presented here are over 350 stimuli for speech topics. This list is not intended to provide specific topics for any of your speeches; it should, however, alleviate any anxiety over "having nothing to talk about" and should stimulate you to develop speech subjects and purposes suitable to you and to your specific audience.

Abolition movement; slavery; Civil War; leaders; rhetoric

Abortion arguments for and against; techniques of; religious dimension; legal views; differing views of

Abstract art meaning of; and emotion; leading artists; Kandinsky; Leger; Mondrian; Picasso; Pollock; contributions of movement; contemporary significance of; value of

Academic freedom nature of; censorship; teachers' role in curriculum development; and government; and research; restrictions on

Acting actors; Actor's Studio; training; fame; styles; film; theater; television; mime

Acupuncture nature of; development of; current practices in; effectiveness of; dangers of

Adoption agencies for; procedures; difficulties in; illegal; concealment of biological parents

Advertising techniques; expenditures; ethical; unethical; subliminal; leading agencies; history of; slogans

Aerospace research; medicine; industry

Age agism; aging processes; aid to the aged; discrimination against the aged; treatment of the aged; different cultural views of aging; sex differences; research in control of aging

Aggression aggressive behavior in animals; in humans; as innate; as learned; and territoriality

Agriculture science of; history of; in ancient societies; technology of; theories of

Air pollution; travel; embolism; law; navigation; power; raids

Air force in combat; training; historical role of; changes in; discrimination in

Alcoholism nature of; Alcoholics Anonymous; Al Anon; abstinence; among the young; treatment of alcoholism

Alien beings; rights; illegal; deportation

American Medical Association (AMA) power of; composition of; and national health insurance; and medical fees

Amnesia nature of; causes and effects of; types of

Amnesty in draft evasion; in criminal law; and pardons; in Civil War; in Vietnam War; conditions of

Animals experimentation; intelligence of; aggression in; ethology; and communication

Architecture nature of; styles of; and engineering; as art; urban and rural

Artists famous; associations; status in different societies; types of; government subsidies of

Arts theater; dance; film; painting; support for; apathy; social aspects of; economic aspects of; styles in the arts

Astrology alchemy; influence of; nature of; significance of; contemporary role of

Athletics professional; little league; college; support for; corruption in; benefits of; little-known sports; records; Olympics

Atomic energy; mass; clock; spectrum; structure; theory

Automation feedback; principles of; technical advantages; economics of

Automobiles development of; economics of; advances in; new developments; mass production

Aviation development of; laws governing; and warfare

Awards Academy; sports; Toni; Cleo; Emmy; scholarship; athletic

Baseball development of; economics of; famous players; rules; changes in; Little League; college; professional

Basketball rules of; development of; college; professional; fixing

Battles decisive in history; techniques and strategies; cultural variations; interpersonal

Bay of Pigs invasion; implications of; Kennedy; Castro; nature of

Bermuda Triangle nature of; myths; structure of; losses

Bicycle racing six-day; Olympic; economics of

Bicycling as exercise; as transportation; touring; development and types of cycles; social aspects; ecological aspects

Bill congressional; of rights; of exchange; of lading

Biological clock; control; warfare; rhythm; sciences

Birth defects; control; rites; racial differences; natural

Blind number of blind persons; training of the blind; Braille; communication and the blind; prejudice against; adjustment of; famous blind persons

Body communication; types; snatchers; disease of; cloning

Books binding; burning; collecting; rare; making; publishing; writing

Botany nature of; scope; methods of research; contributions

Bowling rules of; history of; scoring; amateur; professional

Boxing professional; amateur; great fights; styles of; famous fighters; economics of

Braille development of; mechanics of; alternatives to

Brain trust; washing; damage; genius; intelligence; aphasia

Buildings landmarks; famous; real estate fortunes; structures; functions of

Business cycles; associations; laws; in performing arts; finance

Cable television; underground; development of; economics of

Calorie nature of; and exercise; and diets; and weight gaining

Capitalism nature of; economics of; development of; depression and inflation; philosophy; alternatives to

Cards playing; tarot; fortune

telling; development of games; rules for games

Catholicism Roman; and protestantism; tenets of; changes in; ecumenism; papacy

Censorship arguments for and against; and violence; and sex; television; literacy

Chauvinism and patriotism; and sexism; and learning; changing conceptions of

Child labor; psychology; development; marriage; psychiatry; diseases; welfare; language

Churches famous; and art; architecture of; support for; and taxation

Cities problems of; population patterns; and tourism; crime; government of

Citizenship different conceptions of; acquiring; loss of; naturalization; tests; in different countries

Climate control; changes; adaptation; cycles; forecasting

Cloning nature of; with plants; with humans; with animals; advances in

Clothing changes in; functions of; and communication; designers; fashion; styles

College functions of; economics of; differences among; historical development of; and job training; and education

Communication public; media; intrapersonal; interpersonal; satellite

Communism development of; theories of; religious; ideologies; party organization

Computer memory; music; programming; and communication; chess; personal; and education

Copyright laws; infringements; rules; practices

Corporation law; business; nature of; history; growth of the

Cost of living index; and inflation; throughout world

Counterfeiting laws governing; punishment for; history of; preventions; techniques used in

Country music; dance; furniture; values

Credibility nature of; and persuasion; in advertising; components of

Credit nature of; public; agricultural; card living; unions; bureau

Crime prevention; types of; and law; and punishment

Cults types of; programming; deprogramming; influences of; power of

Culture cultural relativism; lag; drift; diffusion; change; shock

Dance art of; modern; social aspects of; and theater; of death; disco

Death legal aspects of; and religion; and suicide; and life; reincarnation

Debt management; retirement; limit; and credit cards

Defense national; mechanisms; self; techniques; karate

Depression nature of; and suicide; among college students; dealing with

Diet water; Scarsdale; dangers of; alternatives to; fasting; Cambridge

Disasters natural; wartime; prevention of; famous; economics of

Disco growth of; and meeting people; music; dancing; drugs

Discrimination sensory; and prejudice; racial; religious

Diseases major diseases of college students; prevention; detection; treatment; recovery

Divorce rate; throughout world; causes of; advantages of; disadvantages of; proceedings

Draft military Vietnam; dodging; voluntary enlistment

Drugs addiction; treatment; allergies; poisoning; problems; effects

Earnings college students; family; and interest; and taxes; increasing

Earthquakes nature of; famous; Alaskan; San Francisco; volcanos; seismic readings

Ecology nature of; approaches of; applications of

Economics principles of; macro; micro; schools of; of education; in education

Ecumenism nature of; significance of; history of; spread of

Education system of; social; religious; medical; legal; economics of; segregation; desegregation

Election theological; political; and persuasion; and credibility

Electricity theory of; properties of; history of; benefits of; and energy crisis

Emigration migration; changing population patterns; uses of; problems with

Empathy meaning of; in communication; and sympathy acquiring; in therapy

Employment theory; and unemployment; service insurance

Energy conservation; nature of; types of; crisis; sources nuclear; solar

Entertainment industry; benefits; abuses; tax; functions of; and communication

Environment biological; influences; versus innate factors in learning; pollution of

Equal Rights Amendment (ERA) origin of; opposition to; future of; implications of

Ethnicity meaning of; and prejudice; theories of; and culture

Ethology nature of; animal behavior patterns; pioneers; theories of

Evolution philosophical; theological; of human race; theories of; and revolution

Exercise importance of; methods of; dangers of

Exploration space; underwater; behavioral; geographical

Exports and imports; tariffs; taxes; balance of payments

Expressions in music; in drama; in art

Farming techniques; government subsidies; equipment; communal living

Federal Bureau of Investigation (FBI) work of; and propaganda; in war time

Federal Communications Commission (FCC) structure of; powers; functions; and television programming; rulings of; licenses

Feedback positive; negative; uses of; in communication; in mechanical systems; controlling

Feminism meaning of; implications of; changing concepts of

Fetishism types of; causes; treatment; and sexual functioning; theories of

Fishing as sport; for food supply; deep-sea; commercial

Floods prevention of: and dams; major

Folk literature; medicine; music; poetry; society; tales; wisdom

Food health; preservatives; additives; red dye; and allergies; preparation; stamps

Football rules; college; professional; abuses in; training in

Foreign investments nature of; government regulation of; benefits of; problems with

Freedom of speech laws protecting; and Constitution; significance of; abuses of; and censorship; and economics

Freedom of the press and Constitution; revealing sources; importance of; investigative reporting

Fuel types of; conservation; injection; supply crisis

Gambling types of; legal aspects of; casino; houses; and chance; legalization of

Game(s) history of; theory; shows; children's; psychological; destructive

Garden design; flower; vegetable; Victory

Gay rights; lifestyle; laws against; prejudice against; and religion; and lesbian; statistics; relationships

Gender roles; identification; differences

Golf rules of; courses; development of; clubs

Government federal; state; city; powers of

Gravity discovery of; laws of; specific concentration

Guilt causes of; symptoms; dealing with; effects of; and suicide; and religion

Gymnastics exercise; sports; equipment; benefits of experience; competition

Hair styles; and communication; removal of; symbolism of

Health services; human; education; laws; audiology

Heroes nature of; and adolescence; fictional; social role of; real-life heroes

Hinduism philosophy of; teachings; influences on and of; significance of

Holidays development of; economics of; problems with; social aspects of

Horse racing gambling; flats; trotters; structure of; prediction of

Hospital(s) structure; function; and preventive medicine; and concern for community; and cost

Housing urban; cost; inflation discrimination in; subsidized; undergound

Humanism nature of; in art; in literature; tenets of

Humor theories of; nature of; situational; verbal; cultural differences

Hypnotism nature of; and memory; and age regression; potentials of; uses of; dangers of; medical uses of

Ice skating competition; and dancing; techniques; sports

Immigration migration; patterns; laws governing

Impeachment laws governing; nature of; procedures for

Imports and exports; laws regulating; and tariffs; and protection of workers

Income personal; national; and employment theory; tax; statement

Independence in logic; fight for; as motive

Industrialization social aspects; economics of; political

aspects of; development of; psychological aspects

Industrial revolution development of; effects of; causes of; and pollution

Infant mortality causes of; prevention of; racial differences; preventive medicine

Inflation and deflation; causes of; effects of; types of

Information theory development of; communication aspects; problems with; and meaning; and psychology

Insurance compulsory; types of; rate making; development of

Intelligence quotient; tests; theories of; cultural differences

Internal Revenue Service tax rate schedules; auditing; rules of; techniques of

International language development of; advantages of; problems with; and nationalism; Ido; Esperanto

Intolerable Acts developments leading to; effects of; religious aspects of

Invention in music; process of; and genius; and insight

Investment stocks; old; real estate; art; restrictions on; bank; allowance; companies

Islam political aspects of; religious aspects of; economics of; significance of; tenets of; social aspects

Jazz dance; singers; rhythm; origin; spread of; styles of; social implications; aesthetics of

Jehovah's Witnesses beliefs; origin; spread of; influences of

Jewelry significance of; communication by; famous; functional; facial; cultural variations

Journalism as profession; investigative; photojournalism; education

Judaism characteristics of; beliefs; practices; laws; teachings

Kidnapping nature of; famous; laws governing; penalties; Act; Lindberg

Labor types of; division of; hours; in pregnancy; economics of; and management; unions

Languages artificial; sign; natural; learning of; loss of; pathologies of

Laws international; criminal; of nature

League of Nations nature of; structure; contributions of; problems with; Woodrow Wilson and

Liberalism political; religious; significance of; and alternatives

Libraries functions; support; science; design; largest; collections; types of

Life definition of; extraterrestrial; cycle; insurance; support; systems

Liquor types of; and alcoholism; dangers of; sale of; Prohibition

Literacy rate; world distribution; definition; problems in rising rate of

Literature criticism of; art of; types of; education in

Love nature of; theories of; romantic; family; and hate; and interpersonal relationships; of self; and materialism

LSD nature of; uses of; dangers; abuses; and REM; effects of

Machiavellianism nature of; and dogmatism; and persuasion; Niccolo Machiavelli; *The Prince*

Magic nature of; and religion; significance of; types of; and science; history of; and magicians; and sleight of hand

Maoism doctrines of; origin; spread of; philosophy of; significance of

Marriage and divorce; vows; traditions; open; contracts; bans; changing views of; laws against

Medals military; symbolism of; and communication; and behavior

Media forms of; contributions of; abuses; regulations; popularity of; influences of; and violence; and censorship

Medicine preventive; forensic; and health insurance; history of; and poisoning; alchemy; industrial

Men education of; problems of; and women; and chauvinism; changing roles of; and sexism; and prejudice; and homosexuality; in groups; as fathers

Migration animal; human; patterns; causes of; effects of

Military organizations; preparedness; confrontations and conflicts; governments; law

Modern art; architecture; dance; jazz; design

Morality nature of; cultural variations in views; teaching of; and crime

Motorcycle(s) clubs; types of; as sport; fear of; popularity of; laws regulating; transportation

Mottoes functions of; and persuasion; political; commercial

Mountain(s) climbing; building processes; types of; climate; homes

Movie(s) censorship; famous; making; producing; directing;

acting in; history of; economics of

Murder(s) methods of; penalties for; famous; and abortion; and mercy killing

Music festivals; forms; instruments; composition; styles; drama

Myth(s) nature of; origin of; symbolism of; and ritual; contemporary significance of

Narcissism nature of; and Narcissus; Freudian view of; and autoeroticism; and love of others

National Association for the Advancement of Colored People (NAACP) nature of; concerns of; founding of; spread of; accomplishments of; and desegregation; Martin Luther King, Jr.

Nationalism nature of; history of; philosophy of; chauvinism; self-determination

National Organization of Women (NOW) structure of; functions of; influences of; contributions of; beliefs of

Naturalization international law; importance of; requirements for; procedures; quotas

Navy organization of; structure of; regulations; battles; accomplishments; history of

Newspapers functions of; advertising; reporters; famous; structure of; economics of

Nicknames functions of; origins; and intimacy; and self-concept

Nielsen ratings and advertising rates; and level of programming; mechanism for securing; alternative approaches; and the level of programming

Noise pollution; white; and communication; redundancy

and; combating; causes of; types of

Nostalgia social significance of; forms of; and trivia; types of

Novels popular; classics; political; social; writing of

Nuclear plants; explosion; family; war; reaction; weapons; arguments for and against nuclear plants

Numerology function of; systems of; accuracy of predictions; contemporary practices in

Nutrition nature of; functions of food; essential requirements; animal; human; and starvation; and diet

Obscenity nature of; laws prohibiting; and pornography; effects of; influences on

Occupational diseases; psychology; satisfaction; therapy

Olympics events; origin of; and professionalism; summer; winter; structure of

Optics history of; principles of; holography; theories of

Oratory nature of; classical view of; contemporary view of; lecture circuit

Painting(s) elements of; techniques of; styles of; famous

Palestine Liberation Organization (PLO) structure of; functions of; development of; self-determination and

Papacy structure of; and doctrine of infallibility; changes in nature of; problems of; contemporary role of; election of popes; famous popes; influence of

Peace Corps; treaty; pipe; economics of

Pension nature of; different plans; insurance; and unions

Personality development of; measurement of; theories of; disorders; tests

Photography nature of; types of; art of; color; development of; infrared; technology; holography

Poetry types; famous poets; and aesthetic theories; classes of; use of language; imagery in; acoustic devices

Police functions of; structure of; crime prevention; and education; community relations; civilian review; abuses by

Political science; theories, systems; power; philosophy; parties; economy

Pollution air; atmospheric research; chemical radiation; water; and food; sources; effects; laws governing

Population(s) beliefs; theories; Malthusianism; Marxism; and education; and elderly; and family size; world; innate factors; racial typing; evolution; mutation

Pornography and censorship; types of; influences of; restrictions on

Presidents elections of; functions of; famous; impeachment of; powers of

Price system instability; inflation; changes in; taxation; theories of; balance of payments

Priesthood in different religions; roles; training; influences; hierarchy; changes in

Prison reform; systems; security; routine; effect on crime; personality; behavior; and sex; and conditioning

Prohibition history of; effects of; leaders; repeal of; abuses during; and crime

Protestantism history of; origin of; spread of; doctrines of; variations; changes in

Psychic phenomena ESP; psychokinesis; reliability of; and frauds; theories of

Psychoanalysis development of; leaders; impact of; training in; theories of

Public relations in colleges; and propaganda; public opinion; advertising

Public schools support of; changing curriculum; and parochial schools; problems with; PTA's

Publishing economics of; history of; copyright; and media exposure; trade and textbook; magazine and newspapers

Pulitzer prize areas of award; recipients; effects of; established; nature of awards

Racing auto; dog; horse; corruption in; jockeys; fame

Racism nature of; self-hatred; genetic theory; human rights; education; religious; UN position; in United States

Radar air accidents; technology; and space travel; in homes; and transportation; UFO detection

Radio development of; advertising; air traffic control; police; surveillance; radioactivity

Railroads and transportation; population movement; robberies; operation of; financial status; public support

Recording(s) development of; industry; and television; and radio; and dance; styles in

Relativism philosophy; ethical; meaning of; leaders of; influence

Religion different religions;

leaders in; influence of; beliefs of; and agnosticism; and atheism; and God; social dimensions of; and art; and architecture

Rhetoric as persuasion; as style; as propaganda; theories of; in education; and communication

Riots famous; causes of; control of; justification for; effects of

Rivers irrigation; drainage patterns; discoveries; pollution

Royalty payment to inventor; author; artist; English; religious; historical role of; contemporary role of

Saints nature of; devotion to; famous; method of selection; martyrs; canonization process; miracles

Salaries minimum wage; professional; white- and blue-collar; racial variation; and unions; and inflation

Sales advertising; methods; forecasting; and excise taxes; effects on consumers

Satellite communication; launchings; research

Scholasticism nature of; significance of; history of; doctrines of

Sciences history of; procedures in; empirical data; methods of; fiction

Scientology religious dimensions; philosophy of; development of; L. Ron Hubbard; and dianetics

Sculpture elements of; principles of; materials; relief; symbolism; religious; sculptors; famous

Security personal; Social; national

Segregation genetic; racial; leaders in fight against; legal aspects; and legal decisions; effects of; and education

Selection artificial; natural; and adaptation; and evolution

Self-concept meaning of; and communication; and depression; and conditioning

Self-defense in criminal law; international laws; and war; martial arts

Self-determination nature of; and UN charter; and nationalism

Self-disclosure benefits of; cautions in; influences of; influences on; effects of; types of; conditions conducive to

Semantics and communication; linguistic; Alfred Korzybski; connotation and denotation; theories of

Sex education; roles; therapy; surrogate; change; and love; and the concept of deviation; variations; and learning

Shooting as sport; hunting; NRA; folklore; angles; stars; scripts

Singing types; stars; and fame; opera; jazz; popular

Skiing cross country; competitions; as winter sport; as transportation; records; jumping

Skin animal; as money; human; diseases of; grafting; diving; tests; allergies

Slavery forms of; as practice in different times and places; economics of; trade; Civil War; causes and effects of; present-day practices

Soccer development of; rules of; popularity of; origin of

Social Security; facilitation; class; control; differentiation; Darwinism; equilibrium; groups; movement; realism

Solar system; wind; radiation; energy; heating

Sophistry tenets of; and rhetoric; sophists; influence of

Space exploration; fight; probes; age

Sports nature of; psychology of; fans; in college; professional; records; Little League; figures; salaries; international competition; Olympics; invention of; stadiums

Stamps collecting; famous; history; frauds

Stock market; option; common; preferred; Wall Street

Strikes famous; violence; unions; essential-service occupations; teacher; causes and effects

Style elements of; writing; speaking; and criticism; and persuasion; of acting; of dress

Subconscious Freud; development of concept; defense mechanisms

Subversive activities definition of; political; legislation penalties for

Succession lines of; royal; legal; act of; kinship

Suicide causes; among college students; laws regulating; methods; aiding the suicide of another; philosophical implications; religious dimension

Superstition beliefs; mythology; influences on history

Supreme Court judicial review; decisions; make-up of; chief justices; jurisdiction

Swimming in animals; as competitive sport; records; water polo; scuba diving techniques; life saving

Symphony historical development of; composers; famous; and contemporary music; orchestra

Taxation alcohol; cigarette; history of; purposes of; historical methods of; types of; without representation; evasion; tariffs

Teaching methods; teachers; machines; programmed learning; behavioral objectives; and conditioning

Technology benefits of; and undeveloped areas; as threat to workers; and economics; history of

Telepathy nature of; evidence for; tests of; and fraud

Telephone development of; Bell's inventions; Edison's inventions; video; satellite; conference; tapping

Television development of; history of; workings of satellite; commercials; propaganda; and leisure time; programming; economics of; effects of; and violence; and radio; and film; producing; Nielsen ratings

Tennis rules; records; players; deck; paddle; platform; squash

Test-tube babies developments in; opposition to; methods; dangers; variations

Theater Greek; Roman; commedia dell'arte; American; British. Eastern; Italian; French; performers; styles of; and television; and film; Broadway; and critics

Theology forms; development of; different religions; education

Therapy physical; psychological; language; techniques of; schools of

Time management; travel; records

Tobacco production of; smoking; effects of; causes of; methods of stopping; nicotine dangers of; economics of

Trade international; credit; organization; unionism

Traffic control; laws and regulations; bottlenecks

Tragedy as literary genre; in contemporary theater; historical development of; Greek; Elizabethan; theories of

Translation computer; missionary impetus; problems in; history of; kinds of

Transplants nature of; rejection; donor selection; legal aspects; ethical aspects; future of; advances in

Transportation history; urban; water; air; land

Treasury Department Monetary system; origin; functions of; subordinate agencies; and counterfeiting

Trials famous; history of; procedural differences; jury system; admissible evidence; psychological appeals; capital crimes

Trust nature of; and love; and self-disclosure; types of; and communication

UFO's evidence for; types of; reported sightings; theories of; agencies in charge of

Underground in wartime; film; press; theater; houses

Unemployment urban; seasonal; and violence; insurance; disguised

Unions development of; problems with; advantages of; arguments for and against; unionism

United Nations (UN) development of; functions of; agencies; and League of Nations; structure; veto powers; Security Council; Declaration of Rights

Urban living; problems; benefits; stress; crime; transportation; development; decay

Utopianism nature of; criticism of; virtues of; Sir Thomas More's *Utopia*: Christian communism; in classical thought; in literature; and socialism

Vaccine nature of; types; vaccination; immunization

Values and attitudes; and communications; social; economic; changing; religious; axiology; sex differences

Virtue natural; religious; nature of; changing conceptions of; learning and

Vietnam country; people; war; language; rehabilitation

Vitamins deficiency; excess; types of

Voice qualities; voiceprints; and personality; training; and persuasion; paralanguage

Wages minimum; and inflation; and fringe benefits; average; differences among cultures

Wall Street nature of; stock market; fortunes made on; types of stocks

War conduct of; financing; destruction by; causes of; debts; games; casualties; effects of

Water pollution; polo; skiing

Wealth economic; distribution of; primitive economic systems; contemporary views of

Weapons hand and missile; firearms artillery; rockets; automatic; nuclear; biological; psychological

Weather forecasting; hurricanes; control of; rain; snow; heat; cold; and population patterns; and health; and psychology; divining

Weightlifting techniques in; as excercise; as sport; leading weightlifters; competition; dangers in; benefits of; societal attitudes toward; and sexual attraction

Witchcraft meaning of; white and black; and magic; structure of; functions of; theories of; in primitive societies; contemporary

Women and sexism; biology; learning and programming; in different societies; accomplishments of; prejudices against; ERA; social roles

Words history; coinage; foreign contributions; semantics; and meaning

Wrestling amateur; professional; famous wrestlers; rules of; abuses of

Writing styles; forms of; calligraphy; graphology; development of; relationship to speech; picture; shorthand

X-rays uses of; structure of; developments in; dangers of; types of

Youth problems of; crime; education; hostels; music; communication problems; generation gap

Zen meaning of; principles of; historical development of; contemporary interest in; teachings of; influence of

Zodiac nature of; different conceptions of; constellations; myths; surrounding; and horoscopes

Zoology nature of; historical development of; Darwin's concepts; ethology

APPENDIX D

Speeches for study and enjoyment

A variety of public speeches are included in this appendix. A number of thoughts guided my selections. First, speeches that would serve as models of effectiveness were selected; we learn much more easily from the positive than from the negative and so I have purposely only included speeches that would serve as positive models. This is not to say that these speeches could not be improved, but rather to imply that, in the main, they are effective models of what a public speech should be. Second, I sought to include a variety of types of speeches—informative, persuasive, and special occasion speeches. As you read these, however, you will see that many are actually combinations of two or even three types. As noted throughout the text, information and persuasion are in reality seldom separated. Third, only speeches that I felt dealt with significant issues have been included. Speeches on trivial and worthless topics have no place in a public speaking textbook or a public speaking course. Fourth, I included only speeches that would prove interesting and relevant to today's college students. I think you will find all of the speeches included here useful models to follow and analyze and also interesting and relevant to read and think about.

I have annotated the first two of the speeches. These annotations are not full-blown rhetorical analyses but instead are designed to draw your attention to certain elements in the speech that are considered in the text— elements dealing with speaker credibility, organization, the functions and structure of the introduction and conclusion, style, audience analysis and adaptation, the use of supporting materials, persuasive strategies, and a variety of related issues. The purpose here is to make the principles of public speaking that are discussed in the text clearer and more understandable by providing specific and concrete illustrations of them.

MANDATORY RETIREMENT

Claude Pepper

Claude Pepper, United States Representative from Florida, delivered this speech to the National Council of Senior Citizens in Washington, D.C. on June 6, 1977. The rights of the elderly have been so neglected in this youth-oriented society that it is appropriate that specific consideration be given to the elderly. We are all becoming "the elderly" of tomorrow, and people close to us are the elderly of today, so raising our consciousness seems particularly worthwhile. Like the Billups speech ("Black History"), this speech also effectively blends the specific instances with the broad generalizations so important in public speaking effectiveness. The text of the speech is reprinted from *Vital Speeches of the Day* 43 (August 15, 1977):651–653.

In 1776 the Colonists, rebelling against the tyrannies of George the Third, issued a Declaration of Independence and Bill of Rights. In 1848, a group of women, disenfranchised in the country they helped to found, met in Seneca Falls, New York and issued a declaration of sentiments patterned on the Declaration of Independence. In 1948, in the wake of the horrors of Nazi Germany, the U.N. issued a declaration of human rights. Today I call for a declaration of independence for the elderly from mandatory retirement, forced institutionalization, hazardous nursing homes and criminal victimization. I call for a bill of rights guaranteeing the elderly the right to work as long as they are willing and able, the right to home health alternatives to institutionalization, the right to safe nursing homes and security in their homes and in the streets.

Mandatory retirement is a cruel euphemism camouflaging age discrimination and forced unemployment. With the surety of a guillotine, it severs productive persons from their livelihood, shears their sense of self-worth and squanders their talents. The elderly of this country who want to work

Claude Pepper is himself a senior citizen and has spoken widely on the rights of senior citizens and on the obligations of others toward the elderly. In addressing the National Council of Senior Citizens, then, Pepper comes to the speech situation with considerable credibility; he is viewed as a competent spokesperson and as one who has his audience's interest foremost in mind. Because of his previous record in support of the elderly, the audience is already familiar with his position on the issues he raises and, we can assume, will be in basic agreement with him. The speaker is concerned, then not with changing attitudes but with strengthening them and ultimately motivating the audience to specific actions.

In this introduction Pepper accomplishes a great deal. 1. He secures audience favor early in the speech by expressing a position with which they agree. Recall that the audience is composed of senior citizens and that the speaker (also a senior citizen) is committing himself to fight for their rights. 2. Pepper orients the audience by identifying his major points: mandatory retirement, forced institutionalization, hazardous nursing homes, and criminal victimization. The organizational pattern we thus learn is a topical one. 3. Pepper places the issues in historical perspective with a few provocative examples. 4. He gives these issues greater significance by comparing them to, for example, the Declaration of Independence and the United Nations Declaration of Human Rights.

Here Pepper introduces his first major topic: mandatory retirement. Immediately he states his position: "Mandatory retirement is a cruel euphemism . . . ." In the next few paragraphs Pepper gives his arguments against mandatory retirement.

and are able to work deserve the opportunity to work. They are tired of aphorisms. They demand action.

Each day of the year more than 4,000 Americans reach the age of 65. There is no evidence that on that day their ability to function productively in the economy vanishes. There is, in fact, ample evidence to support Shaw's observation that "some are younger at 70 than most at 17." Who would tell Margaret Mead, who is 75, that her contributions to the study of sociology ended at age 65? Who would tell Arthur Fiedler, who is 83, or Leopold Stokowski, who is 94, that those over 65 cannot contribute meaningfully to our appreciation of music? To waste the talents of the older worker is as shameful as it is to waste natural resources.

With just a few specific instances, Pepper makes a good case against mandatory retirement. Who would argue that people like Mead, Fiedler, and Stokowski should be forced to retire. At the same time, he is telling this audience that they are in good company with Mead, Fiedler, and Stokowski and thus stimulates an agreement response from the audience.

Why then does mandatory retirement exist? In part, because social security arbitrarily set a certain age for receipt of benefits. In part because Congress refused to protect workers over 65 in the Age Discrimination in Employment Act. And in part because we have not rid ourselves of the stereotype of the enfeebled older worker. In fact older workers perform as well and often better than younger workers in jobs requiring experience.

Pepper makes the reasons for mandatory retirement seem feeble, at best. They seem, from his analysis, based on accident and misperception. He fails to mention, for example, that one of the major reasons for mandatory retirement is unemployment. Without mandatory retirement, unemployment might be even more serious than it is now. But Pepper's purpose is not to offer an argumentative brief against mandatory retirement, but to strengthen the existing beliefs of the audience.

Mandatory retirement creates a host of additional problems. There is evidence that forced retirement accelerates the aging process, brings on physical and emotional problems, causes economic deprivation, and strains an already overburdened social security system.

Age based mandatory retirement is discriminatory, unjust, unnecessary and a waste of human talent.

Depriving the person who is able and willing to continue to work of the right to work because by some arbitrary standard that person is old is a cruel act. But that is not the only cruel act perpetrated against the elderly.

Here Pepper offers an internal summary of his position and provides a brief transition ("But that is not the only cruel act . . . .") connecting what has been said to what will be said. Pepper thus glides neatly from his first major point (mandatory retirement) to his second point (institutionalization).

Every year, thousands of older Americans are unnecessarily institutionalized. More than one million older people live in nursing homes, mental hospitals, general hospitals, old age and retirement homes and other institutional settings which, in general, suffer from misdirection and inadequate service. Criteria for admission to these facilities are usually vague and variable. For example, one-third of the aged residents of state mental hospitals have no serious mental impairment at all, but simply have no place else to go.

Again Pepper immediately states his position with regard to his second topic: "Every year, thousands of older Americans are unnecessarily institutionalized."

Pepper offers his first major fear appeal—the fear of being institutionalized with inadequate service. He also cites numerous statistics to further impress upon the audience the pervasiveness of the inequities.

Criteria for nursing homes are even hazier. State hospitals discharge many of their elderly, including those who are mentally disturbed and require psychiatric care, to nursing homes. One study of nursing home patients in Massachusetts concluded that as many as 40 percent of its residents could be treated at home for a lower cost if the law allowed. Testimony provided by HEW revealed that between 14 to 25 percent of the one million institutionalized elderly may be unnecessarily

Notice here the clear statement of one of Pepper's major arguments: "Criteria for nursing homes are even hazier." This statment serves to connect the previous argument with the one to follow and clearly signals to the audience that he will now illustrate and document the "haziness" of the criteria. Note too that the statistics cited give us the impression that Pepper is in full command of his subject matter and is therefore a credible spokesperson.

maintained in an institutional setting. Tragically, the federal government perpetuates needless institutionalization of the elderly. Of Medicaid's $3.2 billion budget for the elderly—almost 70 percent goes to nursing homes and only 1 percent for home health alternatives. The vast majority of elderly must rely largely on Medicare and Medicaid support, neither of which will pay for home health care services, and the government compounds the problem. Although preventive health care is far cheaper for both the patients and the government—Medicare and Medicaid do not provide coverage for annual checkups, professional and nutrition counseling and diagnostic services. And while those over 75 suffer visual and hearing losses at rates two to three times that of those less their age, Medicare and Medicaid do not cover the elderly's eyeglasses, hearing aids, and dentures and other necessary medical appliances.

While many nursing homes are properly labelled homes because they offer compassionate care, others are more properly labelled nursing houses or nursing facilities—places where those whom society has abandoned are sent to die—uprooted, isolated, treated with condescension rather than compassion. It is not surprising to discover that death often occurs soon after institutionalization.

The 23 million elderly people in this country want and deserve an alternative to institutionalization. Congress is beginning to view home health care as that alternative. Just last month, the House Committee on Aging, was able to defeat a proposal to cut back funding for home health services.

Institutionalization of the elderly should cease to be society's place of first resort. Rather, it should be the place of last resort—for only those who choose and need such services. Home health care offers the elderly the flexibility of choice and the option to remain independent—an ideal which must be preserved in our democratic society.

Those elderly who require institutionalization deserve federal standards which guarantee that nursing homes are not tinderboxes. After 32 elderly persons died needlessly in a nursing home fire last year, I introduced legislation mandating sprinkler systems in nursing homes funded by Medicare and Medicaid. The legislation authorizes low interest government loans to underwrite the cost of the sprinkler systems. After an investigation, initiated at my request, the General Accounting Office concluded that there has never been a multiple death fire in a nursing home protected by an automatic sprinkler system. The Comptroller General of the United States concluded that "Federal fire safety requirements do not insure life safety in nursing homes" and supported the sprinkler recommendation. Nursing home safety is the special con-

Here Pepper provides the needed transition to connect his second topic (institutionalization) with his third topic, the closely related hazardous nursing home conditions.

Although "23 million" is a huge number, Pepper might have made it more meaningful by relating it to other examples: 23 million represents about one out of every nine people in the country; or, it is the approximate population of California.
Another brief internal summary and a restatement of one of Pepper's major propositions.

Notice how effectively Pepper builds his credibility by noting, for example, that he introduced legislation mandating sprinkler systems in nursing homes and that an investigation was conducted at his initiation. The speaker's record of fighting for the elderly does much to make him a more credible spokesperson.

cern of all persons who will grow old and whose loved ones will grow old and will face the possibility of care in such a facility. These persons are not comforted by a New York State subcommittee report which found that because of fire hazards, nursing homes rank first on a list of unsafe places to live.

The elderly person forced out of a job or forced into an institution is in a very real sense a victim—a victim of societal stereotypes and misdirected legislation. But victimization of the elderly does not stop in the labor force or in health care. Crime against the elderly exacts a financial, physical and psychological cost which is immeasurable. The committee heard elderly victims tell of being raped, beaten, mugged, and assaulted, their savings depleted by medical costs, spending days in hunger waiting for the next Social Security check. Ironically the elderly victim is the least likely to report crime either because he or she fears retaliation or is unable to afford the pursuit of justice.

Every year, nearly 20,000 senior citizens are robbed of their social security checks, usually by direct looting of their mailboxes. During these first days of the month, when social security, pensions, public assistance, and other checks arrive, robberies, burglaries and assaults escalate. The tragedy of crime is compounded for those elderly to whom Social Security checks mean food and shelter. The physical and financial scars of crime are deepened by the psychological scars. One elderly couple in New York City committed suicide rather than live out their lives in fear of being beaten again. Others imprison themselves behind bolted doors and barred windows dreading their next trip to the grocery store, afraid to attend civic and religious functions.

Hearings held by Mr. Roybal have revealed that the elderly are frequently the victims of property crimes—burglary, robbery, and larceny. Older victims, who are most frequently on fixed incomes with little or no savings, are unable to recoup monetary losses. They also lack the resources to replace stolen items or repair damaged property. Even the loss of $20, an amount of money considered too insignificant to register on the FBI crime index, can represent a loss of food, heat or needed medicine to the older person on a small, fixed income. Recognizing this the Committee on Aging has recommended passage of a victim compensation bill, with special provisions to provide coverage for property loss and damage to needy elderly victims.

At the base of governmental response to the elderly are two antithetic stereotypes. One claims that to be old is to be feeble minded and worthless; the other claims that to be old is to be just like everybody else. The misguided belief that an arbitrary age signals senility is perpetuated in the Age Dis-

Note how effectively Pepper connects the previously discussed mandatory retirement and forced institutionalization with his next point, victimization. It is an effective transition and helps us to see the speech as a cohesive whole.

More fear appeal. Notice that Pepper does not draw detailed scenes or portraits of such violent acts. Often overly strong fear appeals may not work as well and cause the audience to withdraw and stop listening. Note too that the incidents that Pepper mentions are probably too familiar to the audience; such acts have probably happened to them or to persons they know, so detailed descriptions are unnecessary.

Note here the use of "guide phrases": "two antithetic stereotypes. One claims that . . .." And, in the next paragraph: "The second stereotype . . .." Phrases such as these help the audience to follow the speaker more closely.

crimination in Employment Act which fails to protect the worker over 65 from age discrimination. That stereotype also fosters the custodial mentality which drives the elderly into costly and often needless institutionalization. By demanding an end to mandatory retirement and by demanding home health alternatives we fracture the hold that stereotype currently has on legislative philosophy.

The second stereotype claims that the elderly do not differ in any significant respect from any other segment of the population. This stereotype spawns legislation which resembles the trickle down theory of economics: design social programs for the population at large and the elderly will presumably benefit. This legislative philosophy ignores the special needs of the elderly. Protection from age discrimination, safety in nursing homes, and protection from fraudulent marketing of hearing aides and dentures are among those special concerns.

We cannot banish these pernicious stereotypes by Congressional mandate. We can guarantee that they are not embodied in legislation.

It is time to declare that the elderly persons in this country will no longer be victimized by mandatory retirement, forced institutionalization, hazardous nursing homes, and criminal assault. I ask you to join in rebellion against the indignities imposed on the elderly.

While you are here for your legislative convention I urge you to talk to and write your congressman, pressing enactment of H.R. 1115, ending mandatory retirement and age discrimination for federal employees, so that the federal government can take the initiative and provide an example for all public and private employers to follow.

Talk to and write your congressman and let him know that you support the upcoming Labor-HEW appropriations bill. This legislation, at the aging committee's urging contains an additional $92 million for programs for the elderly. For example, it doubles the funds for senior citizen centers (from $20 million to $40 million), increases nutrition programs (from $225 to $250 million) and increases home health demonstrations (by $5 million), The National Institute on Aging (also by $5 million), and Senior Companions (a $1/2 million increase) as well as other programs.

Last week, during consideration of this bill in the Appropriations Committee, an amendment was offered to cut many of these increases, together with other labor and health programs. This amendment lost by only one vote and will be offered on the House floor about June 15. I hope you will urge your congressman to support the Labor-HEW bill and oppose the Michel Amendment's cuts and I hope you will write President Carter and urge him to sign the bill.

Note the effectiveness of this restatement of Pepper's main points.

Here Pepper asks for specific action and, in general terms at least, identifies the benefits that such actions could generate. Usually, such statistics are more effective when they are individualized for the members of the audience. For example, the increase from $20 million to $40 million for senior citizens centers is most impressive but more specific figures might help, for example, how many additional seniors these centers might service, what services the centers might provide that they are now unable to provide, and, specifically, what this money will mean to the senior citizens sitting in *this* audience.

Again Pepper asks for specific actions and thereby involves the audience directly. He, in effect, asks the audience to join him in this fight for the rights of the elderly and thus establishes a most effective bond—a working relationship—between himself and the members of his audience.

France supported the colonists in their rebellion against Britain. Men joined women in their battle for suffrage and equal rights. I call on persons of all ages to defend the rights of the elderly because every person in this nation has a stake in the well being of the elderly. Many are themselves elderly; others have elderly loved ones. All will themselves age. And if they do not now join in this rebellion they will find when they become senior citizens that the injustices they have suffered and the problems they have encountered are compounded by age-based mandatory retirement, by a governmental philosophy which favors costly and often needless institutionalization, by nursing homes which are too often tinderboxes, by the spectre of criminal attack, and by pernicious stereotypes.

Let us declare that those who sow promises, reap votes, and then spurn the elderly until the next election will harvest indignation. Contrary to the stereotype, the elderly do not forget the promises of vote seeking politicians. Thus I am particularly pleased that the Carter administration is moving to keep the promises made to the elderly in the 1976 campaign.

As leaders in the cause of the elderly, I ask you to join me in affirming the tenacity of the generation that survived the great depression and two world wars. We have declared our independence. We demand our rights. Thank you.

Although the entire speech was addressed to an audience of senior citizens, Pepper here gives the speech wider appeal and stresses the relevance of this topic and these issues to all people and not just the elderly.

In this conclusion Pepper summarizes his four main points and, in the last paragraph, ends crisply by again identifying himself closely with the audience and by complimenting and praising the audience: "the generation that survived the great depression and two world wars."

BLACK HISTORY

Rufus L. Billups

Rufus L. Billups, Major General, United States Air Force, delivered this speech at a Black Heritage Week Banquet at Chanute Air Force Base, Illinois, on February 10, 1979. I include this speech here for a number of reasons. First, it is a particularly clear example of the merging together of information and persuasion; in large part the speech is one of information—informing the audience of many things they probably did not know, and yet it is also persuasive—attempting to reinforce and even change various beliefs and attitudes. Most "real-life" speeches are a blending of information and persuasion. Second, I include it because Billups has so effectively blended specific instances, examples, and illustrations with broad generalizations— a quality that makes a speech interesting to listen to or read and also memorable. Third, like so many of the speeches included here, this one is included because it raises issues that are significant to all educated citizens. The text is reprinted from *Vital Speeches of the Day* 45 (September 15, 1979):712–714.

I am delighted to be here, and I am grateful for your invitation to meet and talk with each of you about Black Americans. We are once again observing our National Afro-American Heritage in these United States for the preservation and promotion of ethnic understanding, and we are celebrating Black Heritage Week here at Chanute Air Force Base as a part of that need for complete and total education in the United States Air Force.

Our National theme is "Black History, Torch for the Future."

This popular observance, which has become a feature of American life, was the design and plan of Dr. Carter G. Woodson, a native of New Canton, Virginia, who is revered as the "Father of Black History" in America.

In 1915, he founded the Association for the Afro-American Life and History. Later, in 1926, he launched the celebration of Black History Week.

Even before the speech begins, the speaker starts off with considerable credibility. He is a Major General in the United States Air Force. He has risen in the military establishment hierarchy to a level far above 99+ percent of the audience; this is his initial credibility. Further, like most of the audience, he is a military man and black, so he shares two extremely important qualities with the audience and he easily identifies with them. More importantly, they may easily identify with him. Throughout the speech Billups reinforces his credibility through his knowledge of history in general and of black history in particular.

Here the speaker gains attention by complimenting the audience (but not overdoing it) and by relating his speech and his presence here to the specific occasion. He indicates that he is pleased with this speaking encounter: "I am delighted . . .," "I am grateful."

Dr. Woodson wanted more than anything for Black persons to appreciate their heritage. He wanted them to know about Black contributions to the development of America. He wanted all Americans to appreciate the Blacks of our great nation.

His efforts were widely supported by schools, churches, clubs and among Blacks, and the movement gradually found support among institutions of other races in America and abroad. Today, the celebration enjoys widespread participation.

In 1978, Afro-American Black History Month received statements of approval from President Jimmy Carter; Governors of nearly all the States; Mayors and Presidents of City Councils of many larger cities in America; and approval from many of the officials in smaller city governments.

The theme this year, "Torch for the Future" was chosen for the celebration to inspire the search for knowledge about Black accomplishments; to inspire the continued search by many Black citizens for their own ethnic roots: and to encourage a period of introspection about ethnic heritage leading to a fuller participation by all people in the American democracy, and in the American dream.

As I look at the situation in America, today, I could make an assumption that many Black Americans would be surprised and elated to learn of the remarkable achievements by Blacks throughout the history of America, and of the world. I, too, have been enlightened over the years, and consequently, I want very much to share some of that knowledge of our Black people with you at this most appropriate time.

Our great Blacks, past and present, have a history that truly is fascinating and phenomenal. Out of the mists of time has come evidence that the Blacks were prevalent in all of old world culture, and sailed the Indian Ocean from Africa to Japan.

From prehistoric to medieval times, and even later, Black Africans left their mark in India and Melanesia. Nor was the Black race a stranger to Europe. Their blood flowed in the veins of Frenchmen; in King Alexander de Medici of Italy; in professor John Latino of Spain; in Saint Benedict the Moor of Italy; and in painters, sculptors, and authors like Alexander Dumas; and in composers like Samuel Coleridge-Taylor of England.

European art from Ancient Greece through the Renaissance to the Impressionist period reflects clearly how well Europe knew of Black men and women.

African contributions to the Americas from Canada to Argentina have been relatively recent though some go back beyond 400 years. In the light of these realities, we must view

Notice that the speaker stresses the unity of "all Americans." This is a theme that he will return to throughout the speech. He wants the audience, primarily black military men, to see themselves as an integral part of mainstream America.

Here Billups connects "the establishment" with "Black Heritage," a theme that underlies his thesis that blacks should work for advancement within the system, especially within the military system.

Billups orients the audience to his thesis and general purpose here. Note that he explicitly states his informative purpose: "to share some of that knowledge of our black people . . .." But he does not explicitly state his persuasive goal: to persuade the audience to develop more pride in the black heritage and to work within the system to achieve what other blacks have achieved. This is probably an appropriate strategy since the audience is a predominantly Black one and its members might well be hostile to a black Major General stating at the outset that they should work through the system.

Although there are some deviations, the predominant organizational pattern is a temporal one. Billups begins with earliest times, works quickly up to the 1500s, spends considerable time in the eighteenth century, moves to the present, and concludes by making predictions into the future. Although other organizational patterns (e.g., a topical one) could have been chosen, this temporal pattern seems most appropriate, given Billup's purpose.

After providing some specific instances of black contributions and influence on society in general and on specific fields, Billups becomes a bit more direct in stating his thesis: "We must view Black people as a powerful influence in world exploration and settlement." From this statement, he later states his thesis di-

Black people as a powerful influence in world exploration and settlement.

On our own American soil, the first recorded instances of Black settlement in the 1500s were connected with early Spanish explorers, the travels of D'Allyon and DeSoto, and in the old world settlement that became Alabama, and the deep south.

Saint Augustine, Florida, oldest city in the United States, owes much to Black men and women in the early 1500s. The Fort, houses, streets, artillery platforms, and the first Smith's Forge were all built by Black skills and craftmanship.

Blacks were much involved in the history of later Spanish settlements, in Portuguese America, in the Hispanic Americas, in Dutch and English settlements, and in the early American-French colonies.

When British rifles fired in 1770 at the Boston Massacre, a Black man, Crispus Attucks was the first to die for American independence.

At Bunker Hill, in June, 1775, the Black hero was Peter Salem who had also been a crack rifleman at Lexington and Concord.

And, on Christmas, 1776, Oliver Cromwell crossed the Delaware with General Washington and James Monroe, and became one of the first Blacks to attack the British at Trenton.

For the next 200 years, Blacks in America displayed remarkable talents. From the signing of American Independence to the Bicentennial celebration in 1976, and forward, American Black men and women explored, invented, and contributed immensely to the growth and development of this great land of ours. Some of their names and deeds are familiar to us for they excelled in military service, in science and industry, in business enterprise, as leaders and spokesmen and educators, and as writers, playwrights, actors, musicians, and artists.

Today, historic sites, landmarks, monuments and shrines are scattered throughout this nation to commemorate Black men and women as they achieved, often against fierce adversity, often against overwhelming odds. But, they achieved, and you can be proud of them.

Let me acquaint you perhaps for the first time with some of our great people who rose above the catastrophe of war and learned to make constructive use of peace.

There was James Fortin in the late 1700s. A Philadelphian, abolitionist, and writer. The tide for Blacks began to turn as he wrote this:

Has the God who made the white man and the black man left any record declaring us a different species? Are we not sustained by

rectly, then follows with additional specific instances—the settlement of Alabama, the contributions to St. Augustine, and so on.

Observe how these examples—probably unknown to most listeners—help to establish the speaker's credibility.

Notice how the speaker concentrates on examples from the military. Since his purpose is to persuade the audience to work within the system for advancement, his military examples are particularly appropriate. His examples are also appropriate to his own background. As a Major General in the U.S. Air Force, military examples carry a great deal more credibility than any others.

Billups uses quotations five times in the speech. Note that in four of the cases he briefly establishes the credibility of the person he quotes. Note that in the last quotation, he does not "explain" Booker T. Washington on the probably accurate assumption that the audience members are aware of his credentials.

the same power, supported by the same food, hurt by the same wounds, wounded by the same wrongs, pleased with the same delights, and propagated by the same means? And should we not enjoy the same liberty and be protected by the same laws?

Later, the "Golden Voice of Abolition," and one of the greatest spokesmen for the Black people in the 1800s, was Frederick A. Douglass.

Then came Harriet Tubman, "The Black Moses of Her Race." Strong as a man, brave as a lion, cunning as a fox, she led her people to freedom in abolition escapes to the north.

Note the use of simile here; these comparisons make Harriet Tubman's strength, bravery, and cunning most vivid.

And, in that never-to-be-forgotten war between the North and South, Sgt. William H. Carney became the first Black American to win the Congressional Medal of Honor.

From the Civil War forward, through the turn of the century, until today, the reconstruction periods were always quickly followed by a tremendous increase in the discovery and exploration of our nation's resources. Within a span of some 116 years, an impressive 327 Black American inventors gained patents for their original ideas. Everything, and I mean just about everything that you can think of from folding beds, rotary engines, street sprinklers, railway signals, and horse shoes to lawn mowers were invented by Black men and women seeking the unknown.

The list goes on and on, and is truly fascinating.

Note the simplicity of this transition.

Elijah McCoy had 57 patents, mostly for large industry; George Washington Carver, the "Savior of Southern Agriculture" searched and found hundreds of ways to make the soil more productive: and Matthew Hensen, Polar Explorer with Admiral Peary, placed the American flag on the North Pole, 7 April 1909, and is recognized in history as the indispensable Black man for the success of that expedition.

Many other Blacks made their mark during this historical time in America. Ebenezer Bassett became the first American Black Diplomat, representing the United States as Minister to Haiti; Augustus Tolton, first Black American to be ordained a Catholic Priest in America; Ida B. Wells, famous anti-lynch crusader and woman journalist; and Booker T. Washington, Educator, founder of Tuskegee Institute, Alabama. He carried the "Lamp of Learning," and was the first Black to be honored on a U.S. stamp, July 4th, 1881.

Another simple but appropriate transition.

Note how effectively a group of specific instances can be used to make a point. It would be difficult to better highlight the point that blacks contributed greatly to science. Through this barrage of specific instances we learn and become quite convinced that blacks contributed greatly to the development of this country.

It has been said that "When all men know the truth about all men, they will live together in peace."

This was the world that Dr. Martin Luther King wanted. He stood his ground, and could do no other in the struggle against bigotry, injustice, and immorality. Clear vision, courage, and determination were the hallmarks of his life.

Because of the great work that Dr. King did for the Black people of America, and for the work that so many others be-

Note the phrasing Billups uses to describe Martin Luther King: "The struggle against bigotry, injustice, and immorality"; "clear vision, courage, and determination." These word choices and combinations help to further establish the speaker's competence and to show the wide range of King's con-

fore him have done, Black men and women in all walks of life have an opportunity to help themselves as never before in history.

Learn to know your Black ancestors and forefathers, know of their achievements, and you will be amazed and inspired by their deeds and their acts of courage and dedication.

Every field of endeavor has a Black Champion. Since the early 1600s until today, Black Warriors have excelled in wars on this continent and on foreign soil.

Many Blacks earned Medals in World War One and Two, Korea, and Southeast Asia. Some received Medals of Honor, and all were gallant, and gifted Black Americans.

Today, the current situation for Black Americans in the military and in our society is clearly one of total recognition for all. No longer will the successes of many be awarded to only a few. An open door to a future of your own choice has been prepared for you by the personal struggles of Black leaders before you.

In this new year, 1979, our United States Air Force and you can be rightfully proud of retired Lieutenant General Benjamin Davis, Jr.; Major Generals Lucius Theus, and Thomas E. Clifford, and Brigadier General William E. Brown, Jr.

These are the men who have done much to enhance human dignity in our Air Force. Their work is continuing for we are committed to insuring that every Black American in the Air Force has a worthwhile job that is both challenging and rewarding.

In order to achieve this goal for our minorities, every level of command and supervision is totally involved and is aggressively and continually promoting affirmative steps to improve the utilization and dignity of all our people.

What then lies ahead for young Blacks in our country and in our Air Force? This depends upon each of us as individuals, and the social attitudes we develop and perpetuate for the good of our race. No one is going to hand us a thing that we do not deserve. History has revealed that. We will have to earn our future, step by step as others before us have. But, it will be well worth it. The record shows we can meet the challenge, for we have become more and more a successful people.

One of the most inspiring Air Force leaders who believed in the future of young Black Americans was the late General Daniel "Chappie" James, the fourth Black General in American History—and the first to wear four stars.

Listen now to a man who loved America, and his people.

cerns. Note the following use of the phrases "Black Champion" and "Black Warrior." These are phrases that seem particularly appropriate for reinforcing racial pride.

Note how Billups orients the audience to what is to follow. Note the directness of the language: "Learn to know . . . ."

Here the speaker returns to the military field, his area of expertise and the field that both he and the audience are most comfortable with.

Here Billups states one of his most important arguments, namely, that the situation today is one of equality and fairness. Perhaps recognizing that his audience will expect proof of this, Billups provides this proof throughout the speech in the form of examples and quotations from black leaders, especially military leaders.

A useful preview sentence that helps to orient the audience to what follows.

Notice how Billups inoculates his audience, answering possible objections that may be raised to his thesis. He provides the audience with appropriate responses to these potential objections: "No one is going to hand us a thing that we do not deserve. . . ." To the potential objection that Blacks have not contributed sufficiently to society, he says: "We are also the most highly developed Black people in the world . . ." and that "Black Americans are the ninth wealthiest race in the noncommunist world. . . ."

This is my country, and I believe in her, and I believe in her flag, and I'll defend her, and I'll fight for her and hold her hand until in God's given time, through her wisdom and consideration for the welfare of the entire nation, she rights the wrongs of the past generations.

America is a nation of some 25 million Blacks, the third largest number of Blacks within a nation anywhere in the world.

We are also the most highly developed Black people in the world with approximately 7,500 physicians, some 2,700 dentists, over 4,000 attorneys, and thousands of public school teachers. We are an academic, learned, scholarly people, today, in 1979, and we are a family-loving, nation-loving race, a happy people.

Black Americans are the 9th wealthiest race in the non-communist world. In the early 1970s, for example, Blacks earned $51.8 billion dollars, spent some $46 billion, and generated more than $900 million in advertising and public relations.

These figures are growing each year, and could be staggering by the 1980s.

Another statistic: approximately fifty percent of Black Americans are 20 years old or younger. Now, that condition concerns you and your future. Hear how Air Force General David C. Jones, Chairman of the Joint Chiefs of Staff feels about you:

> All our people must have a sense of belonging, and be made aware that they are our most important resource.

Hear, too, how Air Force Major General Lucius Theus feels about your future:

> In the Air Force, Human Goals are established to make the Air Force a model of equitable, fair treatment for all its people. These goals carry the highest priority.

These priorities will succeed for you and for me if we remember our responsibility to our Country—to America. As Black Americans, we must recognize how others are attempting to right the wrongs and improve our way of life. For that we should be grateful and pay our dues, and help make it work. One of the best ways for you to show your goodwill and be an asset to your country is to have faith in your American society, and in your Air Force. Everything and everyone in your life will work out better if you do.

But make no mistake, it has not been easy to reach this time and place in our American way of life. Hard work and determination have preceded you and your place here today.

Billups does not elaborate on these figures. Is 7,500 physicians a lot? It is difficult to say without knowing what percentage these numbers represent. And although $51.8 billion and $46 billion are impressive figures, their meaning is not clear without comparable figures for other groups. Here, it seems, Billups could have used more supporting materials. It is impossible to determine whether the audience also questioned the meaningfulness of these figures.

Notice how Billups identifies with the audience. Throughout his speech he uses "we," "us," and "our," emphasizing his connection with the audience members and the audience's identification with him—a black who has worked his way to the top within the system.

Here Billups answers the potential objection that the "system" does not work for blacks: "As Black Americans, we must recognize how others are attempting to right the wrongs . . .." He further supports this contention by noting specific instances of blacks who have made it and who are now influential parts of the system, as is Billups himself.

Look around our country and see the changes. Black men and women, alive and prominent in our society are voicing their opinions, are making today's Black history, and are building a better life for you and for all Black Americans.

The world acknowledges these talented people: Andrew Young, Ambassador to the United Nations since 1977; Thurgood Marshall, Associate Justice to the Supreme Court with Honorary Degrees from all over the world; Julian Bond, renowned Georgian Senator; Patricia Harris, Law Professor, Howard University; Shirley Chisholm, influential Congresswoman; and Coretta King, President of the Martin Luther King Memorial Center, active in civil rights, and a Black woman of many talents. All are famous Black Americans of our time.

A long time ago, another Black spokesman had this to say to the people of his time, and I feel for your time, and for all time:

> I believe that you who are heirs of the opportunities, the culture, and the wealth of the ages; you who have humanity and justice; you who love our glorious country will recognize that you have a chance to be trained, a chance to be educated, a chance to be efficient, a chance to be useful to your race and country, a chance to be decent, a chance to serve.

That was Booker T. Washington.

And, so, I say to all of you fine young people here with me today, have respect for yourselves! Be understanding of others of all races who reach out for your friendship. Maintain integrity, and perform in a professional manner no matter how complex and demanding your career-field in the Air Force.

Complimenting the audience ("all of you fine young people") seems to work best when it is not overdone. A simple, honest compliment (as in this Billups example) seems universally appreciated by audiences.

I want each of you to remember that there is a chance for you. You can earn respect, and the more difficulties you overcome, the greater will be your success.

I say to you the time is now to look ahead, to strive for individual achievement, but to maintain your true identity. You are following in the footsteps of many gone before you who gave much that you might have a chance in your lifetime, and in the lifetime of your children.

I say to you, hold your head high, be proud and confident of your future, try to attain higher educational goals, and make use of your opportunities on behalf of yourselves, your forefathers, and those who will follow you in times to come.

And, I say to you, above all, have pride in your heritage, pride in your country, pride in yourself, and pride in your United States Air Force.

Thank you.

Note the effectiveness of the parallel structure, "I say to you . . .." in these last few paragraphs. This phrase also signals that the speaker is nearing the conclusion. In these last three paragraphs Billups restates his major thesis and attempts to motivate the audience to act on what he has said.

WHO ARE THE EDUCATED?

Douglas Warner

Douglas Warner, Vice President of Abilene Christian University in Dallas, Texas, delivered this speech at Abilene Christian University on May 13, 1979. This brief speech is interesting particularly because of its unusual development; it is organized as a talk with Socrates, the great Greek philosopher, who taught Plato. I also include the speech here because it raises questions that I think all college students should consider. The text of the speech is reprinted from *Vital Speeches of the Day* 45 (July 1, 1979):571–572.

My dear Socrates, I perceive that you would have me discuss the qualities of an educated man. Your inquiry is well timed; for, I have pondered the subject as of late. Perhaps, I have an answer that will satisfy you.

The educated man is one who knows. The educated man knows because he has carefully learned the teachings of the scholars. He is one who can name the animals; he can name the mountains. The educated man can name the seas and the fishes of the seas; and he has learned the names of the great ones—where they were born, when, and when they died. Indeed, the educated man is he who knows.

My friend, I sense disappointment. Have I said something to displease you? Have I said too much; perhaps, I failed to say enough. I will add; the educated man is he who knows and knows he knows. And, because he knows, he is capable of instructing others as to that which is right or wrong; and in this way, he too, becomes a teacher.

Dear Socrates, I think you frown? You must help me if I have missed the mark. If the educated man is not that which I have said, then, what? Is he something more? Is he something less? Do tell me, dear Socrates, who is educated?

Now you smile. Have I said something humorous? If so, I assure you it was not intended. For my inquiry is honest. I earnestly seek an answer.

You smile again. I know there is something in your smile that I should pursue, but your smile is brought by a question. Am I to conclude that there is something special about my question?

Your look would have me believe that I have struck an answer. But, dear Socrates, I have made no definitive statement. Quite to the contrary, I have posed a disturbing inquiry.

Now, you confuse me. Although your eyes burn brightly, as if I am on the path to something, the answer evades me. I say to you that the educated man is he who knows, and you frown. I ask a question; I show my ignorance, and you smile. Do you comfort a fool or would you have me conclude that, "he who is educated is he who does not know?" Perhaps, you would have me say that the educated man is he who asks questions.

Dear Socrates, I spoke in jest; yet, your feeling of approval would support my summation. And, in truth, even when I spoke, I felt something quicken within. As if I had remembered something forgotten, as if I had come upon a truth once known, but long buried.

But, now, having stumbled into this newly discovered thought, I am confronted with two fresh inquiries. If the educated man is he who asks questions, what kind of questions will he ask. More importantly, dear Socrates, if it is the educated man who asks, who is to answer?

First, I shall explore the nature of questions. Is it who I am that is important or would it not be better to ask, why? Is the question, who were the great ones not overshadowed by the inquiry, why were they great? Is it enough to know the labels given to the universe and yet, never quiz its purpose. Would we give names to the nature of man and yet never understand man himself. Would we classify all the flowers of the field and yet never ponder their origin or splendor.

Could I be so bold as to say, the educated man is, indeed, he who dares to ask. It is he who seeks beyond the names, the labels, beyond that which is, and ponder the unknown, probes beyond that which is understood.

Indeed, is the educated man he who knows and knows he knows, and, if so, what does he really know? Or, can it be that the educated man is one who has learned of his own ignorance and does not find ignorance bliss. But, in recognizing his ignorance, demands to rise above it; he demands to challenge the unknown; he will not accept ignorance.

Indeed, is it not the educated man who can acknowledge his ignorance yet refuses to allow that confession to dampen his curiosity. In fact, his curiosity is aroused to such an audacity that he constantly probes beyond that which is.

Yes, I can see that it is the educated man who asks the questions. Now I am left with a bigger concern, who will answer?

If it is the educated man who asks, indeed, from whom will come the answer? Does it matter? Does it matter who will answer? For, is it not the task of the educated to pose the question. Realizing that a question is like a key, it will unlock curiosity; it will enflame inquiry. Would you have me say that a well posed question will not go unchallenged? That, all men seem to respond to a probing question like a kitten who cannot deny a ball of twine. But the kitten, upon seeing the twine, will pounce upon it and will not relinquish the ball until it is completely unraveled, and the end is exposed.

Is it not also so with man who is given a probing question. He will play with it, he will ponder, he will unravel, he will find its end.

My dear Socrates, have I stumbled into an answer to the inquiry? Have I, too, like a kitten with a ball of twine, unraveled the question of who is educated? Indeed, may I boldly say that the educated man is he who knows that he does not know. But, the educated man does not fear this truth, and because he does not fear ignorance, he will dare to challenge the unknown. And he knows his challenge will not go unanswered.

And what of this occasion, dear Socrates. What of us who have gathered here today to celebrate what we have accomplished. Would you have me tell them that they have learned only the tools of inquiry. That the greatest learning is yet to come.

Should I reveal to them that education is not something given, it is something found.

Should I tell them that the greatest truths are those discovered in one's own mind, and that the greatest questions to be answered are those that are asked of self.

Should I reveal to them that learning is a life-long quest and that the antonym to knowledge is not ignorance, but complacency.

How do we make them understand that learning is never over, it has no end. Indeed, each day is its beginning.

How do we spark the flame of curiosity; how do we encourage them to seek, to ponder, to wonder and to ask. How do we instill within them the courage to dare challenge the other side of tomorrow. How do we get each one to begin the journey inward, the longest journey in life . . .

Dare we share with them the real truth. There are no gifts of knowledge. Each person must become his own teacher and only from within can one unravel his own web of ignorance.

Dear Socrates, please tell me, how do we share with all mankind—a simple, little ball of twine?

MY SPEECH TO THE GRADUATES

Woody Allen

The following speech that appeared in *The New York Times* (August 10, 1979) was written by actor-writer-producer-director-comedian Woody Allen. Copyright © 1979 by The New York Times Co. Reprinted by permission of *The New York Times*.

More than any other time in history, mankind faces a crossroads. One path leads to despair and utter hopelessness. The other, to total extinction. Let us pray we have the wisdom to choose correctly. I speak, by the way, not with any sense of futility, but with a panicky conviction of the absolute meaninglessness of existence which could easily be misinterpreted as pessimism. It is not. It is merely a healthy concern for the predicament of modern man. (Modern man is here defined as any person born after Nietzsche's edict that "God is dead," but before the hit recording "I Wanna Hold Your Hand.") This "predicament" can be stated one of two ways, though certain linguistic philosophers prefer to reduce it to a mathematical equation where it can be easily solved and even carried around in the wallet.

Put in it's simplest form, the problem is: How is it possible to find meaning in a finite world given my waist and shirt size? This is a very difficult question when we realize that science has failed us. True, it has conquered many diseases, broken the genetic code, and even placed human beings on the moon, and yet when a man of 80 is left in a room with two 18-year-old cocktail waitresses nothing happens. Because the real problems never change. After all, can the human soul be glimpsed through a microscope? Maybe—but you'd definitely need one of those very good ones with two eyepieces. We know that the most advanced computer in the world does not have a brain as sophisticated as that of an ant. True, we could say that of many of our relatives but we only have to put up with them at weddings or special occasions. Science is something we depend on all the time. If I develop a pain in the chest I must take an X-ray. But what if the radiation from the X-ray causes me deeper problems? Before I know it, I'm going in for surgery. Naturally, while they're giving me oxygen an intern decides to light up a cigarette. The next thing you know I'm rocketing over the World Trade Center in bed clothes. Is this science? True, science has taught us how to pasteurize cheese. And true, this can be fun in mixed company—but what of the H-bomb? Have you ever seen what happens when one of those things falls off a desk accidentally? And where is science when one ponders the eternal riddles? How did the cosmos originate? How long has it been around? Did matter begin with an explosion or by the word of God? And if by the latter, could He not have begun it just two weeks earlier to take advantage of some of the warmer weather? Exactly what do we mean when we say, man is mortal? Obviously it's not a compliment.

Religion too has unfortunately let us down. Miguel de Unamuno writes blithely of the "eternal persistence of consciousness," but this is no easy feat. Particularly when reading Thackeray. I often think how comforting life must have been for early man because he believed in a powerful, benevolent Creator who looked after all things. Imagine his disappointment when he saw his wife putting on weight. Contemporary man, of course, has no such peace of mind. He finds himself in the midst of a crisis of faith. He is what we fashionably call "alienated." He has seen the ravages of war, he has known natural catastrophes, he has been to singles bars. My good friend Jacques Monod spoke often of the randomness of the cosmos. He believed everything in existence occurred by pure chance with the possible exception of his breakfast, which he felt certain was made by his housekeeper. Naturally belief in a divine intelligence inspires tranquility. But this does not free us from our human responsibilities. Am I my brother's keeper? Yes. Interestingly, in my case I share that honor with the Prospect Park Zoo. Feeling godless then, what we have done is made technology God. And yet can technology really be the answer when a brand new Buick, driven by my close associate, Nat Persky, winds up in the window of Chicken Delight causing hundreds of customers to scatter? My toaster has never once worked properly in four years. I follow the instructions and push two slices of bread down in the slots and seconds later they rifle upward. Once they broke the nose of a woman I loved very dearly. Are we counting on nuts and bolts and electricity to solve our problems? Yes, the telephone is a good thing—and the refrigerator—and the air conditioner. But not every air conditioner. Not my sister Henny's, for instance. Hers makes a loud noise and still doesn't cool. When the man comes over to fix it, it gets worse. Either that or he tells her she needs a new one. When she complains, he says not to bother him. This man is truly alienated. Not only is he alienated but he can't stop smiling.

The trouble is, our leaders have not adequately prepared us for a mechanized society. Unfortunately our politicians are either incompetent or corrupt. Sometimes both on the same day. The Government is unresponsive to the needs of the little man. Under five-seven, it is impossible to get your Congressman on the phone. I am not denying that democracy is still the finest form of government. In a democracy at least, civil liberties are upheld. No citizen can be wantonly tortured, imprisoned, or made to sit through certain Broadway shows. And yet this is a far cry from what goes on in the Soviet Union. Under their form of totalitarianism, a person merely caught whistling is sentenced to 30 years in a labor camp. If, after 15 years, he still will not stop whistling they shoot him. Along with this brutal fascism we find its handmaiden, terrorism. At no other time in history has man been so afraid to cut into his veal chop for fear that it will explode. Violence breeds more violence and it is predicted that by 1990 kidnapping will be the dominant mode of social interaction. Overpopulation will exacerbate problems to the breaking point. Figures tell us there are already more people on earth than we need to move even the heaviest piano. If we do not call a halt to breeding, by the year 2000 there will be no room to serve dinner unless one is willing to set the table on the heads of strangers. Then they must not move for an hour while we eat. Of course energy will be in short supply and each car owner will be allowed only enough gasoline to back up a few inches.

Instead of facing these challenges we turn instead to distractions like drugs and sex. We live in far too permissive a society. Never before has pornography been this rampant. And those films are lit so badly! We are a people who lack defined goals. We have never learned to love. We lack leaders and coherent programs. We have no spiritual center. We are adrift alone in the cosmos wreaking monstrous violence on one another out of frustration and pain. Fortunately, we have not lost our sense of proportion. Summing up, it is clear the future holds great opportunities. It also holds pitfalls. The trick will be to avoid the pitfalls, seize the opportunities, and get back home by six o'clock.

DO NOT REFUSE US

Martha J. Sara

Martha J. Sara, at the time she delivered this speech, was an undergraduate student at the University of Alaska. She delivered this speech on October 17, 1969, at the hearing of the Subcommittee on Indian Affairs of the House Interior and Insular Affairs Committee. The text is reprinted with permission from Lester Thonssen, ed., *Representative American Speeches 1969–1970*, vol. 42 (New York: H. W. Wilson, 1970), pp. 148–153.

Mr. Chairman, members of the board, my name is Martha J. Sara. I'm an Eskimo. I was born and raised in Bethel. I'm a junior at the University of Alaska. My major is sociology and I plan to go on and become a social worker.

On behalf of the Theata Club, which is an organization of native students on the University of Alaska campus, and on behalf of myself, I would like to say that I'm grateful for the right and am happy to take the responsibility to testify on behalf of the Native Land Claims.

Along with hundreds of other native young adults, I've taken the responsibility of becoming educated to better equip myself for our coming responsibilities in the management of our own affairs.

This is not an easy undertaking.

Although I am not the best example available, I will use myself. After high school I entered a school of nursing in Los Angeles. It was difficult for me because I had to overcome handicaps not faced by most American youths. I entered a different culture. Along with the dynamic process of learning what the school offered, I also had to adjust to new values and surroundings. I graduated and became a registered nurse at the age of nineteen. I was filled with a sense of accomplishment and I applied for employment at the Public Health Service Hospital in Bethel. Never before had they employed an associate in arts degree registered nurse—and so young. They had to get permission from Washington; permission was granted. I worked only one year when our community decided to open a prenatal home in Bethel through the assistance of the Office of Economic Opportunity. A director was needed with the qualifications of a registered nurse. I enthusiastically wrote a letter of application even before applications were printed. I knew the people and a lot of the future clients having worked most of the year in the maternity ward in our hospital. To my delight I was hired. Complications arose, however, because someone pointed out that in order to be a director of a prenatal institution in the state of Alaska one had to be twenty-five years old, and I was not yet even twenty-one. Letters were written on my behalf and permission was granted from Juneau for me to keep and fill the position. The funding was unsure because the deadline for occupancy was nearing and the building was unfit for expectant mothers as far as the state sanitarian, state fire marshal, and child welfare institution directors were concerned. Complete renovation of the physical plant and procurement of necessary equipment was urgent. Needless to say, I became an amateur painter, plumber, carpenter, electrician, diplomat, beggar, and petty larcenist. Local men did the plumbing, carpentry, and electrical work in conjunction with the BIA. Local boys under the neighborhood youth program did the painting. Used furniture was procured from the hospital through

GSA. Supplies were ordered and opening day saw us admitting our first lady! We struggled and worked for what we wanted and got it. Of course we had the assistance and backing of the agencies, but the native people involved made it work. We were competent and proved it.

I am here representing a body of eager, willing young adults ready to learn, work, and show our capability in the management of our own affairs. I am just one of many who are willing to struggle for an education, who are willing to work hard, the way we worked on the Bethel Prenatal Home.

We are not asking for all our land—just a portion of it and if you grant it to us, we will have to strive very hard because what we are asking for is less than what we believe is fair. But we are capable of striving very hard.

And how shall you refuse us? You who have centuries of learning, education, civilization, colonization, expansion, domination, exploitation behind you? How shall you refuse us?

Do not refuse us because we are young! In youth there is energy, drive, ambition, growth, and new ideas. Do not refuse us because we are young! For we shall mature!

Do not refuse us because we are undereducated! We are learning fast; and utilizing our newly gained knowledge, comparing and weighing the truths and benefits of this knowledge. We know that the 40 million acres we are asking for will provide a minimum protection to hunting and fishing. We understand that we need the identification with, and the feeling for our own land. We also realize that we need this land as an economic base for our people. The land will be used as a commodity in our economic base. We can accomplish this with 40 million acres. Five hundred million dollars is a lot of money. We understand what a vital role this can play in the economic base of our people. We realize that with proper and careful handling and investment of this money we can make it work for us. We do not plan to make improvements without first establishing a sound economic base which will provide for growth and return. After this is established, then we can begin our improvements. We will then be able to maintain and expand these improvements. We realize that we can not only benefit our people, but all of Alaska. All this for $500 million. Do not refuse us because we are still learning! For we are fast learning!

Do not refuse us the chance to progress! We too have a dream for the progress of our land. We hold a superior position to develop our country because it is our country, and we love it. We will be more cautious in its utilization—and I deliberately use the word "utilization" instead of "exploitation." We will weigh each prospect carefully to assure ourselves that we are making the best decision for our generation and those generations to come. We are not here to grab; we are here to live with the growth of our native land. Do not refuse us the chance for progress. For we too share the dream of progress.

Do not refuse us because you are afraid we don't have competent leaders! I represent a generation of paradoxes. We are paradoxes in the fact that we are the closest links to the parties farthest separated in this issue. One of these groups is our beloved elders whom we left back home only a short time ago, who, along with others, still cling to the old ways and depend upon the land for subsistence. Another group is made up of our able leaders, native and white, who are presently in positions of decision. We are close to the old ones and the people back home because, having recently left them, their problems, worries, and fears burn deep in our hearts. We know what makes them happy; we know what can fill them with contentment; we know what gives them hope. At the same time we are close to our leaders in the fact that we are striving and aspiring to their positions of decision. Native young people are rising up to meet the demands and expectations of a foreign and sometimes hostile society. The day of our leadership is not too far off. When that day of fulfillment comes, I would like to think that we can proudly take our places side by side with the present leaders to direct the affairs of our own people. In their wisdom they can quell our fears, channel our energy, help share our innovative ideas, direct our aggression, and interpret our anxieties. Together we can provide able leadership! Do not refuse us for fear of poor leadership! For we are capable leaders.

Do not refuse us simply because you purchased the sovereign right of our land! Our fathers since time began have paid dearly for our homeland every generation. They struggled against the harshest environment known to man and survived to teach us to do the same. Each generation paved the way for the next. Do not refuse us because you purchased this right! For our forefathers paid for it long before your forefathers had the money.

Do not refuse us because we are a minority! For this is America! We have proved in many ways that, not only do we take advantage of our rights and freedoms along with other Americans, but we are willing to, and have, fought equally for all its privileges. Our native soldiers fought and died for the United States in World War II, the Korean War, and in the present war in Vietnam. As American citizens, we have equal rights and have taken on equal responsibility. So do not refuse us because we are a minority! For this is America!

In closing I would like to say that competence is something that has to be proven. And as young native adults we have demonstrated our abilities and are now proving it.

I would like to add that we are deeply grateful to you all for taking time out of your busy schedules to come and hear our testimonies. It is deeply appreciated. Thank you! Quyana cakneq!

INDEX

84 85 86 87 9 8 7 6 5 4 3 2 1